SECOND EDITION

Teacher's Edition and Lesson Planner

with ActiveTeach

Joan Saslow • Allen Ascher

With Daria Ruzicka

ALWAYS LEARNING

PEARSON

Summit: English for Today's World 2, Second Edition
Teacher's Edition and Lesson Planner

Pearson Education, 10 Bank Street, White Plains, NY 10606

Staff credits: The people who made up the *Summit 2* Teacher's Edition and Lesson Planner team—representing editorial, production, design, and manufacturing—are Rhea Banker, Aerin Csigay, Dave Dickey, Aliza Greenblatt, Caroline Kasterine, Mike Kemper, Nicole Santos, and Martin Yu.

Text composition: TSI Graphics
Text font: Palatino 11/12
Cover photograph: Shutterstock.com
Cover design: Elizabeth Carlson

ISBN 13: 978-0-13-260796-4
ISBN 10: 0-13-260796-4

Photo credits: All original photography by David Mager. Page 2 (top left) AP/Wide World Photos, (top middle) Woods Hole Oceanographic Institution, (top right) AP/Wide World Photos, (middle) AGE Fotostock America, Inc., (bottom left) Shutterstock.com (bottom middle) Frans Lanting/Corbis, (bottom right) Al Giddings Images, Inc.; p. 3 (top) Frans Lanting/Getty Images, (middle) Frans Lanting/Getty Images, (bottom left) Charlotte Thege/Peter Arnold, Inc., (bottom right) AFP/Getty Images/Newscom; p. 4 Cary Wolinsky/Aurora & Quanta Productions, Inc.; p. 6 (left) AP/Wide World Photos, (right) Woods Hole Oceanographic Institution; p. 7 (1) Al Giddings Images, Inc., (2) Dr. Madan Kataria, (6) AP/Wide World Photos, (8) NASA.gov; p. 8 Michael K. Nichols/National Geographic Image Collection; p. 9 (left) Lilly Dong/Getty Images, (middle) Michael McQueen/Getty Images, (right) Digital Vision/Getty Images; p. 10 Diaphor Agency/Photolibrary; p. 21 (top) AP/Wide World Photos, (middle) Bill Irwin/Pearson Education, (bottom) Tony Freeman/PhotoEdit; p. 26 (background) Getty Images, (top) Bettmann/Corbis, (middle) Marc Hauser Photography Ltd/Getty Images, (bottom) Jacques M. Chenet/Corbis; p. 28 (left & right) Kelsey Adventures Ltd.; p. 31 Ghislain & Marie David de Lossy/Getty Images; p. 32 Bettmann/Corbis; p. 34 (top) Ki Ho Park/Kistone Photography, (bottom) AP/Wide World Photos; p. 35 (left) AP/Wide World Photos, (right) Jeffrey Markowitz/Corbis Sygma, (bottom) Shutterstock.com; p. 37 (1) Michael Newman/PhotoEdit, (2) Mary Kate Denny/PhotoEdit, (3) ThinkStock/Photolibrary; p. 38 (Carl) MedioImages Fresca Collection/Alamy, (Karen) AbleStock/Photolibrary, (Bill) Vic Bider/PhotoEdit, (Kate) Michael Newman/PhotoEdit; p. 41 (top left) David Young-Wolff/PhotoEdit, (bottom left) Michael Newman/PhotoEdit, (top right) Michael Newman/PhotoEdit, (bottom right) Andersen Ross/Getty Images; p. 43 (top left) Vicky Kasala/Getty Images, (middle) Elena Rooraid/PhotoEdit, (bottom left) Stockbyte, (bottom right) Stockbyte; p. 44 Giantstep Inc./Getty Images; p. 50 Jack K. Clark/The Image Works; p. 51 (background) Jeff Greenberg/PhotoEdit, (bird) Dennis MacDonald/PhotoEdit; p. 52 (1) Shoot Pty. Ltd./Photolibrary, (2) John Sann/Getty Images, (3) Stockbyte, (4) M. Nader/Getty Images; p. 56 Erik Simonsen/Getty Images; p. 59 Stephen Alvarez/National Geographic Image Collection; p. 63 AP/Wide World Photos; p. 68 Shutterstock.com; p. 70 AP/Wide World Photos; p. 71 (city) Romilly Lockyer/Getty Images, (cruise) Shutterstock.com, (beach) MedioImages/Getty Images, (woods) Ty Allison/Getty Images, (tour) Tim Hall/Getty Images; p. 74 (left to right) David Gould/Getty Images, Photodisc Collection/Getty Images, Stuart Dee/Getty Images, Ryan McVay/Getty Images; p. 75 (background) Adam Jones/Getty Images, (man) Mark Harmel/Photo Researchers, Inc.; p. 76 (top) Michael Newman/PhotoEdit, (1) SuperStock, Inc./SuperStock, (2) Bettmann/Corbis, (3) SPL/Photo Researchers, Inc., (4) Bettmann/Corbis, (5) Bettmann/Corbis, (6) Lynn Gilbert/Pace/MacGill Gallery, (7) Bettmann/Corbis; p. 77 (top) Dennis Degnan/Corbis, (bottom) Jose Luis Pelaez, Inc./Corbis; p. 83 Hulton Archive/Getty Images; p. 86 (1) ©2001 by Randy Glasbergen/www.glasbergen.com, (2) ©The New Yorker Collection 1997 Aaron Bacall from cartoonbank.com. All Rights Reserved, (3) ©The New Yorker Collection 2002 Mick Stevens from cartoonbank.com. All Rights Reserved, (4) ©The New Yorker Collection 1970 Robert Day from cartoonbank.com. All Rights Reserved; p. 87 (1) Meredith Parmelee/Getty Images, (2) Jose Luis Pelaez, Inc./Corbis, (3) Walter Hodges/Getty Images, (4) Frederick Tousche/Getty Images, (5) Photofest, (6) Henry Horenstein/Getty Images; p. 98 Sanford/Agliolo/Corbis; p. 99 John Lamb/Getty Images; p. 101 Johan Visschedijk/1000aircraftphotos.com; p. 102 Shutterstock.com; p. 104 Rainer Grosskepf/Getty Images; p. 105 Richard Green/Mira.com; p. 106 Lester Lefkowitz/Getty Images; p. 110 (Gates) Chris Farina/Corbis, (Welch) Najlah Feanny/Corbis Saba, (Klein) McPherson Colin/Corbis Sygma, (Noor) AP/Wide World Photos, (Roy) Torsten Blackwood/AFP/Getty Images/NewsCom, (Annan) AP/Wide World Photos, (Clinton) Wally McNamee/Corbis; p. 111 Paul Conklin/PhotoEdit; p. 112 (left) Emmanuel Faure/Getty Images, (middle) Stephen Marks/Getty Images, (right) Brooke Slezak/Getty Images; p. 113 (top to bottom) Paul Chesley/Getty Images, Steve Raymer/Corbis, Paul Barton/Corbis, Shao Xian/Photocome/ NewsCom; p. 114 Chen Shuhui/Photocome/ NewsCom; p. 116 Paul Morrell/Getty Images; p. 118 Steve Mason/Getty Images.

Illustration credits: Steve Attoe, pp. 14, 45, 66, 89, 90, 94; Francois Escalmel, pp. 18, 62; Oki Han, p. 23; Marc Mongeau, p. 22; Dusan Petricic, pp. 16, 30, 93, 95; Anna Veltfort, p. 67; Carl Wiens, p. 55.

Text credits: Page 22 "The Silent Couple." Adapted with the permission of Simon & Schuster Adult Publishing Group from The Book of Virtues, edited, with commentary by William J. Bennett. Copyright © 1993 William J. Bennett; p. 106 "World's First 'Green' Dealership." Courtesy of Ford Motor Company; p. 116 Pew Global Attitudes Survey. Pew Global Attitudes Project.

Printed in the United States of America
2 3 4 5 6 7 8 9 10 – V003 – 16 15 14 13 12

PTE Academic - testing real-life English skills

As educators we spend much of our time and energy preparing students for the rigors of study or work in an English-speaking setting. We design our courses and choose our materials carefully so that we can teach students how to communicate effectively in English. When it comes to assessing English skills, we have realized that many high-stakes tests are simply a means to an end in which students dedicate valuable time to passing the test without developing a real ability to communicate in English.

There is an academic test of English, however, that matches our efforts in the classroom. PTE Academic is recognized by institutions around the world and is approved by the UK Border Agency and the Australian Department of Immigration and Citizenship (DIAC) for student visa applications. It is endorsed by, and is the preferred English language test of GMAC®, the Graduate Management Admissions Council.

Why are educators so excited about the test? This state-of-the-art test breaks many of the barriers in testing, but the key concern to teachers is that it truly helps students to become effective communicators in English.

"PTE Academic score data on the enabling language skills such as fluency, grammar, vocabulary and pronunciation, gives us a great tool to assess the language abilities of incoming MBA applicants to ensure they can interact at the levels expected in a small, experienced group of professionals on the Ashridge MBA program."
- Amy Armstrong, Director of Marketing, Ashridge Business School

Relevant tasks
Comprising of 20 different and often innovative items types, PTE Academic assesses the communicative skills of listening, reading, speaking and writing in a number of ways. It assesses a range of enabling skills such as grammar, oral fluency, pronunciation, spelling, vocabulary and written discourse to create a detailed profile of test takers' strengths and weaknesses.

Many of the 20 item types integrate these communicative and enabling skills to provide a real-life measure of a test taker's ability to deal with academic English language in communication.

International English
PTE Academic reflects the international world in which we live. Measures have been taken to ensure that the material in the test is representative of international academic English. Not only are test development professionals based in several regions, including the United Kingdom, Australia, and the United States, but test items are internationally cross-validated to ensure that there is no regional bias.

Targeted preparation for test takers
A variety of dedicated test preparation materials are available for test takers. These include:

- Practice tests with sample answers
- A free PTE Academic Tutorial providing an overview of the test, instruction on each item type that the test taker will encounter and tips on how to navigate through the test
- The *Official Guide to PTE Academic* providing detailed information on administration, descriptions of all item types, analysis of sample answers, test-taking strategies and a wealth of practice items on the accompanying CD-ROM

The skills that students acquire in preparing for PTE Academic will serve them greatly once they arrive at their higher education institutions, or professional and government organizations.

 "As we evaluate candidates, PTE Academic will give us an important tool for measuring their ability to study in an academic environment where English is the primary language of instruction."
- Randall Sawyer, Director of Admissions Cornell University, The Johnson School

For more information on PTE Academic, visit www.pearsonpte.com

Contents

What Is *Summit?*

Instructional levels

Summit is a two-level high-intermediate to advanced communicative series for adults and young adults that can follow any intermediate course book. *Summit* is designed to follow the *Top Notch* series, forming the top two levels of a six-level course.

- *Top Notch* Fundamentals: for true beginners or very weak false beginners
- *Top Notch* 1: for false beginners or for students who have completed *Top Notch* Fundamentals
- *Top Notch* 2: for pre-intermediate students
- *Top Notch* 3: for intermediate students
- **Summit 1: for high-intermediate students**
- **Summit 2: for advanced students**

The following chart shows the correlation of *Summit* and *Top Notch* to International Standards and Tests. For detailed correlations to the "Can do" statements of the Common European Framework (CEFR) and to U.S. federal and state standards, please consult the *Summit* website at: pearsonlongman.com/summit.

Correlations to International Standards and Tests

Course Level	TOEFL (Paper)	TOEFL (iBT)	TOEIC
Top Notch Fundamentals (true beginner)			110 – 250
Top Notch 1 (false beginner)	380 – 425	26 – 38	250 – 380
Top Notch 2 (pre-intermediate)	425 – 475	38 – 52	380 – 520
Top Notch 3 (intermediate)	475 – 525	52 – 70	520 – 700
Summit 1 (high-intermediate)	525 – 575	70 – 90	700 – 800
Summit 2 (advanced)	575 – 600	90 – 100	800 +

Course Level	Common European Framework (CEF)
Top Notch Fundamentals (true beginner)	A1/Breakthrough
Top Notch 1 (false beginner)	A2/Level 1
Top Notch 2 (pre-intermediate)	A2/Level 1
Top Notch 3 (intermediate)	B1/Level 2
Summit 1 (high-intermediate)	B2/Level 3
Summit 2 (advanced)	C1/Level 4

Course Level	Cambridge Exams	
	IELTS	Exam Level
Top Notch Fundamentals (true beginner)		
Top Notch 1 (false beginner)	3.0	KET
Top Notch 2 (pre-intermediate)	4.0	PET
Top Notch 3 (intermediate)	4.0	PET
Summit 1 (high-intermediate)	5.0	FCE
Summit 2 (advanced)	6.0	CAE

Scope

Each level of the *Summit* course contains enough material for 60 to 90 hours of classroom instruction. Split editions are also available. A wide choice of supplementary components makes it easy to tailor *Summit* to the needs of diverse classes and programs or to expand the total number of hours.

Goal

The goal of the course is to make English unforgettable, enabling post-intermediate learners to understand, speak, read, and write English accurately, confidently, and fluently. Three key features are emblematic of the *Summit* course:

- Multiple exposures to new language
- Numerous opportunities to practice it
- Deliberate and intensive recycling

An essential goal of *Summit* is to help post-intermediate students move past the plateau that typically occurs among students at that level.

Language content

Summit has a classic sequential grammatical syllabus. Grammar, vocabulary, and social language are integrated within topical, communicative units. Offering a balance of practical and informational topics, the content is designed to be consciously appealing to the student learning English.

Academic skills and strategies

Each unit in the *Summit* course contains exercises that build key reading, listening, writing, and critical thinking skills and strategies. These are identified at a glance on every page of the Student's Book. A complete list can be seen in the Learning Objectives chart on pages iv–vii.

Conversation syllabus

Experience has shown that post-intermediate students continue to need intensive practice of spoken communication. To this end, *Summit* provides ten essential conversation models that embed crucial conversation strategies and opportunities to personalize. In addition to conversation practice and extension, *Summit* concludes every two-page lesson with free communication activities to ensure adequate practice of speaking skills.

Instructional design

The following is a synopsis of the *Summit* instructional design.

A communication goal for each class session. Each of the four numbered two-page lessons in a *Summit* unit is designed for one class session of 45–60 minutes, and has a clearly stated communication goal.

Three reasons for having a communication goal are to make each class purposeful, to demonstrate progress in each class session, and to enable a more focused evaluation. When teachers and students are unaware of the purpose of each lesson, they often just "go through the motions." Conversely, when teachers and students know the purpose of the lesson, they see value in it and are motivated to achieve a successful outcome.

Integration of skills and content. Research has confirmed that when students encounter new language only once or twice, they find it difficult to master or even remember. For that reason, new vocabulary and grammar are embedded in exercises, conversation models, pair work activities, listening comprehension texts, readings, and other activities to make them unforgettable. In each lesson, new language is examined, explained, integrated, expanded on, and applied so that students receive multiple exposures to the language as well as numerous opportunities to practice it in all skill areas.

Confirmation of progress. The culmination of each of the four lessons is a carefully constructed guided communication activity called Now You Can. Each of these activities is a conversation, discussion, or role play in which students demonstrate their achievement of the goal of the lesson. Students are motivated by their success, and in keeping with the aims of the "Can do" statements of the Common European Framework, continually see the practical value of their instruction.

Explicit presentations of vocabulary, grammar, and social language. In order to allow the *Summit* Student's Books to double as both a teaching and a reviewing tool, language is presented explicitly. Explicit presentations take the guesswork out of understanding meaning, form, and use and provide a concrete reference for students to review. For those who prefer an inductive presentation of grammar, there are printable "Inductive Grammar Charts" on the ActiveTeach disc at the back of this Teacher's Edition. These charts provide an alternative (inductive) approach to each grammar presentation in the Student's Book.

A systematic approach to free expression. Every lesson culminates in a free speaking activity with sequential steps to increase quantity and quality of expression. Planning activities such as idea framing and notepadding lead students to confident productive discussion and role play. Presentations, debates, and projects also provide opportunities for students to develop their spoken expression.

A strategy-based focus on reading and listening comprehension. In addition to the rigorous practice of reading and listening, there is an emphasis on learning strategies. The strategies include understanding meaning from context, distinguishing main ideas from details, comparing and contrasting, determining points of view, drawing conclusions, paraphrasing, and summarizing—all of which enrich students as learners and as communicators.

A systematic writing syllabus. The *Summit* Student's Book contains a writing syllabus that includes clear models and rigorous practice of important rhetorical and mechanical essay writing skills, such as parallelism, summarizing, and punctuation. Each lesson provides practice in the writing process, from prewriting to revision.

A complete course. *Summit* is a complete course with a wealth of supplementary components and a simple integrated technology, allowing the maximum flexibility for all teaching styles, learning settings, and course needs.

For a pictorial presentation of all components of the *Summit* course, please see Student's Book pages ix–xi.

Methodology for a Communicative Classroom

The goal of any post-intermediate communicative language course should be to enable students to express themselves confidently, accurately, and fluently in speaking and writing; to understand authentic spoken and written English; and to function socially in English in a variety of settings, both familiar and unfamiliar. Much practice is needed to reach those goals.

Because the typical student has limited opportunities to observe and practice English outside of class, the goal of the classroom must be to provide rich sources of input for observation as well as intensive opportunities for communication practice. It is the goal of this section and the goal of the *Summit* course to suggest a methodology which makes that possible.

Permitting active observation of language

The world is saturated with English (through the Internet, films, music, and television). Post-intermediate students should be encouraged to seek out and observe English outside of class whenever possible.

On the other hand, students benefit greatly and learn easily from exposure to models of spoken and written English at their own productive level or language just above that level. The level of challenge that benefits students most is often called "i+1" (Krashen and Terrell, 1983[*]) or "comprehensible

input." Comprehensible input is language that contains some unknown words or structures, but is still at a level that students can understand. Such language, especially when it is authentic, is extremely valuable for student progress and is abundant in the *Summit* course.

We believe that each class session should provide students with an opportunity to observe language by reading it and hearing it as well. In order to benefit from the observation process, students should be encouraged to look at and/or listen to reading and listening material for several minutes in order for them to process it and to make connections between what they know and what is new. After students have had ample opportunity to immerse themselves in the observation process they should begin discussing the text or answering questions about it. And to maximize the value of observation, we strongly suggest that students support their opinions or answers by indicating where in an observed text or listening they got the information they needed to answer or to form an opinion. In this way, observation becomes an active process rather than simply a receptive activity.

Encouraging repetition of new language

Some people believe that repetition of language is indicative of an outdated behaviorist audio-lingual approach and (if included at all) only appropriate at the lower levels. Consequently, recent trends in language teaching tend to de-emphasize or discourage repetition

---

[*] Krashen, Stephen and Terrell, Tracy D. 1983. *The Natural Approach: Language Acquisition in the Classroom.* Oxford: Pergamon Press.

of language being learned. However, we have observed that repeating new language is valuable as long as it is not overused and does not interfere with awareness of meaning. Repetition helps students internalize correct pronunciation, stress, and intonation. It is recommended that students listen to and repeat new language for production.

For this reason, when students are learning new vocabulary or new social language, they should be encouraged to listen, or to read and listen, and then to listen again and repeat. When using audio materials as models, students appreciate the opportunity to compare their pronunciation, stress, and intonation with those of the speakers on the audio. We recommend that repetition be a regular feature of the presentation of vocabulary and model conversations.

For activities requiring students to listen and repeat, we suggest having students listen the first time while looking at the written form in their textbooks. This allows students to link the written form in the textbook to the sounds they hear. Next, as students are asked to listen and repeat, have them do it with their textbooks closed. This serves to reduce distractions and allows students to focus exclusively on listening and repeating, rather than reading. It also reduces the confusing effect of English spelling on pronunciation.

It is always beneficial to vary the method and sequence of repetition. Using alternative approaches does not diminish the value of repetition; the approaches add variety and help maintain interest, especially for post-intermediate students. It is best to keep the pace of repetition lively so that the greatest number of students have a chance to participate, maximizing the memorability of the stress and intonation patterns.

It is also beneficial to vary the number of people being asked to repeat. Sometimes it is helpful to have students repeat individually; at other times the whole class, half the class, all the males, all the females, etc. can be asked to repeat as a group. The goal is always served, no matter how the repetition is structured.

It is important, however, not to exaggerate the amount of class time devoted to repetition. A lively pace and a short time period will achieve the desired results; then it is time to move on to more substantive activities.

Ensuring that students use learning strategies

It is important to provide opportunities for students to work toward goals, to access prior knowledge, and to practice strategies such as planning, self-assessing, predicting, etc. These strategies have been proven to have positive results on students' learning. Knowing learning strategies is not enough, however. Research has shown that unless students are aware of the value of strategies, they are unlikely to incorporate them into their own learning initiatives.*

Working toward goals. At the beginning of each term, before beginning instruction, probe students' individual personal goals in learning English. Common goals could be for their profession, travel, academic study, etc. Help students become aware of how their course and/or their textbook will help them reach those goals; for example, by helping them learn to understand and communicate in spoken and written English. It is also worthwhile to encourage students to brainstorm a specific list of what they want to be able to do in English in practical or specific terms. For example:

I want to learn English because I want to:

- *read academic journals or articles.*
- *write e-mails or letters.*
- *discuss news and current events.*
- *have social conversations.*
- *use the Internet.*
- *discuss controversial topics politely.*

Have students look through their textbook to see if it will fulfill any of their goals. Ask them to point out lessons or units that they look forward to learning from.

Make goal-setting or goal awareness an important part of each unit and lesson. Before beginning a unit or lesson, have students look it over and brainstorm what they will be able to do at the end of it. Such awareness builds expectation of results, focuses students' attention on the purpose of instruction, and results in greater satisfaction with each class. Specific techniques for using the goals in class are covered in *Applied Methods: How to Teach a* Summit *Unit,* on page Txx.

Observing progress and self-assessing. When a brief discussion of goals takes place at the beginning of a class session, it then becomes easy for students to observe and confirm their progress that day. One simple way to ensure this is to ask "Did you learn how to describe consumer shopping habits?" "What did you learn today?" and so on. When students confirm that the lesson's goal has been achieved, they value their instruction. Similarly, regularly

---

* The foundational learning strategies that folllow are an intrinsic part of the *Summit* Student's Book. For teachers who would like to teach additional reading, listening, and vocabulary-building strategies, there are numerous printable extension activities on ActiveTeach in the back of this Teacher's Edition.

review progress at the end of each full unit. In general, cumulative positive reinforcement of their study motivates learners to persevere.

Being aware of the instructional process. Make students aware that presentations and activities in class, as well as those assigned for work outside of class (homework, projects, laboratory activities), have a definite purpose and are not random or accidental.

Effective lessons offer students presentations and activities that integrate target content. However, merely *offering* students such lessons is often not enough. The lesson will be more effective if students are *cognitively aware* of the value of each section of the lesson in achieving the lesson goals.

When finishing tasks, projects, and homework, take a moment to review the language students used in the task; for example, ask "Where did you use the passive voice with modals today?" When students become aware that they actually used the passive voice with modals in their conversations, practicing it becomes valuable to them. It is surprising how often students are not aware of the way in which activities help reinforce what they are learning. They often see a conversation practice session as isolated from grammar or vocabulary content, viewing it as just for fun or something to do to fill time.

Reflecting on one's learning. A number of hurdles must be overcome in learning a foreign or second language. One such hurdle is confusing the difference between *understanding* a word and *being able to translate* it into one's own (native) language.

Even post-intermediate learners sometimes attempt to translate everything they read or hear, word-for-word. This is futile for two reasons. First, no one can possibly translate word-for-word quickly enough to follow a speaker speaking at a natural pace. Second, word-for-word translations are impossible for idioms, expressions, metaphors, or other figurative language.

In order to build students' awareness of this fact, we must help them reflect on the meaning of "understanding." Help them to see that they can in fact derive both general and specific meaning from spoken and written texts that contain words they have not heard or seen before. If students say they do not understand the meaning of a new word being learned, help them to describe its meaning, rather than to try to translate it. Ask students to look at the surrounding context to determine connotation—or sense—of the word in order to understand its general meaning. Help them to recognize that not being able to translate a word is different from not understanding it.

This is a profound awareness on which every learner of a new language needs to reflect. This awareness creates the desire and need to depend on context to infer meaning, promoting the development of one of the most important strategies for language learners—understanding meaning from context.

Managing pair, group, and collaborative activities

Collaborative activities, as well as pair and group work, facilitate interaction in English and are a hallmark of communicative language teaching. These activities encourage students to use their own language resources, which in turn makes the lesson more personal and meaningful. They also ensure that students initiate as well as respond in English. Also, by working together, students get to know each other faster and become more independent; they rely on the teacher less for guidance and ultimately take more responsibility for their own learning. We recommend the following approaches for activities featuring pair and group work.

Creating a student-centered environment. Some students, particularly those accustomed to teacher-centered lessons in which teachers spend a lot of time explaining, may not immediately see the benefits of working in pairs or groups. Remind students that working together allows them more time to practice their English and allows you to listen to more students individually. Reassure students that you will circulate to give them individual attention and that this will make you aware of any points that need explanation.

Encouraging cooperative learning and collaboration. Encourage students to help and learn from each other; in other words, to create a community of learners in the classroom. Students can collaborate on written exercises with a partner or group, either by completing the activity together or by comparing their answers. Whenever possible, try to elicit answers from other students before answering a question yourself.

Facilitating a flexible seating arrangement. To ensure that students interact with a variety of partners, have them sit in a different location for each class. When dividing the class into pairs or groups, try to match students of different abilities. One method of forming groups is to have students count off according to the number of groups needed. The "1"s work together, the "2"s work together, and so on.

Monitoring activities. During pair and group work activities, monitor students by moving around the room to keep them on task and to provide help as needed. When possible, avoid participating in pair work yourself, as this will limit your ability to monitor and offer assistance to the rest of the class. If you are faced with an odd number of students, create a group of three students. The third student can work as a helper to encourage eye contact and other socially appropriate behavior and to correct mistakes.

Managing time. To keep students on task, it is best to set time limits for each activity. End activities when most of the class has finished to avoid "dead time" during which students are waiting for others to finish. For students who finish a conversation activity early, have them write out the conversation they created. If you use supplementary activities, it is a good idea to have some of those photocopied and on hand.

Correcting errors purposefully

In general, language learners—particularly adults— like feedback and expect to be corrected when they make a mistake. However, recent research (Brown, 2007*) suggests that correcting errors in students' speech and writing may not be as effective in promoting correct language use as is commonly believed. In fact, research indicates that excessive correction in a communicative course can embarrass or dishearten students and discourage them from attempting the experimentation and practice that is essential for language acquisition.

In view of these findings, we recommend striking a balance between the need for correction and maintaining feelings of success. The following are approaches to provide effective and positive feedback.

Promoting accuracy. For activities where accuracy is the focus, address mistakes shortly after they occur. Students need guidance as they attempt to use new words, phrases, and grammar; immediate correction is important. Ask students to incorporate the corrections as they continue the activity.

Promoting fluency. For freer and more challenging activities where fluency and free expression are the focus (discussions and role plays), refrain from stopping the flow of student discussion with corrections. In these activities, accuracy is less important than communicating ideas, improvising, and remembering and using the full range of language students have learned. Developing the ability to retrieve and use previously learned language is critical if students are to convert the English they have learned in the classroom into the

English they need in their own lives. Interrupting students with corrections discourages this experimentation. Instead, take notes on common student mistakes and then review those errors with the entire class at the end of the activity.

Encouraging self-correction. Students, especially at the upper levels, are often able to correct their own mistakes. First let the student finish the thought, then indicate by sound or gesture that there has been a mistake. Try to point out where the mistake was to give the student an opportunity to self-correct.

Some techniques for eliciting self-correction include pausing at the mistake, or repeating the student's sentence and pausing at the mistake; for example, S: "There were much people." T: "There were . . ." S: "There were *many* people."

A less intrusive method is to correct the student's mistake by reformulating what the student said without stopping the flow of conversation; for example, S: "Many of them has finished." T: "Oh, many of them *have* finished?" S: "Yes, many of them have finished." Note that these techniques often prompt the student to self-correct.

Being selective. Do not try to correct every mistake. Doing so could discourage or overwhelm students. Instead, focus corrections on the skills that are being taught in that particular lesson or on mistakes that interfere with comprehensibility.

Providing emotional support. Above all, be careful not to embarrass students. Be aware that post-intermediate students in particular may be sensitive to criticism in front of their peers and may prefer more private feedback. Give students enough time to think before they answer to avoid making them feel pressured. There is nothing more effective in promoting student participation than reinforcing their belief that you are "on their side." To that end, we suggest that you show approval for student experimentation, even when language is inaccurate. Correction can come later. Experimentation is an essential step on the road to mastery.

Checking and managing homework. Maximizing the amount of time students have to interact and practice English is essential in a classroom environment. It is best to limit the amount of class time devoted to checking answers and correcting homework. For exercises done in class, have students check their answers with a partner. This increases interaction time, ensures that errors get corrected, and encourages students to correct

---

* Brown, H. Douglas. 2007. *Teaching By Principles: An Interactive Approach to Language Pedagogy* (3rd ed.). White Plains: Pearson Education.

their own mistakes. It also helps students avoid the possible embarrassment of giving incorrect answers in front of the entire class.

When the class has finished comparing answers, review the correct answers as a class, either by eliciting the answers from individual students or by having volunteers write their answers on the board. In classes with time constraints, we recommend that you write the answers on the board, as this method is faster.

We suggest that you follow a similar approach with homework by quickly reviewing correct answers. In large classes, you may prefer to systematically select which papers to review out of class in order to give individual feedback and check progress. If five to ten papers are collected every session, each student will receive individual feedback several times per term.

Actively developing free expression

One of the greatest challenges in the post-intermediate classroom is successfully engaging learners in free discussions and role plays. Students are often frustrated by the disparity in level between the complex thoughts they wish to express and the language they have at their command. There are psychological and psychosocial hurdles as well. Adult and young-adult students often worry that they will be judged by their teachers as well as their peers.

The following four techniques form part of a process approach to discussion and are recommended to mitigate the challenge of free discussions and role plays. They support learner confidence and increase quantity, quality, and complexity of expression.

Idea framing. When students are presented—unprepared—with a discussion topic, they typically approach it narrowly; for example, if you propose a discussion about community service, students may only think about one particular aspect of the topic. Worse, students often worry about what you consider appropriate to include in the discussion.

Providing students with a stimulus such as an online or magazine survey or questionnaire can help them frame their ideas by indirectly suggesting topics to be included in the discussion to follow. Surveys and questionnaires you provide also reduce student anxiety by clarifying your expectations of what is appropriate to include in the discussion.

Notepadding. Giving students an opportunity to write notes helps them consider how they will express their ideas. Here again, students may start with a narrow view of what to include in the discussion, but when they are given preparation time beforehand, they will broaden their ideas and plan how they want to express them. Notepadding builds confidence and yields more complex statements than discussion without preparation does.

Text-mining. Although language textbooks usually contain readings that provide students with an opportunity to confront "i+1" comprehensible language, using these readings solely for reading comprehension can be a missed opportunity. One way to make the most of a textbook reading is to ask students to notice and select language from it ("mining its text") that they can use in a discussion or role play. Permit students to circle, underline, or copy "mined" language prior to classroom discussions. Text-mining greatly enhances students' ability to acquire and use more sophisticated language.

Wordposting. Another huge challenge to students is remembering known language—even recently learned language—and using it in discussions and role plays. But when students do not use and reuse learned language, they inevitably forget it.

To ensure that students recycle previously taught language, we suggest that you (or the students themselves) make and keep "wordposts"—lists of relevant recyclable language. Wordposts can be written on the board or photocopied and distributed. To encourage the use of the wordposts during the discussion, you or your students can write a checkmark, cross out, or circle each word or phrase as it is used. Wordposting is one effective recycling technique that makes English unforgettable.

Teaching the receptive skills: reading and listening

Reading and listening are sometimes thought of as receptive skills. In a communicative classroom, however, reading and listening activities can greatly enhance speaking and writing, provide growth of comprehension, and help students cope with authentic language containing unknown words and complex ideas. The following are suggestions for approaching reading and listening in order to gain maximum benefit.

Authentic reading and listening passages will always contain a quantity of unknown language. We know that students can understand more language than they can produce, but they are often hesitant to tackle readings or listening activities that include unknown language. (See the earlier discussion of the value of "i+1" comprehensible input on page Tviii.)

Readings and listening activities should represent real language. However, it is important to avoid language that falls so far above comprehensible level that students can't learn from it. Identifying a zone of comprehensibility enables readings and listening activities to maximize the building of comprehension skills and vocabulary.

As stated earlier, it is important to recognize that language learners instinctively try to translate every word as they read and are frustrated by their inability to create a one-to-one correspondence of the English words to their native language. Adopting an approach that respects the amount of challenge a reading or listening activity presents, discouraging translation, and teaching reading and listening skills and strategies can help students read and listen successfully.

Reading strategies and applied comprehension skills. Reading skills and strategies that help students cope with the challenge of foreign- or second-language reading help prepare them to confront such readings with confidence. Some are practiced before, some during, and others after the actual reading.

Before a reading activity, encourage students to explore their ideas about the topic of the reading. To pique their interest in the reading, get them to access any knowledge they already have about the topic. Another strategy that helps students cope with a reading is identifying its source; for example, is it a magazine article, a website, a series of letters, an advertisement, etc.? These pre-reading strategies will help students approach a reading with the confidence that they know what is coming and will discourage them from focusing on every unknown word.

Some strategies and skills that help students while they read are *skimming, scanning,* and *focusing on the context* in which unknown words occur, to help students understand meaning (instead of trying to translate those words). Encourage students to quickly read the passage from beginning to end without stopping for details. One way to teach skimming is to have students read the first sentence of each paragraph and the first few sentences at the beginning and the end of the passage.

Scanning for specific information is another helpful skill. Before students read line-for-line, they can be asked to find information about dates, names, ages, times, etc. Such information usually identifies itself by format—numbers, isolated words, charts, and the like. Keep in mind, though, that not all readings lend themselves naturally to skimming or scanning. Only choose skimming or scanning with readings that naturally lend themselves to that sort of examination.

As students read and encounter unknown words, help them to find the context clues that "explain" the meaning of those words. In the following sentence, the general meaning of the word *dousing* can be understood from the context: "Songkran is a wild and wonderful festival in which people of all ages have fun *dousing* each other with water for three solid days." Many students would instinctively reach for the bilingual dictionary to look up *dousing* or simply decide the reading was too hard. But asking them to look for the meaning in the surrounding text (the "context," where they will find "with water") helps build the habit of searching for context clues and taking educated guesses.

A good way to help students see the value of searching for context clues is to ask them to explain their reasons for guessing the meaning of a word. Ask them to go into the text to provide support for their opinions. In the case above, students would cite "with water" to support their opinions. Note that a precise definition or translation is not necessarily the goal. Students should also be encouraged to guess the "sense" of a word; for example, whether it is positive or negative, male or female, something you eat or wear, etc. If this is done regularly, students will develop the habit of looking for meaning in the context.

After reading, *summarizing* a text is a valuable applied reading comprehension skill. When students are able to summarize a reading, it indicates that they have identified the main idea and can distinguish it from random facts or details that are included in the article.

One way to provide practice in distinguishing main ideas from details is to ask students to *take notes* as they read and to organize or separate their notes into categories; for example, in a reading about the life of a famous composer, students can be asked to take notes about the key events in that person's life. In a reading about the effects of globalization, students can be asked to jot down information about the pros and cons. Putting notes into categories helps students perceive the details that support the main ideas of a reading and can provide a framework for a logical and articulately expressed summary. A further way to help students understand the main idea of or the point of view expressed in a reading is to ask them to try to *paraphrase* what the author's idea is. As they read, ask students to put the author's words into their own words.

The input/task ratio. When asking comprehension questions about a reading (or a listening activity; see below) it is helpful to keep in mind the relative difficulty of the text. If a text is very challenging and has a lot of difficult or unfamiliar language and complex ideas, questions and tasks should be relatively easy and receptive, such as determining general or main ideas. If a text is relatively easy, the tasks and questions should be commensurately more difficult, productive, and inferential, and should require more critical thinking. In other words, the difficulty of the task should be inversely proportional to the difficulty of the text. If this ratio is respected, even very difficult texts can be used by students at lower levels.

Listening skills and strategies. Listening is often frustrating to students because of factors such as speed, accent, background interference, and the fact that in the real world, a listener usually has only one opportunity to understand. In contrast, a reading text—even if difficult—can be explored, studied, and re-read at the learner's pace.

For most learners, understanding spoken language can be very difficult, especially when the speaker is not seen, as during a phone conversation or when listening to the radio, a podcast, or a classroom audio program. Development of listening skills and strategies can help reduce the natural panic that occurs when students listen to challenging speech. If we want post-intermediate students to be able to cope with real spoken language, it is crucial to expose them to authentic listening passages recorded at a normal rate of speed and in a variety of accents.

As language educators, it is important for us to ask ourselves what the purpose of listening comprehension exercises is in a communicative classroom. Is it to get students to understand every word they hear in a comprehension exercise or is it to help them learn how to successfully understand real spoken English in the world outside the classroom? Although we know the answer is the latter, we struggle with our own feelings of "failure" when post-intermediate students are unable to easily understand everything in the listening texts we bring to class.

To offset our own fears as educators, it is important to explain to students the value of challenging listening experiences and to reassure them that the exercise is not a test of whether or not they understood everything the first time. Be sure students understand that the purpose of this practice is to help them obtain meaning, even from something that is not completely understood, and not simply to answer questions.

In presenting listening comprehension practice in class, be sure students have several opportunities to listen to each passage. Focus students' attention by having them listen for a different purpose each time they listen. Build up the progression of tasks from easier to more challenging ones. Add an extra listening opportunity again after other tasks in order to let students check their work.

The input/task ratio especially applies to constructing listening activities in the classroom. (See pages Txiii–Txiv.) If the listening passage is fast, accented, or otherwise difficult, present a less challenging or receptive task, such as understanding main ideas or identifying the global purpose. On the other hand, if the listening passage is slow or otherwise easy, present more productive or difficult exercises. A convenient way to apply the input/task ratio to listening comprehension exercises is to compare them to the reading skills of skimming and scanning: for more difficult listening passages, expect students to "skim" by listening and getting the main idea, but few details, inferences, or complexities. For easier listening passages, expect them to "scan" for details, make inferences, and draw conclusions based on those.

In all cases, however, make sure students realize that these exercises are meant to increase their ability to cope with natural spoken speech, not a means to judge what they can understand on one listening.

Improving written expression

Writing tasks perform a number of useful functions in a communicative classroom:

- First, they offer yet another vehicle for students to remember, practice, and consolidate language they are learning, reinforcing vocabulary and grammatical conventions.

- Second, they promote the development of accuracy because students and instructors read and edit the writing; errors are visible and can be meticulously corrected.

- Third, they can prepare students for the real writing they will do in their work and social lives: letters, e-mails, reports, articles, messages, and the like.

- Fourth, tasks based on a writing syllabus can teach students the conventions of standard written expression, such as sentence and paragraph development, use of topic sentences, and written rhetorical devices. These cannot be learned through speaking activities.

It's reasonable to expect an increase in both quality and quantity of expression as students develop their writing skills. Students should be reminded and encouraged to actively use the language they have learned, and they should try to vary the vocabulary they use and the way they express themselves. In addition, they should always be encouraged to try and write a little more. If students share their writing in pairs or groups, have other students ask questions about information they want to know more about. Do the same when <u>you</u> read students' work.

Writing is a process that begins with ideas. Encourage students to brainstorm ideas, write lists, take notes, organize their thoughts, use graphic organizers, etc. before they begin writing a first draft. Encourage revision as a regular habit in writing. Students should get feedback from others and look at their own writing critically for clarity of ideas. Then they should rewrite to try and improve what they wrote in the first draft.

When you first read your students' writing, respond to the ideas they are trying to express, rather than focusing on errors. Ask questions that encourage students to say more and clarify what they are saying. Focus on accuracy only after students have had an opportunity to revise and improve the content of their own work.

Students at post-intermediate and advanced level can cope with challenging writing assignments and they should be expected to use high-level grammatical structures in their writing. For example, in an essay about public corruption, students should readily use conditional constructions to examine what they would do if they had the power to change things.

As at all levels of instruction, however, it is important to construct a writing assignment that students are prepared to write about. Many failures in writing occur when students begin translating their ideas from their own language into English, instead of using the words, expressions, and grammar they are familiar with. When assigning a writing task, ask yourself if it will require students to use known language or whether the subject is unrelated to what they know.

To help develop students' abilities in the conventions of writing, it is helpful to link each writing assignment to a particular skill to be applied, such as sequencing events, persuasion, punctuation of dialogue, organizing a comparison and contrast essay, and other features of effective writing. In this way, students practice the language they are learning as well as the conventions expected in English writing. Finally, so that students become familiar with the conventions of formal and informal written expression, vary the text types in assignments, from e-mails to formal letters and essays.

Commonsense Testing and Evaluation

One of a teacher's most difficult challenges is to construct tests that fairly evaluate global student progress. Without pretending to present an exhaustive approach to testing and evaluation, we offer a few principles. First of all, although all teachers accept the principle that "we should test only what we teach," this is easier said than done in a communicative classroom, where more than 50% of class time is spent practicing the oral/aural skills. If we were to "test what we taught" this would require more than 50% of our test items to evaluate listening and speaking. However, oral tests take a lot of time because each student must be tested individually; few programs provide enough time for such testing. For this reason, most programs rely on tests that are largely written.

We would like to suggest procedures that answer the following two questions:

- How can students receive credit for their progress in speaking— the aspects of language learning that have received the most emphasis in class? In other words, how can we evaluate speaking?

- How can we construct a written test that permits students of all ability levels to demonstrate their knowledge of the language they've studied and which measures their abilities in listening and reading comprehension as well as written expression?

Oral tests

As mentioned above, formal oral tests are very time-consuming. In a class of thirty students, administering a five-minute unit oral test to each student would take 150 minutes (two and a half hours). Almost no program could dedicate that much time to oral testing at the end of each textbook unit, so it's only possible to administer a few oral tests per term. However, teachers report that when there are very few oral tests, students tend to panic and perform poorly because the stakes are too high. And a test on which students underperform doesn't accurately assess their progress. A more practical and effective way to measure students' progress is to provide an ongoing, less formal, in-class assessment of speaking skills.

One approach is to keep a record of students' progress in each class session. If a class has thirty students, we suggest focusing on ten students in each session, making a mental note of their spoken responses in whole class, small group, and pair work activities. At the end of the session, make a notation in your record book in a form that makes most sense to you. One simple notation system is to give each student you evaluated a "plus," a "check," or a "minus" for that day's oral work. In the following class session, focus on the next ten students, and in the following session, focus on the final third of the students. In that way, students receive credit for their progress as they begin to retrieve and use target language to communicate in class. You can determine the criteria you wish to use to evaluate your students (e.g. fluency, accuracy, clarity, etc.). The important thing is that you have a record of each student's ongoing progress. At the post-intermediate level, classroom discussions, presentations, and debates all offer opportunities for ongoing informal oral assessment. This set of records can then be factored into the grade each student receives for the marking period, unit, term, etc. The percentage of weight you wish to give to this ongoing oral evaluation in relation to the written test is up to you and your program.

Written tests

How can we construct a written test that enables us to fairly evaluate the progress of all students—those who are gifted as well as those who struggle? All students learn, though not at the same rate, and some learn more from a textbook unit or from a lecture, etc. than others. We suggest that test items in written tests be weighted as follows so that all students who have progressed acceptably can demonstrate that growth on the test. (Note that the item types described below can be mixed throughout the test.)

We propose that 80% of the test items be receptive and literal ones. Examples of these item types would include such things as true and false, multiple choice, and cloze sentences with word banks from which to choose items. These items should "test" students' knowledge of the target vocabulary and grammar they studied in the unit. In terms of difficulty, these items should be at a level that all students who have studied and learned the material can answer successfully.

In turn, 10% of test items should be items that require more thought and more productive responses than those mentioned above. Examples of these items would be an answer to a question, a completion of a conversation response, or cloze sentences in which students have to complete items without benefit of a word bank or a set of choices.

These items should "test" students' knowledge and use of vocabulary and grammar learned in the unit. Regarding difficulty level, these items should target average and above-level students. While it is possible that weaker students will correctly complete these items, it is not probable. It is worth noting that all students sometimes perform above expectation, and that performance should be encouraged.

The final 10% of test items should require responses of multiple sentences or paragraphs, etc. that indicate mastery of vocabulary and grammar and that may require critical thinking, such as inferential understanding of language and ideas in context from reading passages. These items would typically target the strongest students in the class. Again, it is possible, however unlikely, that some weaker and average-ability students might perform well on these items. Any success should be supported.

If a written test is constructed using items apportioned as above, all students can demonstrate progress, with the weakest students (who have worked to their capacity) probably achieving a potential 80% score, average-ability students achieving a potential 90% score, and the best students achieving a potential 100%. Of course, these percentages are not guaranteed, but they do permit even the weakest students to see their progress and the best ones to demonstrate their mastery.

A compelling reason for this approach to constructing written tests is to address teachers' frequent concern that their students don't "do well on the test." Research has shown that teachers often write tests that provide items weighted on the side of the most difficult content taught, under the rationale that "if students can answer these questions, I can assume they could have answered easier items." The consequence of this assumption is that many students don't receive recognition for the language they <u>have</u> learned because they are unable to answer the most difficult and productive items perfectly. However, it is our contention that the easier content, such as the knowledge of the target vocabulary, is at least as important as the ability to use the most difficult grammar. We believe that all of the content should be evaluated.

Global evaluation

Once a score on a written test has been determined, you (or your program) can decide how much weight to give oral tests or the ongoing oral assessment in the student's global evaluation. If we are to truly test what we taught, and the amount of time spent on the oral/aural skills was 75%, then a case could be made for "counting" the written test for 25% of the grade, although few programs would adopt such a scale, for reasons of expediency. Our purpose here is to provide a starting point for discussion to enable programs to consider what weight to assign the oral and written tests so that each student's evaluation meets the goals of the program.

Periodic assessment of writing skills

Since written expression (essays, letters, reports, etc.) is an important part of any post-intermediate syllabus, students' progress should be evaluated regularly. In-class and homework writing assignments and formal writing tests should all be taken into consideration for a global assessment of writing skills.

When evaluating student writing skills on a formal writing test (an essay, for example), take the following criteria equally into account:

- appropriateness (Is the essay on topic?)
- completeness (Does the essay adequately develop the topic?)
- accuracy (Does the essay use complete sentences? Is the grammar, spelling, and punctuation correct? Are vocabulary and idiomatic expressions used meaningfully?)
- clarity (Is the essay well organized? Are ideas presented in a clear and logical manner? Are details used to clarify and illustrate ideas?)
- complexity (Does the essay use a variety of sentence structures? Is the vocabulary varied?)

Again, you or your program can decide how much weight to give assessment of the writing skill in a student's global evaluation.

ActiveTeach For more information on the topics in this section, please consult the ActiveTeach disc in the back of this Teacher's Edition and Lesson Planner.

Summit Unit Format

Summit units contain six two-page lessons, described in detail on pages Txviii–Txxvi.

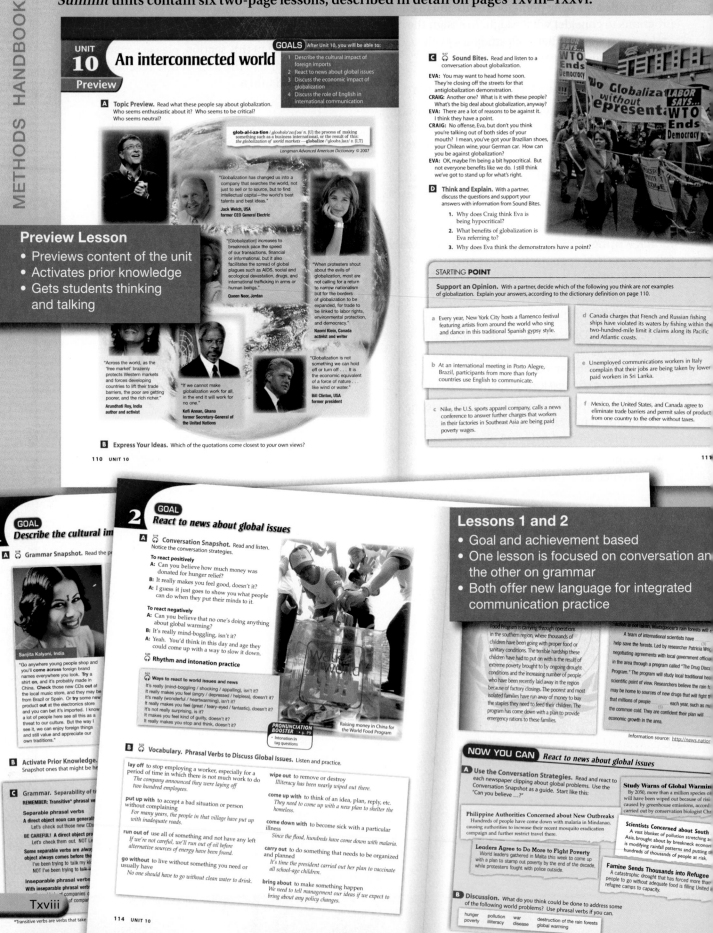

Preview Lesson
- Previews content of the unit
- Activates prior knowledge
- Gets students thinking and talking

Lessons 1 and 2
- Goal and achievement based
- One lesson is focused on conversation and the other on grammar
- Both offer new language for integrated communication practice

Lessons 3 and 4
- Goal and achievement based
- Build reading or listening skills and strategies
- End with a discussion, debate, presentation, or project

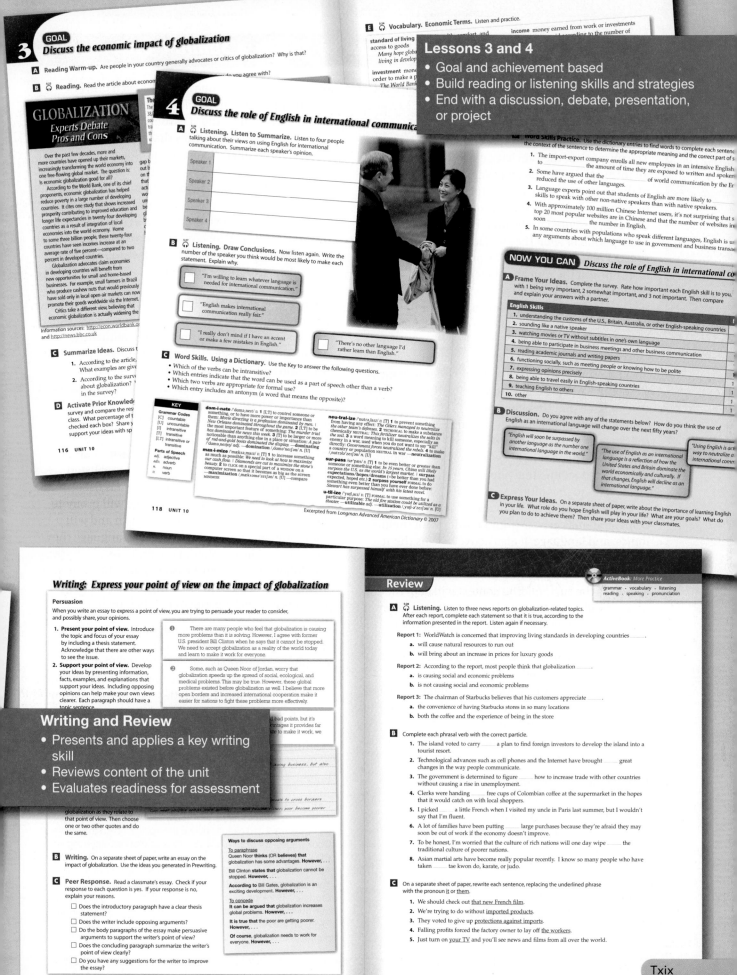

3 GOAL **Discuss the economic impact of globalization**

A Reading Warm-up. Are people in your country generally advocates or critics of globalization? Why is that?

B Reading. Read the article about econom... do you agree with?

GLOBALIZATION
Experts Debate
Pros and Cons

Over the past few decades, more and more countries have opened up their markets, increasingly transforming the world economy into one free-flowing global market. The question is: Is economic globalization good for all?

According to the World Bank, one of its chief proponents, economic globalization has helped reduce poverty in a large number of developing countries. It cites one study that shows increased prosperity contributing to improved education and longer life expectancies in twenty-four developing countries as a result of integration of local economies into the world economy. Home to some three billion people, these twenty-four countries have seen incomes increase at an average rate of five percent—compared to two percent in developed countries.

Globalization advocates claim economies in developing countries will benefit from new opportunities for small and home-based businesses. For example, small farmers in Brazil who produce cashew nuts that would previously have sold only in local open-air markets can now promote their goods worldwide via the Internet.

Critics take a different view, believing that economic globalization is actually widening the ...

Information sources: http://econ.worldbank.or... and http://news.bbc.co.uk

C Summarize Ideas. Discuss t...
1. According to the article, ... What examples are give...
2. According to the surv... about globalization? ... in the survey?

D Activate Prior Knowledg... survey and compare the res... class. What percentage of t... checked each box? Share y... support your ideas with sp...

116 UNIT 10

E Vocabulary. Economic Terms. Listen and practice.

standard of living ... access to goods ... *Many hope globa... living in develop...*

income money earned from work or investments

investment mone... order to make a p... *The World Bank...*

4 GOAL **Discuss the role of English in international communica...**

A Listening. Listen to Summarize. Listen to four people talking about their views on using English for international communication. Summarize each speaker's opinion.

Speaker 1	
Speaker 2	
Speaker 3	
Speaker 4	

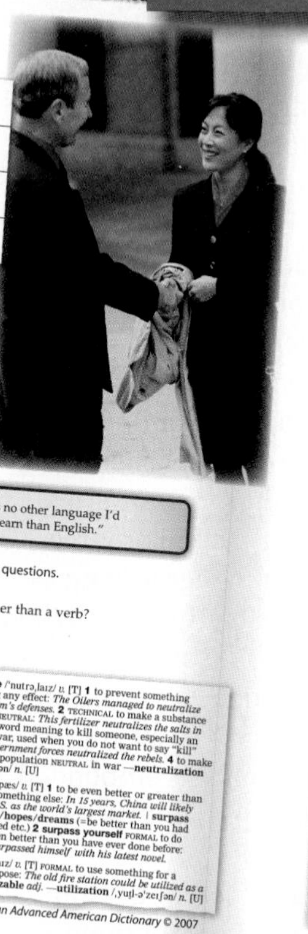

B Listening. Draw Conclusions. Now listen again. Write the number of the speaker you think would be most likely to make each statement. Explain why.

☐ "I'm willing to learn whatever language is needed for international communication."

☐ "English makes international communication really fair."

☐ "I really don't mind if I have an accent or make a few mistakes in English."

☐ "There's no other language I'd rather learn than English."

C Word Skills. Using a Dictionary. Use the Key to answer the following questions.
- Which of the verbs can be intransitive?
- Which entries indicate that the word can be used as a part of speech other than a verb?
- Which two verbs are appropriate for formal use?
- Which entry includes an antonym (a word that means the opposite)?

KEY
Grammar Codes
[C] countable
[U] uncountable
[I] intransitive
[T] transitive
[I,T] intransitive or transitive
Parts of Speech
adj. adjective
adv. adverb
n. noun
v. verb

dom·i·nate /ˈdɑməˌneɪt/ v. **1** [I,T] to control someone or something, or to have more power or importance than them: *Movie directing is a profession dominated by men.* | *New Orleans dominated throughout the game.* **2** [I,T] to be the most important feature of something: *The murder trial has dominated the news this week.* **3** [T] to be larger or more noticeable than anything else in a place or situation: *A pair of red-and-gold boots dominated the display.* —**dominating** /ˈdɑməˌneɪtɪŋ/ adj. —**domination** /ˌdɑməˈneɪʃən/ n. [U]

max·i·mize /ˈmæksəˌmaɪz/ v. [T] **1** to increase something as much as possible: *We need to look at how to maximize our cash flow.* | *Diamonds are cut to maximize the stone's beauty.* **2** to CLICK on a special part of a WINDOW on a computer screen so that it becomes as big as the screen —**maximization** /ˌmæksəməˈzeɪʃən/ n. [U] —compare MINIMIZE

neu·tral·ize /ˈnutrəˌlaɪz/ v. [T] **1** to prevent something from having any effect: *The Oilers managed to neutralize the other team's defenses.* **2** TECHNICAL to make a substance chemically NEUTRAL: *This fertilizer neutralizes the salts in the soil.* **3** a word meaning to kill someone, especially an enemy in a war, used when you do not want to say "kill" directly: *Government forces neutralized the rebels.* **4** to make a country or population NEUTRAL in war —**neutralization** /ˌnutrələˈzeɪʃən/ n. [U]

sur·pass /səˈpæs/ v. [T] **1** to be even better or greater than someone or something else: *In 15 years, China will likely surpass the U.S. as the world's largest market.* | **surpass expectations/hopes/dreams** (=be better than you had expected, hoped etc.) **2 surpass yourself** FORMAL to do something even better than you have ever done before: *Stewart has surpassed himself with his latest novel.*

u·til·ize /ˈyutlˌaɪz/ v. [T] FORMAL to use something for a particular purpose: *The old fire station could be utilized as a theater.* —**utilizable** adj. —**utilization** /ˌyutl-əˈzeɪʃən/ n. [U]

Excerpted from *Longman Advanced American Dictionary* © 2007

118 UNIT 10

Word Skills Practice. Use the dictionary entries to find words to complete each sentenc... the context of the sentence to determine the appropriate meaning and the correct part of s...
1. The import-export company enrolls all new employees in an intensive English ... to ______ the amount of time they are exposed to written and spoken...
2. Some have argued that the ______ of world communication by the En... reduced the use of other languages.
3. Language experts point out that students of English are more likely to ______ skills to speak with other non-native speakers than with native speakers.
4. With approximately 100 million Chinese Internet users, it's not surprising that s... top 20 most popular websites are in Chinese and that the number of websites in... soon ______ the number in English.
5. In some countries with populations who speak different languages, English is us... any arguments about which language to use in government and business transa...

NOW YOU CAN *Discuss the role of English in international co...*

A Frame Your Ideas. Complete the survey. Rate how important each English skill is to you, with 1 being very important, 2 somewhat important, and 3 not important. Then compare and explain your answers with a partner.

English Skills	
1. understanding the customs of the U.S., Britain, Australia, or other English-speaking countries	
2. sounding like a native speaker	
3. watching movies or TV without subtitles in one's own language	
4. being able to participate in business meetings and other business communication	
5. reading academic journals and writing papers	
6. functioning socially, such as meeting people or knowing how to be polite	
7. expressing opinions precisely	
8. being able to travel easily in English-speaking countries	1
9. teaching English to others	1
10. other	1

B Discussion. Do you agree with any of the statements below? How do you think the use of English as an international language will change over the next fifty years?

"English will soon be surpassed by another language as the number one international language in the world."

"The use of English as an international language is a reflection of how the United States and Britain dominate the world economically and culturally. If that changes, English will decline as an international language."

"Using English is act... way to neutralize a... international comm..."

C Express Your Ideas. On a separate sheet of paper, write about the importance of learning English in your life. What role do you hope English will play in your life? What are your goals? What do you plan to do to achieve them? Then share your ideas with your classmates.

Writing and Review
- Presents and applies a key writing skill
- Reviews content of the unit
- Evaluates readiness for assessment

Writing: Express your point of view on the impact of globalization

Persuasion

When you write an essay to express a point of view, you are trying to persuade your reader to consider, and possibly share, your opinions.

1. **Present your point of view.** Introduce the topic and focus of your essay by including a thesis statement. Acknowledge that there are other ways to see the issue.
2. **Support your point of view.** Develop your ideas by presenting information, facts, examples, and explanations that support your ideas. Including opposing opinions can help make your own views clearer. Each paragraph should have a topic sentence...

❶ There are many people who feel that globalization is causing more problems than it is solving. However, I agree with former U.S. president Bill Clinton when he says that it cannot be stopped. We need to accept globalization as a reality of the world today and learn to make it work for everyone.

❷ Some, such as Queen Noor of Jordan, worry that globalization speeds up the spread of social, ecological, and medical problems. This may be true. However, these global problems existed before globalization as well. I believe that more open borders and increased international cooperation make it easier for nations to fight these problems more effectively.

...bad points, but it's ...ntages it provides far ...te to make it work, we

...globalization as they relate to that point of view. Then choose one or two other quotes and do the same.

Ways to discuss opposing arguments

To paraphrase
Queen Noor **thinks (OR believes) that** globalization has some advantages. **However, . . .**

Bill Clinton **states that** globalization cannot be stopped. **However, . . .**

According to Bill Gates, globalization is an exciting development. **However, . . .**

To concede
It can be argued that globalization increases global problems. **However, . . .**

It is true that the poor are getting poorer. **However, . . .**

Of course, globalization needs to work for everyone. **However, . . .**

B Writing. On a separate sheet of paper, write an essay on the impact of globalization. Use the ideas you generated in Prewriting.

C Peer Response. Read a classmate's essay. Check if your response to each question is yes. If your response is no, explain your reasons.

☐ Does the introductory paragraph have a clear thesis statement?
☐ Does the writer include opposing arguments?
☐ Do the body paragraphs of the essay make persuasive arguments to support the writer's point of view?
☐ Does the concluding paragraph summarize the writer's point of view clearly?
☐ Do you have any suggestions for the writer to improve the essay?

120 UNIT 10

Review

ActiveBook: More Practice
grammar · vocabulary · listening · reading · speaking · pronunciation

A Listening. Listen to three news reports on globalization-related topics. After each report, complete each statement so that it is true, according to the information presented in the report. Listen again if necessary.

Report 1: WorldWatch is concerned that improving living standards in developing countries ______.
a. will cause natural resources to run out
b. will bring about an increase in prices for luxury goods

Report 2: According to the report, most people think that globalization ______.
a. is causing social and economic problems
b. is not causing social and economic problems

Report 3: The chairman of Starbucks believes that his customers appreciate ______.
a. the convenience of having Starbucks stores in so many locations
b. both the coffee and the experience of being in the store

B Complete each phrasal verb with the correct particle.
1. The island voted to carry ______ a plan to find foreign investors to develop the island into a tourist resort.
2. Technological advances such as cell phones and the Internet have brought ______ great changes in the way people communicate.
3. The government is determined to figure ______ how to increase trade with other countries without causing a rise in unemployment.
4. Clerks were handing ______ free cups of Colombian coffee at the supermarket in the hopes that it would catch on with local shoppers.
5. I picked ______ a little French when I visited my uncle in Paris last summer, but I wouldn't say that I'm fluent.
6. A lot of families have been putting ______ large purchases because they're afraid they may soon be out of work if the economy doesn't improve.
7. To be honest, I'm worried that the culture of rich nations will one day wipe ______ the traditional culture of poorer nations.
8. Asian martial arts have become really popular recently. I know so many people who have taken ______ tae kwon do, karate, or judo.

C On a separate sheet of paper, rewrite each sentence, replacing the underlined phrase with the pronoun it or them.
1. We should check out that new French film.
2. We're trying to do without imported products.
3. They voted to give up protections against imports.
4. Falling profits forced the factory owner to lay off the workers.
5. Just turn on your TV and you'll see news and films from all over the world.

121

Applied Methods: How to Teach a *Summit* Unit

See pages Txviii–Txix for pictorial examples of the following lessons.

Preview Lesson

The purpose of the Preview Lesson is to provide an introduction to the topic and social language of the unit. A Goals list at the top right of the first page announces the communication goals that are presented in the unit, building students' anticipation of what they will learn in the unit. We suggest that the four goals be pointed out at the beginning of the unit and then individually as each of the four numbered lessons begins.

The Preview Lesson includes highly authentic "i+1" language which should be comprehensible yet challenging for a student in the *Summit* series. It is well known that students make good progress when they are exposed to such language as long as they are not expected to produce it right away. When students see that they can cope with somewhat challenging language, their confidence grows and they enter the unit motivated with the expectation of success. The Preview Lesson contains embedded illustrations, contextual photographs, and other visual cues to meaning.

The material included in each Preview Lesson helps students activate prior knowledge of themes, topics, and language. It also actively helps them build the strategy of determining meaning from context. Encouraging students to use visual cues as well as the surrounding context will help them understand any unknown language in what they are reading or listening to in this first part of the unit.

Preview text. The first page of the Preview Lesson contains a text for students to observe, read, and think about. It may be a website, a catalogue, a quiz, an advertisement, or something similar. In addition to the preview text, you will find one or more exercises that provide practice with the content and language of the preview text.

▶ **Teaching tips** Before discussing the preview text, allow a few minutes for students to silently familiarize themselves with its content and form and explore its details. Always remind students to use the illustrations and context to help determine the meaning of unfamiliar words and phrases. This is an important learning strategy for understanding material above one's productive level. When students have had a few minutes to take in the preview text, ask a few questions about the content

of the text. (Specific questions for each preview text are provided in the interleaved section of this Teacher's Edition—the "Lesson Planner.")

The discussion activities that follow the preview text (usually called "Express Your Ideas") are designed to get students to start talking about the unit topic. These discussion activities help students use both familiar and unfamiliar (new) language from the preview text. Students can discuss in pairs or small groups. After students have concluded their discussions, review by asking a few students to share their ideas with the whole class.

Sound Bites. On the second page of the Preview Lesson, Sound Bites permits students to see a short conversation that contains natural, authentic, corpus-informed social language in a story context. An audio icon 🔊 indicates that the Sound Bites conversation is recorded on the Classroom Audio Program. Alternatively, you might ask students to access the audio directly from their ActiveBook. Sound Bites is not intended to be a conversation model for students to repeat and "learn." Rather, it is an opportunity to observe, read, and listen in order to notice language and how it is used. These examples of natural language will promote comprehension of real spoken English and will ready students for productive social language they will learn in the numbered integrated-skills lessons that follow the Preview Lesson. Sound Bites contains highly appealing idiomatic language that many students can pick up and make their own.

▶ **Teaching tips** Before students read and listen to the Sound Bites conversation, ask questions about the photo, if possible. For variety, and to provide listening practice, you may sometimes want to have students listen with books closed. Another option is to have students read the Sound Bites conversation silently first, then read and listen, or listen without reading. (Specific suggestions for each Sound Bites activity are given in the Lesson Planner, but we encourage you to use the approach you feel is best

FYI: There are several options for accessing the audio. If you are using the Classroom Audio Program audio CDs, CD and track numbers are listed directly above the audio icon on the Student's Book pages; for example, 4:15 indicates that the recording is on CD 4, track 15. If you are using the Digital Student's Book on ActiveTeach, you can click on the audio icons for instant play. Your students can do the same when using their own Digital Student's Book on their ActiveBook. Alternatively, your students can download individual MP3 files of each track directly from a folder on the ActiveBook. These files have the same CD and track numbers used in the Student's Book.

for your group.) No matter which approach you elect to use, however, it is always worthwhile to have students listen to the Sound Bites, whether before or after reading it. (See FYI on page Txx for alternative ways to access *Summit* audio.)

After students have become familiar with the Sound Bites, ask questions to check comprehension. Use the questions that are provided in the Lesson Planner or your own questions. Questions can be presented to the full class, written on the board for students to answer with a partner, or read aloud for students to write answers to. If appropriate, ask additional questions that relate the content of the Sound Bites conversation to students' own lives. Then proceed to the exercises that follow the Sound Bites.

Sound Bites exercises. A series of intensive exercises following each Sound Bites conversation provides practice in determining meaning of new language from context as well as activating previously learned language. One important feature of the second edition of *Summit* is an emphasis on asking students to **explain** their answers. In exercises called Think and Explain, students are asked to notice and cite key language from the Sound Bites to explain the basis of their answers. In addition to building critical thinking skills, explaining provides an opportunity to make receptive exercises productive; it stimulates discussion in class and trains students to use context to support an answer. An added benefit of asking students to find support for answers within a passage is improved performance on standardized tests that expect students to delve into texts to extract meaning. Other exercises ask students to apply key reading strategies to language encountered in the conversation in order to demonstrate understanding.

Starting Point. This final exercise in the Preview Lesson usually asks students to consolidate the information, personalize it, or discuss it before moving on to Lesson 1. In addition, it provides an opportunity for students to activate vocabulary or expressions learned in Sound Bites.

▶ **Teaching tips** The exercise questions can be asked in open class, written on the board for students to answer with a partner, or read aloud for students to write answers to. Specific suggestions are made in the Lesson Planner. When time is short, these exercises can be done as homework and reviewed quickly in class. They remain in the book,

however, as a convenient reminder of meaning when students study and prepare for tests.

Lessons 1 and 2: Conversation or Grammar Focus

Each unit in *Summit* has one lesson focused on grammar and one focused on conversation. They both offer new language as well as integrated communication practice. Lessons 1 and 2 (as all lessons) are always labeled with a communication goal, such as "Discuss your reactions to ads," so students are aware of what they will achieve during the course of the lesson. And these lessons (as all lessons) end with a communication activity in which students demonstrate to themselves mastery of the goal.

Conversation Snapshot. Lessons that focus on conversation always begin with a model conversation entitled Conversation Snapshot. To build awareness and facilitate comprehension, begin by asking questions about the photo or illustration, if appropriate. Conversation strategies that match those listed in the Student's Book Learning Objectives chart (pages iv–vii) are highlighted in boldface blue type. You may or may not wish to share the conversation strategies as they are listed in the Learning Objectives chart with your students. Note that in addition to the conversation strategies, one or more examples of the lesson's grammar or vocabulary may be embedded in the Conversation Snapshot to preview that language.

▶ **Teaching tips** Play the audio of the Conversation Snapshot or read it aloud yourself while the students read and listen with books open. Then check students' understanding of the conversation by asking comprehension questions. Additional questions are provided in the Lesson Planner to help students focus on the essential information in the Conversation Snapshot and determine the meaning of any new language from its context. The questions also prepare students to understand any grammar or vocabulary in the presentation that follows the Conversation Snapshot. Although additional questions are provided in the Lesson Planner, it is not necessary to stop there. When you ask questions, however, be mindful of what students are capable of. Don't elicit language or information that students would not know prior to reading the conversation.

An alternative presentation technique, especially in stronger groups, is to have students listen to the Conversation Snapshot with books closed first. When electing this option, have students look at the photo or illustration first to build a holistic awareness of the social situation of the conversation.

Rhythm and Intonation Practice. Following the Conversation Snapshot is a direction line for Rhythm and Intonation Practice. This second recording of the model directs students to listen and repeat in the pauses. The pause following each line of the model is an opportunity for students to focus on imitating the pronunciation, intonation, rhythm, and stress of the native speaker in the model. The Lesson Planner suggests specific rhythm, stress, and intonation features to call attention to.

▶ **Teaching tips**   Some instructors like to have students look at the text as they repeat. Many prefer to have students do the Rhythm and Intonation Practice with books closed, to avoid the interference of English spelling. We encourage experimentation to see which is more effective. With books closed, students can listen and repeat after each line. Encourage students to imitate the rhythm, stress, and intonation of the conversation as closely as possible, especially those lines that highlight conversation strategies. Correct rhythm, stress, and intonation where necessary and help students to pronounce the language clearly. Encourage students to continue practicing the rhythm and intonation, using the ActiveBook disc included in the back of their textbook.

Pronunciation Booster. In addition to the Rhythm and Intonation Practice that follows each Conversation Snapshot, each unit offers additional pronunciation practice in the Pronunciation Booster in the back of the Student's Book. The Pronunciation Booster provides presentation and practice of important features of pronunciation, intonation, or stress. Each concept in the Pronunciation Booster is linked in some way to the content of the lesson it accompanies.

▶ **Teaching tips**   The Pronunciation Booster should be considered an option for teachers who want to offer a detailed study of pronunciation in class. If teachers prefer not to use class time for these activities, students can do the Pronunciation Booster activities on their own. The listening exercises are on the students' ActiveBook disc.

Extra Pronunciation Activities worksheets can be printed out from your ActiveTeach. These activities provide more practice of the pronunciation lesson from the Pronunciation Booster. The activities use language from Grammar Snapshot (see below), Conversation Snapshot, and Vocabulary activities so students have the opportunity to apply what they've learned to familiar language from the Student's Book, increasing its memorability at the same time. A number of activities suggest that students listen to the Classroom Audio Program in class or on their ActiveBook.

Grammar Snapshot. Lessons that focus on grammar always begin with a Grammar Snapshot, which consists of an article, website, or "interviews" with the target grammar highlighted in boldface text for observation. Each new grammatical structure is previewed in the Grammar Snapshot so students read, hear, and understand the structure in context before they are required to manipulate it. Following each Grammar Snapshot is a strategy-based discussion activity.

▶ **Teaching tips**   Give students a few minutes to read the Grammar Snapshot and observe the grammar usage. Ask students if they notice any patterns in a particular grammar point or differences between two points presented together. Note that all Grammar Snapshots are on the Classroom Audio Program so students can hear the target grammar as well. Its use in class is optional. If you use the audio, you can choose to present it with books closed, while students are reading, or after they're finished reading. We encourage you to experiment and find what works best for your situation. You can also encourage students to listen on their own, using their ActiveBook disc.

Grammar. The new structure highlighted in the Grammar Snapshot is presented through authentic examples and clear, concise, easy-to-understand rules. Controlled exercises follow each grammar presentation in the Student's Book. The exercises provide written and/or oral practice with the structure(s) just taught and offer additional examples of its use in context.

▶ **Teaching tips**   Have students read the information in the Grammar presentation independently. Then ask them to look again at the Grammar Snapshot and try to apply the rules to the grammar highlighted within it. The Lesson Planner offers specific suggestions for presenting and reinforcing the grammar taught in each unit. Students internalize grammatical structures when they have the opportunity to use them in a meaningful and relevant context. Suggestions prompt students to begin using the new structure in the context of their own lives to express opinions, preferences, and other ideas. You can also use an inductive approach by printing out the Inductive Grammar Charts for this lesson from your ActiveTeach disc or by writing the example sentences from the grammar presentation on the board for discussion. The Inductive Grammar Charts are designed to check how well students understand the grammar or to help students figure out how the grammar works. Even if you prefer a more deductive approach, you can use the Inductive Grammar Charts as follow-up activities after the grammar has been presented.

For the controlled exercises that follow each grammar presentation, model the first item in each task if necessary. Have students complete the exercises independently, in pairs, or in small groups. Review answers as a class or have students check answers with a partner. All answers to the exercises are printed in green type on the Student's Book pages across from the Lesson Planner pages in this Teacher's Edition or directly on the Lesson Planner pages.

Grammar Booster. Following most Grammar presentations is an icon referring students to the Grammar Booster in the back of the Student's Book, where grammar from the unit is expanded in some way. In some cases, the Grammar Booster provides a wider focus on the specific grammar point taught in the lesson. In others, it includes related grammar concepts, some of which may be presented in more detail at another time. In still other cases, the Grammar Booster provides targeted review of related concepts students have learned earlier. The Grammar Booster contains confirming exercises for each grammar point presented. Answers are printed in green on the Grammar Booster pages or on the Lesson Planner pages in this Teacher's Edition. The Grammar Booster is an option for teachers who want to go beyond what is normally included in the textbook.

▶ **Teaching tips** If you choose not to use the Grammar Booster for your class, you may wish to selectively assign it to stronger students who are ready for more. Or you may wish to pick and choose those presentations you feel would be most beneficial in certain circumstances. Even if you elect not to use the Grammar Booster, students will appreciate having additional material for permanent reference in their textbook.

Vocabulary. Vocabulary is explicitly presented through context, definitions, and/or pictures. The vocabulary presentations in the Student's Book serve to convey meaning of each new vocabulary item and to provide reference for self-study, which is especially valuable as students prepare for tests.

Vocabulary in *Summit* is presented at word, phrase, and sentence level — including expressions, idioms, and collocations (words that "go together" as phrases).

▶ **Teaching tips** Begin by focusing students' attention on the illustrations, definitions, or sample sentences. Play the audio recording of the vocabulary or read it aloud as a model. Students can listen and repeat to build awareness of correct pronunciation. If necessary, clarify the meaning of any words or phrases students have difficulty understanding. Convey the meaning physically— through gestures, mime, or reference to people or objects in the room—or through examples or a simple explanation. Specific ideas on how to do this are provided in the Lesson Planner.

When possible, personalize the vocabulary. Use the vocabulary to talk about or ask questions about content familiar to your students. In open class, or with pairs and small groups, have students talk about their likes/dislikes, preferences, plans, relationships, belongings, habits, etc. in relation to the vocabulary.

Word Skills. As students advance, they not only need new, previously unknown vocabulary, but they also need to build on their existing productive vocabulary. Students can expand their vocabulary knowledge by learning word transformation, classification, association, and other skills. Word Skills presentations increase students' awareness of word features that can be applied to producing or comprehending new vocabulary. (Word Skills sections sometimes also appear in Lessons 3 and 4).

▶ **Teaching tips** One way to present the Word Skills sections is to begin by focusing students' attention on the definitions, explanations, illustrations, or example sentences included in the presentation. Or, when possible or appropriate, another option is to ask students to divide a word such as *self-critical* into its root (*critical*) and its prefix (*self-*) and define the root. As an example, ask *How would you describe someone who is critical?* (Someone who always finds mistakes or problems.) Then ask *What do you think* self-critical *means?* (Finding a lot of problems or mistakes with oneself.) In this way, students can infer how the prefix *self-* is combined with a number of adjectives and predict similar meaning. Examining words in this way makes it easier to remember them all and expands students' ability to create and understand new words as a group. Worksheets for Vocabulary-Building Strategies can be printed out from your

ActiveTeach. They are designed to help students use and apply new vocabulary and word skills from the unit for more effective learning. The strategies included in these worksheets include associating words, personalizing vocabulary, applying words in new contexts, diagramming, etc. These strategies are effective for students with a variety of learning styles, and students will be able to apply them to other vocabulary they learn as well.

Listening. Lessons 1 and 2 often contain exercises labeled Listening that practice a variety of key listening skills and strategies. These short exercises serve to provide comprehension practice and allow recollection of the vocabulary or grammar. Although short, these tasks require careful listening for sense and critical thinking. The unit's major listening presentation is included in Lesson 3 or 4 (and is more fully described there—see page Txxvi) and includes teaching tips that can be used for all listening activities in the unit.

A note about accented speakers in *Summit*: In order to accustom students to listening to English in today's world, where native speakers of English have a variety of accents and more than two-thirds of English speakers are non-native speakers of the language, *Summit* listening selections include regionally accented native speakers (British, Australian, Canadian, U.S. regional, etc.) as well as accented speakers from a variety of other languages. The Teacher's Edition identifies the regional or language background of speakers included in listening comprehension on the audio (in the printed audioscripts located in the back of this Teacher's Edition and on your ActiveTeach). We encourage you to share this information with your class and to remind students that English is an international language that is used to connect speakers from a variety of cultures and language backgrounds. Important: anything students are supposed to repeat (productive language models), such as Vocabulary and Conversation Snapshots, are always in standard American English.

Now You Can. Lessons 1 and 2 always end with a feature called Now You Can. It is here, at the end of the lesson, that students demonstrate the achievement of the communication goal of the lesson. As students work through the exercises in this section, meaningfully activating the language of the lesson, they will feel motivated by their success and see confirmation of their efforts in achieving the goal. Because each goal has obvious practical and communicative value, students will see their English lessons as worthwhile. Cognitive awareness of progress is exhilarating for language learners and keeps them interested and learning.

Lessons that include a Conversation Snapshot provide a speaking activity called Use the Conversation Strategies. In these activities, students create their own conversations and practice the conversation strategies presented in the Conversation Snapshot. These are usually facilitated by a "starter"—providing the first line of the Conversation Snapshot in order to help students begin their conversation, personalizing it with names, different vocabulary, or other appropriate social language they have learned.

Lessons that include a Grammar Snapshot provide a speaking activity called Use the Grammar. In this structured activity, students use the lesson's target grammar communicatively through discussion or role play.

Frequent planning activities, such as notepadding or idea framing (See page Txii for a description of notepadding and idea framing), help students prepare their ideas before they speak and provide a concrete reference to support them while they speak. Models of appropriate oral and written responses are often included so students know what is expected. For example, a model may show an example of how the target grammar can support their expression. Additional discussion topics are sometimes included to encourage students to extend the topic for further speaking and practice of target language.

▶ **Teaching tips**   The most important way to maximize the value of the Now You Can activity in Conversation Snapshot lessons is to encourage experimentation, showing approval when students create a personal adaptation of the original model conversation and continue it in unscripted ways. Be sure students don't think the purpose of the practice is to test their memory of the original Conversation Snapshot. It is exactly the opposite. As they practice, students should use their own language, as well as the target vocabulary or grammar.

Begin by reading the instructions aloud. Then begin the conversation with a more advanced student to demonstrate that students should use new language from the lesson and draw from other sources. You may wish to remind students of the conversation strategies presented in the Conversation Snapshot. If helpful, point out the language available on the two-page lesson for students to use. Note that the conversations each pair of students creates will vary.

As students practice, circulate and offer help as needed. Remind students to make eye contact during conversations to facilitate authentic communication, and encourage them to use natural pronunciation and intonation. An option is to suggest that students have the conversation a few times with different partners. Also, you can ask a couple of pairs to "perform" or re-create their conversation for the class or for other pairs. When different pairs of students perform in front of the class all students are reminded of how much social language they have learned.

An activity called Conversation Prompts can be printed out from your ActiveTeach disc. These activities are designed to remind students of language they have already learned in the unit—and in previous units—that they can use while they speak. They can be used as additional language support for the Use the Conversation Strategies activity, or they can be used as an alternative approach (with books closed).

For lessons that include a Grammar Snapshot, begin by reading instructions and any example sentences aloud. Then ask a stronger student to demonstrate new language from the lesson, encouraging that student to draw from other sources as well. If helpful, point out the language available on the two-page lesson for students to use. Note that the examples each student creates will vary.

As students practice, circulate and offer help as needed. Keep the lesson's grammar in mind when observing students' discussions. Encourage them to use the structure(s) taught in the lesson. Remind students to make eye contact during conversations, and encourage them to use natural pronunciation and intonation. Vary and change the pairing of students to keep the ideas fresh and interesting.

Lessons 3 and 4: Free Discourse Focus with Reading and Listening

Lessons 3 and 4 also begin with a communication goal such as "Discuss appearance and self-esteem," and culminate in a Now You Can activity in which students achieve that communication goal. These lessons open with either a reading or a listening activity. They provide authentic, interesting, and stimulating language input and lead students to free communication. Vocabulary or Word Skills are usually included and range from one-word items to collocations, idioms, and phrases. Vocabulary meaning is clearly conveyed through illustrations, definitions, and/or contextual sentences. The vocabulary is usually re-entered in the reading or listening and then practiced in the exercises and activities that follow.

Reading Warm-up. This exercise consists of a question or series of questions that prompts students to start thinking about the topic of the Reading. Before students read, they relate the topic of the Reading to their own lives. This process generates interest and aids understanding.

▶ **Teaching tips** Read the Reading Warm-up question(s) aloud. Model the activity by answering the questions yourself. Students can answer the question(s) with a partner or in small groups. To review, ask a few students to share their responses with the class. Specific suggestions can be found in the Lesson Planner.

Before students read the Reading selection itself, have them look at any photos or illustrations. If appropriate, ask questions about these visuals. Give students a few minutes to look at the selection independently. Encourage them to look at the title and any headings to help give them an idea of what the Reading is about.

Reading. All Readings are based on authentic sources. To avoid frustrating students with dense, difficult, lengthy texts, language has often been adapted from the original sources, and most articles have been shortened. However, we have taken great care to maintain the authentic character of the material.

In order to help students grow, Readings contain language that students have not yet learned but that they should be able to comprehend through context and similarity to language they know. However, it is important that students understand that it is not necessary for them to know the literal meaning of every word in order to understand the selection. Note that all Readings are available on the Classroom Audio Program and listening to the Reading is a recommended optional activity. Listening to a native speaker read aloud gives excellent ear training for the rhythm, stress, and intonation of extended (as opposed to conversational) speech. It also helps students learn collocations.

Comprehension or discussion activities always follow the Reading. These activities focus on specific reading skills and strategies such as understand from context, summarize, relate to personal experience, and express and support an opinion. Students are often asked to justify their answers by finding supporting documentation in the text or by providing personal reasoning or examples from their lives or experience. Some of the exercises that follow the Reading prompt students to use context to figure out the meaning of new language or to identify the most important information from the Reading.

▶ **Teaching tips** Ask students to try to answer the question from the Reading instructions as they read. (Then, at the end, after students have read the selection, the question can be asked again to see what conclusions students have come to.) Encourage students to guess at the meaning of new words as much as possible or to comprehend as much as they can without understanding every word. After students read, ask questions that lead them to figure out the meaning of new language, especially language that helps them identify the essential information in the Reading. Always ask students to explain or justify their answers from the text itself. Additional questions and activities are provided in the Lesson Planner.

Read the directions for each Reading exercise aloud or ask for a volunteer to read them. Have students read the exercise items and then reread the selection independently. As students read, they can underline words or information in the Reading that will help them to complete the exercise. Allow students a set period of time to refer to the Reading as necessary to complete the exercise individually, in pairs, or in small groups. Have students check their work with a partner, have pairs or groups check their work with another pair or group, or review answers as a class. For a challenge, have students practice reading the selection aloud in small groups.

It is recommended that students be given an opportunity to read and listen to each Reading. You may treat reading and listening separately, or reading and listening can be done together. We recommend reading first, then listening afterward. However, you may wish to use the Reading as a listening activity with closed books.

Reading Strategies worksheets can be printed out from your ActiveTeach. They are designed to teach specific strategies that support critical thinking and more effective reading. Strategies include classifying information, identifying supporting details, focusing on key causes and effects, etc. A Reading Glossary for each Reading, with simple definitions and paraphrases for selected words and phrases, can also be printed out from your ActiveTeach.

In addition to the Reading Strategies and Reading Glossaries, a Reading Speed Calculator chart can be printed out from your ActiveTeach. It includes total word counts of the main reading selections from every unit and a simple formula for calculating reading speed for each. If you choose to use this optional worksheet, each student should get a copy at the beginning of the term so he or she can record and compare reading speeds throughout the course.

If you want more extensive comprehension questions than the ones that appear in the Student's Book or the Lesson Planner, you can print out Extra Reading Comprehension Questions from your ActiveTeach. These worksheets contain both traditional comprehension and critical thinking questions. You may choose to use either or both with your class. They are also available to your students on their ActiveBook disc.

Listening. Listening activities in Lessons 3 and 4 provide the principal listening comprehension practice of the unit, containing language both at students' productive level as well as at the more challenging receptive (i+1) level. All receptive-level language in the Listening is comprehensible to students through context, intonation, and similarity to language they already know. There are generally two or more activities associated with each Listening. Activities focus on a variety of specific listening skills and strategies such as listen to summarize, infer information, compare and contrast, and identify supporting details. These skills and strategies are labeled on the pages of the text.

▶ **Teaching tips**   Point out to students that a major cause of lack of comprehension is the natural panic that occurs when learners hear unknown words. Explain that it is not necessary to understand every word to understand the selection. To maximize the effectiveness of these activities, avoid providing students with explanations of new language beyond any vocabulary that was taught prior to the Listening. If a student specifically asks about a new word, give the meaning, but do not spend a lot time expanding on it. Exposure to receptive-level language promotes students' language development and prepares them to communicate in the world outside the classroom, where language input is uncontrolled.

In general, it is suggested that students listen to the selection the first time with books closed. (In some cases, the Lesson Planner provides an alternative approach.) In this way, students can focus on the "big picture" without the distraction of completing the exercise. If information about the speakers, the setting, or the situation is included in the directions in the Student's Book, it is helpful to read this information aloud to make sure students focus on it. Alternatively, you might prefer to ask (after the first listening) *Who's talking? Where are the people? What are they doing?* If students are not forthcoming with answers to those questions, you can restate the question, providing two possible answers from which to choose. The value of this approach is to convince students that they have, in fact, understood a good deal, even if they have not understood everything. Demonstrating to students that they have understood something challenging builds their confidence and helps reduce their fear of listening.

Before students listen again and complete an exercise, have them look at the exercise first to focus their attention on the specific listening task required—such as listening for locations or opinions. Play the audio as many times as necessary for students to complete the exercise. Do not approach these exercises as "tests." Repeated exposure to each Listening has substantial instructional value. And increasing students' exposure to challenging language enhances their comprehension and confidence. Review answers as a class, or have students check answers with a partner.

Note that the Listening exercises are all available to your students on their ActiveBook. If you do not wish to play the audio, read the audioscript located at the back of this book (beginning on page AS1) aloud to your students.

Listening Strategies worksheets can be printed out from your ActiveTeach. The worksheets teach specific strategies that support critical thinking and more effective listening. Strategies include inferring point of view, listening for discourse markers, taking notes, predicting, etc.

Now You Can. Both Lessons 3 and 4 also culminate in an activity labeled Now You Can. The goal of Now You Can is to engage students in free and open-ended discussions, role plays, debates, and presentations that demonstrate their achievement of the communication goal of the lesson.

Free discussion is the goal of all language learners. However, foreign language students often have difficulty with free expression because the combination of gathering their thoughts and remembering the language they know is very challenging and often leads to silent panic. But post-intermediate students need to move beyond the controlled safety of models and info gaps they did at beginning and intermediate levels to achieve fuller self-expression. The Now You Can activities are deliberately constructed to provide prepared opportunities for students to experiment and succeed—because each task elicits language that is known.

As in Lessons 1 and 2, pre-speaking preparation activities build confidence and provide concrete support for speaking. Notepadding activities prompt students to make notes that organize their ideas and provide talking or writing points for the discussions, presentations, or debates that follow. Students also frame their ideas by filling out surveys and answering questions. When it is time to actually discuss a topic, students already have the language and the ideas laid out in front of them.

These free-speaking activities have been carefully designed so that students can use language learned from current <u>and</u> previous units. Massive opportunities for recycling language occur throughout *Summit*.

▶ **Teaching tips** If the Now You Can section includes visual stimuli such as photos or illustrations, have students look at these first. Ask questions about them to get students thinking about the topic. If a notepadding activity, a questionnaire, or a survey is included, have students compare their responses afterward or share ideas as they complete the activity. Collaborating in this way generates additional input and provides preparation for speaking. Be sure to point out any models that provide an example of how to begin or how to use target language from the unit lessons.

When Now You Can includes a project or a presentation, students can work individually, in pairs, or in groups. In addition, you can have students present what they've done to the class. For both projects and presentations, an option is to have the class evaluate what their classmates have done and express their reasons. It is important, however, to maintain a positive and supportive atmosphere. Make sure students continue to use English to communicate while they work on the projects or presentations.

Another option is to have students "text-mine" the unit's Reading or Listening passages or the unit's *Summit TV* video segment for language they could use in their discussion or role play. (See page Txii for a description of text-mining).

Discourse Strategies worksheets can be printed out from your ActiveTeach disc. These are designed to help students manage discussion more effectively. Strategies are presented and immediately followed by a pair work activity to practice the strategies before applying them in the actual Now You Can activity on the Student's Book page. Strategies include asking for agreement, showing interest or surprise, paraphrasing an opinion, etc.

Writing and Review

Writing. Each unit of *Summit* contains a page entirely dedicated to building students' writing skills. The *Summit* writing syllabus includes rigorous practice of important writing skills such as parallel structure, persuasion, avoiding sentence fragments, and expressing and supporting opinions clearly. Each writing page begins with a presentation of the writing skill and includes numerous examples. Usually a writing model provides students with a sample of what is expected. When appropriate, there is an error correction exercise. Each assignment is laid out step-by-step, beginning with Prewriting to help students generate ideas. Prewriting usually includes questions to answer, diagrams and charts to complete, or another device to help students organize their thoughts. The next step is Writing. Directions for Writing give clear instructions on the type and length of writing expected. Because revision is an integral part of writing, each writing page has a Self-Check where students are asked focused questions to help them review their own writing. Sometimes an additional step, Peer Response, is included where students review each other's work and can offer suggestions for revision.

▶ **Teaching tips** Encourage students to think and brainstorm ideas freely during the Prewriting activity. Circulate around the room and chat briefly with individual students or pairs to see how they are doing. If a student seems confused about the task, explain it further and make sure other students aren't confused as well.

Allow students to write silently during the Writing activity. Circulate around the room several times so you can keep track of the class's progress. You might want to ask the first student to finish to raise his or her hand. Ask students who have finished earlier than the others to do the Self-Check. They can also use the time to think about any revisions they would like to make.

If there is a Peer Response activity, have pairs of students exchange and read each other's writing. Make sure they focus on ideas first. It doesn't make sense to correct sentences until the writer's ideas have been clarified.

One technique for Peer Response is to have students think of at least three questions they can ask the writer in order to get more information about the writing topic. The writer then can choose whether or not to revise the writing to incorporate that information.

Extra Writing Skills Practice worksheets can be printed out from your ActiveTeach. They offer additional reinforcement through controlled practice of the writing skill taught in the unit's writing lesson. They help students build the confidence to apply these skills in their own free writing.

Review. This section reviews the essential content of the unit and offers students the opportunity to check their progress. It also allows the teacher to identify any areas of particular difficulty that may require additional practice. The Review page begins with a listening comprehension exercise that focuses on target language from the unit. The Review page also includes exercises that review the unit's vocabulary, grammar, and social language.

▶ **Teaching tips** Have students work individually to complete the Review exercises. Circulate to offer help as needed. Review the correct answers as a class. Note any areas of difficulty and provide additional instruction and practice as necessary.

We sincerely hope you enjoy *Summit* and that you and your students find it an effective course.

Joan Saslow and Allen Ascher

How to Use *ActiveTeach*

Other Resources (printable)

📁 How to use the Digital Student's Book

📁 Extension Activities

📁 • *Summit TV* Activity Worksheets
   • *Summit TV* Video Scripts

📁 • Oral Progress Assessment Charts
   • "Can-Do" Self-Assessment Charts

📁 • Audioscripts
   • Workbook Answer Key

ActiveTeach menu screen

Insert the disc into a computer and choose the Digital Student's Book or one of the printable resources.

The Digital Student's Book

Choose a unit and open any two-page lesson.

Choose any of the interactive activities from the student's *ActiveBook*.

Open any segment of the *Summit TV* video program.

Enlarge any section of the page.

Click on ◀ to instantly go to that lesson's Pronunciation Booster or Grammar Booster.

Play the audio.

Write, highlight, erase, create notes, etc.

Note: If you'd prefer to view *Summit TV* as a DVD, insert the disc into a DVD player instead.

Save any work you've created in class.

What is *Summit*?

Summit is a two-level* high-intermediate to advanced communicative course for adults and young adults that can follow any intermediate-level course book.

The goal of the *Summit* course is to make English unforgettable, enabling post-intermediate learners to understand, speak, read, and write English accurately, confidently, and fluently through:

► Multiple exposures to new language
► Numerous opportunities to practice it
► Deliberate and intensive recycling

Each full level of *Summit* contains enough material for 60 to 90 hours of classroom instruction. Alternatively, *Summit* Student's Books are available in split editions with bound-in Workbooks. A wide choice of supplementary components makes it easy to tailor *Summit* to the needs of your classes.

*Summit is designed to follow the Top Notch series, forming the top two levels of a complete six-level course.

The *Summit* Instructional Design

Balanced development of fluency and accuracy

Every two-page lesson culminates in a free discussion, debate, presentation, role play, or project. Planning activities such as idea framing and notepadding lead students to confident spoken expression in those activities. Grammar is tightly integrated with the speaking syllabus for memorability. Grammar charts include clear rules, examples, and explanations of meaning and use. Authentic readings further reinforce target grammar in natural contexts.

Essential conversation models for post-intermediate students

Because post-intermediate students continue to need intensive development of spoken communication, *Summit* provides ten essential conversation models that embed crucial conversation strategies and provide a starting point for personalized communication. Subsequent free communication activities are crafted so students can continually retrieve and use the language from the models. All conversation models are informed by the Longman Corpus of Spoken American English.

Academic skills and strategies

Each unit in the *Summit* course contains exercises that build key reading, listening, and critical thinking skills and strategies, such as paraphrasing, drawing conclusions, expressing and supporting an opinion, and activating prior knowledge. These exercises develop analytical skills while providing additional opportunities for learners to support their answers through speaking.

A high-impact vocabulary syllabus

Vocabulary in *Summit* is presented at word, phrase, and sentence levels, and includes expressions, idioms, and collocations. A concurrent emphasis on word skills enables students to expand their vocabulary by learning word transformation, classification, association, and other skills. Word skills practice increases students' mastery in both comprehending and producing new vocabulary.

A writing syllabus dedicated to the conventions of written English

Summit teaches the conventions of English writing so students will be prepared for standardized tests as well as further academic study. Key writing and rhetorical skills such as using parallel structure, avoiding sentence fragments, expressing and supporting an opinion, and persuading the reader are clearly presented and applied in carefully structured writing tasks. Additional *Grammar for Writing* sections build further awareness of these conventions.

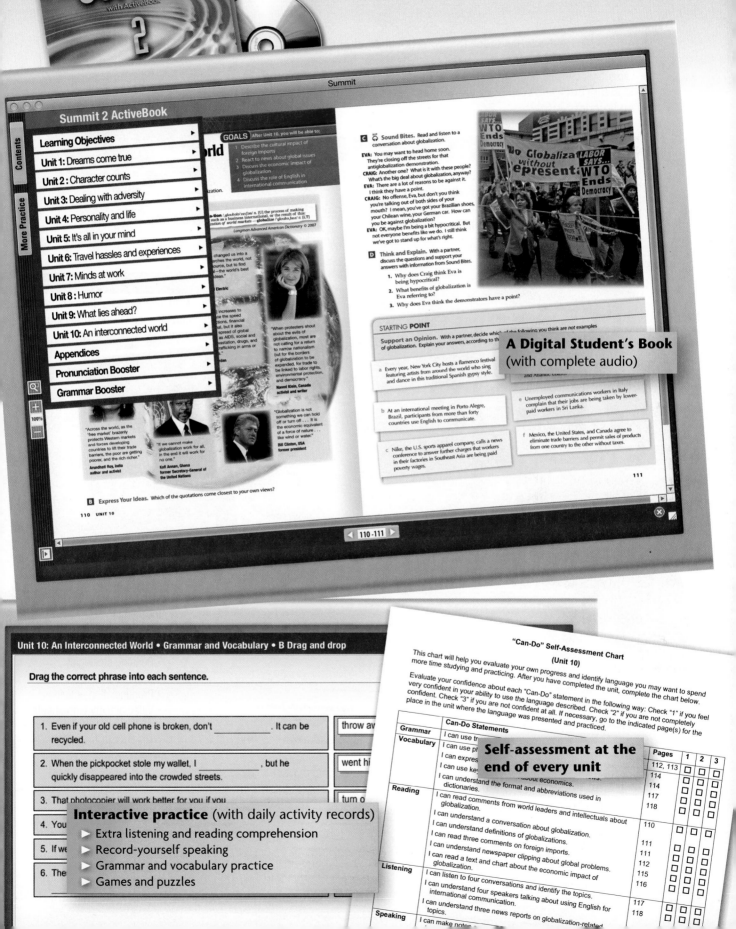

ActiveBook

SECOND EDITION

SUMMIT
with ActiveBook
2

Summit

Summit 2 ActiveBook

Learning Objectives ▶

Unit 1: Dreams come true ▶
Unit 2: Character counts ▶
Unit 3: Dealing with adversity ▶
Unit 4: Personality and life ▶
Unit 5: It's all in your mind ▶
Unit 6: Travel hassles and experiences ▶
Unit 7: Minds at work ▶
Unit 8: Humor ▶
Unit 9: What lies ahead? ▶
Unit 10: An interconnected world ▶
Appendices ▶
Pronunciation Booster ▶
Grammar Booster ▶

GOALS After Unit 10, you will be able to:
1 Describe the cultural impact of foreign imports
2 React to news about global issues
3 Discuss the economic impact of globalization
4 Discuss the role of English in international communication

C 🔊 **Sound Bites.** Read and listen to a conversation about globalization.

EVA: You may not want to head home soon. They're closing off the streets for that antiglobalization demonstration.
CRAIG: Another one? What is it with these people? What's the big deal about globalization, anyway?
EVA: There are a lot of reasons to be against it. I think they have a point.
CRAIG: No offense, Eva, but don't you think you're talking out of both sides of your mouth? I mean, you've got your Brazilian shoes, your Chilean wine, your German car. How can you be against globalization?
EVA: OK, maybe I'm being a bit hypocritical. But not everyone benefits like we do. I still think we've got to stand up for what's right.

D **Think and Explain.** With a partner, discuss the questions and support your answers with information from Sound Bites.
1. Why does Craig think Eva is being hypocritical?
2. What benefits of globalization is Eva referring to?
3. Why does Eva think the demonstrators have a point?

STARTING POINT

Support an Opinion. With a partner, decide which of the following you think are *not* examples of globalization. Explain your answers, according to th

a Every year, New York City hosts a flamenco festival featuring artists from around the world who sing and dance in this traditional Spanish gypsy style.

b At an international meeting in Porto Alegre, Brazil, participants from more than forty countries use English to communicate.

c Nike, the U.S. sports apparel company, calls a news conference to answer further charges that workers in their factories in Southeast Asia are being paid poverty wages.

e Unemployed communications workers in Italy complain that their jobs are being taken by lower-paid workers in Sri Lanka.

f Mexico, the United States, and Canada agree to eliminate trade barriers and permit sales of products from one country to the other without taxes.

A Digital Student's Book
(with complete audio)

-tion /ˌɡloʊbələˈzeɪʃən/ n. [U] the process of making such as a business international, or the result of this: *ization of world markets* —**globalize** /ˈɡloʊbəˌlaɪz/ v. [I,T]

Longman Advanced American Dictionary © 2007

"When protesters shout about the evils of globalization, most are not calling for a return to narrow nationalism but for the borders of globalization to be expanded, for trade to be linked to labor rights, environmental protection, and democracy."
Naomi Klein, Canada activist and writer

"Globalization is not something we can hold off or turn off . . . It is the economic equivalent of a force of nature . . . like wind or water."
Bill Clinton, USA former president

"Across the world, as the 'free market' brazenly protects Western markets and forces developing countries to lift their trade barriers, the poor are getting poorer, and the rich richer."
Arundhati Roy, India author and activist

"If we cannot make globalization work for all, in the end it will work for no one."
Kofi Annan, Ghana former Secretary-General of the United Nations

B **Express Your Ideas.** Which of the quotations come closest to your own views?

110 UNIT 10

111

◀ 110-111 ▶

Unit 10: An Interconnected World • Grammar and Vocabulary • B Drag and drop

Drag the correct phrase into each sentence.

1. Even if your old cell phone is broken, don't _____. It can be recycled.

2. When the pickpocket stole my wallet, I _____, but he quickly disappeared into the crowded streets.

3. That photocopier will work better for you if you

4. You

5. If we

6. The

throw aw

went hi

turn o

Interactive practice (with daily activity records)
▶ Extra listening and reading comprehension
▶ Record-yourself speaking
▶ Grammar and vocabulary practice
▶ Games and puzzles

"Can-Do" Self-Assessment Chart
(Unit 10)

This chart will help you evaluate your own progress and identify language you may want to spend more time studying and practicing. After you have completed the unit, complete the chart below.

Evaluate your confidence about each "Can-Do" statement in the following way: Check "1" if you feel very confident in your ability to use the language described. Check "2" if you are not completely confident. Check "3" if you are not confident at all. If necessary, go to the indicated page(s) for the place in the unit where the language was presented and practiced.

Self-assessment at the end of every unit

	Can-Do Statements	Pages	1	2	3
Grammar	I can use tr		☐	☐	☐
Vocabulary	I can use p	112, 113	☐	☐	☐
	I can expres	114	☐	☐	☐
	I can use ke	114	☐	☐	☐
	I can understand the format and abbreviations used in dictionaries.	117	☐	☐	☐
Reading	I can read comments from world leaders and intellectuals about globalization.	118	☐	☐	☐
	I can understand a conversation about globalization.	110	☐	☐	☐
	I can understand definitions of globalizations.		☐	☐	☐
	I can read three comments on foreign imports.	111	☐	☐	☐
	I can understand newspaper clipping about global problems.	111	☐	☐	☐
	I can read a text and chart about the economic impact of globalization.	112	☐	☐	☐
Listening	I can listen to four conversations and identify the topics.	115	☐	☐	☐
	I can understand four speakers talking about using English for international communication.	116	☐	☐	☐
	I can understand three news reports on globalization-related topics.	117	☐	☐	☐
Speaking	I can make notes	118	☐	☐	☐

The Teacher's Edition and Lesson Planner

Includes:
► A bound-in Methods Handbook for professional development
► Detailed lesson plans with suggested teaching times
► Language, culture, and corpus notes
► Student's Book and Workbook answer keys
► Audioscripts
► *Summit TV* teaching notes

► ActiveTeach

► A Digital Student's Book with interactive whiteboard (IWB) software
► Instantly accessible audio and *Summit TV* video
► Interactive exercises from the Student's *ActiveBook* for in-class use
► A complete menu of printable extension activities

Summit TV

Authentic TV news documentaries and unrehearsed on-the-street interviews

The Digital Student's Book
With zoom, write, highlight, save and other IWB tools.

Printable Extension Activities

Including:
• Discourse strategies
• Extra writing skills practice
• Reading strategies
• Graphic organizers
• Pronunciation activities
• Video activity worksheets and more . . .

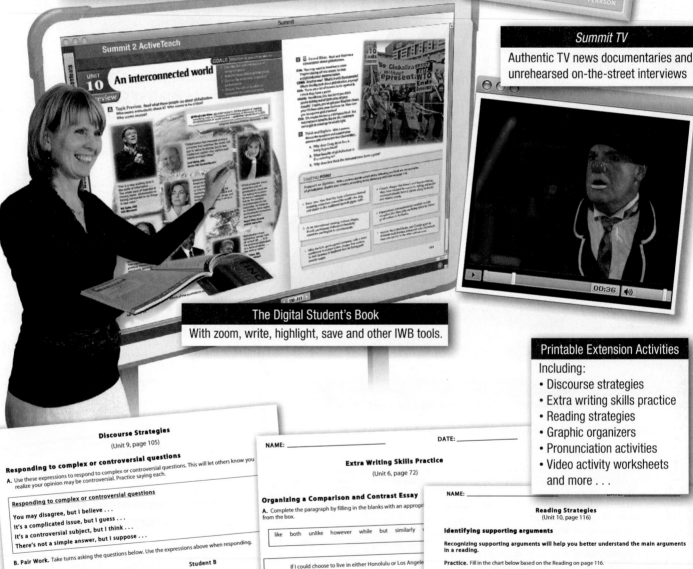

Discourse Strategies
(Unit 9, page 105)

Responding to complex or controversial questions

A. Use these expressions to respond to complex or controversial questions. This will let others know you realize your opinion may be controversial. Practice saying each.

Responding to complex or controversial questions

You may disagree, but I believe . . .
It's a complicated issue, but I guess . . .
It's a controversial subject, but I think . . .
There's not a simple answer, but I suppose . . .

B. Pair Work. Take turns asking the questions below. Use the expressions above when responding.

Student A	Student B
What do you think is the most serious problem the world is facing?	
	What do you think is the biggest problem in our country?
What do you think the biggest problem with the news media is?	
	What do you think the most serious problem with our education system is?

NAME: _____ DATE: _____

Extra Writing Skills Practice
(Unit 6, page 72)

Organizing a Comparison and Contrast Essay

A. Complete the paragraph by filling in the blanks with an appropri
from the box.

| like | both | unlike | however | while | but | similarly | |

If I could choose to live in either Honolulu or Los Angele

❶ _____ Honolulu and L.A. are cities on the Paci
quite different. ❷ _____ L.A. is a big, busy, and e
small, slow-paced, and there isn't much traffic to deal with. You'
lifestyles are relaxed. ❸ _____, Honolulu offers s
❹ _____ L.A., Honolulu has some excellent resta
you can find the same high fashions at the designer boutiques i
❺ _____ both cities have beaches, Honolulu's a
beaches in L.A., the water at Honolulu's beaches are warm all ye

NAME: _____ DATE: _____

Reading Strategies
(Unit 10, page 116)

Identifying supporting arguments

Recognizing supporting arguments will help you better understand the main arguments in a reading.

Practice. Fill in the chart below based on the Reading on page 116.

Arguments for globalization	Arguments against globalization
Benefits that have already occurred:	Problems that have already occurred:

Other components

Workbook

SECOND EDITION
SUMMIT 2
Joan Saslow • Allen Ascher

Workbook
Daily assignments that reinforce each lesson.

Classroom Audio Program

Classroom Audio Program
SECOND EDITION
SUMMIT 2
Joan Saslow • Allen Ascher
PEARSON

Classroom Audio Program
Includes a variety of authentic regional and non-native accents.

Complete Assessment Package

Complete Assessment Package
with ExamView® Assessment Suite Software
SECOND EDITION
SUMMIT 2
Joan Saslow • Allen Ascher

Complete Assessment Package
Ready-made achievement tests. Software provides option to edit, delete, or add items.

Full-Course Placement Tests

TOP NOTCH / SUMMIT
Full-Course Placement Tests
Joan Saslow ■ Allen Ascher
PEARSON Longman

Full-Course Placement Tests
Four test forms to choose from.

MyEnglishLab

An optional online learning tool with:

► An interactive *Summit* Workbook
► Speaking and writing activities
► Pop-up grammar help
► Student's Book *Grammar Booster* and *Pronunciation Booster* exercises
► *Summit TV* with extensive viewing activities
► Automatically-graded achievement tests
► Easy course management and record-keeping

Dreams come true

GOALS After Unit 1, you will be able to:

1 Explain your life choices and plans
2 Describe someone's continuing activities
3 Share your dreams and goals in life
4 Describe your job qualifications and experience

A **Topic Preview.** Look at the Online Edition of *Global Voyager Magazine.* What types of articles would you expect to find on this website?

http://www.globalvoyager.com

Global Voyager Magazine

ONLINE EDITION   Contact us | Shop | Subscribe

▶ **Archives**
Back issues of the Online Edition

▶ **Features List**
Table of contents for this month's stories

▶ **Final Cut**
Outtakes of photos that didn't make it

▶ **Blasts from the Past**
Prize-winning photos from the archives

▶ **Forum**
Readers' opinions

▶ **Voyager Hot Picks**
The editors' must-sees

▶ **Resources**
Links for this month's features

▶ **Our Advertisers**
The best of the best

Dr. Robert Ballard—the man who discovered the *Titanic*. Learn how he turns sunken ships into underwater museums.

Primatologist and ethologist <u>Jane Goodall</u>. Insights into her life, her work, and her dreams.

This Month's Features
Mysteries of the Underwater World

Among the Hmong

The Ancient Fertile Crescent

Pirate Ships of the Future

Airline Food: Ups and Downs

<u>Working in Patagonia</u>

Exotic Jobs
Tour guide Gonzalo Tejeda shares breathtaking photos and scenes of matchless beauty. Download spectacular wallpaper images of Tejeda's "outdoor office."

Monthly Photo Contest

<u>Register</u> to enter

Photo Gallery
Experience a penguin parent-and-chick family reunion through the lens of wildlife photographer Frans Lanting.

<u>The emperor penguin</u>

Online Explorer
Explore the Gulf of Mexico seascape in a mini-submarine with the marine biologist *Time Magazine* named its first "hero for the planet."

<u>Sylvia Earle</u>

B **Express Your Ideas.** What would you click on first? Why? What does your choice "say" about you?

Dreams come true

How to plan a *Summit* lesson

The suggested teaching times for each activity will yield a total teaching time of 45–60 minutes for each two-page lesson. Your actual teaching time will vary from the times suggested, according to your needs, your schedule, and the needs of your class.

Activities labeled "Option" or "Challenge" are additional to the 45–60 minutes, and the estimated teaching time for each is noted with the activity.

In addition, you will see other optional extensions to the material on the Student's Book page. These of course will also increase the time allotted to the lesson:

ActiveTeach An extension activity from *ActiveTeach*, the multimedia disc in the back of this Teacher's Edition

PRONUNCIATION BOOSTER An optional feature at the end of the Student's Book

GRAMMAR BOOSTER An optional feature at the end of the Student's Book

EXTRAS (optional) Available supplementary components to support the lesson.

These optional activities can be assigned as homework or class work. They come from the Workbook, Copy & Go, Top Notch TV, and the Complete Assessment Package.

MySummitLab

This online alternative offers a digital version of the *Summit* Workbook, *Summit TV* Video Program and Activities, and Internet-based projects. A teacher management system enables instructors and programs to monitor progress and tailor content to their students' needs.

The *Summit* authors strongly encourage you to view these lesson plans and accompanying options, challenges, projects, and extension activities as a menu of possibilities in creating the best lesson plan for you. You may wish to construct your lesson entirely without the options, challenges, projects, and extension activities, or to extend the lesson to do all possible activities. The suggested teaching times are provided to help you do that.

A Topic Preview

Suggested teaching time:	10 minutes	Your actual teaching time:	

• Have pairs or small groups discuss the Topic Preview question. Call on several volunteers for their answers.

• Then have students look at the photos and read the captions silently. Ask comprehension questions such as: *What is Dr. Robert Ballard known for?* (He discovered the *Titanic*.) *What is Sylvia Earle's profession?* (marine biologist)

Note: Audio recordings modeling the pronunciation of proper nouns can be found under "Pronunciator" at www.longman.com/summit2e.

• Ask a student to read aloud the titles under *This Month's Features*. Clarify topics as needed.

• Have students focus on the list on the left side of the magazine page. Clarify vocabulary as needed: *back issue* (an old copy of a magazine or newspaper) *outtake* (a version of a photo or movie that is not used in favor of another version) *blast from the past* (something that returns after an absence; here, a photo that is seen again) *hot picks* (popular or favorite selections)

Note: There is more information later in the unit on Dr. Robert Ballard (pages 6 and 13), Jane Goodall (page 8), Frans Lanting (pages 3 and 13), Sylvia Earle (page 7).

Language note: A *primatologist* studies primatology, the branch of zoology that deals with primates. Primates include humans, apes, and monkeys. The suffix *-ologist* means a person who studies, and the suffix *-ology* means science or study. An *ethologist* studies animal behavior. The science is ethology. A *marine biologist* studies animal and plant life in saltwater environments.

Note: Language notes and Culture notes are provided to offer student enrichment or more information. Their use is optional. Usage notes from the Longman Corpus Network are also provided directly on select Student's Book pages with this heading: **CN** Corpus Notes.

Culture note: The Hmong live in the mountainous regions of southeastern China and in northern Vietnam, Laos, and Thailand. The Fertile Crescent is a great arc of cultivable land extending from the Mediterranean coast in the west around the Syrian Desert to the Persian Gulf in the east. Patagonia is located in southern Argentina and Chile between the Andes and the Atlantic Ocean. The emperor penguin, from the Antarctic, is the largest known penguin. Point out these locations on a map.

B Express Your Ideas

Suggested teaching time:	5–10 minutes	Your actual teaching time:	

• Have groups discuss the questions. Then bring the class together and have students share answers and explain their choices.

• Ask *What additional information do you know about the topics on the website?* Invite students to share.

C 🎧 Sound Bites

Suggested teaching time:	10 minutes	Your actual teaching time:

- Before students read and listen to the conversation, have them look at the two photos and read the captions. Ask:
  What skills and qualities do you think a wildlife photographer needs? (photography and artistic skills, patience)
  Would you be interested in a career as a wildlife photographer? Why or why not?

- Have students read and listen to the conversation. To check comprehension, ask:
  What does Max tell Sam? (He's leaving his job at the bank.)
  What is Max going to do instead of working at the bank? (He's going to be a photographer.)
  Is Sam surprised? (No, Max has been talking about changing careers for a long time.)
  What inspired Max to make this move? (Frans Lanting's photos)
  What did Frans Lanting have to do to get the pictures of the penguins? (He had to camp out on the ice in Antarctica for a month.)
  Does Sam think Max could be a good wildlife photographer? (yes)

- Have students read and listen to the conversation again.

> **Language note:** *That* instead of *who* ("You mean the guy that took those penguin pictures on your wall?") is acceptable in spoken English.

Option: [+5–10 minutes] Have students use the answers to the following questions as the basis for a class discussion: *Have you ever quit a job to pursue something else you wanted to do? If yes, give details. What inspired you to make this change? Does anyone want to quit a current job to do something different? If yes, give details. What is keeping you from making this move?*

D Paraphrase

Suggested teaching time:	5–10 minutes	Your actual teaching time:

- Have students do the exercise in pairs. Then bring the class together and have students share their answers. Write the different ways of saying the statements on the board.

- Have two volunteers read the conversation aloud, replacing the four selected statements with other ways of saying them.

Option: [+5 minutes] Have pairs create short conversations using the idioms and expressions from the exercise. For example, A: *I've finally decided to go to art school.* B: *Way to go!*

E Critical Thinking

Suggested teaching time:	5–10 minutes	Your actual teaching time:

- Encourage students to think creatively in pairs or small groups. Ask them to make lists of environmental factors for both animals. (Possible answers: I think penguins developed white and black coloration to hide in snow and rocks. And zebras to hide in trees and bushes.)

STARTING **POINT**

Suggested teaching time:	10 minutes	Your actual teaching time:

- Call on two volunteers to read the information in the speech balloons.

Pair Work

- Circulate as students talk about famous people they admire. Make sure students discuss specific achievements of the people.

- Invite students to tell the class about the person they admire but without mentioning the person's name. Have the rest of the class guess the name of the person.

> **Culture note:** The Nobel Peace Prize is an international award that has been given yearly since 1901. It was established by Alfred Nobel, a Norwegian inventor and industrialist. It is awarded to a person or institution that has made a significant contribution to maintaining peace, resolving international conflicts, or supporting human rights. The winner receives a medal and a financial award. Kenya is located in eastern Africa on the Indian Ocean. The country lies between Somalia and Tanzania. If necessary, locate Kenya on a map.

Challenge: [+5–10 minutes] Have students write a paragraph about a person they admire. Tell students to give details about the person's achievements. Have pairs read and comment on each other's papers before asking volunteers to read their work aloud to the class.

EXTRAS (optional)

- **Workbook:** Exercises 1–4
- **MySummitLab:** Preview

C 🎧 1:02 **Sound Bites.** Read and listen to a conversation between two friends about a career change.

MAX: Well, I gave notice at the bank. In two weeks, I'll be working as a full-time photographer.

SAM: Way to go! You've been talking about doing that for years! What made you finally take the plunge?

MAX: Frans Lanting, believe it or not.

SAM: You mean the guy that took those penguin pictures on your wall?

MAX: Right. I read that in order to get those shots he camped out on the ice in Antarctica for a month.

SAM: Wow! You know, I could really see you doing that.

MAX: So could I. After seeing those photos, I realized I didn't want to spend the rest of my life in a bank. I want to get out and see the world.

King penguins in Antarctica
F. Lanting

D **Paraphrase.** Read the conversation again. Then say each of these statements another way. Answers will vary, but may include:

1. "I gave notice at the bank." I told the bank (that) I'm leaving my job. OR I told the bank I'm resigning.
2. "Way to go!" Good for you! OR Congratulations!
3. "What made you finally take the plunge?" Why did you decide to leave your job now?
4. "You know, I could really see you doing that." I think you would be good at that.

E **Critical Thinking.** Penguins and zebras live in very different parts of the planet, in different environments. What factors might have contributed to their black-and-white coloration?

Zebras in the wild
F. Lanting

STARTING POINT

Pair Work. Think of a famous person you admire. Tell your partner why you admire that person.

Wangari Maathai

"Have you heard of Wangari Maathai? She won the Nobel Peace Prize in 2004. I really admire her. She spent her whole life working to protect the environment. She founded the Green Belt Movement, which has planted more than 45 million trees in Kenya since 1977."

Steve Jobs

"One person I've always really respected is Steve Jobs, the guy who founded Apple Computers. I love how his company's products are both innovative and user-friendly. I think they've had a huge impact on how we live."

1

GOAL
Explain your life choices and plans

A 🎧 1:03 **Conversation Snapshot.** Read and listen. Notice the conversation strategies.

A: You know, I've always wanted to take up fashion design.

B: That's great. What's stopping you?

A: Well, I guess big changes are a little scary.

B: True, but life's short. Go for it!

🎧 1:04 **Rhythm and intonation practice**

PRONUNCIATION BOOSTER ▶ p. P2
- Sentence stress and intonation

B 🎧 1:05 **Vocabulary. Expressions to Describe Life Choices and Plans.** Listen and practice.

take up something you're interested in
Joe was so inspired by the Frans Lanting exhibit that he decided to take up wildlife photography.

decide on a course of study or a career
She decided on a career as a veterinarian because she is interested in medicine and loves animals.

apply for a position or an opportunity to study
He wants to work in the field of conservation, so he applied for a job at the Forest and Wildlife Center.

be accepted to / into a school or a program
When Ann heard she was accepted to medical school, she called all her friends. **CN**

be rejected by a program or a school
It was very difficult for Dan to hide his disappointment when he was rejected by the law school.

sign up for a course or an activity
Over a hundred people signed up for that course because the teacher has such a great reputation.

enroll in a school, organization, or program
Matt plans to enroll in flight school to fulfill his dream of becoming a pilot.

switch to a new course of study or career
People who are unhappy in their career often switch to a completely different field.

CN **Corpus Notes:** When talking about schools or programs, the passive forms of *accept* and *reject* occur more frequently than the active forms.

C 🎧 1:06 **Listening. Activate Vocabulary and Summarize.** Listen to the conversations. Then listen again. After each conversation, summarize the person's situation by completing each sentence with the Vocabulary. Use each expression only once.

1. She has ⸻ engineering school.
enrolled in OR been accepted to

2. She has <u>decided on</u> a career in music.

3. He has <u>taken up OR signed up for</u> meditation.

4. She has <u>been rejected by</u> two graduate programs.

5. He has <u>switched to</u> teaching.

6. She has <u>applied for</u> a position in a medical lab.

1

A 🎧 Conversation Snapshot

Suggested teaching time:	5 minutes	Your actual teaching time:	

These conversation strategies are implicit in the model:
- Use *You know* to ease into a conversation.
- Respond with *That's great* to convey enthusiasm or encouragement.
- Preface a statement with *I guess* to soften an opinion.
- Begin a response with *True, but* to present an alternate view.

- Have students look at the picture. Ask:
  What is the woman's profession? (fashion model)
  What do you think the man's profession is? (fashion designer)
  Who are some famous fashion designers? (Possible answers: Donatella Versace, Coco Chanel, Calvin Klein)
- Have students read and listen. Then ask:
  What career is Student A thinking about entering? (fashion design)
  What is stopping Student A from making this move? (Making a big change is scary.)
  What advice does Student B give Student A? Why? (Go for it. Life is short.)
  Do you agree or disagree with the statement that big changes are scary? Explain your answer.
- Have students read and listen again. Call their attention to the conversation strategies highlighted in the model.

Language note: The phrasal verb *take up* means *enter into a profession*. The idiom *go for it* means *use all one's energy to achieve a specific purpose*. *Life is short* is a saying that suggests that a person should not postpone doing things.

🎧 Rhythm and intonation practice

Suggested teaching time:	5 minutes	Your actual teaching time:	

- Have students repeat chorally. Make sure they:
  - pause briefly after *You know* and *True*.
  - use emphatic stress for <u>always</u> in *I've always wanted to . . .*
  - use falling intonation for *What's stopping you?*

B 🎧 Vocabulary

Suggested teaching time:	5 minutes	Your actual teaching time:	

- Have students listen and practice, and then have pairs think of different expressions to describe life choices and plans. (Possible answers: enter a profession; choose; seek employment / admission; get into; not get into; register for; register at / in; make a change to)
- Have students listen and practice again.

Option: [+5–10 minutes] Have pairs write additional sentences using the Vocabulary. Ask volunteers to share their sentences.

C 🎧 Listening

Suggested teaching time:	5–10 minutes	Your actual teaching time:	

- Tell students to listen carefully to the life plans and choices discussed in the six conversations.
- Then have students read the first two items in the exercise. Have them listen again to the first two conversations and complete the items with the correct expressions from the Vocabulary.
- Have students repeat the procedure with the second two items and then finally with the last two items.
- Have students listen again to all six conversations to check their answers.
- Tell students to compare answers with a partner before reviewing the exercise with the class.

Language note: Students should be able to complete the exercise without understanding every word. You may want to share the following definitions if students ask about specific expressions. Conversation 1: A *whiz* is a person who is very skilled in a specific field. *No surprise there* is an informal way of saying *It's not surprising*. Conversation 3: *What's come over him?* means *What's happened to him?* Conversation 4: *What's with Nina?* is short for *What's wrong with Nina?* or *What's going on with Nina?* To *feel down* is to feel depressed or unhappy. Conversation 5: To *be suited for something* is to have the talent and qualifications to do something. Point out the two different pronunciations of *either* in Conversations 2 and 4.

🔘 **ActiveTeach** • **Vocabulary-Building Strategies**

AUDIOSCRIPT

For audioscript, see page AS1.

D Grammar

Suggested teaching time:	5–10 minutes	Your actual teaching time:

- Write the first example sentence from the Grammar box on the board:

    I love animals and the outdoors, so I've decided to become a naturalist.

    Ask:

    Does the verb have decided *express a past event?* (yes)
    Is this information connected to the present? (yes)

    Point out that because the information is connected to the present, the present perfect is used in this sentence. Call on a volunteer to read the first bold rule in the Grammar box.

- Ask a volunteer to read the information in the Remember box. On the board, write *I enrolled in an art class yesterday.*

    Ask:

    What is the specific past time in this sentence? (yesterday)
    If you wanted to use the present perfect to express a similar idea, how could you change the sentence? (I have enrolled in an art class.)

- Have students read the second bold rule and the examples to themselves. List the adverbs and expressions on the board. Then invite volunteers to suggest additional example sentences using the present perfect. Write these on the board. Ask students whether all the sentences convey information that has relevance to the present. If any of the sentences refer to a specific time in the past, remind students to revise them using the simple past.

- Call on a volunteer to read the remaining bold rule and note and examples. Ask volunteers to think of sentences using *just, recently,* and *lately* to talk about events that have happened to them in the recent past.

ActiveTeach • **Inductive Grammar Charts**

Option: [+10 minutes] Write these sentences on the board and have students identify and correct the ones that are incorrect. Have students explain the errors.

1. *I have recently taken up photography.* (correct)

2. *Mark was not yet accepted to Harvard University.* (incorrect: Mark has not yet been accepted . . . OR Mark has not been accepted . . . yet. OR Mark was not accepted . . . *Yet* is used with the present perfect.)

3. *She just switched to advertising.* (incorrect: She has just switched . . . *Just* describes a past event that has occurred in recent time and is expressed using the present perfect.)

4. *Kelly is a science whiz, so she's decided to study organic chemistry in college.* (correct)

5. *In 1998 she has signed up for her first art class.* (incorrect: In 1998 she signed up . . . The simple past is used to talk about specific times in the past.)

E Integrated Practice

Suggested teaching time:	10 minutes	Your actual teaching time:

- Make sure students understand that they should use the expressions in the Vocabulary on page 4 to write questions about the ideas listed in the box.

- Have a volunteer read the example sentence and then ask for another example. (Possible answer: Have you already signed up for the new computer training?) Suggest that students use the adverbs and expressions listed in the Grammar box as well.

- If necessary, explain that *personal growth* refers to things a person may do or study to improve himself or herself. Circulate as pairs work and assist as needed.

- Bring the class together and have students share questions.

NOW YOU CAN

Suggested teaching time:	10–15 minutes	Your actual teaching time:

A Notepadding

- Refer students to the conversation on page 4 to review explaining life choices and plans for the future. Tell them to review as well the Vocabulary on page 4 of expressions to describe life choices and plans.

- Create a conversation about future plans with a more confident student. Play the role of Student A and include an expression from the Vocabulary to describe your plan. For example, *I've always wanted to sign up for a tap dancing class.* It is not necessary to have a complete conversation but only to get the activity going.

B Use the Conversation Strategies

- After pairs have explained their future plans to each other, ask volunteers to present their conversations to the class. After each presentation, ask *Does anyone have similar plans for the future?*

- Reinforce the use of the conversation strategies; for example, make sure students really sound enthusiastic when they say *That's great!*

ActiveTeach • **Conversation Prompts**

Option: [+5 minutes] Have students use questions from Exercise E to interview another student.

EXTRAS (optional)

- **Grammar Booster**
- **Pronunciation Booster**
- **Workbook: Exercises 5–9**
- **MySummitLab: Lesson 1**

D Grammar. The present perfect for past events related to the present

Although the present perfect expresses a past event or state, it is used to convey information that has relevance to the present.

> I love animals and the outdoors, so I've decided to become a naturalist.

The following adverbs and expressions are often used with the present perfect: <u>ever</u>, <u>never</u>, <u>already</u>, <u>yet</u>, <u>so far</u>, <u>still</u> (with the negative), <u>once</u>, <u>twice</u>, <u>(three) times</u>.

> Have you **ever** thought about a career in law?
> We've **never** considered that course of action.
> She's **already** decided on a career in business.
> I **still** haven't made up my mind about what I'll do after school.
> He's been rejected by medical school **three times**.

The adverbs <u>just</u>, <u>recently</u>, and <u>lately</u> describe past events that have occurred in recent time.

> She's **just** been accepted to a top business school.
> They've **recently** made plans to get married.
> Have you made any progress with your job search **lately**?

NOTE: The adverb <u>lately</u> is rarely used in affirmative statements in the present perfect.

REMEMBER

Use the simple past, not the present perfect, to talk about a specific time in the past.

> She applied for the position at the Science Institute last week.

> **NOT** She ~~has applied~~ for the position at the Science Institute last week.

E Integrated Practice. Using the present perfect and the Vocabulary in Exercise B, write questions you could ask someone about his or her life choices and plans.

Answers will vary, but may include:

IDEAS

educational training
career
personal growth
marriage and family
change of studies
change of job or career

Example: *Have you decided on a career yet?*

1. What jobs have you applied for in the last year?
2. Have you signed up for any interesting courses recently?
3. Have you ever thought about switching to a different line of work / field of study?
4. Have you been accepted to any of the schools you wanted to attend?
5. Have you ever been rejected by a school you really wanted to attend?
6. Have you thought about getting married and starting a family?

NOW YOU CAN *Explain your life choices and plans*

A Notepadding. On your notepad, answer the questions you wrote in Exercise E with true information about yourself.

B Use the Conversation Strategies. Using the information on your notepad, explain your plans for the future to a partner. Use the Conversation Snapshot as a guide. Start like this: "You know, …"

Your life choices and plans

1.
2.
3.
4.
5.
6.

2

Describe someone's continuing activities

A 🎧 1:07 **Grammar Snapshot.** Read the article and notice the use of the present perfect continuous.

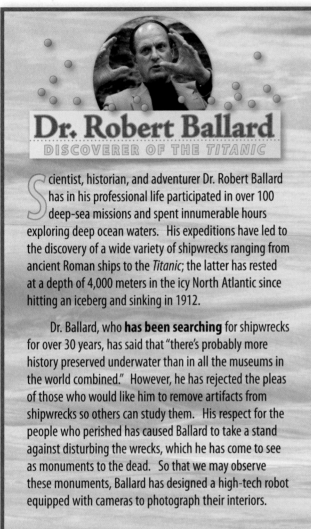

Dr. Robert Ballard
DISCOVERER OF THE *TITANIC*

Scientist, historian, and adventurer Dr. Robert Ballard has in his professional life participated in over 100 deep-sea missions and spent innumerable hours exploring deep ocean waters. His expeditions have led to the discovery of a wide variety of shipwrecks ranging from ancient Roman ships to the *Titanic*; the latter has rested at a depth of 4,000 meters in the icy North Atlantic since hitting an iceberg and sinking in 1912.

Dr. Ballard, who **has been searching** for shipwrecks for over 30 years, has said that "there's probably more history preserved underwater than in all the museums in the world combined." However, he has rejected the pleas of those who would like him to remove artifacts from shipwrecks so others can study them. His respect for the people who perished has caused Ballard to take a stand against disturbing the wrecks, which he has come to see as monuments to the dead. So that we may observe these monuments, Ballard has designed a high-tech robot equipped with cameras to photograph their interiors.

The 1985 discovery of the *Titanic* made Ballard an instant celebrity and has generated thousands of letters from students of all ages. Ballard has been involved in educational projects since then and **has been giving** speeches, **writing** books, and **working** on educational TV programs shown widely across the world.

A high-tech robot designed by Dr. Ballard photographs the Titanic, *which sank after a catastrophic collision in 1912 with an iceberg.*

Information sources: www.pbs.org and www.lordly.com

B **Express and Support an Opinion.** Do you agree with Dr. Ballard's conviction that artifacts should not be removed from shipwrecks? Explain your reasons.

C **Grammar. The present perfect and the present perfect continuous for unfinished or continuing actions**

Use either the present perfect or the present perfect continuous to describe unfinished or continuing actions. Choose the present perfect continuous instead of the present perfect to suggest that the action may continue. Note that this is not a sharp distinction or rule.

> **REMEMBER**
> The present perfect is also used for finished actions.

Ballard **has searched** for shipwrecks for many years. (The speaker is not necessarily suggesting that Ballard will continue to search.)

He **has been searching** for shipwrecks for many years. (The speaker may be suggesting that Ballard will continue to search.)

BE CAREFUL! Certain stative (non-action) verbs are not used in the present perfect continuous: be, believe, hate, have (for possession), know, like, love, own, seem, understand.
I've known about his research for many years.
NOT I've been knowing about his research for many years. **CN**

> **GRAMMAR BOOSTER** ▸ p. G1
> • Stative verbs: non-action and action meanings

CN **Corpus Notes:** A common learner error is using the verbs *be* and *know* in the present perfect continuous. For example, *I have been being a member of this club since 1980.*

A 🎧 Grammar Snapshot

Suggested teaching time:	5–10 minutes	Your actual teaching time:

- To introduce the topic, ask students what they know about the *Titanic*.
- Call on a volunteer to read the title of the article. Then ask another student to read the photo caption.
- Have students read and listen to the article.
- To check comprehension, ask:
  What is Dr. Ballard's profession? (scientist, historian, and adventurer)
  Where and when did Dr. Ballard find the Titanic? (in the North Atlantic, at a depth of 4,000 meters, in 1985)
  Why did the Titanic *sink?* (It hit an iceberg.)
  Does Dr. Ballard remove artifacts from shipwrecks so that others can study them? (no)
  Why is Dr. Ballard against disturbing the wrecks? (He respects the people who died. He considers the wrecks monuments to the dead.)
  How does Dr. Ballard show the world the shipwrecks? (He uses a high-tech robot equipped with cameras.)
- Ask a student to read the sentences that include the present perfect continuous. Ask:
  Did Dr. Ballard perform these activities in the past? (yes)
  Is he still performing these activities in the present? (yes)
- Have students read and listen to the article again.

> **Language note:** *The latter* refers to the second of two items mentioned; here, the reference is to the *Titanic. The former* refers to the first of two items; here, the reference is to ancient Roman ships. Tell students that 4,000 meters can also be expressed as 13,123 feet. An *artifact* is an object that was made and used a long time ago.

Option: Interested students may want to use the Internet to find out more about the *Titanic.* They may also want to see the 1997 U.S.–made film about the 1912 collision.

Challenge: [+5–10 minutes] Have students use the Internet to find photos taken by Dr. Ballard's high-tech robot. Tell students to share the addresses of the websites with the class.

B Express and Support an Opinion

Suggested teaching time:	5 minutes	Your actual teaching time:

- To prepare, ask students to make two short lists of reasons why removing the artifacts is (a) a good idea and (b) a bad idea.

C Grammar

Suggested teaching time:	10 minutes	Your actual teaching time:

- Ask a student to read aloud the bold rule and the two example sentences in the Grammar box.
- On the board, write part of the last sentence from the article: *Ballard . . . has been giving speeches, writing books, and working on educational TV programs shown widely across the world.* Make sure students understand that the complete verbs are *has been writing* and *has been working.*
- Ask a student to change the present perfect continuous to the present perfect. Write this sentence on the board as well: *Ballard has given speeches, [has] written books, and [has] worked on educational TV programs shown widely across the world.*
- Point out the subtle difference between the two sentences: the use of the present perfect continuous suggests that Dr. Ballard will continue giving speeches, writing books, and working on TV programs. The use of the present perfect does not necessarily suggest that Ballard will continue these activities.
- Call on a volunteer to read the information in the Be Careful! box. Remind students that stative verbs are also known as non-action verbs.
- Ask a student to read the information in the Remember box. Then have students find examples in the Grammar Snapshot article of the present perfect used for finished actions. (has . . . participated, [has] spent; have led; has rested; has said; has rejected; has caused; has come; has designed; has generated; has been involved)

🔘 **ActiveTeach** • **Inductive Grammar Charts**

Project: Have students research Dr. Robert Ballard on the Internet. Tell them to use the present perfect and the present perfect continuous to write down six additional facts about Dr. Ballard and his work. Bring the class together and have students combine their information in a short article.

D Grammar Practice

Suggested teaching time:	10–15 minutes	Your actual teaching time:

- Have students read the names of the people mentioned in the exercise. Ask *Which names do you recognize?* (Students should recognize Sylvia Earle, who has already been mentioned in this unit.) Invite students to share any information they might know about the people.

- Before students do the exercise, have them scan the text and circle the stative verbs. (1. be, 2. understand, 3. have, 5. believe, 6. know, 7. believe) Remind students that these verbs should not be used in the present perfect continuous. Refer students to the Be Careful! box in the Grammar box on page 6 for examples of stative verbs. Also remind students that the present perfect is used for finished actions at an unspecified time in the past.

- After students complete the exercise, have them check answers with a partner. Then bring the class together and answer any questions. If students used the present perfect for continuing or unfinished actions, point out that this is correct but that the directions ask for the present perfect continuous.

Option: [+5–10 minutes] Have pairs write biographical notes on another person who has had an impact on the world. Have them use the present perfect continuous and the present perfect. Remind them not to use the present perfect continuous with stative verbs. Have students share their notes with the class.

Answers for Exercise D

1. has been studying (unfinished action), has been (stative verb), has been designing (unfinished action)
2. has understood (stative verb), has been teaching (unfinished action)
3. has had (stative verb), have been educating (unfinished action)
4. has been helping (unfinished action), has built (finished action)
5. has been negotiating (unfinished action), has believed (stative verb)
6. has known (stative verb), has made (finished action), have contributed (finished action), has been working (unfinished action)
7. has believed (stative verb), has been donating (unfinished action)
8. has been participating (unfinished action), have expressed (finished action)

NOW YOU CAN

Suggested teaching time:	15–20 minutes	Your actual teaching time:

A Frame Your Ideas

- Call on a volunteer to read the example for *Strongest-held belief about life.*
- Circulate as students complete the questionnaire. Assist as needed.

B Use the Grammar

- In preparation for the project, have students make notes about the information they learn about their partner.
- Ask several students the question in the speech balloon. Listen for the correct verb forms. For example, *Yes, I have. I went to London last spring.*
- Circulate as students ask each other questions. Make sure they use correct verb forms in both the questions and answers.

C Project

- Have students review their notes about their partner. If they are missing any information, have them ask their partner.
- Remind students to use the correct verb forms in their biographies. Review that they should use the present perfect when talking about past events that connect to the present. However, when talking about past events with a specific past time reference, they should use the simple past.

EXTRAS (optional)

- **Grammar Booster**
- **Workbook: Exercises 10–13**
- **MySummitLab: Lesson 2**

D **Grammar Practice.** Complete the following biographical notes. Use the present perfect continuous for unfinished actions, except with the stative verbs that are not used in the continuous. Use the present perfect for finished actions. Explain your reason for each answer.
(See page T7 for answers to Exercise D.)

"The first sentence in number 1 is an unfinished action."

❶ Sylvia Earle .... (study) the plant and animal life of the world's oceans for close to forty years. She .... (be) fascinated by the ocean ever since she moved to the Gulf of Mexico as a young girl. For more than twenty years, she .... (design) equipment for exploring the ocean floor.

❷ For many years **Madan Kataria** .... (understand) that laughter can have health benefits. Since 1995, when he started the Laughter Club of India, he .... (teach) "laughter yoga," a technique for making people laugh in order to improve their health.

❸ Ever since her childhood, when she accompanied her physician mother into remote areas of Venezuela and Colombia, **Magdalena Hurtado** .... (have) a great curiosity about different cultures. For many years now, she and her husband, anthropologist Kim Hill, ... (educate) people about the influence of biology and ecology on human life.

❹ Millard and Linda Fuller created Habitat for Humanity, a worldwide organization that for almost thirty years .... (help) people build houses for themselves. Since its founding in 1976, Habitat for Humanity .... (build) more than 175,000 houses around the world.

❽ Chiaki Mukai, a medical doctor as well as Japan's first female astronaut, ... (participate) in space flights since 1994. John Glenn, the famous U.S. astronaut, and many others .... (express) admiration for her achievements.

❺ Martthi Ahtisaari, who won the Nobel Peace Prize in 2008, ... (negotiate) international conflicts for more than thirty years. Ever since he began serving as United Nations Commissioner to Namibia in 1977, he .... (believe) that all conflicts can be resolved.

❻ For a long time **Zahi Hawass**, an Egyptian archeologist, ... (know) that many great monuments still lie buried beneath the ground. Dr. Hawass .... (make) many important discoveries that .... (contribute) significantly to our knowledge of ancient Egypt. Since 1987 he .... (work) on conserving and restoring the Pyramids.

❼ For many years **Charles Wang**, the successful businessman who founded Computer Associates, ... (believe) that people with means should help others in need. He .... (donate) money to worthy causes for many years.

NOW YOU CAN   *Describe someone's continuing activities*

A **Frame Your Ideas.** Complete the questionnaire about your life, achievements, and beliefs.

Strongest-held belief about life *I believe if people communicated better, the world would be a better place.*

Name .... Address ....
How long have you lived there? .... Where did you live before? ....
How long have you been studying English? ....
What else have you studied? ....
Marital status .... If married, when were you married? ....
Travel history ....
Awards or prizes ....
Strongest-held belief about life ....

When did you develop that belief? ....

B **Use the Grammar.** Get to know your partner. Use the questionnaire as a guide to ask questions. Use the present perfect and the present perfect continuous correctly.

"Have you traveled outside of the country anytime in the last year?"

C **Project.** Write a one-page biography of your partner, using the information you learned about him or her in Exercise B. Either make a scrapbook of all your classmates or post the biographies on a bulletin board. Include pictures if you can.

A **Reading Warm-up.** Have you ever heard of Jane Goodall? What do you know about her work?

B 🎧 1:08 **Reading.** Read the biography of Jane Goodall. What factors in her early life contributed to her interest in Africa?

BIOGRAPHIES

JANE GOODALL

Born in London on April 3, 1934, world-renowned primatologist Jane Goodall got an early start on animal study, spending much of her childhood observing animals that lived right in the backyard of her house. Later, Kipling's *Jungle Book* and the Tarzan stories fascinated her as well, and those, coupled with her love for animals, led her to plan a life in the African jungle. When she finally ventured into Africa at the age of 23, Goodall was fulfilling her childhood dream.

Goodall worked as a secretary for a year in Kenya until, having learned that anthropologist Louis Leakey was doing research in Zaire, she made a trip to meet him. Leakey had been searching for someone to carry out a field study on chimpanzees at the Gombe National Reserve in Tanzania and decided Goodall would be ideal for the project because her lack of formal training would prevent prior knowledge from interfering with her observations and conclusions. Leakey told her the research might take ten years; she thought it might take just three. They were both mistaken. Goodall has been researching chimps at Gombe for over 40 years now.

Progress in the first months at Gombe was slow and discouraging, as the chimps would not let Goodall approach. Complicating matters, Goodall spent weeks in bed, sick with malaria. But one day Goodall observed a chimp in the camp looking at a banana on the table inside a tent. This was Goodall's first chance to get close to a chimp, and from that day on, bananas were always kept nearby for

any curious visitors. Patience enabled Goodall to win the chimps' trust and gradually make friends with them.

In a lifetime of study, Goodall has discovered many interesting and formerly unknown similarities between chimps and humans. Among those discoveries: chimps are not herbivorous—they also eat meat, just like humans; chimps make and use tools; they adopt orphan infants; they know and use medicinal plants (by chewing).

Today Goodall divides her time between traveling and lecturing about her findings at Gombe and running the Gombe Stream Research Center, where she has been the director since 1967. She has also established a home for injured or orphaned chimps and created a program for schoolchildren to learn about wild animals and conservation of the environment.

> On your ActiveBook disc: *Reading Glossary* and *Extra Reading Comprehension Questions*

Information source: *Jane Goodall*, by Adrian G. Weiss

C **Confirm Content.** Complete the chart, based on information in the biography.

Difficulties at Gombe	Discoveries at Gombe	Other achievements
The chimps would not let Goodall approach. Goodall spent weeks in bed, sick with malaria. Progress was slow and Goodall was discouraged.	*Chimps eat meat.* Chimps make and use tools. Chimps adopt orphan infants. Chimps know and use medicinal plants.	Goodall travels and lectures about her findings at Gombe. She runs the Gombe Stream Research Center. Goodall established a home for injured or orphaned chimps. She created a program for schoolchildren to learn about wild animals and conservation.

D **Express and Support an Opinion.** With a partner, create a description of Jane Goodall's personality. Use information from the text to support your description.

3

A Reading Warm-up

| Suggested teaching time: | 5 minutes | Your actual teaching time: | |

- After pairs discuss the questions, bring the class together. Have students share what they know about Goodall's work. Students should remember from page 2 that she is a primatologist and ethologist. From the photo, they can infer that she works with chimpanzees.

- Ask *What kinds of qualities do you think a person needs to be a primatologist?* (Possible answers: fascination with and love of animals, desire to learn about them, patience)

B 🎧 Reading

| Suggested teaching time: | 10–15 minutes | Your actual teaching time: | |

- Display a map of Africa and have students locate Kenya, the Democratic Republic of the Congo (formerly Zaire), and Tanzania. Ask students to share anything they know about these countries.

- Before students read, have them look at the photo. Ask *What is Goodall doing?* (observing chimps) Then have students predict the content of the reading. Ask *Do you think working with chimpanzees was a lifelong dream for Goodall?*

- Have students read and listen to the article and then answer the Reading question.

- Ask *What contributed to Goodall's interest in animals?* (As a child, she spent a lot of time observing animals in her backyard. *The Jungle Book* and the Tarzan stories fascinated her.)

- To check comprehension, ask:
  How old was Jane Goodall when she first went to Africa? (twenty-three)
  What was her first job in Africa? (secretary)
  After meeting Louis Leakey, what did Goodall start working on? (a field study on chimpanzees)
  How long has Goodall been researching chimps? (over 40 years)
  Why do you think this project is taking so long? (Possible answer: There is always something new to learn.)
  How did Goodall get a closer look at chimpanzees? (She used bananas to win their trust.)
  What does Goodall do today? (She lectures about her findings at Gombe and runs the Gombe Stream Research Center.)

- Have students read the article again.

Culture note: *The Jungle Book* (1894) is a children's book by English writer Rudyard Kipling. It tells the story of Mowgli, a human child who is raised by wolves. The first of twenty-four <u>Tarzan stories</u> written by American author Edgar Rice Burroughs appeared in 1914. They relate the adventures of Tarzan, a boy who is adopted by a band of apes in Africa. <u>Kenya</u> and <u>Tanzania</u> are located in eastern Africa on the Indian Ocean. <u>Zaire</u>, currently known as the Democratic Republic of the Congo, is located in central Africa. <u>Gombe</u>, short for the Gombe National Reserve, is located in Tanzania and is the site of Goodall's chimpanzee research. <u>Louis Leakey</u> was an English / Kenyan archaeologist and anthropologist known for his studies on human origins.

C Confirm Content

| Suggested teaching time: | 5 minutes | Your actual teaching time: | |

- Copy the headings from the chart on the board: *Difficulties at Gombe, Discoveries at Gombe, Other achievements.* Have students volunteer information they remember from the biography. Write the information on the board.

- Then have students look at the biography again and write any additional information in their books.

- After students have completed the activity, have them compare answers with a partner.

- Have students compare the list of difficulties with the lists of discoveries and achievements. Ask *Do you think the difficulties have been worth it? Would you like to have Jane Goodall's job? Why? Why not?*

D Express and Support an Opinion

| Suggested teaching time: | 5 minutes | Your actual teaching time: | |

- To prepare, ask students to underline any words, phrases, or sentences in the Reading that describe or provide clues to Goodall's personality.

- Have students discuss what they found in the Reading and make a list of her key personality traits.

- Invite pairs to present their findings to the class. Ask other students to add their ideas.

 • **Reading Strategies**
• **Reading Speed Calculator**
• **Extra Reading Comprehension Questions**
• **Reading Glossaries**

E 🎧 Vocabulary

Suggested teaching time:	5 minutes	Your actual teaching time:

- Have students skim the Vocabulary and note the phrases they are less familiar with.
- After students listen and practice, ask volunteers to read the first two example sentences, substituting the alternative phrase. (Living in the jungles of Africa had been her *lifelong dream*. She finally *realized her dream* . . .)
- Have pairs create additional sentences about Goodall, using the phrases they are less familiar with. Circulate and assist as needed.
- Then have students listen and practice again.

F Vocabulary Practice

Suggested teaching time:	5–10 minutes	Your actual teaching time:

- Tell students to skim the paragraph. Point out that in some sentences an adjective is missing (1. childhood / lifelong; 4. short-term; 5. long-term), while in others a verb is missing (2. fulfilled / realized; 3. set; 6. achieve / reach; 7. took). Make sure students understand that they may need to change verb forms in some items.
- After students complete the paragraph, have them check answers with a partner. Then go over answers as a class, making sure students read both possible expressions when appropriate.

Option: [+5 minutes] Ask *How old was Jane Goodall when she fulfilled her childhood dream?* (twenty-three) *Do you think it is unusual to fulfill a lifelong dream so early in life? Has anyone already fulfilled a lifelong dream?*

NOW YOU CAN

Suggested teaching time:	10–15 minutes	Your actual teaching time:

ActiveTeach • **Discourse Strategies**

A Frame Your Ideas

- Have students look at the pictures of the family, the hammock, and the engineers. Ask *Do you see yourself in these pictures? Is one of your dreams to have a family? Is one of your long-term goals to become an engineer? Does your lifelong dream include retiring to a tropical paradise?*
- On the board, write *short-term goal, long-term goal, lifelong dream.* Provide an example of each from your own life and share one or more steps you have taken to achieve your goals and dreams.
- As students complete the chart, circulate and assist as needed.

B Pair Work

- In preparation for Exercise C, have students take notes as their partner shares information about goals and dreams.
- Tell students to share any difficulties they have had in achieving their goals and dreams.

C Presentation

- After each student presents, invite the class to ask questions. Students may want to ask for specific dates, difficulties involved in realizing a dream, changes in long-term goals, or current dreams and goals.
- Finally, ask each student to share his or her greatest achievement to date.

ActiveTeach • **Vocabulary-Building Strategies**

Option: [+5–10 minutes] Have students write their partner an informal letter giving advice on things the partner can do to help achieve his or her dreams.

EXTRAS (optional)

- **Workbook: Exercises 14–16**
- **MySummitLab: Lesson 3**

E 🎧 1:09 **Vocabulary. Dreams and Goals.** CN
Listen and practice.

> **childhood / lifelong dream**
> *Living in the jungles of Africa had been her childhood dream.*
>
> **fulfill / realize a dream**
> *She finally fulfilled her dream of setting up a home for injured or orphaned chimpanzees.*
>
> **short-term / long-term goal**
> *Her short-term goal was to get to Africa. Her long-term goal was to have an impact on science.*
>
> **set goals for oneself**
> *When she heard that Leakey was in Zaire, she set a goal for herself to meet him.*
>
> **take steps to achieve / reach a goal**
> *It was clear that she needed to take some difficult steps to reach her goal.*

F **Vocabulary Practice.** Use the Vocabulary to complete the paragraph about Jane Goodall's dreams and goals. In some cases, more than one word is possible.

> Jane's Goodall's ___childhood / lifelong___ dream was to live
> in Africa. She ___fulfilled / realized___ (1) this dream when she
> was only in her twenties. She was able to do
> this because she ___set___ (3) goals for herself at the
> beginning of her research. When she started
> her field study, her ___short-term___ (4) goal was to win
> the chimps' trust, and her ___long-term___ (5) goal was
> to discover new similarities between chimps
> and humans. It was not easy for Goodall to
> ___achieve / reach___ (6) her goals, but she was able to do so
> because she ___took OR had taken___ (7) all the necessary steps.

CN **Corpus Notes:** In expressing wishes for the future, *dream of* occurs more frequently than *dream about*.

NOW YOU CAN *Share your dreams and goals in life*

A **Frame Your Ideas.** Complete the chart with your own goals. Use the pictures for ideas.

	Goal or dream	Steps taken to achieve it
a short-term goal		
a long-term goal		
a lifelong dream		

B **Pair Work.** Share the information in your chart with a partner.

C **Presentation.** Tell the class about your partner's dreams and goals.
Your classmates ask questions to find out more.

GOAL
Describe your job qualifications and experience

A 🎧 **1:10 Word Skills. Using Collocations with Have for Job Qualifications.**

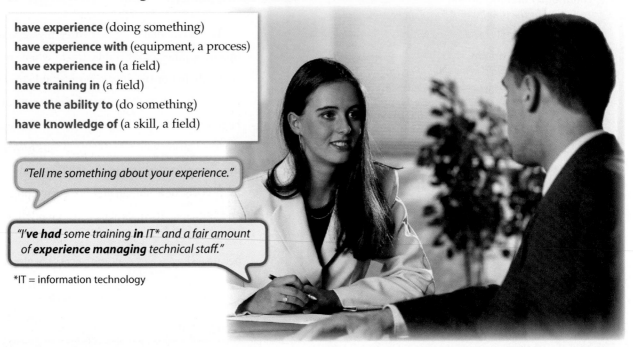

have experience (doing something)
have experience with (equipment, a process)
have experience in (a field)
have training in (a field)
have the ability to (do something)
have knowledge of (a skill, a field)

"Tell me something about your experience."

"I've had some training in IT* and a fair amount of experience managing technical staff."

*IT = information technology

B **Activate Word Skills.** Read the ad and explain why you would or wouldn't apply for this job. Use the collocations with <u>have</u>.

"I wouldn't apply for this job because I've had no experience planning large events."

ASSISTANT CRUISE DIRECTOR

Have you ever dreamed of seeing the world? Here's your opportunity to get paid to do it! One-World Vacation Lines has a number of openings for Assistant Cruise Directors, responsible for all shipboard entertainment. Interested candidates will have experience in the travel or hotel industry and will have the ability to arrange parties, games, and other events for large groups of people. You should love being around people from different cultures. Experience planning recreational activities a plus. Knowledge of languages desirable but not necessary.

C 🎧 **1:11 Listening. Listen to Take Notes.** Listen to the job interview with Marcos Ferrante. Then listen again and take notes about his qualifications for the job. Answers will vary, but may include:

Experience: has been working as an assistant hotel manager for two years

Abilities: a real people person; very friendly and easily wins people over; very organized; able to deal with the unexpected; flexible; able to make quick decisions

Training: instructed in hotel's emergency procedures

Goals: to get experience working on a cruise ship and to start his own travel agency

D **Express and Support an Opinion.** Do you think Ferrante is a good candidate for the job? Why or why not? Listen again if necessary for details to support your opinion.

4

A 🎧 Word Skills

Suggested teaching time:	5 minutes	Your actual teaching time:

- Have students listen and practice. Then ask two volunteers to read the interviewer's question and the applicant's response. Ask for other responses based on the students' own experience. Encourage students to use the collocations to talk about their job qualifications.

- Tell students that the prepositions are an important and inseparable part of these collocations. Remind them to learn the prepositions together with the phrases.

- Then have students listen and practice again.

> **Language note:** If students are unfamiliar with the term *collocation*, explain that it refers to the use of certain words together. For example, we say *a tall building*, not *a high building*.

ActiveTeach • Vocabulary-Building Strategies

Option: [+5–10 minutes] Have pairs role-play an interviewer and an applicant in a job interview. Have them ask and answer questions about the applicant's qualifications, using the collocations in Exercise A. Ask pairs to present their role plays to the class.

B Activate Word Skills

Suggested teaching time:	5–10 minutes	Your actual teaching time:

- Read the question in the first line of the ad. Ask for a show of hands to answer the question. Then have a volunteer read the rest of the paragraph.

- Ask *What are the qualifications for this job?* As students state the qualifications, write them on the board. (have experience in the travel or hotel industry; have the ability to arrange parties . . . ; love being around people from different cultures; have experience planning recreational activities; have knowledge of languages) Underline the verb *have* and circle the preposition in each collocation. Leave the qualifications on the board for use with Exercise D.

- Ask several students if they would apply for this job and to explain why or why not. Encourage students to use the collocations in Exercise A.

C 🎧 Listening

Suggested teaching time:	10–15 minutes	Your actual teaching time:

- To introduce the topic, tell students to recall a job interview they've had. If necessary, have students think about an interview they've had to gain admission to a school or course. Ask:
  What kinds of questions did the interviewer ask?
  What was the result of the interview?

- Have students listen to the job interview and then scan the headings in the exercise (Experience, Abilities, Training, Goals). Then have students listen again and complete the activity. Pause the audio as needed to allow students enough time to write their responses.

- If necessary, have students listen again before comparing notes with a partner.

AUDIOSCRIPT

For audioscript, see page AS1.

ActiveTeach • Listening Strategies

D Express and Support an Opinion

Suggested teaching time:	5 minutes	Your actual teaching time:

- Refer students to the list of job qualifications written on the board in Exercise B, or have the class review the ad in Exercise B.

- Tell students to compare the job qualifications with the applicant's qualifications that they noted in Exercise C. Have students discuss why they think Marcos Ferrante is or isn't a good candidate for the job.

- On the board, write additional discussion questions:
  Do you think Ferrante gave good answers to the interviewer's questions?
  Did he sound confident?
  Do you think Ferrante's interview was successful?
  If you were the interviewer, would you hire him?

Challenge: [+10 minutes] Have pairs write a letter from the interviewer to Ferrante, either offering him the job or turning him down. Tell students to refer to details in the interview to explain the reason for Ferrante's acceptance or rejection. If necessary, allow students to listen to the interview again.

E Draw Conclusions

Suggested teaching time:	10–15 minutes	Your actual teaching time:	

- To introduce the topic, ask:
  Have you ever written a resume? What job were you applying for?
  Did you include a goal?
  What other information did you include? What categories—such as Goal, Experience, Special Training—did you use?

- Have students read the two resumes and then review the job qualifications in the ad in Exercise B. Tell pairs to compare each person's qualifications with the job qualifications.

- As students discuss which candidate is better qualified, encourage them to use the collocations in Exercise A.

- Bring the class together and have students explain their choice of candidate. Ask *Does the candidate you chose lack any qualifications?* (Possible answer: Yes, Alice Shanker lacks knowledge of languages.) Then ask *Do you think Shanker can still get the job?* (Yes, because knowledge of languages is desirable but not necessary.)

Culture note: The Czech Republic is a small country in Europe bordering Poland, Germany, Austria, and Slovakia. *Praha* is the Czech name for Prague, the capital of the country. If necessary, have students locate the Czech Republic on a map.

NOW YOU CAN

Suggested teaching time:	10 minutes	Your actual teaching time:	

A Notepadding

- On the board, write *dream job*. Ask *What does this expression mean?* (an ideal job, a job one would very much like to have) *Does anyone have a dream job? What is it?*

- Ask a volunteer to read the headings on the notepad. Tell students to write the name of their dream job after Position.

- Have students complete the details on the notepad.

B Discussion

- Ask a volunteer to read Ways to become qualified in the box. Remind students that the prepositions are important and inseparable parts of these collocations.

- Then have a student read aloud the advice in the three speech balloons. Ask *What is each person's dream job?* (journalist, nurse, website designer)

- Circulate as groups discuss dream jobs and give advice on how to become qualified for these jobs. Encourage students to use the collocations in the box to give advice.

- Bring the class together and invite students to share their dream jobs. Make a list of dream jobs on the board. See whether any students have the same dream job. Take a poll and ask *How many of you think you will get your dream job someday?*

Option: [+5–10 minutes] Have students write down their dream jobs and the things they need to do to become qualified for these jobs. If some students already have their dream job, have them outline the steps they took to become qualified for the job. Ask volunteers to share their information with the class.

EXTRAS (optional)

- **Workbook: Exercises 17–18**
- **MySummitLab: Lesson 4**

E **Draw Conclusions.** Look at the resumés of the two candidates for the assistant cruise director job. With a partner, discuss their qualifications. Which candidate is better qualified for the job? Use the collocations with <u>have</u>.

Ivan Urban
Václavské nám. 32
11 525, Praha 1
Czech Republic

Goal: Seeking a position in the travel business in which I can use my knowledge of languages and ability to motivate people.

Experience:
Sept 08–present: East Euro Airlines (Prague, Czech Republic): Customer Service Representative
Handle customer inquiries about flight schedules. Book flights and assist customers with other travel arrangements.

June–Aug 08: Camp Friendship (Quebec, Canada): Assistant Director of international summer camp for teens. Organized daily activities and weekly trips.

Languages: Fluent in Czech, English, German; some Spanish and Japanese.

Special Training: Lifesaving procedures

Alice Shanker
28 Lancer Street
Winter Park, FL 32793 USA

GOAL: To use my ability to work with people from different cultures and gain experience in the tourism industry.

EXPERIENCE:

(Feb 07–present) *Front Desk Clerk, Beachfront Hotel and Resort, Miami Beach, Florida.*
Check in hotel guests and assist them during their stay.

(Jan 05–Jan 07) *Executive Assistant, International Print Associates, Miami, Florida.*
Organized conferences, sales meetings, and customer events worldwide. Helped solve customers' problems.

NOW YOU CAN *Describe your job qualifications and experience*

A **Notepadding.** On your notepad, write notes to describe the details of your "dream job."

Position:
Type of employer:
Responsibilities:
Qualifications you might need:
Qualifications you already have:
Desired salary:
Other:

Ways to become qualified
get (some) **experience** (doing something)
get training in (something)
learn how to (do something)
get a degree / certificate in (something)
get certified in (something)

B **Discussion.** Take turns describing your dream jobs. Encourage each other by suggesting steps you can take to become qualified for those jobs.

"You may want to **get some experience writing** articles for your school newspaper."

"It seems like you might need to **get a certificate in** nursing first."

"I'd suggest you let them know you **have the ability to** build websites."

Writing: Write a biography

Common Sentence Errors: Review and Extension

Sentence Fragments

A dependent clause is not a complete sentence—it is a *sentence fragment*. To make a fragment a complete sentence, attach it to an independent clause. Use a comma if the dependent clause comes first.

~~Although Isabel Carter has painted many portraits.~~
Although Carter has painted a lot of portraits,
she hasn't sold any yet.   Answers will vary, but may include:
~~Who paints a lot of portraits.~~
Carter is an artist who paints a lot of portraits.

1. painter who
2. young, but she
3. portraits because
4. world, and they
5. support, she

Run-on Sentences

Joining two independent clauses with neither a conjunction nor punctuation is a *run-on sentence*.

~~Carter is a very talented artist she has won many awards.~~

Joining two independent clauses with a comma but no conjunction is a type of run-on sentence called a *comma splice*.

~~Carter is a very talented artist, she has won many awards.~~

To correct run-on sentences:

- Add a coordinating conjunction. (A comma is optional.)
  Carter is a very talented artist **and** she has won many awards.
- Separate the clauses into two sentences. Use a transition word if possible.
  Carter is a very talented artist. **In fact**, she has won many awards.
- Add a subordinating conjunction.
  Since Carter is a very talented artist, she has won many awards.
- Use a semicolon. (However, it is a good idea to avoid overusing semicolons.)
  Carter is a very talented artist; she has won many awards.

ERROR CORRECTION

Find and correct the errors.

An Artist in Our Community

Isabel Carter is a talented portrait painter.[1] Who is much admired in our community. She is quite young she has already achieved [2] a great deal. Her portraits, which have been exhibited in local galleries and art shows, use bold strokes of color to express character and mood. Everyone in our community is familiar with Ms. Carter's portraits. Because many of [3] them depict people we all know. Her vision and technique make you see a person you thought you knew in a completely different way, which is quite remarkable. Ms. Carter has painted many beautiful portraits of people whom she has encountered around the world, they are as fascinating to us as the [4] portraits of people we know. If she can get financial support. She will study painting in [5] Italy next year.

Coordinating Conjunctions		Subordinating Conjunctions
and	for	because
but	so	although
or	yet	even though
nor		if

A **Prewriting. Clustering Ideas.** Look at the idea cluster. On a separate sheet of paper, create your own idea cluster about a living person you admire. Write ideas in circles and expand each new idea. Include jobs, achievements, hobbies, places traveled to, interests, etc.

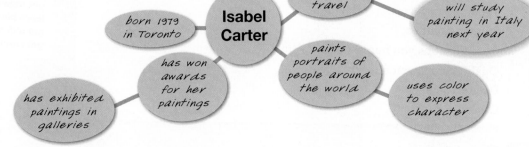

B **Writing.** On a separate sheet of paper, write a biography of the person you chose, using your ideas.

C **Self-Check.**

☐ Did you write any sentence fragments? If so, correct them.

☐ Did you write any run-on sentences or comma splices? If so, correct them.

Writing

Suggested teaching time:	25–30 minutes	Your actual teaching time:	

Common Sentence Errors . . .

- On the board, write *sentence fragment*. Invite students to define what it means.

- Tell students to read the section on sentence fragments. Remind students that an independent clause has a subject and a verb, and it expresses a complete idea.

- Ask students to define dependent clause. (It has a subject and a verb, but it does not express a complete idea.)

- Ask students to explain when you have to use a comma. (when you combine an independent clause and a dependent clause, if the dependent clause comes first)

- Now write on the board *run-on sentence*. Invite students to define what it means. (two independent clauses joined without a conjunction or punctuation)

- Tell students to read the section on run-on sentences. Ask *What is a comma splice?* (It's a run-on sentence with two independent clauses combined with only a comma.)

- Write three sentence errors on the board:

    Carter loves to travel she will study painting in Italy next year.

    Because Carter paints portraits of people around the world.

    Carter was born in 1979, she grew up in Toronto, she loves to paint.

    Ask students to correct and rewrite each sentence two different ways. Encourage them to use the conjunctions in the boxes or their own ides. Invite students to share their corrections.

- Point out that a semicolon should not be substituted for *but, or, nor, for*, or *so* when joining independent clauses.

Language note: A *biography* is a written history of a person's life. *Bio-* comes from the Greek word that means *life*, and *-graphy* comes from the Greek verb *to write*. An *autobiography* is a written history of a person's life that is written by the person. The prefix *auto-* comes from the Greek word for *self*.

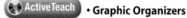 • **Extra Writing Skills Practice**

Error Correction

- Ask students to read the paragraph titled "An Artist in Our Community" and complete the Error Correction activity.

- Have students compare error corrections with a partner. Ask them to explain their corrections. Bring the class together and go over any difficulties.

A Prewriting

- Have students read and study the idea cluster independently. Bring the class together and have students tell who they will write about.

- Remind students that an idea cluster doesn't have to be perfectly written. It is a tool to help generate ideas rather than a finished piece of writing.

- To help students get started, brainstorm possible ideas to include in their idea cluster. Create an idea cluster on the board by writing in students' ideas. (Possible answers: jobs, achievements, hobbies, places traveled to, interests, future plans, strengths, birth date) Note: A blank idea cluster appears on *ActiveTeach*.

- As students create their idea clusters, circulate and assist as needed.

B Writing

- Tell students to look at their own idea cluster from Exercise A Prewriting and then the biography of Isabel Carter in the Error Correction exercise to see how the ideas were used in the writing.

- As students begin to write their biographies, tell them they can omit any ideas from their cluster or add any details they forgot.

C Self-Check

- After students complete the Self-Check, have them correct any sentence fragments or incorrect verb forms.

- Then have students exchange biographies or read them to the class.

ActiveTeach • **Graphic Organizers**

A 🎧 Listening

Suggested teaching time:	10 minutes	Your actual teaching time:

- Have students listen to all four conversations first and then look over the chart.

- Have students listen again to the first conversation and answer the questions for that conversation. Continue with the remaining conversations and questions.

- After students complete the chart, have them compare answers with a partner.

- Then have students listen again. Stop after each conversation and have students identify the line that reveals whether the speaker is confident or not. (Conversation 1: *I don't think I'll ever really be able to outdo them.* [not confident] Conversation 2: *I'm starting to feel like maybe it's time to just give up. I'm really not sure I'll ever have a house of my own.* [not confident] Conversation 3: *I've already applied for a loan.* [confident] Conversation 4: *You're probably right.* [confident]) In Conversation 4, point out that although at first the woman is not confident, she becomes confident after talking about her qualifications.

- Ask students if they answered most questions correctly. Replay conversations as needed.

Challenge: [+5–10 minutes] Using the conversations in the Listening Comprehension as models, have pairs create their own conversation about a lifelong dream. Tell students to decide if they are confident or not about achieving their dream. Invite pairs to present their conversations to the class. Ask the class to determine whether the speaker is confident or not. Have the class identify the line in the conversation that revealed the level of confidence.

AUDIOSCRIPT

For audioscript, see page AS2.

B Complete the sentences ...

Suggested teaching time:	5–10 minutes	Your actual teaching time:

- Have students read the sentences first before filling in the prepositions.

- If students have difficulty completing the sentences, refer them to the Vocabulary on page 4 and the Word Skills on page 10.

- Have students compare answers with a partner. Go over any questions with the class.

C Complete the biographical notes ...

Suggested teaching time:	5–10 minutes	Your actual teaching time:

- Before students do the exercise, have them scan the text and circle the stative verbs. (1. believe; 2. be, have) If necessary, refer students to the Be careful! box on page 6 for examples of stative verbs. Remind students that these verbs cannot be used in the present perfect continuous.

- If necessary, review that the present perfect is used for finished actions at an unspecified time in the past.

- After students complete the exercise, have pairs compare answers. Bring the class together and clarify any difficulties. If students used the present perfect for continuing or unfinished actions, point out that this is correct but that the directions ask for the present perfect continuous.

- Have three volunteers read the biographical notes aloud.

EXTRAS (optional)

- **Workbook: Page 12**
- **Complete Assessment Package**

- **ActiveTeach:**
  Summit TV Video Program and Activity Worksheets
  Printable Audioscripts
  "Can-Do" Self-Assessment Charts
  Workbook Answer Key

- **MySummitLab:**
  Writing
  Summit TV Video Program and Activity Worksheets
  Achievement Test 1

A 🎧 **Listening.** Listen to the conversations. Then read the
questions in the chart and listen again. Complete the chart after each conversation.

	What is the speaker's dream or goal in life?	Is the speaker confident about achieving his / her dream or goal?	
1	to have the biggest stamp collection in the world	☐ yes	☑ no
2	to have a house of his own	☐ yes	☑ no
3	to start her own business	☑ yes	☐ no
4	to be a flight attendant	☑ yes	☐ no

B Complete the sentences with the correct prepositions from the box.

1. She has always wanted to take __up__ the piano and has enrolled __in__ a program that teaches the basics of music.

2. Anyone applying __for__ a job in the newspaper business should have training __in__ journalism.

3. He has decided __on__ a career as a chef and has been accepted __to__ a world-renowned cooking school in France.

4. Her experience __in OR with__ the diplomatic service and her knowledge __of__ international law make her an excellent candidate for the position at the UN.

5. People who switch __to__ a different line of work in mid-career must be prepared to start at the bottom.

6. The ability __to__ solve problems is a valuable skill in all professions.

7. There is almost no field in which experience __with OR in__ computers is not important.

for
in
of
on
to
up
with

C Complete the biographical notes about people who have had an impact on the world. Use the present perfect continuous for unfinished actions, except with the stative verbs that are not used in the continuous. Use the present perfect for finished actions.

1. Robert Ballard's achievements as a deep-sea explorer and inventor are impressive. He __has published__ (publish) over 50 scientific articles and __has received__ (receive) more than 30 awards. He __has designed__ (design) a robot that can enter sunken ships and photograph them. Ballard __has always believed__ (always believe) that more history is preserved underwater than in museums.

2. Frans Lanting __has been documenting__ (document) wildlife from the Amazon to Antarctica for more than two decades. His photographs __have been dazzling__ (dazzle) people for just as long, and he __has been__ (be) an inspiration for nature photographers and environmentalists all over the world. Lanting __has had__ (have) a deep love of the natural world ever since he was a child.

3. Arundhati Roy __has won__ (win) worldwide acclaim and literary prizes for her novel, *The God of Small Things*. Since its publication, however, she __has been devoting__ (devote) her energies to political writing on a number of global issues. For example, she __has spoken__ (speak) at various events worldwide, such as at protests against nuclear weapons tests and against large hydroelectric dam projects.

Character counts

GOALS After Unit 2, you will be able to:
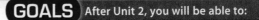
1 Discuss the social uses of lying
2 Express regret and take responsibilty
3 Discuss ways to help people in need
4 Tell a story with a "moral"

A **Topic Preview.** Look at the proverbs and try to explain what each one means. Do you know any similar proverbs in your own language? Can you translate those proverbs into English?

1. A sleeping cat will not catch a rat. (India)

2. Write injuries in sand, kindnesses in marble. (France)

3. Because we focused on the snake, we missed the scorpion. (Egypt)

4. Tell the truth—and run. (Serbia)

5. People who live in glass houses shouldn't throw stones. (Germany)

B **Critical Thinking.** With a partner, classify the proverbs according to their themes.

Themes	Proverb Number
Being honest	4
Being lazy	1
Criticizing others for faults we also have	5
Paying too much attention to one thing while neglecting another	3
Being mindful of the lasting effects of praise and criticism	2

C **Express Your Ideas.** Which proverbs do you like best? Why?

Character counts

A Topic Preview

Suggested teaching time:	10 minutes	Your actual teaching time:

- On the board, write the word *proverb*. Ask *What is a proverb?* (a short popular saying that expresses a belief or a truth and often includes general advice)

- Focus on each proverb and illustration separately. Have volunteers read the proverbs and explain what's happening in the illustrations. Point out that the illustrations interpret the proverbs literally. The meanings, however, are figurative.

- Then discuss the Topic Preview questions as a class. Make sure students understand the meaning of each proverb. (Note that Exercise B focuses on the themes of the proverbs.) Write on the board any proverbs that students suggest.

> **Language note:** A *literal* word or expression is its basic meaning. A *figurative* word or expression is used in a different way from its usual one.

Challenge: [+5–10 minutes] Divide the class into five groups and assign each one a proverb. Have students think up a situation in which it would be appropriate to say the proverb and then create a role play for the situation. Invite groups to present their role plays to the class and have students guess the proverb.

B Critical Thinking

Suggested teaching time:	5–10 minutes	Your actual teaching time:

- Call on a student to read the themes. If necessary, explain that *being mindful* means being aware of something.

- After pairs classify the proverbs, bring the class together and go over the answers. If students disagree about the classifications, have them explain their reasons.

- Point out that the image of sand in illustration 2 suggests impermanence, something that will be quickly forgotten. The image of marble suggests permanence, something that will be remembered for a long time. In proverb 4, note that it's important to be honest even if people disagree with you.

Option: [+5–10 minutes] Have students use the Internet to look up an additional proverb, including its country of origin, for each theme. Advise students to choose proverbs they understand and will be able to explain. Encourage students to be creative in choosing search words. For example, search words for proverb 1 might be *lazy* and *proverb*. Invite volunteers to present their proverbs to the class and have students guess the themes.

C Express Your Ideas

Suggested teaching time:	5 minutes	Your actual teaching time:

- Have groups discuss the questions.

- Then bring the class together and have students share their answers. Take a poll to determine the class favorite(s).

Option: [+5 minutes] Have students prepare a pie chart or a bar graph to show the results of the poll of class favorites.

D 🎧 Sound Bites

Suggested teaching time:	10 minutes	Your actual teaching time:

- Before students read and listen, have them look at the photo. Ask:
  Where are these people? (probably in an office)
  What is the man doing? (making a lot of photocopies)
  What do you think the woman is saying? (Possible answer: Her hand gesture implies a question, so perhaps "What in the world are you doing?")
- After students read and listen to the conversation, ask comprehension questions:
  What does Sandy remind Frank? (The procedures memo is due today.)
  Why is Frank doing so much photocopying? (He's helping out his colleague, Chris.)
  Why does Frank want to help Chris? (Chris helped him last week, and he feels it's his turn to be helpful.)
  What advice does Sandy give Frank? (He shouldn't do so much work for Chris that he misses his own deadline.)
- Have students read and listen to the conversation again.
- Write the following proverb on the board: *One good turn deserves another.* Ask *Which statement in the conversation has the same meaning as this proverb?* (I figure I owe him one.)

Language note: *Have a hard time* means have difficulty doing something.

Culture note: Xerox is the name of a company that manufactures photocopiers, printers, scanners, and other office machines. In the 1950s, Xerox was the first company to introduce a photocopier, and so the word *xerox* came to be used as a verb meaning to photocopy and as a noun meaning a photocopy. *Xerox* is still used with the same meaning today even though not all photocopiers are made by the Xerox company.

Option: [+5 minutes] Have students use the answers to the following questions as a basis for a class discussion: *Have you ever been in a situation similar to Frank's in which someone asked you for help when you had a lot of work yourself? What did you do? When a colleague helps you at work, do you usually try to return the favor?*

E Paraphrase

Suggested teaching time:	5–10 minutes	Your actual teaching time:

- After students do the exercise in pairs, bring the class together and have students share their answers. Write the different ways of saying the statements on the board.
- Have two volunteers read the conversation again, replacing the five selected statements with other ways of saying them.

Option: [+5 minutes] Have pairs create short conversations using the idioms and expressions from the exercise. For example, A: *I lost the file Mr. Peterson gave me.* B: *You're going to be in hot water!*

F Relate to Personal Experience

Suggested teaching time:	5 minutes	Your actual teaching time:

- Have groups discuss the questions and give explanations.
- Then bring the class together and have students share their answers. Find out whether students find it difficult to say no in the same kinds of situations. Ask *What makes it difficult to say no in certain situations?*

STARTING POINT

Suggested teaching time:	5–10 minutes	Your actual teaching time:

- On the board, write *favor*. Ask:
  What is a favor? (a kindness or a service that a person performs for someone else)
  Do you often do favors for other people?
  Do people often ask you to do favors for them?
- Ask a volunteer to read the favors people ask for. Have students think of other favors. Write these on the board.

Pair Work

- After pairs discuss the questions, bring the class together and have students share answers. Take a poll to find out how many students consider themselves pushovers. Ask *What is the difference between finding it difficult to say no and being a pushover?*

EXTRAS (optional)

- Workbook: Exercises 1–4
- MySummitLab: Preview

CN **Corpus Notes:** Some other frequent collocations with *bind* in the phrase *be in a bind* are *a terrible bind* and *a major bind*.

D 🎧 1:13 **Sound Bites.** Read and listen to a conversation between two colleagues about the difficulty of saying no.

SANDY: Why are you doing all that xeroxing? Isn't that procedures memo due today?

FRANK: Yeah, but Chris is in a real bind, and he **CN** asked me to help him out. I guess I have a hard time saying no.

SANDY: You really are a pushover, you know.

FRANK: But Chris helped me out last week. I figure I owe him one.

SANDY: I suppose. But don't go overboard. If you don't get that memo in on time, you're going to be in hot water.

E **Paraphrase.** Read the conversation again. Then say each of these statements another way.

Answers will vary, but may include:

1. "Chris is in a real bind."
   Chris is in a difficult situation.
2. "You really are a pushover."
   You are easy to influence.
3. "I figure I owe him one."
   It's my turn to help him.
4. "Don't go overboard."
   Don't do too much.
5. "You're going to be in hot water."
   You're going to be in trouble.

F **Relate to Personal Experience.** Do you ever find it difficult to say no? Discuss the situations in which you have this difficulty. Use at least two of the expressions from Exercise E in the discussion.

STARTING **POINT**

Pair Work. Tell your partner about some favors others have asked you to do. How easy is it for you to ask others for favors? Are you a pushover?

Some favors people ask for

watering their plants

picking up their mail

taking care of their child or children

taking care of their pets

picking up groceries for them

giving them a ride

lending them money

? other: _____

15

GOAL

Discuss the social uses of lying

A 🎧 1:14 **Grammar Snapshot.** Read the article. Notice how adjective clauses are introduced.

To Tell the Truth

Lying is part of everyday life, says psychologist Bella DePaulo, **who** carried out a study **in which** 147 people were asked to keep a diary of the lies they told over the course of a week. Here is what their diaries revealed:

- There wasn't a day **when** the participants didn't tell at least one lie.
- Over the week they deceived about 30 percent of the people **with whom** they interacted.

The most common lies **that** people tell are those **in which** they pretend to like something to avoid hurting others or those **in which** they make up excuses to get out of trouble.

According to psychologist Leonard Saxe, we live in a world **where** we are often rewarded for lying and punished for telling the truth. "If we admit we just overslept, we're punished much more than if we lie and say we were stuck in traffic."

Professor Jerald Jellison of the University of Southern California did an experiment. He proved that the people **whose** professions require the most social contacts—for example, shop assistants, salespeople, politicians, and journalists—tell the most lies.

The truth is, we *all* tell lies. Occasionally, one of the participants in Dr. De Paulo's study would insist that he or she could be entirely truthful for three or four weeks. None of them ever succeeded.

Information source: www.psychologytoday.com

B **Relate to Personal Experience.** Discuss and then make a list of times in your life when you . . .

told a lie to avoid hurting someone else's feelings.

told a lie to make an excuse.

were punished after telling the truth.

C **Critical Thinking.** With a partner, brainstorm one or more additional situations in which people are likely to lie. Explain why. Answers will vary, but may include:

People lie at job interviews to make their background more impressive. People lie to avoid revealing an uncomfortable truth about themselves.

D **Express and Support an Opinion.** Do you agree with Saxe's view that we live in a society in which we are often rewarded for lying and punished for telling the truth? Explain, using examples from real life if possible.

1

A 🎧 Grammar Snapshot

Suggested teaching time:	5–10 minutes	Your actual teaching time:	

- To introduce the topic, ask *Do you always tell the truth?* If no, ask *In what situations don't you tell the truth?*

- Have students read and listen to the article. Remind them to take note of the words in bold that introduce adjective clauses.

- Call on a volunteer to read the first adjective clause. (who carried out a study) With the class, identify the noun it modifies. (Bella DePaulo)

- Tell students to underline each adjective clause in the article and circle the noun it modifies. Go over the answers together. (in which 147 people were asked . . . / a study; when the participants didn't tell at least one lie / a day; with whom they interacted / people; that people tell / lies; in which they pretend . . . / those [lies]; in which they make up excuses . . . / those [lies]; where we are often rewarded . . . / a world; whose professions require . . . / people)

- Point out the adjective clause that is not introduced by a relative pronoun. In line 3, the pronoun *that* has been left out: *lies [that] they told.*

- To check comprehension, ask:
  What did the people in Bella DePaulo's study do? (They kept diaries of lies they told during one week.)
  What did the study reveal? (The participants told at least one lie every day; in a week, the participants told lies to about 30 percent of the people with whom they interacted.)
  Which lies are most common? (pretending to like something to avoid hurting others and making up excuses to get out of trouble)
  According to psychologist Leonard Saxe, are you likely to get in trouble for telling your boss you overslept? (yes)
  According to Professor Jerald Jellison, in which professions do people lie most? (professions that require the most social contact, such as shop assistants, salespeople, politicians, and journalists)

- Have students read the article again.

Project: Ask *How many lies do you think you tell in one week?* Have students replicate Bella DePaulo's study by keeping a diary of the lies they tell during one week. Do the students' diaries reveal the same findings as those in DePaulo's study?

B Relate to Personal Experience

Suggested teaching time:	5 minutes	Your actual teaching time:	

- Ask *Do you think it's OK to lie to avoid hurting someone's feelings? Is it OK to lie to make an excuse? Why? Why not?*

- Have students look at the three illustrations and read the speech balloons.

- Ask *Have you ever lied to a friend about your reaction to a new haircut or other physical change? Have you ever lied to your boss about why you'll be late for work?* Have students respond with a show of hands.

- Then have pairs work together to complete the exercise.

- Bring the class together and have students share their examples for the first two situations. Have students note similarities. Students will use the examples for the third situation in Exercise D.

C Critical Thinking

Suggested teaching time:	5 minutes	Your actual teaching time:	

- To prepare, ask the class to think of two situations in which people might feel they need to lie to someone.

- After pairs have brainstormed more ideas, ask them to share their list with the class.

- Encourage further discussion with each example; for example, *Would you tell a lie in this situation too? Why or why not?*

D Express and Support an Opinion

Suggested teaching time:	5–10 minutes	Your actual teaching time:	

- Have students discuss the question in groups, referring to the examples they listed in Exercises B and C.

- Then bring the class together and have groups report how many people agreed or disagreed with Saxe. Encourage students with opposing points of view to ask each other questions in order to better understand the other viewpoint.

Challenge: [+10 minutes] Have students write a short essay summarizing their answer to the discussion question. Have them include the examples they noted during the group discussion. Collect the essays and give students feedback.

E Grammar

Suggested teaching time:	10 minutes	Your actual teaching time:

- To introduce the topic, ask students to give some examples of words that introduce adjective clauses. If necessary, refer students to the bold words in the Grammar Snapshot on page 16. (who, in which, when, with whom, that, where, whose)

- On the board, create a two-column chart titled *People, Things*. Ask *Which words introduce adjective clauses about people?* (who, whom, that) *About things?* (that, which) If students have difficulties, have a volunteer read the Remember box. Write the words in the appropriate columns. You may want to use the term *relative pronoun* to refer to these words that introduce adjective clauses: *who, whom, whose, that,* and *which. Where* and *when* also introduce adjective clauses, but these words are relative adverbs, not pronouns.

- Write on the board the following sentences with adjective clauses about people:
  1. DePaulo is a psychologist <u>who</u> did a study about how often people lie.
  2. The people <u>who</u> (or <u>whom</u> or <u>that</u>) DePaulo studied were asked to keep diaries.

  Point out that in sentence 1, *who* functions as the subject of the adjective clause. In sentence 2, *who, whom,* and *that* function as the object of the adjective clause.

- Call on a student to read the first bold point in the Grammar box and the three example sentences. Ask *What nouns do the adjective clauses modify?* (people, world, time) Point out that in spoken English, *where* is sometimes used instead of *when* to introduce adjective clauses about time. On the board, write:
  There are occasions <u>when</u> telling the truth may not be a good idea. OR
  There are occasions <u>where</u> telling the truth may not be a good idea.

- Ask a volunteer to read the second bold point. Then call on students to read the pairs of formal and informal sentences. Remind students that the informal example sentence in each pair can be further reduced by omitting the relative pronoun. For example, *The participants in the study deceived many of the people they interacted with.* Have students reduce the other informal example sentences. (Money is a subject people are rarely honest about. The researcher we received the survey from is studying attitudes about lying. Most people save their biggest lies for the person they are closest to.)

- Have students note the different placements of the preposition in the sentences. Point out that *whom* is less and less frequent in informal spoken English. When *whom* occurs in informal speech, the preposition is usually at the end of the sentence. For example, *The participants in the study deceived many of the people whom they interacted with.*

- Have students read the Be careful! note to themselves. Remind students that *who* is a subject and *whom* is an object.

● ActiveTeach • **Inductive Grammar Charts**

F Grammar Practice

Suggested teaching time:	5 minutes	Your actual teaching time:

- Have students look at the words in the box. Review the information in the Grammar box by asking the following questions:
  Which words are used for people? (who, whom, that) *For things?* (that, which) *For possession?* (whose) *For location?* (where) *For time?* (when; where, in spoken English)

- Before students do the exercise, have them scan the sentences for clues that will help them decide if the adjective clause is about people, things, possession, location, or time. (1. *place:* location; 2. *people:* possession; 3. *people with:* people; 4. *people:* people; 5. *situations in:* location; 6. *times:* time; 7. *people to:* people; *people:* people; 8. *times:* time; *times:* time; 9. *action for:* things; 10. *people:* possession)

- After students complete the exercise, have them compare answers with a partner. Circulate and assist as needed, and then go over answers as a class.

NOW YOU CAN

Suggested teaching time:	10–15 minutes	Your actual teaching time:

A Notepadding

- As a preview, call on volunteers to read the headings for the three categories. For each heading, ask:
  What is the adjective clause? (in which we shouldn't tell lies, in which lying is the best solution, to whom I'd never lie)
  What noun does the adjective clause modify? (situations, situations, people)

- Have students complete the exercise independently.

- Then bring the class together and have students compare their examples. Invite students to explain why they listed the specific situations and people.

B Use the Grammar

- Tell students they can also incorporate examples from Exercise D on page 16. Circulate and assist as needed.

- After students have completed their paragraphs, tell them to reread their paragraphs and check that they used formal forms with adjective clauses.

C Discussion

- Before groups start the discussion, refer them to Exercises B and C on page 16 to review the lists of examples of situations in which lying might be beneficial.

- After groups discuss, bring the class together. Invite groups to summarize their ideas for the class. If groups hold different opinions, have them give reasons for their views.

EXTRAS (optional)

- **Grammar Booster**
- **Workbook: Exercises 5–9**
- **MySummitLab: Lesson 1**

E Grammar. Adjective clauses

Whose, where, and when introduce adjective clauses about possession, location, and time.

People **whose jobs require frequent social contact** have the most opportunity to lie. (possession)

There's no place in the world **where people are completely honest all the time.** (location)

There has never been a time **when some form of lying wasn't a part of everyday life.** (time)

In formal English, when a relative pronoun is the object of a preposition, the preposition appears at the beginning of the clause. In informal English, the preposition usually appears at the end.

FORMAL: The participants in the study deceived many of the people **with whom** they interacted.

INFORMAL: The participants in the study deceived many of the people **who** (or **that**) they interacted **with.**

FORMAL: Money is a subject **about which** people are rarely honest.

INFORMAL: Money is a subject **which** (or **that**) people are rarely honest **about.**

FORMAL: The researcher **from whom** we received the survey is studying attitudes about lying.

INFORMAL: The researcher **who** (or **whom**) we received the survey **from** is studying attitudes about lying.

FORMAL: Most people save their biggest lies for the person **to whom** they are closest.

INFORMAL: Most people save their biggest lies for the person **who** (or **whom**) the are closest **to.**

BE CAREFUL! Use **whom**, not **who**, directly after a preposition. Use **which**, not **that**, after a preposition.

> **REMEMBER**
>
> <u>Who</u>, **whom**, and <u>that</u> introduce adjective clauses about people.
>
> <u>That</u> and <u>which</u> introduce clauses about things. **CN**

CN Corpus Notes: A common learner error is using *which* with people. For example, *I don't like people which smoke.*

> **GRAMMAR BOOSTER ▸ p. G2**
>
> • Adjective clauses: overview
> • Adjective clauses with quantifiers
> • Adjective clauses reduced to adjective phrases

F Grammar Practice. Complete the sentences with one of the words from the box.

1. The workplace is the place _where_ people tend to tell the most lies.
2. The people _whose_ lies are discovered lose the trust of those they work with.
3. The people with _whom_ I work are trustworthy.
4. People _who_ break their promises cannot be trusted.
5. There are situations in _which_ it's impossible to tell the truth.
6. There are times _when_ being honest can cause you problems.
7. The people to _whom_ I never lie are the people _who_ are really close to me.
8. There are times _when_ I lie to avoid getting into trouble and times _when_ I lie to avoid hurting others.
9. Telling the truth is an action for _which_ there is sometimes no reward.
10. The people _whose_ lies were recorded said they would tell about 75 percent of the lies again.

who	whom
which	whose
where	when

NOW YOU CAN *Discuss the social uses of lying*

A Notepadding. Write examples for each category.

Situations in which we shouldn't tell lies	Situations in which lying is the best solution	People to whom I'd never lie

B Use the Grammar. Write three paragraphs about lying, with each paragraph based on one of the categories above. Use the examples from your notepad as a guide. Use the formal forms with adjective clauses.

C Discussion. Why is it difficult to be entirely truthful all the time? Do you think it would be desirable? Compare your views.

2 GOAL
Express regret and take responsibility

A 🎧 ^1:15 **Conversation Snapshot.** Read and listen. Notice the conversation strategies.

A: Tim, I hate to tell you this, but I dropped the camera you lent me, and it can't be fixed.

B: Oh, no. How did *that* happen?

A: Well, I tripped, and it fell out of the bag. I feel awful about it.

B: Are you sure it can't be fixed?

A: Pretty sure. I took it to the camera shop, and **CN1** they said to forget it. But I can replace it with a newer model.

B: That's really not necessary.

A: No, I insist. And please accept my apology. **CN2**

🎧 ^1:16 **Rhythm and intonation practice**

PRONUNCIATION BOOSTER ▸ p. P3
· Emphatic stress and pitch

CN1 **Corpus Notes:** The expression *forget it* is common in spoken English but is rarely written.

CN2 **Corpus Notes:** The most frequent apology in spoken English is *I'm sorry.* Also common is *I apologize. Please accept my apology* is forr

🎧 ^1:17 **Ways to express regret**
I'm so sorry.
I feel awful (about it).
I feel (just) terrible.

B 🎧 ^1:18 **Vocabulary. Ways to Take and Avoid Responsibility.** Listen and practice.

Statement		Attitude or action
He said, "I'm sorry. I'll pay for the damage."	➡	He took responsibility for the damage.
He said, "It wasn't my fault. I'm not paying for it!"	➡	He avoided taking responsibility for the damage.
He said, "I'm sorry. It was my fault."	➡	He admitted making a mistake.
He lied and said, "It was Bob's fault."	➡	He shifted the blame to someone else.
He overslept but said, "Sorry. The train was late."	➡	He made up an excuse.
After he broke the camera, he said, "I'll buy you a new one."	➡	He made up for it. (He made up for breaking the camera by buying a new one.)

C 🎧 ^1:19 **Listening. Infer Information.** Listen to the conversations. Then listen again. After each conversation, choose the expression that best completes each statement.

1. She .... the damage.
  (a.) took responsibility for   **b.** avoided taking responsibility for

2. He .... the damage.
  a. took responsibility for   **(b.)** avoided taking responsibility for

3. He ....
  a. admitted making a mistake   **(b.)** shifted the blame to someone else

4. She ....
  (a.) admitted making a mistake   **b.** made up an excuse

5. She .... for being late.
  (a.) made up an excuse   **b.** made up

6. She .... losing the scarf.
  a. avoided taking responsibility for   **(b.)** made up for

2

A 🎧 Conversation Snapshot

Suggested teaching time:	5 minutes	Your actual teaching time:

These conversation strategies are implicit in the model:
- Use *I hate to tell you this, but* to soften bad news.
- Begin a sentence with *Well* to allow time to think.
- Use expressions such as *I feel awful about it* to convey regret.
- Use *That's not necessary* to decline help politely.
- Say *Please accept my apology* to repeat a regret.

- Have students read and listen to the conversation. Then ask:
  What did Student A do? (She dropped Tim's camera.)
  How did this accident happen? (Student A tripped, and the camera fell out of the bag.)
  Is Student A going to have the camera fixed? (No, it can't be fixed.)
  What does she offer to do instead? (She offers to replace the camera with a newer model.)

- Finally, have students read and listen to Ways to express regret. Have a volunteer read Student A's second line and use another way to express regret. Note that the sentence *I'm so sorry* does not conclude with *about it*. The sentences *I feel awful / (just) terrible* can conclude with *about it*.

- Call students' attention to the conversation strategies highlighted in the model.

🎧 Rhythm and intonation practice

Suggested teaching time:	5 minutes	Your actual teaching time:

- Have students repeat chorally. Make sure they:
  - use emphatic stress for <u>that</u> in *How did that happen?*
  - use falling intonation for *How did that happen?*
  - use emphatic stress for <u>awful</u> in *I feel awful about it.*
  - use rising intonation for *Are you sure it can't be fixed?*

B 🎧 Vocabulary

Suggested teaching time:	5–10 minutes	Your actual teaching time:

- Have a student read the first statement on the left and then the first sentence under the heading Attitude or action. Then have a volunteer give the base form for the highlighted phrase under Attitude or action. (take responsibility for) Continue the same procedure for the remaining five items, giving the base form for the way to take or avoid responsibility. (avoid taking responsibility for, admit making a mistake, shift the blame to, make up an excuse, make up for)

- Have students listen and practice. Then ask students to describe Student A's attitudes and actions in the Conversation Snapshot using phrases in the Vocabulary. (Student A took responsibility for the damage. Student A admitted making a mistake. Student A is going to make up for the damage.)

- Have students listen and practice again.

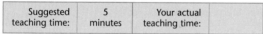 • **Vocabulary-Building Strategies**

C 🎧 Listening

Suggested teaching time:	5–10 minutes	Your actual teaching time:

- Tell students to listen carefully to the attitudes and actions expressed in the six conversations.

- Then have students read the first two items in the exercise. Have them listen again to the first two conversations and complete the items with the correct expressions.

- Have students repeat the procedure with the second two items and then finally with the last two items.

- Have students listen again to all six conversations to check their answers.

- Tell students to compare answers with a partner before reviewing the exercise with the class.

Language note: Students should be able to complete the exercise without understanding every word. You may want to share the following definitions if students ask about specific expressions. *Cut someone off* means pass someone's car abruptly, without signaling or giving any warning. *Buy something* means believe something. The expression is often used in the negative: *They didn't buy my excuse.*

AUDIOSCRIPT

For audioscript, see page AS2.

NOW YOU CAN

Suggested teaching time:	25–30 minutes	Your actual teaching time:

A Frame Your Ideas

• Have students read the questions in the survey. Make sure they understand the meanings. Ask *Which situations have you been in?*

• After pairs discuss the questions, have students complete the survey individually. Then have pairs compare answers.

B Notepadding

• Have students make notes about two situations on their notepad.

• Then ask *Have you ever regretted something you said or did? Why? What did you do to fix the situation?*

C Use the Vocabulary

• Have students share their situations with a partner, using the Vocabulary from page 18.

• Encourage pairs to ask questions and say what they would do in the same situation.

D Use the Conversation Strategies

• Refer students to the Conversation Snapshot on page 18 to review expressing regret and taking responsibility. Have them review as well the Vocabulary on page 18.

• Brainstorm with the class different ways to complete the sentence. For example, *I hate to tell you this, but I had a terrible accident when I was driving your car.*

• Role-play a conversation with a more confident student. Play the role of Student A and take responsibility for what happened. It is not necessary to create a complete conversation but only to get the activity started.

• Then have pairs create their own conversations, changing roles so that each student plays the role of Student A.

• Reinforce the use of the conversation strategies; for example, make sure that the student expressing regret sounds sincere.

• Ask volunteers to present their role plays to the class. After each presentation, ask *Have you ever been in a similar situation? Did you do the same thing?*

(ActiveTeach) • **Conversation Prompts**

Option: [+5–10 minutes] Have students write a summary of the situation they discussed in the role play. Have pairs exchange and check the summaries before students read them to the class.

EXTRAS (optional)

• Pronunciation Booster
• Workbook: Exercises 10–12
• MySummitLab: Lesson 2

A **Frame Your Ideas.** With a partner, discuss each question in the survey and fill in the answer that best describes what you would do.

How hard is it for you to accept responsibility?			
What would you do if you ...			
✳ made a serious mistake at work?	Ⓐ	Ⓑ	Ⓒ
✳ broke or lost something you had borrowed?	Ⓐ	Ⓑ	Ⓒ
✳ forgot to give back something you had borrowed?	Ⓐ	Ⓑ	Ⓒ
✳ forgot to do an assignment at work or in school?	Ⓐ	Ⓑ	Ⓒ
✳ fell behind schedule at work?	Ⓐ	Ⓑ	Ⓒ
✳ were late for an appointment?	Ⓐ	Ⓑ	Ⓒ
✳ were stopped for exceeding the speed limit?	Ⓐ	Ⓑ	Ⓒ
✳ were reminded about a promise you hadn't kept?	Ⓐ	Ⓑ	Ⓒ
✳ were caught telling a lie?	Ⓐ	Ⓑ	Ⓒ
✳ forgot a friend's birthday?	Ⓐ	Ⓑ	Ⓒ

Ⓐ = I would tell the truth.
Ⓑ = I would make up an excuse.
Ⓒ = I would shift the blame to someone else.

B **Notepadding.** Choose two situations from the survey that have actually happened in your life. Make notes about what happened and what you said and did.

Situation:
I forgot a friend's birthday.

Situation:	Situation:
What I said:	What I said:
What I did:	What I did:

C **Use the Vocabulary.** Compare notes with a partner. Use the Vocabulary from page 18 to summarize what you did in each situation.

D **Use the Conversation Strategies.** Role-play a conversation in which you express regret and take responsibility for having lost or broken something of your partner's. Then change roles. Use the Conversation Snapshot as a guide. Start like this: "I hate to tell you this, but . . .

GOAL
Discuss ways to help people in need

CN Corpus Notes: *Feel sorry for* occurs more frequently than *have compassion for*, in both written and spoken English.

A 🎧 **Vocabulary.** Expressions Related to Compassion and Admiration. Listen and practice.

1:20

do (someone) a favor do something someone has asked you to do for him or her

help (someone) out do a kind or useful thing for someone

give (someone) moral support give someone encouragement by expressing approval or interest, rather than by giving practical help

find (something) rewarding feel happy and satisfied because you feel you did something useful or important

feel sorry for / have compassion for (someone) **CN** feel sympathy for someone because something bad has happened to that person or because he or she is suffering

look up to (someone) admire or respect someone for his or her experience or achievements

be proud of (someone) feel pleased with someone's achievements

B **Vocabulary Practice.** Complete the sentences with the Vocabulary, using the correct verb forms. More than one answer may be possible. Compare answers with a partner.

1. They ____are proud of____ their daughter because she has achieved so much already.
2. She ____is proud of OR looks up to____ her father because he worked hard to send his children to college.
3. Mike's a nice guy. Whenever I ask him for a ride to work he always says yes, even if it's out of his way. He's always willing to ____help me out OR do me a favor____
4. I ____feel sorry for OR have compassion for____ my cousin Mary. Her father died and her family has suffered.
5. When someone is upset about something, you can help by ____giving moral support____. Often just being a good listener is enough to help someone through a time of trouble.
6. I volunteer at a camp for children with disabilities. Whenever I have a free weekend, I ____help (them) out____ by setting up the equipment or preparing snacks for the kids. When I see the big smiles on their faces, it makes me feel really good. I ____find it rewarding____.

C 🎧 **Listening. Listen for Details.** Listen to a radio program in which two people talk about helping others. Then read the statements and listen again. Check <u>Vivian</u> and/or <u>James</u>.

1:21

	Vivian	James	
1.		✓	work(s) with children.
2.	✓		work(s) with the aged.
3.	✓		volunteer(s) two days a week.
4.		✓	work(s) in a public library.
5.	✓		do(es) favors and run(s) errands.
6.		✓	provide(s) snacks.
7.	✓		was (were) inspired by a family member.
8.	✓	✓	has (have) compassion for others.

3

A 🎧 Vocabulary

Suggested teaching time:	5 minutes	Your actual teaching time:

- Have students listen and practice.

- Make sure students understand the difference between *finding something rewarding* (deriving moral satisfaction from doing something) and *being rewarded for doing something* (receiving material compensation for an action).

- Explain that someone who looks up to a person is usually younger and/or less accomplished than that person. The expression *look up to* is often used to describe the feelings of a child toward a parent but not usually those of a parent toward a child.

- Have students listen and practice again.

> **Language note:** *Feel sorry for* someone means feel pity or sympathy for someone in a bad situation. *Feel compassion for* someone means have a strong feeling of sympathy for someone.

B Vocabulary Practice

Suggested teaching time:	5–10 minutes	Your actual teaching time:

- Before students complete the sentences, have them scan the exercise and note which sentences require the word *someone* or the use of a pronoun. (3. do someone a favor / help someone out; 5. giving him or her moral support; 6. find it rewarding)

- Remind students to check their completed sentences for correct verb forms. Then have them compare answers with a partner.

- Bring the class together and go over any problems. Focus on sentences for which more than one answer is possible and encourage students to suggest the different options.

ActiveTeach • **Vocabulary-Building Strategies**

Option: [+5–10 minutes] Read aloud the following situations and have volunteers use the expressions in the Vocabulary to make a statement about each situation. You may prefer to photocopy and distribute the situations and then have pairs or groups make statements about them.

1. Peter's boss is a very successful man. He started his own company when he was only twenty-seven. Peter has learned a lot from this man.

2. Jen volunteers at a local school by helping kids with their homework. She loves doing this.

3. Maria's parents died when she was ten, and she had a very difficult childhood. I feel sympathy for her.

4. Helen recently lost her job and is having trouble finding a new one. I talk to her every day and encourage her to keep trying.

5. Richard has three deadlines this week, so you're working on one of his projects.

6. My sister graduated with honors from a top university.

(Answers: 1. Peter looks up to his boss. 2. She finds volunteering rewarding. 3. I have compassion / I feel sorry for her. 4. I'm giving her moral support. 5. You're helping him out / doing him a favor. 6. I'm proud of her.)

C 🎧 Listening

Suggested teaching time:	5–10 minutes	Your actual teaching time:

- To introduce the topic, ask:
  What are some volunteer programs in your community for helping people? What do the programs do?
  (Possible answers: programs to tutor children or provide meals for the homeless)
  Have you ever been involved in a similar volunteer program? What did you do?

- Have students listen to the radio program with their books closed. Tell students to listen for the expressions related to compassion and admiration listed in the Vocabulary in Exercise A.

- Then have students read the statements and listen again. Have them complete the exercise.

- If necessary, have students listen again to check their answers.

- Go over the answers with the whole class.

> **Language note:** If you are *confined to a nursing home* it means you have to live in a nursing home. When something *rubs off* on someone, it has an influence or effect on someone. A *drop-in center* is a place you can go to during certain hours without an appointment or reservation. *One good turn deserves another* is a proverb that means when someone does you a favor, you should do a favor in return. Point out the double meaning in the organization name All Kids Count. The program tutors children in math, which involves counting. *Count* also means be important or matter.

AUDIOSCRIPT

For audioscript, see page AS3.

ActiveTeach • **Listening Strategies**

T20

D 🎧 Listening

Suggested teaching time:	5 minutes	Your actual teaching time:

- Circulate as students discuss Vivian's and James's volunteer activities. Have students listen to the radio program again if they have trouble remembering details.
- Then bring the class together and ask:
  What do you think are the challenges of volunteering for Reach Out? The rewards?
  What do you think are the challenges of volunteering for All Kids Count? The rewards?
  Which program would you prefer to volunteer for? Why?

NOW YOU CAN

Suggested teaching time:	25–30 minutes	Your actual teaching time:

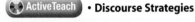 **ActiveTeach** · **Discourse Strategies**

A Pair Work

- Call on volunteers to read the statements in the speech balloons. Have students note the expressions from the Vocabulary on page 20. (look up to [someone], have compassion for [someone], give [someone] moral support)
- Have pairs complete the discussion and then bring the class together. Call on students to share what kinds of people they admire. Ask *What have you learned from these people?*

B Frame Your Ideas

- Have students look at the three photos and read the captions.
- Then ask students to suggest some volunteer activities. Allow students to repeat some of the community programs they mentioned in the introduction to Exercise C on page 20. Write the suggested activities on the board.
- Then have students read the list of volunteer activities in the book and compare it with the items on the board. Ask *Which activities appear both on the board and in the book? Which appear only on the board? Which appear only in the book?* Clarify vocabulary as necessary.
- Have students complete the exercise individually and then compare their choices with a partner.
- Bring the class together. Ask *Did anyone add an activity in the Other category? What was it? Why are you interested in this activity?*

Language note: *Elderly* is the polite way to refer to people who are old. *Old* is used in talking about the age of someone or something. For example, *How old is your son?* People who are *shut in* can't go out. They may be confined to a nursing home or other facility. *Raising money* means collecting money. In the phrase *relief effort*, *relief* refers to food, clothing, medical supplies, and other necessities. A *relief effort* is an attempt, often headed by an organization, to collect these supplies and distribute them to people who are victims of a flood, fire, or other disaster.

C Presentation

- Make sure students understand that to *motivate* is to inspire or make someone want to do something. Review what motivated Vivian and James to start their programs. (Vivian's mother motivated her. James's own difficulties learning math motivated him.)
- After groups discuss the question, bring the class together. Invite students to share their ideas. Ask *Do you / Would you find it rewarding to help people you don't know? Why? Why not?*

Option: [+10 minutes] Have students interview a person they know who is active in a volunteer organization. Tell students to find out details about the organization and how the person became involved in it. Encourage students to find out what motivated the person to join the organization. Then have students present their findings to the class.

EXTRAS (optional)

- Workbook: Exercises 13–15
- MySummitLab: Lesson 3

1:22 🎧 **Listening. Listen to Summarize.** Listen again and summarize what Vivian and James do. Explain how and why they got involved in their programs.

NOW YOU CAN *Discuss ways to help people in need*

A **Pair Work.** Discuss what kinds of people you admire and look up to and what kinds of people you have compassion for. Use the expressions from the Vocabulary on page 20.

> *"I admire people who give up everything to help people who have nothing. I could never do that myself, but I really look up to them for their sacrifice."*

> *"The people I have the most compassion for are those who are sick. If you don't have your health, everything is more difficult! It's important to give these people the most moral support you can."*

Raising money for disaster relief

B **Frame Your Ideas.** If you were to volunteer to help other people, what types of activities on the questionnaire would you be most interested in? Compare choices with a partner.

○	Visiting sick children in a hospital
○	Visiting elderly people in a nursing home
○	Running errands or doing favors for people who are sick or shut in
○	Tutoring children who are having trouble in school
○	Driving an ambulance
○	Cooking and serving meals to the needy
○	Collecting money or clothing to help the poor
○	Donating money to a charity
○	Raising money for a charity
○	Traveling to another city or country to help out in a relief effort
○	Other: ....

Visiting an elderly person in a nursing home

C **Presentation.** Present your ideas about what motivates people to help others, especially people they don't know. Use the questionnaire to help you provide specific examples from your own or others' experiences.

Tutoring a young child

GOAL
4 *Tell a story with a "moral"*

A **Reading Warm-up.** Why do you think stories that "teach a lesson" exist in all cultures? What purpose do they serve?

B 🎧 **Reading.** Read the story about a newlywed couple. Do you think they will have a good marriage?

The Silent Couple

There was once a very stubborn young man and an equally stubborn young woman who met, fell in love, and got married. After the wedding ceremony, they had a grand feast at their new house. The celebration lasted all day.

When all the guests had left, the husband noticed that the last guest had failed to close the door.

"My dear," he said, "would you mind getting up and shutting the door?"

"Why should I shut it?" yawned the wife. "I've been on my feet all day. You shut it."

"So that's the way it's going to be!" snapped the husband. "Just as soon as you get the ring on your finger, you turn into a lazy good-for-nothing!"

"How dare you!" shouted the bride. "We haven't even been married a day, and already you're calling me names and ordering me around!"

They sat glaring at each other for a full five minutes. Then an idea popped into the bride's head.

"My dear," she said, "neither of us wants to shut the door, and both of us are tired of hearing the other's voice. So I propose a contest. The one who speaks first must get up and close the door."

"It's the best idea I've heard all day," replied her husband.

So they made themselves comfortable and sat face-to-face without saying a word.

They had been that way for about two hours when a couple of thieves passed by and saw the open door. They crept into the house, which seemed perfectly deserted, and began to steal everything they could lay their hands on. They took tables and chairs, pulled paintings off walls, even rolled up carpets. But the newlyweds neither spoke nor moved.

"I can't believe this," thought the husband. "They'll take everything we own, and she won't make a sound."

"Why doesn't he call for help?" the wife asked herself.

Eventually the thieves noticed the silent, motionless couple and, mistaking them for wax figures, stripped them of their jewelry, watches, and wallets. But neither husband nor wife uttered a sound.

The robbers hurried away with their loot, and the newlyweds sat through the night. At dawn a policeman walked by and, noticing the open door, stuck in his head to ask if everything was all right. "Is this your house? What happened to all your furniture?" And getting no response, he raised his hand to hit the man.

"Don't you dare!" cried the wife, jumping to her feet. "That's my new husband, and if you lay a finger on him, you'll have to answer to me!"

"I won!" yelled the husband. "Now go and close the door."

> On your ActiveBook disc: *Reading Glossary* and *Extra Reading Comprehension Questions*

Source: Traditional tale adapted from *The Book of Virtues*, 1993

C **Express and Support an Opinion.** Discuss the questions. Do you think the wife should have closed the door when her husband first asked her to? Why? Do you agree that the husband "won"? In what way? If you had to write a moral for this story, what would it be?

A Reading Warm-up

Suggested teaching time:	5 minutes	Your actual teaching time:

- After students answer the question, ask *How do stories that "teach a lesson" influence you?* Then invite students to share some popular stories with a "moral."

B 🎧 Reading

Suggested teaching time:	10–15 minutes	Your actual teaching time:

- Have students look at the picture. Ask *What's happening in the picture?* (The newlyweds are sitting across from each other, looking at each other angrily. There are two men in the background, but the newlyweds don't seem to notice them.) *Does this picture remind you of any story you know that teaches a lesson? Which one?*
- Call on a volunteer to read the title of the story. Ask *Why do you think the couple is silent?* (Possible answer: because the man and woman are angry at each other)
- Have students make predictions about the story. Ask *What do you think the story is about?*
- Have students read and listen to the story and then answer the question. Tell students to explain why they think the couple will or won't have a happy marriage.
- Review students' predictions about the story. Ask *Were your predictions correct?*

- To check comprehension, ask:
  What caused the dispute between the newlyweds? (Neither of them wanted to close the door.)
  What did the bride suggest to solve the problem? (The first person to speak would have to close the door.)
  What happened while the couple was sitting and looking at each other? (Thieves entered the open door and stole all their belongings.)
  In the end, who was the first to speak? (the bride)
  Why did she speak? (She wanted to stop the policeman from hitting her husband.)
- Have students read the story again.

C Express and Support an Opinion

Suggested teaching time:	5–10 minutes	Your actual teaching time:

- Have students discuss the questions in groups.
- Then bring the class together and have students share answers. Write the suggested morals on the board. If the morals are very different, discuss them in more detail and decide which ones are best reflected in the story. Then take a poll. Ask *How many of you agree that the husband won?*

Challenge: [+5–10 minutes] Ask *If you were the bride, what would you have done? If you were the groom?* Have pairs retell the story, changing it according to what they would have done as the bride or groom. Have students share their versions with the class.

ActiveTeach
- **Reading Strategies**
- **Reading Speed Calculator**
- **Extra Reading Comprehension Questions**
- **Reading Glossaries**

D Associate Ideas

Suggested teaching time:	5 minutes	Your actual teaching time:	

- Call on students to read the proverbs. Tell pairs to look at the illustrations on page 14 to help them recall the meaning of the proverbs.

- After pairs choose a proverb, bring the class together and have students share answers. Review the message of the proverbs as needed.

- Ask *What other proverbs do you know that match the message of this story?* Write these proverbs on the board.

Option: [+5–10 minutes] Have pairs write their own proverb that matches the message of the story. Ask students to share their proverbs with the class.

NOW YOU CAN

Suggested teaching time:	20–25 minutes	Your actual teaching time:	

A Pair Work

- To introduce the topic, ask:
  Who was Aesop? (Aesop was the real or possibly legendary ancient Greek creator of fables. He is supposed to have lived in the late sixth century B.C.E.)
  What are some of Aesop's most popular fables? ("The Tortoise and the Hare," "The Fox and the Grapes") Have a volunteer tell one of these stories or another of Aesop's fables.

- Invite volunteers to read the stories to the class. Encourage them to read them enthusiastically, as if they were presenting them to an audience. Ask *Have you ever heard these stories before?*

- Have pairs read the stories again and answer the questions.

- Bring the class together and ask pairs for the moral of each story. Write these on the board. Discuss any differences of opinion. Then have pairs tell which story they preferred and why.

Language note: Students may see *B.C.E.* (Before the Common Era) as well as *B.C.* (Before Christ) to show that a date is a certain number of years before the birth of Christ.

Option: [+5 minutes] Write the following two proverbs on the board: *Think before you leap. Every cloud has a silver lining.* Ask *What do you think these proverbs mean?* Then have students match each proverb to a story: *Think before you leap* for "The Frogs and the Well" and *Every cloud has a silver lining* for "A Traditional Chinese Tale."

B Project

- Have volunteers read the boxed Ideas. Then have students read the beginning sentences of the two stories in Exercise A for additional ways to begin a story.

- As groups create their story, circulate and assist as needed.

- Then bring the class together and have a spokesperson tell each group's story. Have the class write a moral for each story. Make sure each group agrees with the moral for their story.

- Have the class vote for their favorite story and most appropriate moral.

Language note: Using the boxed Ideas gives students more practice with adjective clauses. *Once upon a time* is another way to begin a story.

EXTRAS (optional)

- **Workbook: Exercises 16–18**
- **MySummitLab: Lesson 4**

D **Associate Ideas.** With a partner, decide which proverb gives the same message as the story. Explain your answer.

"A sleeping cat will not catch a rat."

"Write injuries in sand, kindnesses in marble."

"Because we focused on the snake, we missed the scorpion."

"Tell the truth—and run."

"People who live in glass houses shouldn't throw stones."

NOW YOU CAN *Tell a story with a "moral"*

A **Pair Work.** Read the stories. What do you think is the moral of each story? Which one do you prefer? Why?

The Frogs and the Well
from Aesop's Fables

Two frogs lived together in a pond. One hot summer the pond dried up, and they set out to look for a new place to live. Eventually they passed by a deep well, and one of them looked down into it and said, "There's plenty of water here, and it looks like a nice cool place! Let's jump in and make this our home."

But the other, who was wiser and more cautious, replied, "Not so fast, my friend. If this well dried up like the pond, how would we get out?"

A Traditional Chinese Tale

There was a young man living in the north of China whose horse ran away. Everyone felt sorry for him.

"Perhaps this will soon turn out to be a blessing," said his father.

After a few months, the horse came back followed by another, very beautiful, horse. Everyone congratulated the man for his good fortune.

"Perhaps this will soon turn out to be a cause of misfortune," said his father.

The man loved to go riding, and one day he fell from the beautiful horse and broke his leg. Everyone felt sorry for him.

"Perhaps this will soon turn out to be a blessing," said his father.

A month later, war broke out, and there was a big invasion in the north. All able-bodied young men had to join the army to fight the invaders. Nine out of ten men died in the terrible battles that were fought. The man had not joined in the fighting because of his injured leg, and so he survived.

B **Project.** With a small group, create a story that teaches a lesson. (It can be an original story or one you already know.) Collect your stories and with your class write a moral for each story.

IDEAS

This story / tale takes place in a town where . . .
It's set in a time when . . .
It's about a . . . who / to whom / for whom . . .
The moral of the story is . . .

A 🎧 **Listening**

Suggested teaching time:	10 minutes	Your actual teaching time:

- Have students listen to the conversations with their books closed.
- Have students read the chart headings and then listen again to complete the activity.
- After students complete the chart, have them compare answers with a partner.
- Then have students listen again. Stop after each conversation to allow students to check their answers.

Language note: Conversation 1: A *tough call* is a difficult decision. *Be short of cash* means not have enough cash to spare. Conversation 2: *So much for buying a new one* means that the idea of buying a new jacket is not a possible solution. Conversation 3: *Give something a go* means try something.

Option: [+5 minutes] Have pairs discuss what they would do in each of the three situations.

AUDIOSCRIPT

For audioscript, see page AS3.

B **Complete the sentences ...**

Suggested teaching time:	5–10 minutes	Your actual teaching time:

- Have students review the Vocabulary on page 18. Note that the phrases *express regret* and *tell the truth* are not included in the Vocabulary, but students should know what they mean.
- Tell students to use the context of the sentences when choosing the phrases.
- Have students compare answers with a partner. With the whole class, go over any questions.

C **Complete the paragraph ...**

Suggested teaching time:	5–10 minutes	Your actual teaching time:

- If necessary, refer students to the Grammar box on page 17 to review adjective clauses and words used to introduce them.

- Before students do the exercise, have them scan the sentences for clues that will help them decide if the adjective clause is about people, things, possession, location, or time. (1. people, 2. people, 3. time, 4. things, 5. things, 6. things, 7. things, 8. people, 9. location) Have students also note the sentences in which pronouns are used as objects of prepositions and remind them to use *whom* (not *who*) and *which* (not *that*) after a preposition. (1. with, 5. on, 6. about, 7. in)
- While students complete the exercise, circulate and assist as needed. Note that both pronouns *that* and *which* are acceptable for item 4. Remind students that *which* may be used in restrictive clauses in informal English.
- Have students compare answers with a partner.

Language note: The phrase *one of* takes a singular verb. For example, in item 8, *Nora was one of those persons who fails . . .*

Challenge: [+5–10 minutes] Have students scan the adjective clauses and identify which are restrictive (2, 3, 4, 7, 8, 9) and which are non-restrictive (1, 5, 6). Remind students that a restrictive adjective clause gives essential information and is *not* set off from the sentence by commas. A non-restrictive adjective clause gives additional information and is set off by commas. Go over each sentence and discuss whether the clause gives information that is essential to identify the noun it modifies.

D **On a separate sheet of paper, ...**

Suggested teaching time:	5 minutes	Your actual teaching time:

- Call on volunteers to read the topics.
- After students write their personal examples and explanations, bring the class together and have students share.

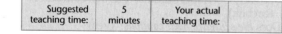

EXTRAS (optional)

- **Workbook: Page 25**
- **Complete Assessment Package**
- **ActiveTeach:**
    Summit TV Video Program and Activity Worksheets
    Printable Audioscripts
    "Can-Do" Self-Assessment Charts
    Workbook Answer Key
- **MySummitLab:**
    Writing
    Summit TV Video Program and Activity Worksheets
    Achievement Test 2

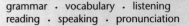

A 🎧 **Listening.** Listen to the conversations. Then listen again and complete the chart after each conversation.

Answers will vary, but may include:

	What is the person concerned about?	What will he or she do about it?
1	lending people money	make up an excuse
2	telling Mary she lost her jacket	tell the truth and offer to buy Mary something else
3	community programs not getting enough volunteers	get involved in some volunteer work

B Complete the sentences with phrases from the box.

> shift the blame   express regret   make up for it
> tell the truth   make up an excuse

1. If Matt makes a mistake, he never admits it and instead tries to ___shift the blame___ to other people in his office.

2. Dan forgot to prepare his report for the sales meeting. He didn't want to admit his mistake, so he decided to ___make up an excuse___. He told his boss that his computer deleted the file.

3. After borrowing my umbrella, Alice forgot it on the train. She offered to buy me a new one to ___make up for it___.

4. Jane has really poor manners. For example, she never thinks to ___express regret___ when she does something wrong. I believe it's important to say that you're sorry when you make a mistake or cause problems for other people.

5. I really believe that in some situations it's better not to ___tell the truth___, especially when you are protecting someone's feelings. For example, if my grandmother spent all day cooking dinner, but it tasted terrible, I would still tell her it was delicious.

C Complete the paragraph with words from the box.

> who   whom
> that   which
> where   when

Nora Richards, with ___whom___ I worked for five years, was a person ___who OR that___ could never get her
(1)   (2)
work done on time. I still remember the time ___when___ she asked me to help her write a long report
___that OR which___ was due the next day! The report, on ___which___ she had been working for an entire month, was
(4)   (5)
needed for a business deal with a very important client. The deal, about ___which___ Nora talked all the
(6)
time (instead of writing the report), fell through, and Nora was fired. There are situations in ___which___
(7)
you simply have to meet your deadlines. Nora was one of those persons ___who OR that___ fails to understand
(8)
that the office is a place ___where___, as the proverb says, "Actions speak louder than words."
(9)

D On a separate sheet of paper, give a personal example of each of the following situations. Explain what happened in each case.

1. A favor I did for someone or that someone did for me
2. A person (or group of people) I feel sorry for
3. A person I look up to or feel proud of
4. An experience I found rewarding

Dealing with adversity

GOALS After Unit 3, you will be able to:

1 Describe a dangerous or challenging experience
2 Express frustration, empathy, and encouragement
3 Describe how people confront adversity
4 Discuss the nature of heroism

A **Topic Preview.** Read the quotations. What attitude toward adversity do they express?

> **❝** I'm not afraid of storms for I'm learning to sail my ship. **❞**
>
> **Louisa May Alcott, writer**

> **❝** Obstacles don't have to stop you. If you run into a wall, don't turn around and give up. Figure out how to climb it, go through it, or work around it. **❞**
>
> **Michael Jordan, athlete**

> **❝** When it gets dark enough, you can see the stars. **❞**
>
> **Lee Salk, psychologist**

B **Express Your Ideas.** Do you agree that adversity can be a positive experience? Do you find any of the quotations inspiring or relevant to your own life? Explain.

Dealing with adversity

A Topic Preview

Suggested teaching time:	10–15 minutes	Your actual teaching time:

- Have a student read the title of the unit. Ask *What is adversity?* (a situation in which someone has a lot of problems or difficulties) *What does the title mean?* (managing or coping with difficulty)

- Have students scan the names under the quotations. Ask *Which names do you recognize?*

- Then divide the class into groups and assign each group a quotation. Tell students to read their quotation carefully and think about the meaning. Have them note any interesting or symbolic images in the quotation. For example, a storm can symbolize a difficult situation. You may want to assign groups one or more of the additional quotations in the Option following.

- Circulate as students work and assist as necessary.

- Then bring the class together and have group spokespersons read their quotation and give the group's interpretation. Ask groups if their quotation had any interesting images or symbolic meanings. (Possible answers: <u>Alcott</u>: Sailing a ship can symbolize going through life. Alcott suggests that she is not afraid of difficult situations, because she is learning to find her way through life. <u>Jordan</u>: This quotation suggests that you shouldn't give up when you encounter a difficult situation but rather find a way to overcome it. <u>Salk</u>: Darkness can symbolize a difficult situation. The quotation suggests that even in a difficult situation you can see something beautiful or inspiring.)

- Ask *When you find yourself in a difficult situation, what do you do?* (Possible answers: I try to overcome the difficulty. I get discouraged or depressed.) Then ask *What attitudes toward adversity do these reactions express?* (Possible answers: courageous or determined attitude; discouraged or depressed attitude)

- Then discuss the question in the Topic Preview as a class.

> **Culture note:** <u>Louisa May Alcott</u> (U.S., 1832–1888) is famous for her children's books. She is best known for her novel *Little Women*. <u>Michael Jordan</u> (U.S., 1963–) is a famous basketball player and one of the most popular athletes of all time. <u>Lee Salk</u> (U.S., 1926–1992) was a child psychologist, an expert on family relationships, an author, and a consultant.

Option: [+10–15 minutes] Write one or more of the following quotations on the board. Have pairs or groups read the quotations and discuss both the literal and the symbolic meanings. Keep the quotations on the board for further use in Exercise B. *"The greatest glory in living lies not in never failing but in rising every time we fall."* Nelson Mandela, statesman. *"Adversity causes some men to break, others to break records."* William A. Ward, writer and educator. *"A certain amount of opposition is of great help to a man. Kites rise against, not with the wind."* Lewis Mumford, philosopher.

> **Culture note:** <u>Nelson Mandela</u> (South Africa, 1918–) is a political leader. He was president of South Africa from 1994 to 1999. <u>William A. Ward</u> (U.S., 1921–1994) was an author, scholar, and college administrator. <u>Lewis Mumford</u> (U.S., 1895–1990) was an architectural critic, urban planner, and historian.

B Express Your Ideas

Suggested teaching time:	5–10 minutes	Your actual teaching time:

- Tell students to reread the quotations in Exercise A. As appropriate, refer students to the quotations on the board. Then ask the first discussion question.

- Then have students answer the second discussion question. Tell them to give specific examples to explain why the quotation was inspiring or relevant.

Option: [+5 minutes] Write this informal expression on the board: *When the going gets tough, the tough get going.* Ask *What does this expression mean?* (Possible answer: When a situation becomes difficult, hardworking, determined people try to overcome the difficulty.) *Which quotations in Exercise A have a similar meaning?* (Jordan's quotation; also Ward's) Have students explain their answers.

Challenge: [+5–10 minutes] Have pairs think of different words to symbolize adversity, hope, and courage, such as *darkness* (adversity) and *sunshine* (hope, courage). Tell students not to use any of the words in the quotations in Exercise A. Then have students write their own quotation about dealing with adversity, using the images they thought up. Bring the class together and have students share their quotations.

C 🎧 Sound Bites

Suggested teaching time	5–10 minutes	Your actual teaching time:

- Before students read and listen, have them look at the photo. Ask:
  Where are the man and woman? (in a hallway, probably in an office building)
  What is happening in the background? (People are entering an elevator.)
  What can you tell from the woman's body language? (Possible answers: She's upset, worried, or unhappy.)
  What can you tell from the man's body language? (Possible answer: He's concerned.)
  What do you think the two people are talking about? (Possible answer: The man is asking if the woman is OK, and she's explaining how she feels.)

- Have students listen to the conversation with their books closed. To check comprehension, ask:
  What happened to Anne? (She was just stuck in an elevator.) *For how long?* (twenty minutes)
  What made the experience in the elevator so scary? (It was totally dark / pitch black.)
  How did Anne feel? (She was scared to death.)

- Have students listen again as they read the conversation.

Language note: *Be stuck in a place* means not be able to get out of a place. *Go off* means shut off or turn off. *I couldn't see "a thing"* is an emphatic expression. Normally people say *I couldn't see "anything."* To be *going out of your mind* is to feel extremely afraid or nervous.

D Paraphrase

Suggested teaching time	5 minutes	Your actual teaching time:

- Have pairs think of different ways to say each statement.

- Then bring the class together and have students share their answers. Write the different ways of saying the statements on the board.

- Have two volunteers read the conversation again, replacing the selected statements with one of the statements on the board.

Option: [+5 minutes] Have pairs create short conversations using the idioms and expressions from the exercise. For example, A: *Are you OK? You look a little shaky.* B: *I'm OK. But I was almost in a terrible car accident.*

E Think and Explain

Suggested teaching time	5 minutes	Your actual teaching time:

- Make sure students show where the text of the conversation supports their answers. (1. He says, "Are you OK?" 2. She says she was stuck in the elevator for twenty minutes. 3. She says she couldn't see a thing. 4. He says, "You must have been going out of your mind.")

F Make Personal Comparisons

Suggested teaching time	5 minutes	Your actual teaching time:

- Before students answer the questions in groups, make sure they understand the meaning of *keep your cool* (stay calm).

- After groups complete the exercise, bring the class together and have students share how they would feel in Anne's situation. Have them also explain why this situation is frightening to some people. Ask *Has anyone ever been stuck in an elevator? What happened? How did you feel?*

STARTING POINT

Suggested teaching time	10 minutes	Your actual teaching time:

A Frame Your Ideas

- To introduce the topic, ask *What do you think is scarier—being in an earthquake or other natural disaster or having to give a speech to a roomful of strangers?* Ask students to give their reasons.

- Then call on a student to read the list of situations. Ask *Which situations have you experienced?*

- Have students individually rate the situations.

B Pair Work

- After pairs compare their ratings, bring the class together and discuss.

- Ask *Which situation is the most frightening? The least frightening?*

Option: [+5 minutes] Have pairs discuss what they would do if they found themselves in the situations listed.

EXTRAS (optional)

- **Workbook: Exercises 1–2**
- **MySummitLab: Preview**

CN **Corpus Notes:** This emphatic use of *like* occurs very frequently in informal spoken English. However, it almost never occurs in writing.

C 🎧 **Sound Bites.** Read and listen to a conversation between two friends about a scary experience.

MATT: Hey! You look a little shaky. Are you OK?

ANNE: I'm not sure. I was just stuck in the elevator.

MATT: Are you serious? You mean when the power went off? How long were you in there?

ANNE: Like twenty minutes. And it was pitch black, and I couldn't see a thing. **CN**

MATT: You must have been going out of your mind.

ANNE: Yeah. I was scared to death.

D **Paraphrase.** Read the conversation again. Then say each of these statements another way.
Answers will vary, but may include:

1. "You look a little shaky."
   You look nervous.
2. "It was pitch black."
   There was no light.
3. "You must have been going out of your mind."
   You must have felt very scared.
4. "I was scared to death."
   I was very frightened. OR I was very scared.

E **Think and Explain.** Mark each statement <u>true</u> or <u>false</u>. Then explain your answer with a quotation from Sound Bites.

<u>true</u> **1.** Matt is concerned about Anne.
"Are you OK?"

<u>true</u> **2.** Anne couldn't get out of the elevator.
"I was just stuck in the elevator."

<u>false</u> **3.** Anne spent the time in the elevator reading.
"I couldn't see a thing."

<u>true</u> **4.** Matt imagines that Anne was scared.
"You must have been going out of your mind."

F **Make Personal Comparisons.** Discuss the questions. If you were stuck in an elevator, would you be scared, or would you keep your cool? Why does getting stuck in an elevator frighten some people?

STARTING **POINT**

A **Frame Your Ideas.** What scares *you*? Rate the following situations from 1 to 3, with 1 being very frightening, 2 being somewhat frightening, and 3 being not at all frightening.

◯ getting stuck in an elevator	◯ being caught in a burning building
◯ being stung by a bee	◯ riding in a speeding car
◯ driving in very bad weather	◯ going to the dentist
◯ eating in a dirty restaurant	◯ walking down a dark street
◯ riding a horse	◯ experiencing turbulence during a flight

B **Pair Work.** Compare and explain your ratings.

GOAL
Describe a dangerous or challenging experience

A 🎧 **Grammar Snapshot.** Read the article and notice how past actions and events are described.

Stranded climbers rescued by text message

Two climbers stranded on a Swiss mountain during a snowstorm **were rescued** by a helicopter yesterday. Two days before, they **had sent** an SOS text message from a cell phone to a friend in London.

Rachel Kelsey, 34, and Jeremy Colenso, 33, both experienced climbers, **had checked** the weather forecast for a week before they **set out**. And on the way up the weather **was** perfect. However, as they **were climbing** down from the summit of Piz Badile, they **were forced** to stop and take shelter behind a large rock. A severe snowstorm **had** suddenly **begun** and their descent **had become** impossible. At 1:30 A.M., Kelsey **sent** a text message asking for help and providing details of their location. By 5:00 A.M., her friend in London **had responded**, saying that he **had made** contact with a team of rescuers.

It **was snowing** heavily and the winds **were** fierce. The climbers **got** several messages from the rescue team, telling them to be strong. The rescuers' helicopter **had been unable to take off** because of the severe weather. By the time the helicopter **found** the climbers, their food supplies **were running out**—they **had eaten** just two peanuts each in 12 hours—and they **had** already **spent** a night in temperatures of -15° C. Kelsey **explained**, "We **knew** if they **didn't reach** us, we **had** little chance of surviving. It **was** such a relief when they finally **reached** us."

Rachel Kelsey

Jeremy Colenso

Information source: www.guardian.co.uk

B **Draw Conclusions.** What problems did the climbers face while waiting for the rescuers? Why do you think they survived?

C **Grammar.** Describing the relationship of past events and actions to each other

The <u>simple past tense</u> can be used to describe a past event or action that occurred right after another past event or action.
> When they arrived, I **sent** an SOS message.
> (First they arrived. Then I sent the message.)

The <u>past perfect</u> can be used to describe an event or action that occurred before another past event or action.
> When they arrived, I **had** already **sent** an SOS message.
> (First I sent the message. Then they arrived.)

The <u>past continuous</u> can be used to describe an event or action that continued at the same time as another past event or action.
> When they arrived, I **was sending** an SOS message.
> (They arrived while I was sending the message.)

The <u>past perfect continuous</u> can be used to describe an event or action that had continued before another past event or action occurred.
> When they arrived, I **had been trying** to send an SOS message for an hour.
> (I was trying to send the message for an hour. Then they arrived.)

GRAMMAR BOOSTER
▸ p. G4
• Describing past actions and events: review

1

A 🎧 Grammar Snapshot

Suggested teaching time:	10 minutes	Your actual teaching time:

- Have students look at the photos. Ask *Do you think mountain climbing is a dangerous or challenging experience?* Have students explain their answer and then ask *Have you ever gone mountain climbing?*

- Call on a volunteer to read the title of the article. Then ask *Do you think most climbers take a cell phone with them? Would you? Why? Why not?*

- Have students read and listen to the article. Tell students to note the verb forms used for past actions and events.

- To check comprehension, ask:
  What mountain were the two climbers climbing? (Piz Badile)
  Where is the mountain located? (in Switzerland)
  How was the weather on the way up the mountain? (perfect)
  What happened on the way down? (A sudden, severe snowstorm made their descent impossible. They took shelter behind a large rock.)
  Who did Kelsey send an SOS text message to? (a friend in London)
  At what time did her friend respond? (5:00 A.M.)
  Who else did the climbers get messages from? (the rescue team)
  Why did it take so long for the rescuers to get to the climbers? (The severe weather made it impossible for the helicopter to take off.)

- Have students read the article again.

> **Language note:** An *SOS* is a call for help. SOS is an internationally recognized distress signal.

> **Culture note:** The north side of Piz Badile is located in Switzerland, the south side in Italy. –15° C (Celsius) can also be expressed as 5° F (Fahrenheit).

Option: [+5–10 minutes] Have students use the answers to the following questions as a basis for a class discussion: *What modern technology do you think people should take when they go hiking or climbing?* (Possible answers: cell phones, PDAs, small computers, GPSs) *Do you think hikers and climbers can rely on these devices? Why? Why not?* (Possible answer: No, because reception can be poor or nonexistent, or their batteries can die.) *Why wouldn't hikers and climbers take such items?* (Possible answers: They're heavy, they take up space, they may stop working if they get wet.) Make a class list of the most important items climbers and hikers should carry.

B Draw Conclusions

Suggested teaching time:	5 minutes	Your actual teaching time:

- Discuss the questions as a class. List the problems the climbers faced on the board.

- Then ask *How would you react if you were faced with similar problems? Do you think you could survive in such cold weather with so little food? Explain.*

C Grammar

Suggested teaching time:	10 minutes	Your actual teaching time:

- Ask *What past forms are used in the article in Exercise A?* (simple past tense, past perfect, past continuous) Then have students identify the past form used for each action and event in bold in the article. (*were rescued*—simple past; *had sent*—past perfect; *had checked*—past perfect; *set out*—simple past; *was*—simple past; *were climbing down*—past continuous; *were forced*—simple past; *had begun*—past perfect; *had become*—past perfect; *sent*—simple past; *had responded*—past perfect; *had made*—past perfect; *was snowing*—past continuous; *were*—simple past; *got*—simple past; *had been unable to take off*—past perfect; *found*—simple past; *were running out*—past continuous; *had eaten*—past perfect; *had spent*—past perfect; *explained*—simple past; *knew*—simple past; *didn't reach*—simple past; *had*—simple past; *was*—simple past; *reached*—simple past)

- Go over the past forms as a class. Have students explain each one. Make sure students understand that the first sentence in paragraph 1 (Two climbers . . . were rescued . . .) and the third sentence in paragraph 2 (. . . they were forced . . .) include the passive voice forms of the simple past.

- Call on a volunteer to read each rule and example in the Grammar box. Write each example sentence on the board and underline the verbs. Refer to sentences 1, 2, and 4 and ask *Which action happened first?* (1. They arrived. 2. I sent the message. 4. I was trying to send the message.) In sentence 3, point out that the actions took place at the same time. Answer any questions.

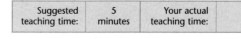 • **Inductive Grammar Charts**

> **Language note:** Point out that in informal speech, the simple past tense rather than the past perfect is increasingly common.

Option: [+5–10 minutes] Have pairs write an additional example sentence for each different past form. Bring the class together and ask volunteers to share their work.

D Grammar Practice

Suggested teaching time:	5–10 minutes	Your actual teaching time:

- Before students begin the exercise, tell them to read the order of the events in each sentence.

- Work through the first item together. Have students continue to work independently and then compare answers with a partner.

- Bring the class together. For each sentence that includes the past perfect or the past perfect continuous, ask *Which event took place first?* (1. The plane took off. 2. They left the airport. 4. They canceled the expedition. 5. I locked all the doors. 6. I lost my cell phone. 7. They were walking for an hour. 8. I was working hard all day.) Then ask:
    Which verb form did you use for the first past event in these sentences? (past perfect: 2, 4, 5, 6; past perfect continuous: 7, 8)
    Which verb form did you use for the second past event? (simple past)

Point out that the order of past events in a sentence can vary. In item 2, for example, the first event is mentioned first, but in item 7, the second event is mentioned first.

- Point out the alternative simple past tense (*lost*) in item 6. Tell students that in informal speech the simple past tense is more likely to be heard today.

Option: [+5 minutes] Read these sentences or write them on the board. For each one, have students say or write which event happened first.

1. When Sam graduated from college, he had won four academic awards. (Sam won four academic awards.)

2. By the time I got off the Internet, she had been trying to call me for three hours. (She was trying to call me.)

3. Kim didn't go to the movies with Charlie because she had already seen the film. (Kim saw the film.)

4. Mark's clothes were dirty because he had been painting the kitchen. (Mark was painting the kitchen.)

5. Because I had worked really hard, I took the weekend off to go skiing. (I worked really hard.)

E Grammar Practice

Suggested teaching time:	5–10 minutes	Your actual teaching time:

- Ask a volunteer to read the words and phrases in the box titled Expressing sequence. Point out that *suddenly* is used when one event interrupts another event or series of events. For example, *I had been sleeping peacefully when suddenly there was a loud knock on the door. In the meantime* means *during the period between events.* For example, *The rescue team will arrive in two days. In the meantime, the climbers will try to stay warm.*

F Summarize

Suggested teaching time:	5 minutes	Your actual teaching time:

- Circulate as pairs retell the story and listen for correct use of sequence words. Write down any errors you hear.

- Then bring the class together and go over any recurring errors.

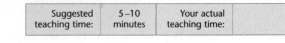

NOW YOU CAN

Suggested teaching time:	5–10 minutes	Your actual teaching time:

A Notepadding

- Ask *Have you or has someone you know ever been in a dangerous or frightening situation? What was it? Why was it dangerous or frightening?* Tell students to focus on this situation and fill in the notepad.

- If students can't think of a situation, tell them to make one up or use one from a current news story.

B Use the Grammar

- Have students review the expressions in Exercise D on page 27.

- Then call on a volunteer to read the idioms in the box. Remind them that they know the idiom *keep one's cool* from Exercise F on page 27.

- Ask two volunteers to read the short conversation in the speech balloons.

- Tell students to refer to their notepad as they tell their story to a partner, using correct past verb forms for clarity. Encourage the partner to ask questions, following the model in the speech balloon and using sequence words.

EXTRAS (optional)

- **Grammar Booster**
- **Workbook: Exercises 3–6**
- **MySummitLab: Lesson 1**

D **Grammar Practice.** Look at the order in which the events occurred and complete the sentences with the simple past tense, the past perfect, the past continuous, or the past perfect continuous. Explain which event occurred first.

> "First the plane took off."

1. (The plane took off. Then they arrived.)

   The plane ___had taken off___ when they ___arrived___ at the airport.

2. (They left the airport. Then the plane took off.)

   They ___had left___ the airport by the time the plane ___took off___.
   First they left the airport.

3. (The plane took off at the same time they arrived.)

   When they ___arrived___ at the airport, the plane ___was taking off___.
   Both actions happened at the same time.

4. (They canceled the expedition. Immediately the sky cleared.)

   When they ___canceled___ the expedition, the sky ___cleared___.
   First they canceled the expedition.

5. (I locked all the doors. Then I went to bed.)

   I ___had locked___ all the doors by the time I ___went___ to bed.
   First he/she locked all the doors.

6. (I lost my cell phone. That's why I didn't phone for help.)

   I ___didn't phone___ for help because I ___had lost OR lost___ my cell phone.
   First he/she lost his/her cell phone.

7. (They were walking for an hour. Then they realized they were lost.)

   When they ___realized___ they were lost, they ___had been walking OR had walked___ for an hour.
   First they were walking for an hour.

8. (I was working hard all day. That's why I was exhausted.)

   I ___had been working OR had worked___ hard all day, so I ___was___ exhausted when I went to bed.
   First he/she was working hard all day.

E **Grammar Practice.** Read the article on page 28 again. On a separate sheet of paper, write the events in sequence.

F **Summarize.** Use your notes to retell the story of the climbers.

EXPRESSING SEQUENCE

One day . . .
Suddenly . . .
Then . . .
Afterwards . . .
By the time that . . .
When . . .
In the meantime . . .
Finally . . .

NOW YOU CAN   *Describe a dangerous or challenging experience*

A **Notepadding.** Have you (or has someone you know) ever been in a dangerous or frightening situation? Write notes about it on the notepad.

B **Use the Grammar.** Tell each other your stories in sequence, using correct past verb forms for clarity. Respond and ask questions as you listen. Use idioms from the box.

> "What happened next?"

> "Well we **had told** our family where we were going, so they **knew** where to look for us."

IDIOMS
be a little shaky
be going out of one's mind
be scared to death
keep one's cool

The location, time, date, season:

The people involved:

The danger or fear:

The sequence of events:

GOAL
Express frustration, empathy, and encouragement

A 🎧 **Conversation Snapshot.** Read and listen. Notice the conversation strategies.

A: I give up!

B: What's the matter?

A: No matter how carefully I eat, my cholesterol just won't come down.

B: Well, **maybe** you just need to give it a little more time.

A: I've already given it six months! It's starting to get me down.

B: **I know what you mean.** I'd be frustrated, too.

🎧 **Rhythm and intonation practice**

🎧 **Frustration**

I give up!
I'm fed up! **CN**
I can't take it any more!
I've had it!
I'm at my wits' end!

🎧 **Empathy**

I know what you mean.

That must be { discouraging.
frustrating.
disappointing.

CN **Corpus Notes:** The expressions *be fed up* and *have had it* are frequently followed by the preposition *with*. For example, *I'm fed up with living in that apartment*.

B **Grammar. Clauses with <u>no matter</u> . . .**

<u>No matter</u> often introduces clauses in statements that express frustration or encouragement.

<u>No matter</u> is commonly combined with <u>who</u>, <u>what</u>, <u>when</u>, <u>why</u>, <u>where</u>, or the intensifier <u>how</u> + an adjective or adverb.

No matter how carefully I eat, my cholesterol won't come down.
No matter who makes the coffee, it's always too strong.
No matter who(m) they asked, the answer was always the same.
I can't seem to get it right, **no matter what** I do!
No matter when we call, it's always the wrong time.
No matter where she looked, she couldn't find what she needed.
You have to keep trying, **no matter how** tired you are.

C **Grammar Practice.** With a partner, take turns completing the following statements with personal information.

"No matter how much coffee I drink, I can't seem to stay awake."

1. No matter how much coffee I drink, . . .
2. No matter what everyone says, . . .
3. No matter who(m) I talk to, . . .
4. No matter how much money you make, . . .
5. No matter how long you live, . . .
6. No matter what my parents think, . . .
7. . . . , no matter what you want.
8. . . . , no matter where my friends are.

30 UNIT 3

2

A 🎧 Conversation Snapshot

Suggested teaching time:	5 minutes	Your actual teaching time:

These conversation strategies are implicit in the model:
- Use expressions such as *I give up* and *I've had it* to get a listener's attention.
- Soften a suggestion with *Maybe*.
- Use expressions like *I know what you mean* to encourage the listener to say more.

- To introduce the topic, write on the board *frustration, empathy, encouragement*. Ask *What do these words mean?* (*Frustration* refers to a feeling of irritation because you can't do something you want to. *Empathy* refers to understanding another person's problems or feelings. *Encouragement* refers to support you give to help someone overcome a problem.)

- Have students read and listen to the conversation. Then ask comprehension questions such as:
  How long has Student A been trying to lower his cholesterol? (for six months)
  Is Student A or B feeling frustration? (Student A)
  Which lines show frustration? (I give up! It's starting to get me down.)
  Which lines show empathy? (I know what you mean. I'd be frustrated, too.)
  Which line expresses encouragement? (Well, maybe you just need to give it a little more time.)

- Have students read and listen to the expressions of frustration and empathy. Clarify meanings as needed.

- Then have students look at the two pictures. Ask:
  How is the woman on the left feeling? (sad, upset)
  How is the woman on the right trying to help? (She's expressing empathy and offering tissues.)
  Why is the man feeling frustrated? (He's been trying unsuccessfully to put a cabinet together.)

- Call students' attention to the conversation strategies highlighted in the model.

Language note: When something *gets you down*, it makes you sad or depressed. *I give up* means that I don't want to continue trying to do something. *I'm fed up* means that I'm annoyed with a situation and want it to change. *I can't take it anymore* means that I can no longer bear an unpleasant situation. *I've had it* means that I have no more patience to continue in a difficult situation. *I can't take it* and *I've had it* are very close in meaning. *I'm at my wits' end* means that I'm upset because I can't solve a problem.

🎧 Rhythm and intonation practice

Suggested teaching time:	5 minutes	Your actual teaching time:

- Have students repeat chorally. Make sure they:
  - use falling intonation for *What's the matter?*
  - pause briefly after *No matter how carefully I eat.*
  - use emphatic stress for <u>I'd</u> in *I'd be frustrated, too.*

B Grammar

Suggested teaching time:	5–10 minutes	Your actual teaching time:

- Write on the board *No matter how carefully I eat, my cholesterol just won't come down.* Ask *What's another way of saying this?* (Possible answer: It doesn't matter how carefully I eat. My cholesterol won't come down.) Write students' suggestions on the board.

- Ask a student to read the two bold points in the Grammar box and then the first example sentence. Point to the restatements on the board.

- Call on volunteers to read the remaining example sentences and then say them in a different way. (*No matter* can be restated as *It doesn't matter* + *who, when,* or another question word.) After a student reads the third example, remind students that *whom* is rarely used in spoken English.

- Ask *Can the clauses introduced by* no matter *stand alone?* (No. Because they are dependent clauses, they need to be attached to an independent clause.) Point out that a clause introduced by *no matter* can appear before or after the independent clause. Ask *In which example sentences does the clause introduced by* no matter *come after the independent clause?* (examples 4, 7)

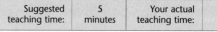 • **Inductive Grammar Charts**

C Grammar Practice

Suggested teaching time:	5 minutes	Your actual teaching time:

- Restate the sentence in the speech balloon, beginning with the independent clause. (I can't seem to stay awake, no matter how much coffee I drink.) In each item, point out the comma after the first clause, whether it is the independent clause or the clause with *no matter*.

- Circulate as pairs work and assist as needed. Then ask students to choose one of their statements from items 1 through 6 and restate it, placing the clause with *no matter* after the independent clause.

D 🎧 Vocabulary

Suggested teaching time:	5–10 minutes	Your actual teaching time:

- Have students skim the Vocabulary and note the phrases they are less familiar with.
- Have students listen and practice. Then bring the class together and answer any questions.
- Tell students to choose one of the phrases and use it to write a sentence about their own life, following the example. Have students share their sentences. Listen for correct use of the vocabulary items.
- Have students listen and practice again.

 • **Vocabulary-Building Strategies**

E 🎧 Listening

Suggested teaching time:	10 minutes	Your actual teaching time:

- Have students skim the exercise to be sure they understand the answer choices.
- Have students listen to the conversations and then complete as many statements as they can. Then have them listen again and circle the remaining statements.
- Play the conversations again and have students check their answers. Have them compare answers with a partner.
- Then bring the class together and go over each statement. Play the conversations again and tell students to listen for the sentences that reveal the answers. (1. Well, I wouldn't worry too much about it. 2. But you've got two more days to finish it. So I'll give you some help, OK? 3. Well, you've got to talk her out of it. 4. . . . if that's what he really wants, I'd suggest you encourage him.)
- Have students look at the photograph. Then ask *What do you think the woman on the right is trying to do?* Encourage students to use expressions from the Vocabulary in their answers. (Possible answer: She's trying to lift her friend's spirits.)

Language note: Students should be able to complete the exercise without understanding every word. You may want to share the following definitions if students ask about specific expressions. *Going through a stage* means being at a particular point in the development process. This expression is used to talk about a child's behavior. *Go over the edge* means go crazy. *Dead serious* means very serious. *Talk someone out of something* means convince the person not to do something.

AUDIOSCRIPT

For audioscript, see page AS4.

NOW YOU CAN

Suggested teaching time:	10–15 minutes	Your actual teaching time:

A Notepadding

- Ask a student to read the example career problem. Invite students to suggest other career problems. (Possible answers: My company doesn't allow for advancement. I always have to work late, but I'm not compensated for my time.)
- After pairs complete the exercise, bring the class together and have students share problems.

B Use the Conversation Strategies

- Refer students to the Conversation Snapshot on page 30 to review expressing frustration and empathy. Have them review expressions of encouragement in the Vocabulary on this page.
- Reinforce the use of the conversation strategies; for example, when students express frustration, make sure they sound like they mean it.
- Remind students to start their conversations with an expression of frustration.
- After pairs have created a conversation, invite students to share their role plays. Have the class identify the type of problem they're talking about.

C Use the Grammar

- After groups give each other advice and encouragement, bring the class together. Ask:
  Do you usually stick with a difficult problem, or do you give up?
  What do you do when you get frustrated?
  What cheers you up when you're feeling discouraged?

🔵 ActiveTeach • **Conversation Prompts**

Challenge: [+5–10 minutes] Have students write each other letters giving advice and encouragement to help deal with the problems they spoke about in their groups. Tell them to include the expressions of encouragement in the Vocabulary. Invite students to read their letters to the class.

EXTRAS (optional)

- **Grammar Booster**
- **Pronunciation Booster**
- **Workbook:** Exercises 7–8
- **MySummitLab:** Lesson 2

CN **Corpus Notes:** *Keep at it occurs more frequently in written English.*
Stick with it occurs more frequently in spoken English.

D 🎧 2:08 **Vocabulary. Encouragement and Discouragement.** Listen and practice.

---

encourage someone (to do something)

My mother always encouraged me to become a dancer. When I was a child, she took me to dance classes and predicted that I would be a star one day.

discourage someone (from doing something) /
talk someone out of (something)

I wanted to quit school, but my mother discouraged me from doing it (OR talked me out of it). She thought it was important for me to complete my studies.

cheer someone up / lift someone's spirits

It really cheered me up (OR lifted my spirits) when my friends visited me in the hospital. I smiled for the first time in weeks.

let something get to you / let something get you down

My boss has been very critical of my work recently. I try not to let it get to me (OR let it get me down), but I am still upset by his comments.

keep at it / stick with it / refuse to give up **CN**

At first, I could speak only a few words of French. I kept at it (OR stuck with it OR refused to give up), however, and after some hard work, I was finally able to speak with some fluency.

feel like giving up / feel discouraged

I've been a car salesman for six months, but I haven't sold a single car. It just makes me feel like giving up (OR feel discouraged).

E 🎧 2:09 **Listening. Infer a Speaker's Purpose.** Listen to the people discussing problems. Then listen again and circle the statement that best characterizes each person's advice.

1. He's telling his friend ....
   a. not to let it get to her
   b. to cheer her son up

2. She's ....
   a. encouraging him to get the job done on time
   b. trying to talk him out of it

3. She thinks he ....
   a. shouldn't let it get him down
   b. should discourage his sister from doing it

4. She doesn't think her friend should ....
   a. talk her son out of it
   b. feel discouraged

PRONUNCIATION BOOSTER ▸ p. P4
• Vowel reduction

NOW YOU CAN *Express frustration, empathy, and encouragement*

A **Notepadding.** Look at the categories of problems on the notepad. Then discuss and list typical examples of each type of problem.

B **Use the Conversation Strategies.** Role-play a conversation in which you encourage your partner to overcome a difficulty. Use the Conversation Snapshot and ideas from your notepad as a guide. Start with an expression of frustration.

C **Use the Grammar.** In small groups, tell each other about other difficulties you face, using clauses with <u>no matter</u>. Give each other advice and encouragement, using expressions of empathy.

Career problems: *a boss who doesn't give enough recognition for employees' achievements*

Career problems:

Academic problems:

Money problems:

Family problems:

Health problems:

A **Reading Warm-up.** Are you familiar with Helen Keller's story? What do you know about her life?

B 🎧 **Reading.** Read the article. What obstacles did Helen Keller have to face in her life?

> On your ActiveBook disc: *Reading Glossary* and *Extra Reading Comprehension Questions*

TRIUMPH
Out of
TRAGEDY

Helen Keller playing chess with her teacher, Anne Sullivan

For the first eighteen months of her life, Helen Keller was a normal infant who had learned to recognize the voices of her parents and take joy in looking at their faces. Then illness closed her eyes and ears and plunged her into a world of darkness and silence. The illness erased not only her vision and hearing but also, as a result, her power of speech.

Keller's life thereafter became a triumph over crushing adversity. In time, she overcame her disabilities and was a full and happy participant in life. She learned to see and hear in her own way, making use of her senses of touch and smell, and eventually she even learned to talk. She realized goals no similarly handicapped person had ever achieved — university study, success as a writer, worldwide recognition as a great humanitarian.

Although Keller was able to cope with some of her limitations, her early childhood was filled with frustration. She had to hold the hands of other people to learn what they were doing, and she was only able to recognize her parents and their friends by feeling their faces and clothes. She was able to communicate with her family, using signs she had invented to let them know what she wanted. For example, she would pretend to cut bread when she wanted to eat bread. However, communication with her family was one-sided. She wanted to communicate in the same way that her family did but was unable to talk. She expressed this frustration in outbursts of anger and bad behavior — "a wild, unruly child" who kicked, scratched, and screamed was how she later described herself.

Her parents were losing hope — until they found her a teacher. Anne Sullivan, partly blind herself, had learned to communicate with the deaf and blind through a hand alphabet. She came to live in the Keller home.

Keller's first lessons were far from encouraging. When Sullivan first arrived, Keller looked for candy in her bag. When she found none, she kicked and screamed. No matter how often Sullivan used the hand alphabet, Keller could not understand, which only made her frustrated and angry.

One day Sullivan had an idea. She took her student, who was not quite seven at the time, to the water pump and placed one of her hands under the spout while she spelled the word "water" into the other. Later Keller wrote about this experience, "Somehow the mystery of language was revealed to me. I knew then that 'w-a-t-e-r' meant the wonderful cool something that was flowing over my hand. That living word awakened my soul, gave it light, hope, joy, set it free. There were barriers still, it is true, but barriers that in time could be swept away."

Keller's progress from then on was amazing. She and Sullivan became lifelong companions, touring the world together. Keller worked tirelessly for the blind and inspired many other disabled people to similar accomplishments.

Keller once remarked, "I seldom think about my limitations, and they never make me sad. Perhaps there is just a touch of yearning at times, but it is vague, like a breeze among flowers. The wind passes, and the flowers are content."

Information source: Alden Whitman, "Triumph Out of Tragedy," *The New York Times*

3

A Reading Warm-up

Suggested teaching time:	5 minutes	Your actual teaching time:	

- Have pairs discuss the Warm-up questions. Then bring the class together and write on the board *Helen Keller*. Have students share what they know about her. If no one has ever heard of Helen Keller, inform students that she was a remarkable woman who, although both blind and deaf, triumphed over adversity.

> **Cultural note:** Helen Keller (U.S., 1880–1968) was the first blind and deaf woman to attend college. She was a writer and lecturer as well as an activist for blind people.

Option: To give students more background information on Helen Keller, suggest that they try to see one or both movies made about Keller. *The Miracle Worker* (1962) deals with Anne Sullivan's struggle to teach the young Helen Keller to communicate. *Helen Keller: The Miracle Continues* (1984) deals with Keller's college years at Radcliffe and her early adult life. Interested students may also want to use the Internet to do further research about her.

B 🎧 Reading

Suggested teaching time:	10–15 minutes	Your actual teaching time:	

- Before students read, have them look at the photo. Ask:
  What are the two women doing? (playing chess)
  Are you surprised that Helen Keller is playing chess? Explain your answer. (Students may be surprised that Keller played chess because she was blind.)
- Call on a volunteer to read the title. Ask *What do you think this story will be about?* (how Helen Keller overcame the tragedy of her deafness and blindness)

- Have students read and listen to the article. Call on students to name the obstacles Keller faced and write them on the board. Ask *What does a person need in order to overcome such obstacles?* (Possible answers: the ability to overcome challenges, frustration, and discouragement; courage; strength; optimism)
- To check comprehension, ask:
  What caused Helen Keller's blindness and deafness? (illness)
  After her illness, did she speak? (no)
  How did she communicate with her family? (with signs she made up)
  What frustration did Helen Keller experience as a child? (She wanted to communicate in the same way that her family did—by speaking.)
  What did her teacher Anne Sullivan teach her? (the hand alphabet)
  Was the hand alphabet easy for her to learn? (no)
  What word helped Helen Keller begin to understand the hand alphabet? (water)
  What goals did Keller realize in her life? (university study, success as a writer, and worldwide recognition as a humanitarian)
- Have students read the article again.

Challenge: [+10 minutes] Have students reread the quotation at the end of the article. Then tell them to write a paragraph responding to it. They can apply the quotation to their own life or to someone else's situation, or they can comment on how the quotation applies to Helen Keller's life. Have students share their paragraphs with small groups.

🔘 **ActiveTeach**
- **Reading Strategies**
- **Reading Speed Calculator**
- **Extra Reading Comprehension Questions**
- **Reading Glossaries**

C Summarize

Suggested teaching time:	10 minutes	Your actual teaching time:	

- Have a volunteer read the quotation. Ask *Based on the quotation, what kind of outlook on life do you think Helen Keller had?* (Possible answers: positive, optimistic, courageous)
- If necessary, tell students to refer to the article on page 32 to review details of Helen Keller's life.
- After pairs complete the chart, bring the class together and have students share their answers.

D Draw Conclusions

Suggested teaching time:	5–10 minutes	Your actual teaching time:	

- While students discuss the questions in groups, circulate and assist as necessary.
- Bring the class together and discuss the answers. Then ask *What are the benefits of having a character like Helen's?* (Possible answer: One can overcome suffering and obstacles.)

Option: [+5 minutes] Have a student reread the quotation from Michael Jordan on page 26. Ask *How does Helen Keller's experience illustrate this quotation?* Have pairs or groups discuss. (Possible answer: Some people would not have been able to handle Helen Keller's situation, but she refused to give up. She achieved more than any handicapped person had ever been able to.)

Challenge: [+10–15 minutes] Following the discussion, have students write a short essay explaining what Helen Keller's life teaches us about confronting adversity. Have pairs exchange papers and suggest changes or additions. Ask volunteers to share their essay with the class.

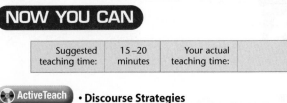

NOW YOU CAN

Suggested teaching time:	15–20 minutes	Your actual teaching time:	

ActiveTeach • Discourse Strategies

A Notepadding

- Ask a student to read the list of adversities in the Ideas box. Have students think of someone who has faced one of these types of adversity or another kind of obstacle. Tell students that the person can be someone famous or someone in their own family or circle of friends. Ask *Do you think this person has a character like Helen Keller's?*
- Circulate and assist as needed while students write notes.

B Pair Work

- Give students a few minutes to organize their notes before they tell their partners about the people they chose.
- Circulate and encourage students to ask questions about the people presented. For example, *How do you think the person's attitude affected the way he or she faced the adversity? How do you try to help this friend or family member?*

C Discussion

- Bring the class together and call on students to share how the person they chose confronted adversity. Have students compare how different people confront adversity.
- As students answer the second question, write their ideas on the board.
- Ask *What kind of attitude or character do you think is most helpful in overcoming obstacles?*

Option: [+5–10 minutes] Have students use the prompts on the notepad in Exercise A Notepadding to take notes about adversity they have faced in their own lives. Then have students write a paragraph about the experience. Students can share paragraphs with a partner.

EXTRAS (optional)

- **Workbook:** Exercises 9–10
- **MySummitLab:** Lesson 3

C **Summarize.** With a partner, complete the chart.
Answers will vary, but may include:

Obstacles Keller faced	Ways in which she overcame them
She lost her vision, hearing, and power of speech because of an illness.	She learned to communicate through a hand alphabet. She made use of her senses of touch and smell and even learned to talk.

D **Draw Conclusions.** Using information from the text and your own ideas, discuss the questions.

1. What do you think there was in Helen Keller's character or experience that enabled her to be successful in her life?

2. What does Keller's life teach us about confronting adversity?

NOW YOU CAN *Describe how people confront adversity*

A **Notepadding.** Frame your ideas for the discussion. Think of a person who faces (or has faced) adversity. Write discussion notes about the person.

IDEAS
- Overcoming illness or a physical handicap
- Facing racial, ethnic, or sexual discrimination
- Coping with the effects of a natural disaster
- Experiencing political instability or war
- Lacking money, education, or support

Name:

Type of adversity:

Steps taken to overcome it:

The person's attitude:

What can be learned from this person's experience?

B **Pair Work.** Tell each other about the people you took notes about. As you listen, ask questions to find out more.

C **Discussion.** Generalizing from your notes and the Pair Work, how do people differ in the way they confront adversity in their lives? What do people who successfully overcome obstacles have in common?

4

GOAL
Discuss the nature of heroism

A 🎧 2:11 **Word Skills. Using Parts of Speech.** Study the three different forms of each word. Check the meaning of unfamiliar words in the dictionary.

noun	adjective	adverb
bravery	brave	bravely
confidence	confident	confidently
courage	courageous	courageously
fearlessness	fearless	fearlessly
generosity	generous	generously
heroism	heroic	heroically
pride	proud	proudly
willingness	willing	willingly

Seol Ik Soo after the crash

B 🎧 2:12 **Listening. Activate Word Skills.** Listen to a news report. Then complete each statement about the story, using a word in the correct part of speech from the Word Skills chart. Compare your answers with the class.

1. Seol's decision to go back to the plane wreckage was very ......courageous....... .

2. Although aware that the airplane could explode at any moment, Seol ......fearlessly...... returned to the plane again and again to rescue wounded passengers.

3. Seol's boss was ......proud...... of him for his ......bravery...... .

4. The story suggests that anyone, even an apparently ordinary person, is capable of ......heroic...... acts.

5. Seol's ......willingness...... to risk his life to save others was extraordinary.

6. Frankly, I'm not ......confident...... that I could do what Seol Ik Soo did.

The plane wreckage

C 🎧 2:13 **Listening. Listen to Summarize.** Listen again and write a summary of the report. Include as many details as possible.

Seol Ik Soo, a twenty-five-year-old tour guide from Korea, was flying home with a group of tourists from China when his plane crashed into a mountaintop, killing more than 120 passengers. Seol survived. He crawled through a hole in the plane and escaped. He heard other people inside the plane calling for help, so he went back and carried as many as ten survivors to safety. He tore his shirt into bandages for the wounded and used his belt to bind a man's badly bleeding leg.

Answers will vary.

4

A 🎧 Word Skills

Suggested teaching time:	5–10 minutes	Your actual teaching time:

- To introduce the topic, write the following words on the board: *noun, adjective, adverb.* Review each part of speech. (A *noun* names a person, place, thing, or abstract idea; nouns can be concrete—people, places, and things—or abstract—an idea, emotion, feeling, or quality you cannot touch. An *adjective* describes a noun. An *adverb* describes a verb, an adjective, or another adverb.)

- After students listen and practice, have students focus on the nouns. Ask *Are these nouns concrete or abstract?* (abstract)

- Clarify the meaning of any words students ask about. Then ask *What do all these words have in common?* (Possible answer: They can all be used to discuss people who have had difficult or challenging experiences or have overcome adversities.)

- Have students listen and practice again.

Language note: *Bravery* is the state of being able to face danger without fear. *Confidence* is a belief that you or someone else can do something well. *Courage* is the state of being able to control fear in dangerous or difficult situations. *Fearlessness* is the state of not being afraid. *Generosity* is the willingness to give money, time, or other things to help someone. *Heroism* is the state of being very brave or courageous. *Pride* is the feeling of satisfaction when you or someone you know does something good. *Willingness* is the state of being happy, ready, and able to do something.

Option: [+5–10 minutes] Photocopy and distribute the following sentences, or write them on the board. Tell students to close their books, and then call on volunteers to identify the part of speech of each underlined word.

1. The volunteers were praised for their <u>heroic</u> actions during the emergency.
2. We have <u>confidence</u> that Jane will pass her entrance exam.
3. The soldiers fought <u>courageously</u> in the war.
4. The climbers were <u>brave</u> when they were stranded during a snowstorm.
5. The woman <u>generously</u> dedicated all her free time to working at the animal shelter.
6. Her <u>willingness</u> to help impressed her manager.
7. Bill's parents were <u>proud</u> of his volunteer work in the community.
8. The firefighter <u>fearlessly</u> entered the burning building.

(Answers: 1. adjective, 2. noun, 3. adverb, 4. adjective, 5. adverb, 6. noun, 7. adjective, 8. adverb)

B 🎧 Listening

Suggested teaching time:	5–10 minutes	Your actual teaching time:

- Have students look at the two photos on the page and read the captions. Tell students that they are going to learn about a man's heroic act after a plane crash.

- Tell students to look at the sentences and decide if each missing word should be a noun, an adjective, or an adverb. (1. adjective; 2. adverb; 3. adjective, noun; 4. adjective; 5. noun; 6. adjective)

- Have students listen to the news report and complete the sentences. If an answer is an adjective or an adverb, tell students to circle the word it modifies.

- Bring the class together and go over the answers. (1. courageous: decision; 2. fearlessly: returned; 3. proud: boss; 4. heroic: acts; 6. confident: I)

C 🎧 Listening

Suggested teaching time:	10 minutes	Your actual teaching time:

- Have students listen to the news report and take notes for their summary.

- After students write their summary, have them listen again to check their information and add any details they may have overlooked.

- Have pairs exchange summaries. Circulate while students work and answer any questions.

- Bring the class together and go over common errors. Then have students listen again for words from Exercise A. (heroic, courage, heroically, proud, fearlessly)

Option: [+10 minutes] Tell students the source of the news report: http://www.time.com/time/asia/features/heroes/seol.html. Encourage interested students to learn more about Seol Ik Soo and report their findings to the class.

Challenge: [+10 minutes] On the board, write these questions: *1. How would you have acted in Seol's situation? 2. Do you think you would have done what Seol did? 3. What makes a person act heroically? 4. Where does this kind of courage come from?* Have students write a paragraph summarizing their answers. Then bring the class together and have students share.

AUDIOSCRIPT

For audioscript, see page AS4.

 ActiveTeach
- **Vocabulary-Building Strategies**
- **Listening Strategies**

T34

NOW YOU CAN

Suggested teaching time:	25–30 minutes	Your actual teaching time:

A Notepadding

• On the board, write *heroism*. Have students brainstorm things that come to mind when they see this word. (Possible answers: courage, bravery, willingness to risk one's life) Write students' responses on the board.

• Have pairs complete their definition. Then bring the class together and have students share. Discuss any significant differences in definitions. Refer to the list of responses on the board as applicable.

• Then invite a student to look up *heroism* in a dictionary and read the definition to the class.

B Discussion

• To preview, have students look at the photos and ask volunteers to read the captions. Ask students to share what they know about the three people.

• While students read the profiles, create a three-column chart on the board. Write each person's name at the top of a column. Have groups discuss the question and suggest ways in which each person is a hero. Write students' suggestions in the chart. Note: the three-column chart appears on *ActiveTeach*. You may want to copy and distribute charts for students to work on individually.

• Then ask *Which adjectives from Exercise A could you use to describe these people?* Write the adjectives in the chart under the appropriate name(s).

> **Language note:** *Heroine* is a feminine form of *hero*. Generally, however, a neutral form is preferred—*chairperson*, for example, rather than *chairman* or *chairwoman*. Sometimes the traditionally masculine form is used for both men and women—*hero*, or *actor* rather than *actress*.

> **Culture note:** Malden Mills is located in Lawrence, Massachusetts, in the northeastern U.S. Henry Feuerstein founded the company in 1906, and it has remained a family-owned business. Václav Havel was born in 1936. He remains an important intellectual and political figure.

Option: [+5–10 minutes] Have students use the answers to the following questions as a basis for a class discussion: *How did Aaron Feuerstein treat his workers after the fire?* (He kept all employees on the payroll with full benefits for three months.) *How do you think this helped his company in the long run?* (Possible answers: Company morale was high. People were grateful. They returned to work and worked harder than ever.) *What might have happened if Feuerstein had not kept the workers on the payroll?* (Possible answer: He might have lost a lot of workers who had to get jobs elsewhere.) *Do you think most businesspeople do things because they are "the right thing to do"? Why? Why not?* Have students give examples.

C Presentation

• Refer students to Exercise A on page 34. Remind students to use correct forms of the words in their presentation.

• When students have completed their preparation for the presentation, have them practice presenting with a partner.

• Poll how many students chose to write about each person. Invite students to explain their choices before presenting to the class.

Challenge: [+5–10 minutes] Divide the class into three groups and assign each group one of the heroes discussed on this page. Tell each group to find out additional information about this person to present to the class.

Project: Have students reread their definition of *heroism* in Exercise A Notepadding. Then tell them to think of a person they consider a hero. It can be someone famous, a friend or acquaintance, or a family member. Tell students to write a paragraph about this person, including words from Exercise A on page 34. Have students bring in pictures of their hero. Create a class poster with the photos and descriptions of the heroes.

🔘 ActiveTeach • **Graphic Organizers**

EXTRAS (optional)

• **Workbook: Exercises 11–13**
• **MySummitLab: Lesson 4**

A **Notepadding.** Frame your ideas for the discussion. With a partner, discuss and write a definition of heroism. Use words from the Word Skills chart.

Heroism is . . .

B **Discussion.** Read the three profiles. Would you call each of these people a hero, based on the definition you wrote? Why or why not?

Malden Mills, which makes fleece, a fabric used in sweaters and jackets, burned to the ground in 1995. Aaron Feuerstein, the owner of Malden Mills, spent millions of dollars of his own money to keep all 3,000 employees on the payroll with full benefits for three months until Malden Mills could be rebuilt. Feuerstein, a generous man who believes that his responsibility goes beyond just making money for investors in his company, said, "I have an equal responsibility to the community." He added, "I think it was a wise business decision, but that isn't why I did it. I did it because it was the right thing to do."

The 1995 fire that burned most of Malden Mills to the ground could have put 3,000 people out of work. But owner Aaron Feuerstein refused to let that happen.

Czech playwright and poet Václav Havel was a leader of the movement to establish a democratic Czechoslovakia. In 1968, after opposing the Soviet invasion of Czechoslovakia, Havel's plays were banned, his passport was taken away, and he was imprisoned three times — spending a total of almost five years in prison. In spite of this, Havel remained an activist, and when the Soviets left in 1989, he was elected president of the Czech Republic. Havel has spent his entire life speaking the truth, even at great personal risk.

Václav Havel opposed Soviet rule of Czechoslovakia and led the struggle for democracy.

60-year-old hero Alicia Sorohan rescued her friend from the jaws of a giant saltwater crocodile like this one.

On October 11, 2004, while camping in Queensland, Australia, Alicia Sorohan awoke to the sound of someone screaming. Rushing out of her tent, she came across her friend Mike Kerr in the mouth of a 14-foot (4.2 m) saltwater crocodile. The 60-year-old grandmother immediately jumped on the back of the giant crocodile, which dropped Kerr and attacked her, biting her in the face and arm. When shot and killed by another member of the group, the crocodile had Sorohan's arm in its mouth and was dragging her into the water. Sorohan and Kerr both survived the incident, though both had serious injuries. Family members of the victims, in shock after the horrible attack, said that Sorohan's bravery had been astonishing. "She deserves an award of some kind," said Wayne Clancy, her son-in-law.

C **Presentation.** Choose one of the people in this lesson. Summarize details from the person's life and experiences. Explain how the person's experiences and actions make him or her a hero. Use words from the Word Skills chart.

Writing: Narrate past events logically

Using Adverbial Clauses and Phrases to Clarify Time Relationships in a Story

REMEMBER: Adverbial clauses are dependent clauses that contain a subject and verb and modify the time relationships of actions within sentences. They are always connected to an independent clause.

Adverbial clauses can be reduced to adverbial phrases when the subject of the independent clause and the adverbial clause are the same. Adverbial clauses and phrases help clarify the time relationship of events.

Adverbial clauses	Reduced to adverbial phrases
When I fell off my bike, I hurt my back.	**Falling off my bike**, I hurt my back.
We saw a bear **while we were hiking**.	We saw a bear **while hiking**.
Before I left, I sent my parents a letter.	**Before leaving**, I sent my parents a letter.
After I had shared my news, I felt better.	I felt better **after having shared my news**.

Be careful! When the subject of the adverbial clause is different from the subject of the independent clause, it should not be reduced.

Whenever **someone** tried to help me, I refused.

Kyle and I were close friends until **he** lied to me.

We told her the plan as soon as **she** arrived.

Punctuation note: When adverbial clauses or phrases appear before the independent clause, they are usually followed by a comma. When they appear after the independent clause, they are not preceded by a comma.

Before I left, I sent my parents a letter. / I sent my parents a letter before I left.

A Prewriting. "Freewriting" to Generate Ideas.

- Choose a topic. On a separate sheet of paper, write, for five to ten minutes, all the details about the topic you can think of. Write quickly. Do not take time to correct spelling, punctuation, verb forms, time order, etc.
- Read what you wrote. Choose ideas you would like to develop and put them in logical order.

Topics
A dangerous, frightening, or exciting personal experience
An obstacle you or someone you know had to overcome

B Writing. On a separate sheet of paper, tell your story. Use adverbial clauses and phrases.

C Self-Check.

☐ Is the sequence of the events in your narrative clear and logical?

☐ Did you use correct punctuation?

☐ Did you use correct past verb forms?

WRITING MODEL

While camping with my friend Eric last summer, I had some scary neighbors—bear cubs! In books and on TV, they are cute creatures. However, when they are steps away from you, it is a different story.

One morning, when eating a snack by my tent, I heard a rustling noise behind me. I thought it was Eric until I turned around and saw a bear trying to open a garbage can. I tried to remember the different rules for scaring away bears. But before I could do anything, the bear noticed the apple I was holding in my hand . . .

Writing

Suggested teaching time:	20–25 minutes	Your actual teaching time:

Using Adverbial Clauses ...

- Make sure that students understand that *narrate* means *tell* or *describe.*

- Ask students to read the explanations above the two charts and the example sentences in the charts.

- Ask the class how the adverbial phrases are different from the adverbial clauses. (When an adverbial clause is reduced to an adverbial phrase, there is no subject and the form of the verb changes.)

- Have students read the Be Careful! explanation and example sentences. Ask *When can you reduce an adverbial clause to an adverbial phrase?* (when the subject of the independent clause and the adverbial clause are the same) *When can't you reduce an adverbial clause?* (when the subjects are not the same)

- Ask a volunteer to read aloud the punctuation note. Ask *When is it OK to use a comma with adverbial clauses and phrases?* (when the clause or phrase comes before the independent clause)

- Remind students that sequencing words and phrases (First, Next, Then, After that, Finally) and prepositional time phrases (on Fridays, in May, from January to May, at 8:00, By January, During that time) are two other ways to clarify time relationships.

ActiveTeach • **Extra Writing Skills Practice**

A Prewriting

- Ask a student to read the choices in the Topics box, and have students choose the one they will write about.

- If students need help to get ideas flowing, work with them individually and prompt with questions. For example, for the first topic, ask *When did this experience happen? Who was involved?*

- After students "freewrite," tell them they can use numbers or other symbols to order their ideas logically.

Writing Model

- Have students read the Writing Model to themselves. Tell them to notice the different past verb forms.

- Have pairs point out to each other the prepositional time phrases (last summer, One morning) and adverbial time clauses. (when they are steps away . . . , when eating a snack . . . , until I turned around . . . , before I could do anything . . .)

B Writing

- Before students begin writing, refer them to the Grammar box on page 28 to review past forms and to the box on page 29 to review sequence words.

- Tell students they can provide additional information even if it isn't in their freewriting notes. Remind students to use the tools discussed to clarify the order of events.

C Self-Check

- After students read the Self-Check questions, tell them to correct any problems in their writing with sequencing, punctuation, and past verb forms.

- Then have students exchange stories or read their stories to the class.

Review

A 🎧 Listening

Suggested teaching time:	10 minutes	Your actual teaching time:

- To introduce the topic, review different problems people might have, such as health problems, career problems, or family problems. Elicit a sentence with *No matter* to illustrate one of the problems students name. For example, *No matter what I do, I can't lose any weight.*

- Have students listen with their books closed to the descriptions of the three problems.

- Then have them look at the names and photos. Have students reread the task before they listen again and complete the exercise. If necessary, allow students to listen again to review each person's problem and make sure their summary sentences are applicable.

- Go over the *No matter* sentences as a class. Have students compare the different responses they provided.

- Then ask:
   What type of problem does Felix Tan have? (a work or career problem) *Robert Reston?* (a health problem) *Eva Garcia?* (a personal or family problem) *Which problem do you think is the most serious? The least serious? Why?*

Option: [+5 –10 minutes] Tell pairs to create a brief description of a problem, following the models in the Listening Comprehension. Have students read them to the class and invite students to summarize each person's frustration with a sentence beginning with *No matter.*

AUDIOSCRIPT

For audioscript, see page AS4.

B Complete this excerpt . . .

Suggested teaching time:	10 –15 minutes	Your actual teaching time:

- Refer students to page 28 to review past forms, if necessary. Encourage students to study the context of each sentence carefully. Point out that more than one past form is correct in some sentences.

- After students complete the excerpt individually, have them compare answers with a partner. Bring the class together and go over the sentences that have more than one possible completion. (6. had understood, understood; 9. hoped, had hoped, had been hoping, was hoping; 13. had been working, had worked; 18. had destroyed, destroyed; 19. was working on, had been working on)

Language note: Tell students that in spoken English, the past perfect is being used less frequently. The simple forms are being used more and more and can no longer be considered incorrect.

Culture note: *Vaudeville* was a kind of theater entertainment that was popular from the 1880s to the 1930s. A vaudeville show included many different short performances such as dancing, singing, and scenes from plays.

Option: [+5 minutes] To emphasize the past forms, have students take turns reading the sentences in the exercise aloud to a partner or group.

Challenge: [+5 minutes] Have students skim the excerpt and underline sequence words, prepositional time phrases, and adverbial time clauses. (After Helen Keller's graduation; by 1918; While Keller was performing; While Keller and Sullivan were touring; After this; since 1914; in 1936; While Keller was abroad; not finished yet; not long before) Go over in class and answer any questions.

C Write what you would say . . .

Suggested teaching time:	5 –10 minutes	Your actual teaching time:

- Refer students to pages 30 and 31 to review expressing frustration, empathy, and encouragement and clauses with *No matter.*

- Give students an example: *No matter how hard it is, don't give up. Your health is very important.* Ask students for situations in which this response would be appropriate. (Possible situations: A friend is trying to stop smoking. A co-worker is starting a new exercise program.)

- Have students complete the exercise and then bring the class together. Have students share their answers. Compare the different responses and poll the class for the most encouraging statements.

Option: [+5 –10 minutes] Have pairs use one of the items from Exercise C as a starting point for a conversation. Then have pairs role-play their conversations for the class.

EXTRAS (optional)

- **Workbook: Page 36**
- **Complete Assessment Package**

- **ActiveTeach:**
   Summit TV Video Program and Activity Worksheets
   Printable Audioscripts
   "Can-Do" Self-Assessment Charts
   Workbook Answer Key

- **MySummitLab:**
   Writing
   Summit TV Video Program and Activity Worksheets
   Achievement Test 3

Review

A 🎧 2:14 **Listening.** Listen to the descriptions of difficulties three people are having. Then listen again to each description and use a clause with <u>no matter</u> to write a sentence summarizing each person's frustration.

Answers will vary, but may include:

1. Felix Tan

No matter how often he asks for help, his boss ignores his requests.

2. Robert Reston

No matter what he does, his blood pressure just won't come down.

3. Eva Garcia

No matter where she looks, she just can't find the right gift for her husband.

B Complete this excerpt from a biography of Helen Keller, using the simple past tense, the past continuous, the past perfect, or the past perfect continuous. In some cases, more than one answer is possible.

After Helen Keller's graduation with honors from Radcliffe College, she and Anne Sullivan <u>made</u> (make) a good living (1) from their lectures around the world. Keller <u>spoke</u> (speak) of (2) her experiences and beliefs, and Sullivan <u>interpreted</u> (interpret) (3) what she said, sentence by sentence. However, by 1918, the demand for Keller's lectures <u>had diminished OR diminished</u> (diminish) considerably, so they (4) <u>started</u> (start) a vaudeville show that demonstrated how Keller (5) <u>had understood OR understood</u> (understand) the word "water" for the first time. While (6) Keller <u>was performing</u> (perform) in this show, she was offered the (7) chance to make a film about her life. Keller <u>accepted</u> (accept), (8) but the film was not the success she (See below.) (hope) for. (9)

While Keller and Sullivan <u>were touring</u> (tour) the world with (10) their vaudeville show, Sullivan <u>came down with</u> (come down with) (11)

an illness that <u>left</u> (leave) her unable to speak above a (12) whisper. After this, Polly Thompson, who <u>had been working OR had worked</u> (work) for (13) Keller and Sullivan as a secretary since 1914, <u>took on</u> (take on) (14) the role of explaining Keller to the theater public.

Sullivan <u>died</u> (die) in 1936, but Keller <u>kept on</u> (15) (16) (keep on) touring the world with Thompson, raising money for the blind. While Keller was abroad, she <u>learned</u> (learn) that a (17) fire <u>had destroyed OR destroyed</u> (destroy) her home as well as the latest book she (18) (See below.) (work) on. This book, which Keller <u>had not finished</u> (not (19) (20) finish) yet, was about Sullivan, and it was called *Teacher.* Once again, Keller showed her capacity to struggle against the odds. It was not long before she had rewritten the entire book.

9. had hoped OR hoped OR had been hoping OR was hoping
19. had been working OR was working

Information source: www.rnib.org.uk

C Write what you would say in each situation, using an expression of frustration, empathy, or encouragement.

Answers will vary, but may include:

1. You want to encourage someone to stick to a diet, for medical reasons.

YOU Keep at it! OR Stick with it! OR Don't give up! OR Maybe you just need to give it a little more time.

2. A friend is having marital difficulties, and you want to cheer him up.

YOU Don't let it get to you! OR Don't let it get you down.

3. You want to express frustration to a classmate about a project you're having trouble with.

YOU I give up! OR I'm fed up! OR I've had it! OR I can't take it anymore! OR I'm at my wits' end!

4. A co-worker tells you about difficulties she's having at work, and you want to let her know you understand how she feels.

YOU I know what you mean. OR That must be discouraging. OR That must be frustrating.

Personality and life

GOALS After Unit 4, you will be able to:
1 Describe your shortcomings
2 Talk about ways to manage stress
3 Discuss how you handle anger
4 Describe your values

A **Topic Preview.** Look at the catalogue of self-help workshops. Which workshops seem the most or least interesting to you?

THE LEARNING Center

Dedicated to helping you reach your goals

UPCOMING EVENTS

Get Organized Now Discover how getting organized can help you increase your productivity many times over. Learn practical tips that will help you start putting your life in order today!
May 4, 2:00–3:00 P.M.

Say Good-bye to Procrastination Don't put off till tomorrow what you could do today! Eliminate time wasters. Easy-to-apply strategies that will get you using your time more efficiently than ever!
May 4, 3:00–4:00 P.M.

Make It Happen You've got big dreams, but you don't know how to get there? Discover how to achieve success by taking small, realistic steps that will help you reach your goals!
May 5, 7:00–8:00 A.M.

Test Like a Champion Find out how you can turn low scores into mega-scores! Tips from the experts will help you overcome test-taking jitters and achieve success.
May 5, 8:00–9:00 A.M.

Boost Your Self-Esteem Do you lack self-confidence? Discover the causes of low self-esteem and what you can do about them. Learn a simple and effective technique you can perform daily to turn your life around!
May 6, 7:00–8:00 P.M.

Bite Your Tongue! Hate your boss? Can't stand your co-workers? Learn how to get along with people and manage difficult relationships with six essential techniques for handling anger successfully.
May 6, 8:00–9:00 P.M.

Sedentary No More Are you a hopeless couch potato? Get out of that chair and get active today! Develop an exercise program that not only works but motivates you to stick with it!
May 7, 8:00–9:00 A.M.

End to Insomnia Having trouble sleeping? Finding it hard to get through the day with your eyes open? Identify the causes of your sleep problems and learn new techniques for coping with them.
May 7, 7:00–8:00 P.M.

FEATURED SPEAKERS

"Get Organized Now"
Carl Hernandez, author, *Finding Your Efficiency Zone*

"Make It Happen"
Karen Kringle, Ph.D., author, *Seven Essential Habits for Success*

"Say Good-bye to Procrastination"
Bill Heiden, CEO, Marcus Industries

"Test Like a Champion"
Kate Yang, Director, Harley Testing Center

B **Express Your Ideas.** Which workshops might be useful in the following situations? Discuss with a partner and explain your choices.

- You're thinking about applying for a new position, but you're not sure you're smart enough.
- You often get into arguments with people at work.
- You've always wanted to find a job overseas, but you're not sure where to begin looking.
- Because your desk is such a mess, you sometimes have difficulty finding important files and information.
- You have trouble getting started on big projects.

Personality and life

A Topic Preview

Suggested teaching time:	10–15 minutes	Your actual teaching time:

- To introduce the topic, write on the board *self-help workshop*. Ask:
  What is a workshop? (a short intensive course that focuses on a specific topic)
  What is a self-help workshop? (a short intensive course that teaches participants how to improve themselves in some way)
  Have you ever attended a self-help workshop?
  What did you learn during the workshop?

- Have students individually read the catalogue, including the section on featured speakers, and circle the workshops they might like to take. Then have groups discuss the Topic Preview question and give reasons for their answers.

- To check comprehension, ask:
  Which workshop would someone attend to learn how to manage anger? (Bite Your Tongue!)
  Who is the featured speaker for the workshop called Make It Happen? (Karen Kringle)
  Which workshop can help motivate participants to exercise regularly? (Sedentary No More)
  What will Kate Yang speak about? (test-taking tips)
   What is her job? (director of Harley Testing Center)
  Which workshop should someone who has low self-confidence attend? (Boost Your Self-Esteem)
  Which speaker has written a book about efficiency? (Carl Hernandez)
  During which month are the workshops taking place? (May)

- As a class, have students look at the workshop descriptions for Bite Your Tongue! and End to Insomnia. Point out the condensed questions: *Hate your boss? Having trouble sleeping? Finding it hard to get through the day with your eyes open?* Explain that dropping the subject and *be* or *do* is frequent in informal English and in advertising. Ask a volunteer to express the first question in the traditional way. (Do you hate your boss?) Then tell students to write the remaining condensed questions in the traditional way. Share answers as a class. (Are you having trouble sleeping? Are you finding it hard to get through the day with your eyes open?)

Language note: *Procrastination* is postponing doing something that you should be doing. *Don't put off till tomorrow what you could do today* is a proverb that advises against procrastinating. *Mega* is a prefix that means *large. Jitters* is an informal word for *nervousness. Bite your tongue* is an idiom that means *be quiet, keep yourself from speaking. Sedentary* means *used to sitting and not being active or doing a lot of exercise. A couch potato* is a slang term for a sedentary person who spends a lot of time watching TV. *Insomnia* is chronic difficulty sleeping.

Option: [+5 minutes] Ask *Which workshop would you be qualified to run?* Invite students to suggest themselves as a workshop leader by describing their qualifications such as a job that relates to the workshop, a book he or she has written, or previous experience leading or taking a similar workshop.

Challenge: [+10 minutes] Have pairs create a title and description for an additional self-help workshop, following the models in the catalogue. Then have pairs present their descriptions. After each presentation, ask *Who would be interested in attending the workshop?*

B Express Your Ideas

Suggested teaching time:	5–10 minutes	Your actual teaching time:

- Call on volunteers to read the situations. Then have pairs discuss the situations and match them with the appropriate workshops.

- Bring the class together and call on pairs for their answers and explanations.

- Then start a class discussing by asking *Have you ever been in one of these situations? Do you think taking a workshop would have been helpful? What else might have been helpful?*

C 🎧 Sound Bites

Suggested teaching time:	10 minutes	Your actual teaching time:	

- Before students read and listen, have them look at the photo and read the caption. Ask:
  Where do you think these people are? (in an office)
  What can you tell about the situation from their body language? (The woman, Carla, is angry at the man, Phil. He's feeling defensive.)
- Point out that the conversation is between two colleagues, Meg and Pat. They are talking about Carla and Phil, their co-workers shown in the photo. Then have students read and listen to the conversation.
- To check comprehension, ask:
  Who are Meg and Pat talking about? (their co-workers Carla and Phil)
  Why are the women talking about them? (because Carla and Phil are making a lot of noise; Carla is yelling at Phil)
  Is Phil good at keeping secrets? (No, he's a gossip.)
- Call on a student to read Meg's second line about Carla. Ask *Which workshop on page 38 could help Carla deal with her problem? Why?* (Bite Your Tongue! She can't manage her anger.)
- Have students read and listen to the conversation again.

> **Language note:** *Shame on you* is an expression that means you should be ashamed of yourself.

Challenge: [+10 minutes] Have pairs continue the conversation for two to three more exchanges. Tell students they can also include Carla and Phil in the conversation. Invite pairs to read their conversations to the class.

D Paraphrase

Suggested teaching time:	5–10 minutes	Your actual teaching time:	

- After pairs complete the exercise, bring the class together and have students share their answers. Write the different ways of saying the statements on the board.
- Have two volunteers read the conversation in Exercise C, replacing the six selected statements with other ways of saying them.

Option: [+5 minutes] Have pairs create short conversations using the idioms and expressions from Exercise D. For example, A: *What's wrong with Jack?* B: *He's really ticked off at his boss. He just found out he has to work this weekend.* Ask pairs to share their conversations with the class.

E Think and Explain

Suggested teaching time:	5 minutes	Your actual teaching time:	

- After pairs answer the questions, bring the class together and ask:
  Does Pat tell Meg where Carla was offered a job? Why or why not? (No, because she doesn't feel comfortable talking behind Carla's back.)
  Who do you think is more of a gossip—Meg or Pat? Why? (Meg, because she gossips about Phil to Pat and wants Pat to share the details about Carla's job offer.)
- Then have students share their predictions about what will happen next.

STARTING **POINT**

Suggested teaching time:	10 minutes	Your actual teaching time:	

- Have a student review the list of workshop topics in Exercise A. Ask *Which workshop deals with inability to follow through?* (Make It Happen) *Which deals with getting angry easily?* (Bite Your Tongue!)

Pair Work

- Encourage students to provide specific examples as they discuss possible consequences of the problems. They can use examples from their own lives if they are comfortable talking about themselves.
- Then bring the class together and ask *Do you think a one-hour workshop might help someone with one of these problems? Why or why not?*

EXTRAS (optional)

- **Workbook: Exercises 1–4**
- **MySummitLab: Preview**

CN **Corpus Notes:** The expressions *not feel comfortable* and *not be comfortable* occur with about the same frequency in both spoken and written English.

C 🎧 **Sound Bites.** Read and listen to a conversation
2:15 between two colleagues.

MEG: What's all that racket?

PAT: Carla. Yelling at Phil. She's really ticked off at him.

MEG: Oh, Carla's always ticked off about something or other. She needs to get hold of herself. What's she so angry about now?

PAT: Well, it seems she confided in Phil, and …

MEG: Big mistake. Phil can't keep a secret. Everyone knows what a gossip he is … So what did she tell him?

PAT: Shame on you! Well, she told him she'd been offered a new job and that she was thinking of taking it.

MEG: No kidding. Where?

PAT: Hey, I don't feel comfortable talking behind her back. **CN** Now that it's out in the open, why don't you just ask her yourself?

D **Paraphrase.** Read the conversation again. Then say each of these statements another way.
Answers will vary, but may include:

1. "What's all that racket?"
   What is all the noise about?
2. "She's really ticked off at him."
   She's really mad / angry at him.
3. "She needs to get hold of herself."
   She needs to calm down.
4. "Well, it seems she confided in Phil."
   She told Phil something personal.
5. "Everyone knows what a gossip he is."
   Everyone knows he likes talking about other people's private lives.
6. "I don't feel comfortable talking behind her back."
   I don't want to talk about her when she's not here.

E **Think and Explain.** With a partner, discuss the questions and support your answers with information from Sound Bites.
Answers will vary, but may include:

1. Why is Carla mad at Phil?
   She confided in him and he told her secret to someone.
2. Why do you think Pat says, "Shame on you!" to Meg?
   (See answer below.)
3. What was Carla's secret?
   She was offered a new job and was thinking of taking it.
4. What do you think will happen next? Answers will vary.
2. Because Meg called Phil a gossip and then she started to gossip about him.

"Carla's yelling at Phil. She's always ticked off about *something*."

STARTING **POINT**

Pair Work. Discuss the possible consequences of each of these problems in a person's life.

Disorganization   **Low self-esteem**   **Procrastination**

Getting angry easily   **Poor test-taking skills**

A sedentary lifestyle   **Insomnia**

D Grammar Practice

Suggested teaching time:	10 minutes	Your actual teaching time:

- Have students skim the sentences and underline the verbs and adjectives of urgency, obligation, and advisability. (2. essential; 4. critical; 5. demanded; 6. crucial; 8. proposed; 9. insisted; 11. important) These sentences will use the subjunctive form. Be sure that students understand that the base form is used even when the statement refers to the past—for example, items 5, 8, and 9.

- Then have students complete the exercise.

- Go over the answers as a class. Have volunteers explain each answer. Ask *Are any of these sentences in the passive voice?* (yes, item 5) *Does this sentence require the subjunctive?* (Yes, because *demand* is a verb of urgency, obligation, or advisability.)

- Then focus on the sentences that do not require the subjunctive. (1, 3, 7, 10) Point out that the verbs and adjectives in these sentences do not express urgency, obligation, or advisability. (1. thinks, 3. agrees, 7. hope, 10. true)

NOW YOU CAN

Suggested teaching time:	15–20 minutes	Your actual teaching time:

A Pair Work

- Call on volunteers to read the descriptions while students look at the photographs. Clarify vocabulary as needed. Explain that a *workaholic* has an obsessive need to work.

- Tell pairs to use the expressions in the box when giving advice. Remind students that these verbs and adjectives of urgency, obligation, and advisability require the subjunctive.

- Then bring the class together and ask students to share their advice. Write the names of the people on the board and list students' advice under the appropriate name. Have the class vote on the best advice for each person.

B Use the Grammar

- Call on a volunteer to read the Ideas in the box. Tell students that they can use these causes of stress or one of their own ideas. Then have pairs interview each other.

- Bring the class together. Have students share their partner's causes of stress and the tips they suggested. Take a poll to find out the most common cause of stress.

Challenge: [+10 minutes] Have students choose one of the people from the exercise and write this person a letter giving advice on his or her problem. Tell students to use the subjunctive with the verbs and adjectives of urgency, obligation, and advisability listed on page 42 in the Grammar box. Collect the letters and give students individual feedback on their use of the subjunctive.

EXTRAS (optional)

- **Grammar Booster**
- **Workbook: Exercises 7–8**
- **MySummitLab: Lesson 2**

D Grammar Practice. Decide whether to use the subjunctive and circle the correct form. Explain each answer. Verbs and adjectives of urgency, obligation, and advisability are underlined below.

> *"Don't use the subjunctive. Thinks isn't a verb of urgency."*

1. Sue thinks that Jack (overreact / (overreacts)) to problems.
2. It's <u>essential</u> that your father ((avoid) / avoids) taking on more than he can handle.
3. Everyone agrees that a certain amount of stress (be / (is)) unavoidable.
4. It's <u>critical</u> that Shelly ((learn) / learns) how to deal with pressure at work.
5. Bill's manager <u>demanded</u> that he ((be) / is) fired immediately.
6. It's <u>crucial</u> that she (doesn't accept / (not accept)) more projects than she can handle.
7. I really hope that this plan (be / (is)) successful.
8. John <u>proposed</u> that he ((continue) / continues) cooking dinner while we clean the house.
9. Our manager <u>insisted</u> that no one ((be) / is) late for the divisional meeting.
10. It's true that humor (help / (helps)) people handle major crises in their lives.
11. It's <u>important</u> that Bruce ((try) / tries) to exercise more.

NOW YOU CAN   *Talk about ways to manage stress*

> I suggest . . .
> I recommend . . .
> I think it's important . . .
> I believe it's essential . . .

A Pair Work. Discuss each person's situation. Take turns giving advice, using the subjunctive.

Marie Klein has four exams to study for. She has to take care of her younger brother because her mother is away on a business trip.

Paul Nakamura is working on a huge project. He needs help to finish it, but he prefers working alone.

Mark Chambers is a workaholic. He's losing weight because he never eats a proper meal. Lately he's just been grabbing a quick bite and eating in the car on the way to work. His family is starting to worry about him.

Elaine Pace hasn't been sleeping well. She's tired all the time and finds it hard to function effectively during the day, probably the result of stress at work.

Jan Orlini thinks her co-workers are talking about her behind her back. It has her so worried that it's affecting her work.

B Use the Grammar. Interview your partner about the causes of stress in his or her life. List them on your notepad. Then write a tip for each one, using the subjunctive.

IDEAS
- too much pressure at work or school
- poor use of time
- conflicts between family members
- communication problems between family, friends, or co-workers

Causes of stress	Your tips
deadlines at work	It's essential that you learn to organize your time better.

Causes of stress	Your tips

43

It's all in your mind

GOALS After Unit 5, you will be able to:
1 Present your views on superstitions
2 Evaluate suspicious claims
3 Discuss fears and phobias
4 Describe and interpret a dream

A **Topic Preview.** Look at the website. Have you heard of any of these superstitions? Do you know others in the same categories?

Good Luck | Bad Luck | Animal | General | Baby | Death | Wedding | New Year's

OldSuperstitions.com
The Largest List of Superstitions on the Web

Good Luck Superstitions
A frog brings good luck to the house it enters.

Seeing a spider spinning in the morning brings good luck.
Click here for more . . .

Bad Luck Superstitions
Putting shoes on a table is bad luck.

Breaking a mirror brings seven years of bad luck.
Click here for more . . .

Animal Superstitions
A dog eating grass brings rain.

Rats leaving a ship mean the ship will sink.
Click here for more . . .

General Superstitions
An itchy nose means you will have a fight with someone.

A bed changed on a Friday will bring bad dreams.
Click here for more . . .

Baby Superstitions
Babies born with teeth become extremely selfish.

It's unlucky to wash a baby's head for the first twelve months.
Click here for more . . .

Death Superstitions
A bird flying through the window is a sign that someone has died.

A pregnant woman at a funeral brings bad luck.
Click here for more . . .

Wedding Superstitions
If the groom drops the wedding ring during the ceremony, the marriage is doomed.

After the wedding, the spouse who goes to sleep first will be the first to die.
Click here for more . . .

New Year's Superstitions
Empty pockets on New Year's Eve mean a year of financial trouble.

It's bad luck to let a fire go out on New Year's Eve.
Click here for more . . .

Good Luck | Bad Luck | Animal | General | Baby | Death | Wedding | New Year's

Information source: www.OldSuperstitions.com

B **Express Your Ideas.** Why do you think people believe in superstitions? What purpose do superstitions serve?

It's all in your mind

A Topic Preview

Suggested teaching time:	10 minutes	Your actual teaching time:

- To introduce the topic, on the board, write *superstitions*. Ask:
  What is a superstition? (a belief that some things are lucky and other things are unlucky)
  What are some superstitions? (Possible answers: The number 13 is unlucky. Having a black cat cross your path is unlucky. A horseshoe or a four-leaf clover will bring good luck.)

- Call on volunteers to read the superstitions on the website. Make sure students understand the meanings. Then ask:
  Are the superstitions listed under Baby Superstitions good luck or bad luck? (bad luck)
  Are the superstitions listed under New Year's Superstitions good luck or bad luck? (bad luck)
  Are the superstitions listed under Wedding Superstitions good luck or bad luck? (bad luck)
  What are some examples of good luck baby superstitions, New Year's superstitions, or wedding superstitions? (Possible answers: A lock of hair from a baby's first haircut should be kept for good luck. Eating black-eyed peas on New Year's Day will bring good luck. Throwing rice at a bride and groom brings good luck—fertility and prosperity—to the newly married couple.)

- Go over the Topic Preview questions as a class.

Language note: *A spider spinning . . .* refers to a spider web, as can be seen in the picture. *Empty pockets* means having no money. *A bed changed* refers to changing the sheets on a bed. *Doomed* means certain to fail.

Culture note: The superstition about a broken mirror goes back to ancient times. Ancient Greeks believed that a person could see the will of the gods in a mirror. If a person broke a mirror, the belief was that the gods did not want the person to see the future, because it held something unpleasant. Ancient Romans believed that a mirror reflected a person's health. If a mirror was broken, it meant a person would have health problems for seven years.

Option: [+10 minutes] Have students choose one of the categories of superstitions and do research on the Internet. Tell students to write down two or three superstitions to share with the class. Have students also find information about the origin of the superstitions if possible.

B Express Your Ideas

Suggested teaching time:	5–10 minutes	Your actual teaching time:

- Have students discuss the questions in groups. Then bring the class together and have students share answers.

- Ask the following questions to extend the discussion:
  What are the logical explanations for some of the superstitions on this page?
  Are there more good luck superstitions or bad luck superstitions? Why do you think this is so?

C 🎧 Sound Bites

Suggested teaching time:	5–10 minutes	Your actual teaching time:

- Before students read and listen to the conversation, have them look at the picture. Ask:
  What do you think the items in the picture stand for? Have you ever had a dream that included any of these objects? How did you feel?

- Have students read and listen to the conversation. To check comprehension, ask:
  What are the man and woman talking about? (Carolyn's dream)
  In what way was Carolyn's dream realistic? (As usual, her car was shaking and making funny noises.)
  In what way wasn't it realistic? (Carolyn was on the back of a giant bird.)

- Have students read and listen to the conversation again.

Language note: A *clap of thunder* is the very loud noise you hear during a storm, usually after you see a flash of lightning. A person's *unconscious* is the part of the human mind that contains thoughts and feelings that one is not aware of and cannot control.

D Think and Explain

Suggested teaching time:	10 minutes	Your actual teaching time:

- Have students read the questions and think about their answers.

- Have several students share their answers to the questions.

- Then ask:
  Do you take dreams seriously? Why? Why not?
  When you dream, what do you think your unconscious is trying to tell you?
  Do you usually tell people about your dreams? Why? Why not?

Option: [+5–10 minutes] Have pairs role-play a conversation about a dream, using Carolyn and Andrew's conversation as a model. Ask volunteers to present their conversation to the class.

E Relate to Personal Experience

Suggested teaching time:	5 minutes	Your actual teaching time:

- After pairs are finished talking, invite students to tell the class about their partner's dream. The class can vote on which dream is the strangest or the most interesting.

STARTING POINT

Suggested teaching time:	10–15 minutes	Your actual teaching time:

A Pair Work

- Have students scan the list of dream topics and then complete the checklist.

- Have students discuss their answers with a partner.

B Discussion

- Encourage students to talk about dreams they've had that deal with the specific topics. As a class, discuss possible meanings of these dreams.

- Take a class poll. Ask:
  How many people never dream?
  How many people rarely remember their dreams?
  How many people usually have pleasant dreams?
  How many people often have nightmares?

- Then ask individual students:
  Are your dreams usually realistic or unrealistic? Explain.
  Do you usually remember the details of your dreams? Give examples.

- Finally, invite students to answer the Discussion questions.

Option: [+5–10 minutes] Have students create a bar graph or pie chart to record the information from the class poll. Students can then poll class members to find out how many people usually dream about each topic. Students can graph this information as well.

Challenge: [+10 minutes] Have students write a paragraph describing the strangest dream they ever had. Then tell them to exchange papers with a partner. Tell the partner to identify key themes in the dream and to try to interpret it.

EXTRAS (optional)

- Workbook: Exercises 1–2
- MySummitLab: Preview

CN **Corpus Notes:** The expression *drive in a car* can mean *operate a car* or *ride in a car as a passenger*. In the present, *drive in a car* occurs almost exclusively in the continuous aspect. *Drive a car* means only *operate a car*.

C 🎧 3:02 **Sound Bites.** Read and listen to a conversation about a strange dream.

CAROLYN: You won't believe the dream I had last night!

ANDREW: Oh yeah?

CAROLYN: I was driving in the car and, as usual, it started shaking and **CN** making funny noises.

ANDREW: What's so weird about that?

CAROLYN: Well, listen to what happened next. There was this clap of thunder, and suddenly I was on the back of some giant bird.

ANDREW: OK. Then what happened?

CAROLYN: Nothing. The alarm went off, and I woke up.

ANDREW: Huh. Sounds like your unconscious is trying to tell you something.

CAROLYN: Like what?

ANDREW: Like maybe it's time to buy a new car?

D **Think and Explain.** With a partner, answer the questions, using information from Sound Bites and your own ideas.

1. Why do you think Carolyn tells Andrew her dream?

2. Why do you think Andrew says Carolyn's unconscious is trying to tell her something?

E **Relate to Personal Experience.** Have you ever had a dream that was strange? Tell your partner about it.

STARTING **POINT**

A **Pair Work.** What kinds of dreams do you usually have? Check all the items that apply. Compare and discuss your answers with a partner.

☐ I never dream. ☐ I rarely remember my dreams. ☐ My dreams are very pleasant. ☐ I have scary nightmares.

My dreams are usually about . . .

☐ family
☐ friends
☐ strangers
☐ famous people

☐ food
☐ water
☐ fire
☐ animals

☐ flying
☐ falling
☐ being chased
☐ other: _____

B **Discussion.** Do you think dreams have meanings? Why do you think people dream?

4 GOAL
Describe and interpret a dream

3:09

Some participial adjectives

confusing	confused
depressing	depressed
disappointing	disappointed
disturbing	disturbed
embarrassing	embarrassed
enlightening	enlightened
exciting	excited
fascinating	fascinated
frightening	frightened
shocking	shocked
startling	startled
surprising	surprised

A **Word Skills. Using Participial Adjectives.**

REMEMBER

A present participle can be used as an adjective to describe a noun or noun phrase.
The dream I had last night was very
disturbing. ("Disturbing" describes the dream.)

A past participle can be used as an adjective to describe a noun or noun phrase, but it has a passive meaning.
After I woke up from the dream, I felt very **disturbed** by it. ("Disturbed" describes how the dream made me feel.)

B **Word Skills Practice.** Circle the correct participial adjective. Make a check mark next to those with a passive meaning.

1. The violent images that appear in dreams can be very (shocking / shocked). But psychologists say we shouldn't be (shocking / shocked) by anything that appears in our dreams. ✓

2. Mark found his frequent nightmares extremely (depressed / depressing).

3. I was (surprising / surprised) to learn that everyone has dreams, even if they don't remember them. ✓

4. Researchers were (fascinating / fascinated) by the discovery that young children do not dream about themselves until the age of three or four. ✓

5. Sometimes nightmares are so (startling / startled) that the brain reacts, causing some people to jerk their arms and legs suddenly while they sleep.

C 3:10 **Listening. Listen for Details.** Listen to the radio call-in program. After each call, answer the questions about each dream. Answers will vary, but may include:

Margo's dream	Simon's dream
1. How often has she had the dream? Every night for about two weeks.	1. How often has he had the dream? Once
2. How does she feel during the dream? Helpless, terrified	2. How does he feel during the dream? The dream put him in a great mood.
3. What effect does the dream have on her afterward? She feels nervous and worried for the rest of the day.	3. What effect does the dream have on him afterward? He felt really optimistic.

D 3:11 **Listening. Compare and Contrast.** Listen to the two calls again. Then after each call, summarize and compare and contrast:

1. Margo's and Dr. Walker's interpretations of Margo's dream

2. Simon's and Dr. Walker's interpretations of Simon's dream

E **Discussion.** Do you agree with what Dr. Walker says about dreams? If not, what purpose do you think dreams serve? Do you believe they predict the future? Listen again if necessary.

4

A Word Skills

Suggested teaching time:	5–10 minutes	Your actual teaching time:

- As a review, write on the board *present participle*. Remind students that a present participle is the base form of a verb + *–ing*. Write on the board *satisfy, annoy, excite*. Elicit the present participles of these verbs. (satisfying, annoying, exciting) Then write on the board *past participle*. Remind students that a past participle of a regular verb is the base form of a verb + *–ed*. Elicit the past participles of these verbs. (satisfied, annoyed, excited)

- Call on a student to read the first bold rule and example sentence. Have students look at the list of present participles in the left column of the chart. Ask students to repeat the example sentence using one of the present participles; for example, *The dream I had last night was very confusing / exciting / surprising.*

- Then have a volunteer read the second bold rule and example sentence. Have students look at the list of past participles in the right column of the chart. Ask students to repeat the example sentence using one of the past participles; for example, *After I woke up from the dream, I felt very confused / excited / surprised by it.*

- Make sure students understand the difference between the first and second example sentences. In the first sentence, *disturbing* describes the dream. In the second sentence, *disturbed* describes the speaker, how the dream made him or her feel.

- Point out that past participles used as adjectives are sometimes followed by *by* + the agent that causes the action. In the second example sentence, the agent is *it*, referring to the dream.

- On the board, write *1. The class was very boring. 2. Jill was very bored in class.* Ask *Do these sentences have a similar meaning?* (yes) Then write *3. Jill was very boring in class.* Ask *Does this sentence mean the same thing as the other two?* (no) *What does it mean?* (Jill is a boring person. *Boring* describes Jill.)

∩ Some participial adjectives

- Have students read and listen to the participial adjectives in the chart. Then invite students to suggest pairs of sentences using pairs of words from the chart; for example, *I was disappointed by the movie. It was very disappointing.*

B Word Skills Practice

Suggested teaching time:	5–10 minutes	Your actual teaching time:

- To provide more practice, have students rewrite each sentence, using the other type of participial adjective.

 ActiveTeach • **Vocabulary-Building Strategies**

C ∩ Listening

Suggested teaching time:	10 minutes	Your actual teaching time:

- To introduce the topic, ask a couple of volunteers to describe a good or bad dream they've had. If no one wants to share, give an example of your own; for example, *I often dream that I'm climbing up a hill, but I can never get to the top.* Then ask *What do you think this dream means?* Tell students that they will learn something about interpreting dreams in the listening.

- Have students listen to the entire radio call-in program with their books closed.

- Then have students listen to the first call and Dr. Walker's interpretation. Ask *What's Margo's dream?* (She's falling into a dark, endless tunnel.)

- Have students listen to the second call and Dr. Walker's interpretation. Ask *What's Simon's dream?* (He's flying like a bird.)

- Have students listen again. Tell them to complete the left side of the chart after the first call and the right side of the chart after the second call.

- Have students check answers with a partner. Review the chart with the class.

> **Language note:** *My heart is pounding* means my heart is beating very fast. *Shake someone up* means upset someone or make the person nervous.

AUDIOSCRIPT

For audioscript, see page AS6.

 **ActiveTeach** • **Listening Strategies**

D ∩ Listening

Suggested teaching time:	5–10 minutes	Your actual teaching time:

ActiveTeach • **Listening Strategies**

- Tell students to take notes as they listen in order to support their opinions during the Discussion.

- After pairs discuss the questions, bring the class together. Ask *Do you agree more with Margo's and Simon's interpretations or Dr. Walker's? Why?*

E Discussion

Suggested teaching time:	5 minutes	Your actual teaching time:

- Discuss the questions as a class. Ask *Does anyone believe that dreams have no purpose at all? Why do you think so?*

- As students answer the third question, have them explain the reasons for their belief. Ask *Has anyone ever had a dream about the future? Did it come true?*

NOW YOU CAN

Suggested teaching time:	15 minutes	Your actual teaching time:

A Pair Work

- Tell students to look at the picture at the bottom of the page. Ask:
  Do you think this is a picture of a good dream or a bad dream? Why?
  Have you ever had a dream about walking up a dark staircase? Was it a good dream or a bad dream?

- Have students use a piece of paper to cover up the Possible meanings box on the right. Then have students read the items in the Common dreams box. Ask *Have you had any of these dreams? Describe one of them. What do you think the dream meant?*

- Then have students read the items in the Possible meanings box on the right and match the interpretations to the dreams. Students can also suggest other interpretations.

- Bring the class together and have pairs share the interpretations they wrote.

B Notepadding

- To introduce the topic, take a poll by asking *Who has had a recurring or memorable dream?* Then ask *Was it a good dream or a bad dream?*

- Tell students to complete their notepad individually. If students don't remember a recurring or a memorable dream, tell them to make one up.

C Pair Work

- After pairs discuss, have several volunteers share their dream with the class.

- After each presentation, ask the class:
  What interpretation of this dream could you suggest? Who has had a similar dream?

- Read the list of Common dreams in Exercise A and take a class poll to find out which are the most common among students. Ask *Why do you think these dreams are the most common?*

Option: [+10 minutes] Have students write a paragraph about their dream and a possible interpretation. Collect the paragraphs and give individual feedback.

Challenge: [+5 –10 minutes] Write these four dream subjects on the board: *1. You are back in grade school. 2. You are walking alone in a large field. 3. You are in a tornado. 4. You are jumping out of an airplane.* Have students role-play conversations about the dreams, using participial adjectives. Refer students to the list of participial adjectives in Exercise A on page 58. For example, A: *I've been having a disturbing dream lately.* B: *Tell me about it. I'm fascinated by dreams. Maybe I can interpret it.* A: *Well, I'm walking alone in a large field and I'm disturbed about something. It's actually kind of depressing, because I really hate being alone.* B: *Maybe that's what the dream is reflecting—how much you dislike being alone.* Ask volunteers to role-play their conversations for the class.

EXTRAS (optional)

- **Workbook: Exercises 12–13**
- **MySummitLab: Lesson 4**

Describe and interpret a dream

A **Pair Work.** If it is true that a dream can indicate the fears and wishes of the dreamer, how would *you* match the common dreams below with some possible meanings? If you don't find a meaning you agree with, write your own interpretation.

Common dreams
falling from a steep cliff
flying in a hot-air balloon
being chased by a terrible monster
climbing an endless flight of stairs
failing an important exam
winning a sports event or contest

Possible meanings
desire to escape a responsibility or task
fear of failure
high self-esteem
pride in one's achievements
desire for success
lack of self-confidence

B **Notepadding.** Write some notes on your notepad about a recurring dream—a dream you've had more than once—or a particularly memorable dream.

Who was in the dream?	How often have you had this dream?
What was it about?	What do you think it means?

C **Pair Work.** Tell your partner your dream, using the notes on your notepad. Discuss alternative interpretations.

C 🎧 Sound Bites

Suggested teaching time:	10 minutes	Your actual teaching time:

- Before students read and listen, have them look at the photo. Ask:
  How do you know these people are at an airport? (The signs give directions to different gates.)
  What kinds of hassles do people experience at an airport? (Possible answers: delayed or canceled flights; missed flight connections; very long waits)
  How do you deal with hassles at the airport?

- Have students read and listen to the conversation. Then ask:
  How do you think the two colleagues are feeling? (probably stressed or anxious because of the very long lines)
  How do you usually feel at the airport—Anxious? Calm? Stressed?

- Have students read and listen to the conversation again.

Option: [+5–10 minutes] Have students write a paragraph describing their most horrendous airport experience. If they are more familiar with other kinds of transportation, have them describe any unpleasant travel experience, such as travel by train or car. Invite students to read their paragraphs to the class.

D Summarize

Suggested teaching time:	5 minutes	Your actual teaching time:

- Have pairs discuss the questions. Call on students to share their answers.

- Ask *If you were Susan, would you have declined Peter's offer? Why? Why not?* Listen for correct use of the verb form. (I would / would not have declined Peter's offer because . . .)

E Paraphrase

Suggested teaching time:	5–10 minutes	Your actual teaching time:

- Have pairs think of different ways to say each statement.

- Then bring the class together and have students share their answers. Write the different ways of saying the statements on the board.

- Have two volunteers read the conversation again, replacing the selected statements with one of the statements on the board.

Option: [+5 minutes] Have pairs create short conversations using the idioms and expressions from the exercise. For example, A: *I'd like to buy a magazine for the flight. Do you think you could watch my bags a sec?* B: *Sure, no problem.*

STARTING **POINT**

Suggested teaching time:	10–15 minutes	Your actual teaching time:

- Review the travel hassles students spoke about in the Topic Preview on page 62. Then call on a student to read the locations and topics in the chart. Have students refer to the travel supplies catalogue on page 62 and match the products with the locations and topics. (Possible answers: at airports: Luggage Spotters; on planes, trains, or buses: the Docu-Pouch; with language: the Point-O-Gram; with money: the Conversion Wizard and the Cash Stash Key Ring) Encourage students to think of other products or ideas.

Brainstorm Ideas

- Then have pairs discuss and list hassles and useful products or ideas on the chart. Circulate and brainstorm with students if they need ideas.

- Call on students to share hassles and products or ideas. For each product suggested, ask *Have you seen such a product for sale? If not, do you think people would buy it if it were available? Why? Why not?*

Project: Have pairs prepare a plan for selling one of the products they thought of in the Starting Point exercise. Tell them to search online to find out if a similar product already exists. If yes, have them decide how their product could be different or better, and then create the plan. To help students write their plans, write these questions on the board or photocopy and distribute them:

What is the product?

What is it called?

Does a similar product exist on the market?

Who is the target audience?

Why would people buy this product?

How much would this product cost?

How much would it cost to make this product?

Where would you advertise and sell this product?

Suggest that students illustrate the new product as well. Then invite pairs to present their plans to the class.

EXTRAS (optional)

- **Workbook:** Exercises 1–3
- **MySummitLab:** Preview

CN1 **Corpus Notes:** *A sec*, used in place of *a second* in informal spoken English, always occurs in a singular form (NOT *Wait* ~~two secs~~).

C 🎧 3:13 **Sound Bites.** Read and listen to a conversation between two business colleagues at the airport.

SUSAN: Hi, Pete. What a horrendous line!

PETER: It's always like this lately. You'd think they'd get the message and hire some more people to deal with these crowds.

SUSAN: Yeah. This isn't moving at all. Hmm. Do you think you
CN1 could watch my bags a sec? I need to make a quick phone call and I don't have my cell. **CN2**

PETER: Go for it. Or on second thought, why don't you just use mine?

SUSAN: Thanks. But it's an international call. I'd better use the public phone. I can charge it to the office.

D **Summarize.** Answer the questions.
Answers will vary, but may include:
1. What's the problem?
   They're stuck in a long line at the airport.
2. What favor does Susan ask of Peter?
   To watch her bags while she makes a call
3. Why does Susan decline Peter's offer?
   Because she has to make an international call and it is expensive.

E **Paraphrase.** Read the conversation again. Then say each of these statements another way.
Answers will vary, but may include:
1. "What a horrendous line!"
   The line is terribly long.
2. "You'd think they'd get the message."
   You would think they'd learn from experience.
3. "Do you think you could watch my bags a sec?" Could you look after my bags for a few moments?
4. "Go for it." Sure. Go ahead.
5. "On second thought, . . ." Instead

CN2 **Corpus Notes:** *Phone call* occurs much more frequently than *telephone call*, particularly in spoken English.

STARTING **POINT**

Brainstorm Ideas. With a partner, discuss and list some of the kinds of hassles that occur when people travel. Write the name of a product or idea that might help in dealing with each problem.

	Hassle	Useful product or idea
at airports		
in hotels		
on planes		
on trains		
on buses		
with language		
with money		
with food		

C 🎧 Sound Bites

Suggested teaching time:	5 minutes	Your actual teaching time:

- Before students read and listen to the conversation, have them look at the photo. Ask:
    What do you think this man does for a living?
    What types of intelligences do you think he possesses?
    Do you think you can judge a person's intelligence by his or her looks? Why? Why not?

- Have students read and listen to the conversation. Then ask comprehension questions:
    Who are Olivia and Charles talking about? (a former classmate, Johnny Nolan)
    What was Johnny like in school? (He was always failing and getting into trouble.)
    What is he doing as an adult? (He's CEO / head of MegaStar Foods.)
    Why is Charles surprised that Johnny is so successful? (Possible answer: When Johnny was in school, he didn't seem likely to become successful.)

- Have students share similar stories. Ask *Do you know anyone who was not very good in school but went on to become a success? Do you know anyone who was very successful in school but didn't do much with his or her life afterward? Give examples.*

- Have students read and listen to the conversation again.

D Paraphrase

Suggested teaching time:	10–15 minutes	Your actual teaching time:

- Have students do the exercise in pairs. Then bring the class together and have students share their answers. Write the different ways of saying the statements on the board.

- Have two volunteers read the conversation aloud, replacing the six statements with other ways of saying them.

Option: [+5 minutes] Have pairs create short conversations using the idioms and expressions from the exercise. For example, A: *Did you hear that Richard Burns plays the violin with the City Symphony Orchestra?* B: *Wow, he's really turned his life around. He was always struggling in high school.*

E Apply Ideas

Suggested teaching time:	5 minutes	Your actual teaching time:

- Have groups talk about Johnny Nolan and decide which intelligences they think he had and didn't have. Tell them to use information from the conversation. (He was always failing in class and getting into trouble.) If students need help, hint that he may not have had mathematical or linguistic intelligences needed to succeed in the classroom, but he may have had intuitive and interpersonal ones.

- Ask *Do you think Johnny Nolan developed other intelligences later in life? If yes, how do you think he did this? If no, how do you think he was able to become successful?*

STARTING **POINT**

Suggested teaching time:	10–15 minutes	Your actual teaching time:

- Have volunteers read the phrases in the box. Clarify vocabulary if needed.

Access Prior Knowledge

- Have pairs name people they know or know about who can be described by these phrases. If students have trouble thinking of someone, suggest they consider people in the entertainment world or politics.

- Have students refer to the quiz on page 74 to talk about the intelligences each person has or had.

Option: [+5–10 minutes] Have groups ask and answer the following questions: *How do people discover their intelligences? Why do some people never discover some intelligences or discover them later in life? At what point in your life did you discover your different intelligences?*

EXTRAS (optional)

- Workbook: Exercises 1–2
- MySummitLab: Preview

CN **Corpus Notes:** The expression *Get out of here!* is common in very informal spoken English. It is used to show strong surprise at something another person has said.

C 🎧 **Sound Bites.** Read and listen to a conversation about someone who turned his life around.

4:02

OLIVIA: Do you remember Johnny Nolan?

CHARLES: I think so. Wasn't he the kid who was always failing in class and getting into trouble?

OLIVIA: That's the one. Well, he's apparently turned his life around. I just heard he's the CEO of MegaStar Foods.

CN **CHARLES:** Get out of here! Johnny Nolan? Head of a multimillion-dollar company?

OLIVIA: I guess he turned out to have a real head for business.

CHARLES: That's for sure. I didn't think he had it in him.

OLIVIA: It just goes to show you—you can't judge a book by its cover.

D **Paraphrase.** Read the conversation again. Then say each of the statements another way.

Answers will vary, but may include:

1. "He's turned his life around."
   He's made positive changes in his life.
2. "Get out of here!" You're kidding!
3. "He turned out to have a real head for business." He's very good at business.
4. "That's for sure." That's very true.
5. "I didn't think he had it in him."
   I didn't think he could do it.
6. "You can't judge a book by its cover."
   You can't form an opinion about someone or something based only on outward appearance.

E **Apply Ideas.** What kinds of intelligences do you think Johnny Nolan might have? Why?

STARTING **POINT**

Access Prior Knowledge. Describe people you know or have heard of who…

turned their lives around.	**did well in both school and life.**
did well in school but not in life.	**struggled in school or in life.**
did poorly in school but well in life.	**always got into trouble.**

What kinds of intelligences do you think these people have (or had)?

D 🎧 Listening

Suggested teaching time:	5–10 minutes	Your actual teaching time:	

- Have students read and listen to the jokes. Ask group members to share their reactions.
- Refer students to the article on page 92 to review the theories about what makes jokes funny. Then have groups discuss which theory best explains the humor of each joke.

Option: [+5–10 minutes] Have students choose one of the jokes on this page and tell it to the class or to a group. Have the other students use the Vocabulary on page 90 to respond.

NOW YOU CAN

Suggested teaching time:	15 minutes	Your actual teaching time:	

A Class Survey

- On the board, copy the chart below. Poll the class and fill in the blanks, or have students complete their own charts individually. Print out and distribute charts from *ActiveTeach.*
- Invite students to draw conclusions based on the poll. For example, *Most people thought that Joke 1 was the funniest. This shows that most people appreciate the humor in unexpected and illogical situations.*

Funniest joke	Most popular joke (men)	Most popular joke (women)
Joke number_____	Joke number_____	Joke number_____

ActiveTeach
- Graphic Organizers
- Discourse Strategies

B Presentation

- After each student tells about a funny experience, ask the class *Do you agree that the situation was funny? Explain.*
- Then ask *Who has had a similar experience? Did you think it was funny? Why or why not?*

EXTRAS (optional)

- **Workbook:** Exercises 9–10
- **MySummitLab:** Lesson 3

D 🎧 **Listening. Apply Ideas.** Read and listen to each joke. With a partner, discuss what you think of each one. Decide which theory from the reading best explains the intended humor of each joke and why.
Accept any theory students can support.

4:22

The Superiority or Incongruity Theory

Joke 1

"How much do you charge?" a woman asks a lawyer. "I get $50 for three questions," the lawyer answers. "That's awfully steep, isn't it?" says the woman. "Yes, it is," replies the lawyer. "Now what's your final question?"

The Superiority Theory

Joke 2

A couple of dog owners are arguing about whose dog is smarter.
"My dog is so smart," says the first owner, "that every morning he waits for the paperboy to come around. He tips the kid and then brings the newspaper to me, along with my morning coffee."
"I know," says the second owner.
"How do you know?"
"My dog told me."

The Incongruity Theory

Joke 3

A man is hitting golf balls at a driving range with his nine-year-old son. Each time he hits the ball, his son cheers him on. "Great shot, Dad!" "Perfect!" "Way to go!"
A woman hitting balls next to them watches as each of the man's shots flies farther and farther away.
After a few minutes, the woman walks over and asks, "Do you think I could borrow your son for a few minutes?"

NOW YOU CAN *Explain why something is funny*

A **Class Survey.** Poll the class. Which joke in Exercise D do most students think is the funniest? Which was the most popular among the men? Which among the women? What conclusions can you draw based on the poll?

B **Presentation.** Take turns telling the class about something funny that happened to you or someone you know. Discuss why you think the experience was funny.

Writing: Write a story that includes dialogue

Punctuation of Dialogue

When writing a story that includes dialogue, you can use a combination of direct and indirect speech. Review the punctuation rules for writing direct speech.

When the reporting verb comes before a quotation,
- put a comma after the reporting verb.
- put the end punctuation inside the quotation marks.

Mr. King said, "Please turn off the lights."

When the reporting verb comes after a quotation,
- put a comma, question mark, or an exclamation point at the end of the quoted sentence, inside the quotation marks.
- put the speaker's name before or after the reporting verb.

"Please turn off the lights," Mr. King said.
"Did anyone turn off the lights?" asked Mr. King.

When the reporting verb comes within a quotation, put quotation marks around each part of the quotation.

"Mark and Jan," Mr. King said, "please turn off the lights."

If the reporting verb comes between complete sentences, put a period after the reporting verb.

"Mark and Jan, please turn off the lights," Mr. King said. "I'm going to show the video."

NOTE: When writing indirect speech, don't use a comma after the reporting verb.

NOT Mr. King said, not to turn off the lights.

About a year ago, my grandmother was walking down the street, stopping from time to time to look in shop windows. At one store, she stopped to admire a dress in the window. Just as she turned to enter the store, a businessman walking very fast and, not looking where he was going, bumped into her, knocking her down.

"Oh, I'm so sorry!" said the man. "Are you OK?"

My grandmother was too stunned to reply. But then after a moment she said she was fine.

"Look!" she heard someone say from across the street. "An old woman just fell down!"

She quickly sat up and looked around with great concern and said, "Where?"

When she told us this story, we all laughed.

A **Prewriting. Ordering Events.** Think about an anecdote—a funny story—you can tell. It can be something you've experienced, or it can be something you've heard about, read, or seen in a movie or on television. Write a summary of the events in the order in which they happened.

1. ....
2. ....
3. ....
4. ....
5. ....

B **Writing.** On a separate sheet of paper, write the story, telling what happened and what people said, using a combination of direct and indirect speech. Each time you use the direct speech of a new speaker, begin a new paragraph.

C **Self-Check.**

☐ Did you use both direct and indirect speech in your story?

☐ Did you punctuate direct and indirect speech correctly?

☐ Did you make appropriate shifts in tense, pronouns, and expressions of time and place in indirect speech when needed?

Writing

Suggested teaching time:	20–25 minutes	Your actual teaching time:

Punctuation of Dialogue

- To review direct and indirect speech, have students read the Writing Model individually. Tell them to notice the punctuation in sentences that include dialogue. Point out that a change in speaker may be indicated by starting a new paragraph, as in the Writing Model. However, this is not required. Quotations of different speakers may be run into a single paragraph.

- Then call on a student to read the introduction. Have volunteers read the four punctuation rules and example sentences and the note. Point out that when the reporting verb comes after a quotation, there is a comma at the end of the quoted speech, even though the original statement ended with a period. (original statement: Please turn off the lights. quoted speech: "Please turn off the lights," Mr. King said.)

- Stop after each example sentence and ask students to write additional examples on the board.

ActiveTeach • **Extra Writing Skills Practice**

A Prewriting

- Have students think about a funny story they would like to write about. Circulate and assist as needed. If students can't think of anything to write about, work with them individually, prompting them with questions that can help get ideas flowing.

- Then have students write the events in the order in which they happened. If students need more room, tell them to use a separate sheet of paper. Explain that the notes don't need to be perfectly written. The goal is to generate ideas.

B Writing

- As students prepare to write, refer them to the Writing Model.

- Tell students to feel free to provide any additional information they think of even though it may not be in their notes.

C Self-Check

- After students complete the Self-Check, have them correct any errors in punctuation or in the use of tense, pronouns, and expressions of time and place. Refer students to the Grammar box on pages 88 and 89 to review changes in verbs and in expressions of time and place from direct to indirect speech.

Option: [+10 minutes] Peer review. Have students exchange papers with a partner. Tell them to read their partner's story and check the punctuation and shifts in tense, pronouns, and expressions of time and place in indirect speech. Have students note any errors and suggest corrections.

Review

A 🎧 Listening

Suggested teaching time:	10 minutes	Your actual teaching time:

- Elicit the different types of humor discussed in the unit. If necessary, refer students to the types of verbal humor in the Vocabulary on page 91. Write the types of humor on the board: *verbal humor: a joke, a riddle, a pun, an anecdote, a blooper, a limerick; a practical joke.*

- Have students listen without writing to the three examples of humor. Then have them listen again to identify the type of humor each example represents.

- Bring the class together to share answers. Then ask *Which example do you think was the funniest? Why?*

AUDIOSCRIPT

For audioscript, see page AS11.

B Write the response . . .

Suggested teaching time:	5 minutes	Your actual teaching time:

- Refer students to the Vocabulary on page 90. You may want to have them listen again to the ways to respond to a joke.

- Before students do the exercise individually, point out that more than one answer is possible for some situations.

- Have pairs compare answers. Then go over the situations that have various possibilities. (1. I'm sorry, but that's pretty silly / lame / ridiculous. 3. I don't get it. That went over my head. 4. What a riot / scream / hoot! That's hilarious / hysterical / too much! That cracked me up! That really tickled me.)

C Change each of the following . . .

Suggested teaching time:	5–10 minutes	Your actual teaching time:

- Before students rewrite the sentences, remind them not to use a comma after the reporting verb in indirect speech. Also tell students to make appropriate shifts in tense, pronouns, and expressions of time and place.

- Have students compare answers with a partner. Then go over any questions. Tell students that in item 3 it is not incorrect to omit *that* (*My father admitted that . . .*). However, because of the change in subject from the expected *he* to *twenty-five years of practicing medicine,* the use of *that* makes the sentence clearer.

- Then ask:
  Which sentence is in the past unreal conditional? (sentence 7)
  What happened to the verbs when you changed this sentence to indirect speech? (They stayed the same.)

D On a separate sheet of paper, . . .

Suggested teaching time:	5–10 minutes	Your actual teaching time:

- Before students rewrite the sentences, tell them to make appropriate shifts in tense and pronouns. Remind them also to include appropriate punctuation.

- Go over the answers as a class. Have volunteers write the sentences on the board.

EXTRAS (optional)

- **Workbook: Page 100**
- **Complete Assessment Package**

- **ActiveTeach:**
  Summit TV Video Program and Activity Worksheets
  Printable Audioscripts
  "Can-Do" Self-Assessment Charts
  Workbook Answer Key

- **MySummitLab:**
  Writing
  Summit TV Video Program and Activity Worksheets
  Achievement Test 8

Review

ActiveBook: *More Practice*

grammar · vocabulary · listening
reading · speaking · pronunciation

A 🎧 **Listening.** Listen to three examples of humor and write
the type of humor that each example represents. Listen again if necessary.

1. a practical joke OR an anecdote   2. a joke   3. a riddle

B Write the response you would give in each situation. Use the Vocabulary.

1. Someone tells you a joke you don't find very funny. **YOU** That's pretty silly / lame / ridiculous.

2. You hear a joke that insults an ethnic group. **YOU** That's in poor taste.

3. Someone tells you a joke that uses complicated words or facts you don't understand.

   YOU I don't get it. / That went over my head.

4. You hear a joke that you find very funny. **YOU** What a riot / a scream / a hoot!

5. Someone tells you the same joke that you heard last week. **YOU** I've heard that one already.

   Additional responses for 4: That's hilarious / hysterical / too much! That cracked me up! / That really tickled me!

C Change each of the following to indirect speech.

1. Mary admitted, "I didn't get the joke." Mary admitted (that) she didn't get / hadn't gotten the joke.

2. The students insisted, "We weren't telling dirty jokes at lunch yesterday." The students insisted (that) they

   weren't / had not been telling dirty jokes at lunch yesterday / the day before.

3. My father admitted, "Twenty-five years of practicing medicine have taught
   me that laughter can be the best medicine." My father admitted that twenty-five years of practicing medicine

   had taught him that laughter can / could be the best medicine.

4. Jeff told his friends, "I'll tell you about a blooper I made at my job interview
   yesterday if you promise not to laugh." Jeff told his friends (that) he would tell them about a blooper he made /

   had made at his job interview yesterday / the day before if they promised not to laugh.

5. "I can't understand British humor," said Anne. Anne said (that) she can't / couldn't understand British humor.

6. She said, "I may not have enough knowledge of British culture to understand
   all the pop culture references." She said (that) she might not have enough knowledge of British culture to

   understand all the pop culture references.

7. John insisted, "If I had known the joke was offensive, I wouldn't have told it." John insisted (that) if he had

   known the joke was offensive, he wouldn't have told it.

D On a separate sheet of paper, write what the people actually said, using direct speech.

1. Jane said I was a good sport for not getting angry about the practical joke
   she had played on me. Jane said, "You're a good sport for not getting angry about the practical joke I played
   on you."

2. He admitted that he hadn't gotten my joke about the penguin. He admitted, "I didn't get your joke about
   the penguin."

3. The host told his guests not to tell any political jokes at the party. The host told his guests, "Don't tell any
   political jokes at the party."

4. He promised that he would explain the joke to me later.
   He promised, "I'll explain the joke to you later."

What lies ahead?

GOALS After Unit 9, you will be able to:

1 Discuss the feasibility of future technologies
2 Describe applications of innovative technologies
3 Discuss future trends
4 Discuss ways to protect the environment

A **Topic Preview.** Read these two quotations from the past. How were they wrong?

> "There is no reason for any individual to have a computer in his home."
>
> Kenneth Olsen, President of Digital Equipment, 1977

> "Everything that can be invented has been invented."
>
> Charles H. Duell, Commissioner of the U.S. Patent Office, 1899

B **Express Your Ideas.** Why do you think Duell and Olsen, who were specialists in their fields, were unable to foresee the future? If you had to make a statement in one sentence about the future, what would it be?

What lies ahead?

A Topic Preview

Suggested teaching time:	5 minutes	Your actual teaching time:	

- To introduce the topic, have students look at the picture and share their associations. (Possible answers: city, Earth, universe)
- Call on volunteers to read the quotations.
- Then have students read the Topic Preview question and discuss the answer in small groups.
- Ask:
  What important inventions have been made since 1899? (Possible answers: the space shuttle, penicillin, television)
  What reasons are there for people to have a computer at home? (Possible answers: to use e-mail to communicate with friends; to do research on the Internet; to write reports)

B Express Your Ideas

Suggested teaching time:	5–10 minutes	Your actual teaching time:	

- Have groups discuss the first question. Then bring the class together and have students share answers.
- Invite students to write their statements about the future on the board. Ask *In fifty years, how do you think people will respond to these statements?*

Option: [+10 minutes] Have pairs list the most important inventions that had been made by 1899. (Possible answers: the telephone, the automobile, the electric light bulb) Encourage students to research inventions online. Then have pairs speculate why Charles H. Duell may have thought that these items represented everything that could be invented. Bring the class together and have pairs share inventions and speculations.

C 🎧 Sound Bites

Suggested teaching time:	10 minutes	Your actual teaching time:

- Have students read and listen to the conversation. Clarify vocabulary as needed.
- Ask:
  What would Olga like to do? (travel to another planet like a tourist)
  Do you think a space tourism company would be a good investment? Why? Why not?
  What do we do today that people fifty years ago never would have imagined?
- Have students read and listen to the conversation again.

Language note: *Far off* in this context means far in the future. *Astronomical* means very high. *Far-fetched* means unbelievable or unlikely. Focus on Olga's second line, "There was this piece on the news . . . " Students may remember that gerunds are supposed to be preceded by possessives: *someone's trying*. Note that this rule is less and less observed in informal spoken English.

Option: [+5 minutes] Have pairs look at the photo and write a caption for it. Bring the class together and have students share their captions.

Option: [+5 minutes] Have pairs create short conversations about events of the future, using the expressions *I think it's pretty far-fetched* and *It's not as far off as you think*. For example, A: *Wouldn't it be great if we could have free high-speed Internet access?* B: *Actually, that's not as far off as you think. Many places are already talking about citywide wireless connections.*

D Think and Explain

Suggested teaching time:	5 minutes	Your actual teaching time:

- Discuss the questions as a class. Then ask:
  Who do you agree with—Olga or Kate? Why?
  Would you travel to space as a tourist if this were possible? Why? Why not?

E Focus on Language

Suggested teaching time:	10–15 minutes	Your actual teaching time:

- Before students do the exercise, make sure they understand that a *decade* is ten years and a *century* is 100 years. To check comprehension, ask:
  What year marks the end of this decade?
  What year marks the end of this century?
- Have pairs share their opinions about the future events. Then bring the class together and have students compare points of view. Encourage students to give reasons for their opinions.

Challenge: [+15 minutes] On the board, write *Affordable space tourism will happen in our lifetime.* Divide the class in half and assign each half the negative or the affirmative position. Tell each group to prepare arguments to support the assigned position. Then bring the class together and have groups present their arguments. Allow each side to respond. Write the arguments on the board. Then have students review the arguments to determine which side had the stronger arguments.

STARTING POINT

Suggested teaching time:	10–15 minutes	Your actual teaching time:

- If necessary, suggest some examples of modern innovations or technologies. (Possible answers: air conditioning, computers, airplanes, DVD players, calculators)

Pair Work

- Then have pairs discuss why each innovation or technology would have surprised a person 100 years ago.

Project: Have pairs think up a product that will be a common household item in the year 2100 but that we can't imagine existing today. Encourage students to be creative and innovative and to provide illustrations. Have pairs present their product and explain what it does. After each presentation, ask the class *Do you think such a product could realistically exist in 100 years? Why? Why not?*

EXTRAS (optional)

- Workbook: Exercise 1
- MySummitLab: Preview

C 🎧 5:02 **Sound Bites.** Read and listen as two women discuss the future.

OLGA: Wouldn't it be great if there were some way to be flown to another planet? I mean comfortably. Like a tourist.

KATE: Forget about it. That's not happening in our lifetime.

OLGA: Don't be so sure. There was this piece on the news about someone trying **CN** to get investors to start up a space tourism company. There are even a couple of space tourism websites. It's not as far off as you think.

KATE: Yeah, right! Who would invest in that? The cost would be astronomical. And then, to top it off, no one would go.

OLGA: I think you're wrong. Lots of people would. I would. I think it would be a great investment.

KATE: Well, I think it's pretty far-fetched.

OLGA: Hey, fifty years ago, who would have thought we'd be able to do all the things we do today?

D **Think and Explain.** Why does Olga think space tourism may not be so far off? Why does Kate think the possibility is far-fetched?

E **Focus on Language.** In your opinion, when might the following future events occur: in the next decade, by the end of the century, or never? Use the expressions from Sound Bites.

- space tourism
- the widespread use of non-petroleum-dependent technology
- the elimination of cancer as a health threat
- the widespread use of flying automobiles

EXPRESSIONS

- Wouldn't it be .... if . . .?
- Who would have thought . . .?
- .... isn't as far off as you think.
- Forget about it.
- Don't be so sure.
- be far–fetched
- [not] in our lifetime

STARTING POINT

Pair Work. Make a list of one modern innovation or technology in each of the following categories that would have surprised a person who lived 100 years ago. How has each one changed people's lives?

	innovation or technology
the home	
the workplace	
transportation	
leisure	
education	

GOAL
Discuss the feasibility of future technologies

A 🎧 5:03 **Grammar Snapshot.** Read the article and notice the passive forms.

JULES VERNE

(1828–1905) was internationally renowned for his science fiction and adventure stories, many of which dealt with exploration of the sea, the interior of the Earth, and outer space. The 19th century in Europe was a time of great interest in developing science and technology, and Jules Verne was among the first writers to explore in fiction how people **would be affected** by technology in the future. Verne's great writings deal with contemporary scientific innovation and its potential for human benefit or destruction.

Three of Verne's early novels, *Twenty Thousand Leagues Under the Sea*, *Journey to the Center of the Earth*, and *From the Earth to the Moon*, expressed optimism that nature **would be understood** and **controlled** by humans through new technologies. In these books, Verne's heroes are scientists who travel to unknown places to gain knowledge that will benefit humanity.

In his later works, Verne is less optimistic about the future. In *The Eternal Adam*, for example, Verne is extremely pessimistic, portraying scientists as unscrupulous and willing to allow others to use their scientific discoveries and inventions for war and destruction.

Although a beloved storyteller, Verne **will** always **be credited** with having foreseen the invention of many modern machines and technologies.

Predicted by Verne:
- Long-distance travel by balloon • Interplanetary travel • A moon landing • The electric engine
- The tank • The picture telephone • Scuba-diving gear • The helicopter • The satellite

B **Express Your Ideas.** Jules Verne was able to envision many future technologies. What technologies do you predict for the future?

C **Grammar.** The passive voice: the future, the future as seen from the past, and the future perfect

The future
Use <u>will be</u> or <u>be going to be</u> + a past participle to make predictions and statements about the future in the passive voice.
> In the future, appliances **will be linked** to each other and to the Internet as well.
> In coming years, our lives **are going to be made** easier by new home technologies.

The future as seen from the past
Use <u>would be</u> or <u>was / were going to be</u> + a past participle to make statements about the future as seen from the past in the passive voice.
> Verne predicted that spaceships **would be taken** into outer space.
> He thought that one day nature **was going to be controlled** by humans.

The future perfect
Use <u>will have been</u> + a past participle to make statements in the future perfect in the passive voice.
> By 2025, commercial space travel **will have been started**.
> Cities **will have been built** on the moon by the end of the century.

> **NOTE:** The passive voice is often used when discussing science and technology. Use a <u>by</u> phrase when it's important to name the agent (the performer of the action).
>
> Our lives will be improved **by technology**.

> **GRAMMAR BOOSTER**
> ▸ p. G13
> • When to use the passive voice

D **Grammar Practice.** Look at the ad for the "home of the future." Then, on a separate sheet of paper, change the four statements in the ad from active to passive voice.

Household chores will be done by robots. Heating and air-conditioning will be turned on and off by computers. Appliances will be linked to the Internet by space-age wiring. Your home will be fully powered by solar energy.

Build your home of the future today with our complete kit.

In your home:
- robots will do household chores.
- computers will turn heating and air-conditioning on and off.
- space-age wiring will link appliances to the Internet.
- solar energy will fully power your home.

1

A 🎧 Grammar Snapshot

Suggested teaching time:	5–10 minutes	Your actual teaching time:

- Before students read and listen, write on the board *Jules Verne.* Ask *What do you know about Jules Verne?* If students don't know anything about him, have a volunteer read the first sentence of the article.

- Call on a student to read the list of inventions that Verne predicted. Ask:
    How do you think people reacted to these predictions?
    In your opinion, which of these inventions did people think were most unlikely?

- Have students read and listen to the article. Clarify vocabulary as needed.

- To check comprehension, ask:
    What is Jules Verne known for? (science fiction and adventure stories)
    What were some of his popular topics? (exploration of the sea, the interior of the Earth, and outer space)
    What did Verne explore in his fiction? (how people would be affected by technology in the future)
    What message was expressed in three early novels? (optimism that nature would be understood and controlled by humans through new technologies)
    Who are the heroes in Verne's books? (scientists who travel to unknown places to gain knowledge that will benefit humanity)
    In which book was he less optimistic about the future? (*The Eternal Adam*)
    How does Verne portray scientists in this book? (Scientists are unscrupulous and willing to allow others to use their scientific discoveries for war and destruction.)

- Have students read and listen to the article again, noticing the passive forms in bold.

> **Culture note:** Jules Verne was a French novelist. Other inventions that he predicted include the television, the submarine, and the airplane. Additional novels include *Around the World in Eighty Days* and *Around the Moon.*

B Express Your Ideas

Suggested teaching time:	5 minutes	Your actual teaching time:

- After students discuss the questions in groups, bring the class together and have students share answers.

- On the board, write the future technologies that students mention. Ask *Which of these technologies do you think will really be invented? Why? When?*

C Grammar

Suggested teaching time:	5–10 minutes	Your actual teaching time:

- Review the difference between the active and passive voice. On the board, write *Jules Verne wrote Twenty Thousand Leagues Under the Sea.* Ask *Is this sentence active or passive?* (active) *How do you know?* (The verb *wrote* has a direct object, *Twenty Thousand Leagues Under the Sea.*) Have a student restate this sentence in the passive voice. (*Twenty Thousand Leagues Under the Sea was written by Jules Verne.*) Explain that this grammar section focuses on the passive voice to talk about the future, the future as seen from the past, and the future perfect.

- Remind students about the difference between the future and the future perfect. The future with *will* or *be going to* expresses future time. For example, *Every student in the world will be connected to the Internet.* The future perfect expresses the idea that one event will happen before another event or a time in the future. For example, *By 2050, every student in the world will have been connected to the Internet.*

- Then call on a volunteer to read the first bold rule about the future and the example sentences. Elicit additional sentences. Repeat the procedure for the next two bold rules (the future as seen from the past and the future perfect). Point out that the future as seen from the past often appears as indirect speech, as in the example sentences.

- Ask *Which passive forms are used in the article in Exercise A?* **(the future as seen from the past:** would be affected; would be understood and controlled; **the future:** will be credited)

- Call on a student to read the Note. Elicit additional example sentences with an agent. For example, *In 2100, homes will be cleaned by robots.*

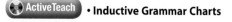 **· Inductive Grammar Charts**

D Grammar Practice

Suggested teaching time:	5–10 minutes	Your actual teaching time:

- Have students read the ad to themselves and then complete the exercise independently.

- Bring the class together to go over the answers. For each sentence, ask:
    What is the agent in the sentence? (1. robots, 2. computers, 3. space-age wiring, 4. solar energy)
    Is the agent important to the meaning of the sentence? (yes)

Project: On the board, write *Build your office of the future today with our complete kit.* Have pairs write four passive sentences describing an office of the future. For example, *All administrative tasks will be done automatically by a computer robot.* Bring the class together and have students share their ideas. Compile the descriptions in a series of ads based on the ad in Exercise D.

E Grammar Practice

Suggested teaching time:	10 minutes	Your actual teaching time:

- Call on students to read the predictions. Clarify vocabulary as needed. Have a student read the example advertisement for Smell-O-Vision. Point out the use of the passive voice. Ask *What is the agent in this sentence?* (the smells of the scenes on the screen)

- While pairs write their own advertisement, circulate and assist as needed. Remind students to use the passive voice to explain the future benefit of the technology.

- Bring the class together and have students share their advertisements. After each ad, ask *How would you react if you saw this ad in a magazine or newspaper?*

- Have a student read the quote under the directions. Ask individual students *Which of the four ideas sounds like a good idea to you? Why?*

> **Language note:** A *flop* and a *bust* are both informal terms for a failure. *Take off* means *become successful*. *Catch on* means *become popular*.

Challenge: [+15 minutes] Have pairs think up their own invention and write an advertisement explaining the future benefit of the technology. Tell students to include the passive voice, using the advertisements in Exercise E as models. Have pairs read their ads to the class and instruct students to respond to the idea, using one of the following expressions: *That will be a flop. That will never take off. That will never catch on. That will be a bust.* Encourage students to explain why they think the idea won't be successful.

F Draw Conclusions

Suggested teaching time:	5 minutes	Your actual teaching time:

- Discuss the statement as a class, using the terms in the box.

- Then ask *Do you think any of the ideas could still catch on with further research and development? Which one(s)? Why?*

NOW YOU CAN

Suggested teaching time:	10 minutes	Your actual teaching time:

- Have a volunteer read the phrases in the speech balloon. Make sure students understand that *claim* means *say* or *state*. *Theorize* means *speculate* or *hypothesize*.

- Tell students that they will be doing two things in the exercise. First, they will change the quotations in direct speech to indirect speech, using one of the phrases in the box to begin each sentence. Then they will change the quotation from active voice to passive voice.

- Rewrite a quotation together as a class. On the board, write *The technologies of the future will greatly benefit humankind.* Then write *Verne thought . . .* Ask a student to complete the sentence in indirect speech. (Verne thought [that] the technologies of the future would greatly benefit humankind.) Point out that *will* changes to *would* in indirect speech.

- Next, ask students to rewrite the sentence in the passive voice. If they have difficulty, remind them that, in a passive sentence, the receiver of the action (in this case, *humankind*) appears at the beginning of the sentence. (Verne thought [that] humankind would be greatly benefited by the technologies of the future.)

A Use the Grammar

- Have pairs rewrite the quotations in the exercise, following the two steps for each one. Circulate and assist as needed. Remind students to change *will* to *would* and *are going to* to *were going to*. Although the passive voice with *were going to* is correct (*Verne thought that trips to outer space were going to be taken one day*), many speakers would restate the sentence using *would* (*Verne thought that trips to outer space would be taken one day*) because it sounds less awkward.

Pair Work answers
Verne thought (believed, etc.) that ordinary people would one day purchase picture telephones.
Verne thought (believed, etc.) that people were going to take trips to outer space some day.
Verne thought (believed, etc.) that the military would use tanks in the future.
Verne thought (believed, etc.) that scuba-diving gear would protect divers searching for undersea treasures.

Sentences in the passive voice
Verne thought (believed, etc.) that picture telephones would one day be purchased by ordinary people.
Verne thought (believed, etc.) that trips to outer space were going to be taken some day.
Verne thought (believed, etc.) that tanks would be used by the military in the future.
Verne thought (believed, etc.) that divers searching for undersea treasures would be protected by scuba-diving gear.

- Go over the answers as a class. Then ask pairs to share some of their wild predictions about the future. After the presentations, ask *Which predictions do you think are most unlikely? Do any seem likely? Which ones?*

B Discussion

- Have pairs discuss the questions. Then bring the class together and ask for examples of future technologies students think will become successful.

- Take a poll to find out how many students are optimistic or pessimistic about the future use of science and technology. Have optimistic and pessimistic students explain their point of view.

EXTRAS (optional)

- **Grammar Booster**
- **Pronunciation Booster**
- **Workbook: Exercises 2–6**
- **MySummitLab: Lesson 1**

E **Grammar Practice.** Read about some failed predictions from the past. With a partner, create an advertisement for one prediction. Use the passive voice, explaining the future benefit of the technology.

"Run, don't walk, to see Smell-O-Vision at your local theater. You'll be surrounded by the smells of the scenes on the screen!"

"It sounded like a good idea at the time."

Smell-O-Vision. In 1960, the movie *Scent of Mystery* combined visual images with releases of odors into the theater. The movie-maker predicted this technology would be used in all movies of the future.

(Smell-O-Vision was a flop.)

The flying car. On November 17, 1947, the New York Times reported that a prototype of a flying car, the ConvAIRCAR, had circled San Diego, California, for one hour and eighteen minutes. The maker of the car predicted that the flying car would be a commercial success.

(The flying car never caught on.)

Cryonics for immortality.

In the 1960s, Robert Ettinger's book *The Prospect of Immortality* argued that people with fatal illnesses could have their bodies frozen before death and, once a cure for the illness was found, could then be thawed and cured. This would permit us to live beyond our natural life.

(This technology never took off.)

Rocket-delivered mail.
On June 8, 1959, a rocket carrying 3,000 letters was launched from a submarine in the ocean and delivered to a U.S. naval station in Florida. Some people believed the age of rocket-delivered mail had begun.

(But rocket-delivered mail was a bust.)

Information source: http://retrofuture.com

F **Draw Conclusions.** Discuss why you think each of these ideas failed to catch on.

- failed to [catch on / take off]
- never [caught on / took off]
- was / were a bust

PRONUNCIATION BOOSTER ▸ p. P9
- Formal pronunciation, rhythm, and intonation

NOW YOU CAN *Discuss the feasibility of future technologies*

A **Use the Grammar.** First, restate each Jules Verne "quotation," using the future as seen from the past. Next, on a separate sheet of paper, rewrite each sentence, using the passive voice. Then, with a partner, make three wild predictions about the future.

- "Ordinary people will one day purchase picture telephones."
- "People are going to take trips to outer space some day."
- "The military will use tanks in the future."
- "Scuba-diving gear will protect divers searching for undersea treasures."

(See page T101 for answers.)

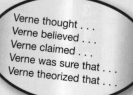

Verne thought . . .
Verne believed . . .
Verne claimed . . .
Verne was sure that . . .
Verne theorized that . . .

B **Discussion.** What future technologies do you think will catch on? Are you optimistic or pessimistic about the use of science and technology in the future? Why?

E 🎧 Listening

Suggested teaching time:	5–10 minutes	Your actual teaching time:

- Before students listen, tell them to skim the statements in order to know what to listen for. Make sure students understand that item 7 refers to the rate of population growth, not to population.
- If students have difficulty keeping up with the lecture, stop after each section to let them complete the statements.
- Have students listen again to check their work. Then have them compare statements with a partner.

Challenge: [+10–15 minutes] Draw the following chart on the board for students to copy on a piece of paper, or print out and distribute copies from *ActiveTeach*.

Population	Answers: 2015	Answers: 2000
World	7.2 billion	6.1 billion
India	1.2 billion	900 million
Pakistan	195 million	140 million
South Africa	38.7 million	43.4 million
Russia	130–135 million	146 million

Then have students listen to the lecture again and fill in the chart with the numbers cited. Go over the completed chart as a class.

 • **Graphic Organizers**

F Support an Opinion

Suggested teaching time:	5 minutes	Your actual teaching time:

- Discuss the questions as a class. Encourage all students to share their thoughts and opinions.
- Then ask *How will the population in this country change between 2000 and 2015? What will influence it?*

NOW YOU CAN

Suggested teaching time:	5–10 minutes	Your actual teaching time:

 • **Discourse Strategies**

A Notepadding

- Have students look at the photo. Ask *What trend do you think this picture illustrates?* (birth trends) *What are the birth trends in this country?*
- Call on a volunteer to read the list of social trends. Invite students to suggest other topics, and write these on the board for reference.
- Ask a student to read the comment about marriage and divorce trends. Then have students write independently about trends that concern them. Have pairs compare answers and note any similarities.

B Discussion

- Bring the class together and have students form small groups with others who chose the same topic.
- Circulate as groups discuss the concerns and predict consequences. Assist as needed.

C Summarize Ideas

- Write the following tips on the board:
  Paragraph 1: Explain the problem and give examples.
  Paragraph 2: Explain what will happen as a result of the trend.
- Then have students write independently about the trend they discussed in their group.
- If time permits, have students exchange papers with a partner or read their paragraphs to the class. Alternatively, collect student assignments and give individual feedback.

EXTRAS (optional)

- **Workbook: Exercises 12–13**
- **MySummitLab: Lesson 3**

E 🎧 5:13 **Listening. Infer Information.** Read the statements. Then listen to the lecture again. Circle the word or phrase that best completes each statement, according to the information presented in the lecture.

In comparison with the year 2000, . . .

1. the world's population in 2015 will be (**higher** / lower / the same).
2. birthrates in developed countries will be (higher / **lower** / the same).
3. populations in India and Pakistan will be (**higher** / lower / the same).
4. the population in African countries with high birthrates and high AIDS mortality will be (higher / **lower** / the same).
5. populations in Russia and Eastern Europe will be (higher / **lower** / the same).
6. populations in Japan and Western Europe will be (higher / **lower** / the same).
7. the rate of population growth in North America, Australia, and New Zealand will continue to be (**higher than** / lower than / the same as) in other developed countries.

F **Support an Opinion.** Do any of the statistics about future world demographics concern you? Why or why not?

NOW YOU CAN *Discuss future trends*

A **Notepadding.** With a partner, discuss some social trends in your country that concern you. Write them on your notepad. Do you and your partner have similar concerns?

> Marriage and divorce: *Fewer and fewer people are getting married.*

Government and politics:

The news media:

Education:

Marriage and divorce:

Family life:

Other:

B **Discussion.** On the board, write the trends that students discussed. Choose one topic you're concerned about and meet in small groups with others who have chosen that topic. Discuss your concerns and predict at least three consequences if the trend continues.

C **Summarize Ideas.** On a separate sheet of paper, write two paragraphs about the trend you discussed. In the first paragraph, explain the problem and give examples. In the second paragraph, explain what will happen as a result of the trend.

> *In this country, there has been a trend toward getting married at an older age . . .*

A **Reading Warm-up.** What are some ways we can save energy and water?

B 🎧 5:14 **Reading.** Read the article. What do you think about the steps the dealership took?

World's First "Green" Dealership

GreenZone, believed to be the world's first "green" dealer facility, was opened in Umeå in northern Sweden. It is expected to pave the way for other green facilities worldwide. The project was developed by Ford dealer Per Carstedt, in conjunction with Ford, McDonald's, and Statoil. It includes three different buildings—a car dealership, a restaurant, and a gas station.

GreenZone uses solar collectors to absorb energy from the sun.

The GreenZone project has two very challenging goals: to conserve resources by using only renewable energy sources to meet energy demands and to reduce energy consumption by 60–70% by using green technologies.

The car showroom building is heated by a geothermal system that collects heat energy from within the earth and from solar collectors that absorb the energy from the sun. In addition, the dealership, restaurant, and gas station are all linked by pipes. Water in the pipes carries heat from one building to another. For example, excess heat from the restaurant kitchen is used to heat the car showroom.

The energy used for lighting is provided by augmenting electricity from the national power company with power generated by a local wind generator. This cuts down on the amount of power that needs to be purchased. And to reduce the need for lighting, skylights have been installed in the roofs to give better light during the day.

Fresh water from the public water supply is needed only for the kitchen and the restaurant. Rainwater is collected for other uses within the facility, and used water is always filtered and reused. In this way, the demand for fresh water is reduced by 90%.

All the materials used in the construction of the facility were either reused or recycled, cutting down on waste and pollution. Living plants, known as "green filters," are used to purify air that circulates in the ventilation system in the buildings.

The entire staff has been educated in environmental matters so that they are also committed to the dealership's environmental goals.

renewable can be replaced so it is never used up

energy power that is used to produce heat and make machines work

consumption amount used

pipes tubes through which gas or liquid can travel

generator a machine that produces electricity

recycle to process used objects so they can be used again

waste unwanted materials that are left after something has been used or consumed

On your ActiveBook disc: *Reading Glossary* and *Extra Reading Comprehension Questions*

Information source: Ford Motor Company

C **Activate Vocabulary from a Text.** Complete each statement about the GreenZone project.

1. Reducing .... demands is the purpose of green technologies.
   a. pollution **b.** energy **c.** renewable

2. At GreenZone, a decision was made to avoid using .... energy sources.
   a. nonrenewable **b.** renewable **c.** power

3. Waste and pollution are reduced by .... materials at the dealership.
   a. using **b.** recycling **c.** linking

4. Employees know that one way to protect the environment is to protect its ....
   a. wastes **b.** solar power **c.** resources

5. The GreenZone project uses a variety of .... sources: electric, wind, geothermal, and solar.
   a. pollution **b.** waste **c.** power

4

A Reading Warm-up

Suggested teaching time:	5 minutes	Your actual teaching time:	

- Discuss the Warm-up question as a class. Then ask *Do we currently follow these ways to protect the environment? If not, why not?*

B 🎧 Reading

Suggested teaching time:	10–15 minutes	Your actual teaching time:	

- Call on a student to read the title. Ask *What do you think the adjective* green *means here?* (beneficial to the environment)
- Have students read and listen to the article. Refer them to the box at the bottom right corner of the article to clarify essential vocabulary.
- To check comprehension, ask:
  Where was the first "green" dealer facility established? (in Sweden)
  What is it called? (GreenZone)
  What three companies joined together to form GreenZone? (Ford, McDonald's, and Statoil)
  What are the two main goals of GreenZone? (to conserve resources by using only renewable energy sources and to reduce energy consumption by 60 to 70 percent by using green technologies)
  In what areas is GreenZone working to help meet these goals? (heating, lighting, fresh water supply, and ventilation)

- Have students read and listen to the article again. Then call on students to answer the question in the direction line.

Option: [+10 minutes] Have a student reread the last paragraph of the article. Ask *What type of environmentally friendly behavior do you think is expected of GreenZone employees?* (Possible answers: recycling paper; using washable cups and plates and not paper or plastic) *Would you feel comfortable working in such an environmentally conscious workplace? Why? Why not?*

- **Reading Strategies**
- **Reading Speed Calculator**
- **Extra Reading Comprehension Questions**
- **Reading Glossaries**

C Activate Vocabulary from a Text

Suggested teaching time:	5 minutes	Your actual teaching time:	

- Have students do the exercise individually. Then have them compare answers with a partner.
- Bring the class together and go over any questions.

D Explain a Process

Suggested teaching time:	5–10 minutes	Your actual teaching time:	

- Have students look at the chart. Point out that the article on page 106 discusses four systems at GreenZone: Heating, Lighting, Water, and Ventilation. Have students locate and label the paragraphs that discuss each system. (paragraphs 3, 4, 5, and 6, respectively)
- Then have pairs fill in the chart, referring to the information in the article.
- Bring the class together and go over the answers.

Option: [+5–10 minutes] Use the answers to the following questions as a basis for class discussion: *Which energy sources used at GreenZone are used in your workplace? In your home? What other energy sources and processes could you recommend?* (Possible answer: cooling systems that work via water circulation)

E Infer Information

Suggested teaching time:	5 minutes	Your actual teaching time:	

- Have groups discuss the questions and take notes. Then bring the class together and go over the answers.
- As a follow-up to the last question, ask:
  How committed do you think people are to using recycled materials? Explain.
  What can we do to encourage people to use recycled materials? (Possible answers: incentives like tax cuts; laws and regulations; fines for not adhering to laws)

Option: [+10 minutes] If students are interested, suggest that they research one or more of these topics on the Internet. Have students report their findings to the class and answer any questions.

F Draw Conclusions

Suggested teaching time:	5 minutes	Your actual teaching time:	

- Discuss the questions as a class.
- Then ask *What kinds of companies do you think would make good partners for a green dealership?*

NOW YOU CAN

Suggested teaching time:	10–15 minutes	Your actual teaching time:	

A Frame Your Ideas

- Have students complete the self-test individually. Then have them compare answers with a partner.
- Bring the class together and ask pairs:
  Who is more environmentally conscious?
  How important is it to you to be environmentally conscious?

B Discussion

- Go over the tips in the self-test. For each one, make sure students understand the reason for the suggestion. For example, *Covering a pot when boiling water makes the water boil faster and therefore uses less energy.*
- Call on students to read the opinions in the speech balloons. Ask *Which comment do you agree with more?*
- Then call on individual students to answer the Discussion questions.
- Invite students to suggest additional ways to protect the environment at home.

EXTRAS (optional)

- Workbook: Exercises 14–16
- MySummitLab: Lesson 4

D **Explain a Process.** Complete the chart about the systems at GreenZone, according to the
reading. Write the sources of energy for each system and describe the process.

System	Source of energy	Process
Heating	*geothermal and solar*	*Heat is transported from one building to another.*
Lighting	power company; wind generator; skylights	Wind generator reduces amount of power purchased. Skylights reduce need for lighting.
Water	public water supply and rainwater	Rainwater collected and used except in kitchen and restaurant. Used water filtered and reused.
Ventilation	living plants	Plants purify air that circulates in ventilation system.

E **Infer Information.** Answer the questions, based on what you learned in the reading and from
your own general knowledge.

1. What are some renewable energy sources?

2. What are some nonrenewable energy sources?

3. How do solar collectors work?

4. What are the benefits of using recycled materials?

F **Draw Conclusions.** Why do you think a car company, a gas station, or a fast-food restaurant would
be interested in a green dealership? What might motivate a company to create a project such as this?

NOW YOU CAN *Discuss ways to protect the environment*

A **Frame Your Ideas.** Complete and discuss the self-test with a partner. How differently did you
respond? Who seems to be more environmentally conscious, according to the self-test?

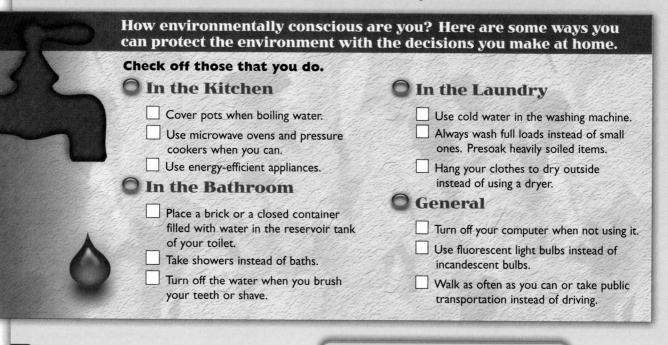

**How environmentally conscious are you? Here are some ways you
can protect the environment with the decisions you make at home.**

Check off those that you do.

◉ **In the Kitchen**
- ☐ Cover pots when boiling water.
- ☐ Use microwave ovens and pressure cookers when you can.
- ☐ Use energy-efficient appliances.

◉ **In the Bathroom**
- ☐ Place a brick or a closed container filled with water in the reservoir tank of your toilet.
- ☐ Take showers instead of baths.
- ☐ Turn off the water when you brush your teeth or shave.

◉ **In the Laundry**
- ☐ Use cold water in the washing machine.
- ☐ Always wash full loads instead of small ones. Presoak heavily soiled items.
- ☐ Hang your clothes to dry outside instead of using a dryer.

◉ **General**
- ☐ Turn off your computer when not using it.
- ☐ Use fluorescent light bulbs instead of incandescent bulbs.
- ☐ Walk as often as you can or take public transportation instead of driving.

B **Discussion.** What do you think of the tips
in the self-test? Do you think any of them
are practical ideas or are they just a waste of
time? Why? Do you think it's important to
protect the environment for the future? Why or
why not?

*"I think it's silly to worry about how much water
you use at home. I don't think it makes a bit of
difference to the environment."*

*"I totally disagree. I think protecting
the environment starts at home."*

Writing: Predict life in the future

The Essay
When writing an essay, present your personal view on a topic and give reasons, facts, or examples to support that view. The outline on the left and the sample essay on the right indicate an effective way to organize an essay.

thesis statement

WRITING MODEL

I. Introduction:
- Include a thesis statement—a sentence that presents the topic and focus of the entire essay.
- Write general statements about your topic that suggest what the body paragraphs will be about.

In twenty years, cars will be very different from today's cars. The car of the future will probably be powered by an alternative energy source, and it will be equipped with new technologies brought about by advances in computing.

II. Body paragraphs: Develop the idea presented in the thesis statement in two or more paragraphs. Each paragraph should have a topic sentence, followed by supporting examples.

Experts predict the car of the future will be powered by electricity. This will benefit the environment in several ways. First of all, [other details] . . . In addition, [other details] . . .

Advances in computing will also bring a lot of changes in car design. The car of the future will have many advanced technological features. For example, [other details] . . .

III. Conclusion: Summarize the main points and restate the thesis.

Although we cannot predict exactly what the car of the future will be like, we can make some educated guesses based on the direction the car industry is heading in. In twenty years, we will probably not remember . . .

A Prewriting. Planning Ideas. Choose a topic and write a thesis statement.

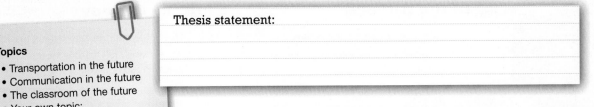

Thesis statement:

Topics
- Transportation in the future
- Communication in the future
- The classroom of the future
- Your own topic: ....

On a separate sheet of paper, plan the body paragraphs of your essay. Write a topic sentence for each paragraph you plan to write. Follow each topic sentence with a list of supporting examples.

Body paragraph 1:
topic sentence
supporting example
supporting example

Body paragraph 2:
topic sentence
supporting example
supporting example

B Writing. On a separate sheet of paper, write an essay about your topic. Use your thesis statement and your topic sentences and develop your supporting examples.

C Self-Check.

☐ Does your thesis statement announce what the essay will be about?
☐ Does the body of the essay give sufficient support for your point of view?
☐ Does your conclusion summarize the main points of your essay and restate its thesis?

Writing

Suggested teaching time:	20 minutes	Your actual teaching time:	

The Essay

- Ask *Have you ever written an essay? What was it about?*
- Call on a volunteer to read the introduction. Tell students that essays usually give the writer's point of view. Allow students time to look at the outline and read the Writing Model. Then ask:
  What is the thesis statement? (In twenty years . . .)
  What is the topic sentence in the second paragraph? (Experts predict . . .)
  What is the topic sentence in the third paragraph? (The car of the future . . .)
  Does the conclusion restate the thesis? (yes)
- Invite students to complete the incomplete sentences with supporting examples. For example, *First of all, cars will no longer need gasoline.*

 • Extra Writing Skills Practice

A Prewriting

- Call on a volunteer to read the Topics. Invite students to suggest other topics. Then focus on one topic and write it on the board: *The classroom of the future.* Ask:
  What thoughts and opinions do you have about the classroom of the future?
  What statement could you make about the classroom of the future to present the topic of the essay?

Explain to students that this statement is the thesis statement. It introduces the topic and suggests what the body paragraphs will be about. For example, *In the future, online classrooms will become more popular than the traditional face-to-face classrooms.*

- Circulate as students write their thesis statements and read each one. Make sure that the thesis statement voices the student's opinion on the chosen topic and that it is clear what the body paragraphs will be about.

- Then have students write a topic sentence for each paragraph and list supporting examples. Tell students that their examples don't need to be perfectly written. The goal of the prewriting stage is to organize their ideas and get their thoughts flowing. If students have difficulty with topic sentences and supporting sentences, refer them to page 48 in Unit 4 for a review.

B Writing

- As students write, encourage them to refer to their outline. Remind them to include general statements about their topic in the introduction. Tell students to write two body paragraphs, each consisting of a topic sentence and supporting examples. Finally, remind them to summarize the main points and restate the thesis in the conclusion.

C Self-Check

- After students complete the Self-Check, have them correct any organizational problems in the introduction, body paragraphs, or conclusion.

Option: [+15 minutes] Peer review and response. Have students exchange essays with a partner. To direct students' responses, write on the board *Can you suggest reasons or examples to make your partner's essay stronger?* Then ask *Do you agree or disagree with your partner's point of view?* Have students write a short response starting *I agree / disagree with your point of view because . . .*

Option: [+15 minutes] To provide more writing practice, have students write an essay about one of the innovative technologies presented on page 102. Tell students to follow the outline and to be sure to include a thesis statement in the introduction, a topic sentence and supporting examples in each body paragraph, and a restatement of the thesis in the conclusion. Collect the essays and offer feedback.

Review

A 🎧 Listening

Suggested teaching time:	10 minutes	Your actual teaching time:	

- Have students review the innovative technologies presented on page 102. Point out that the actual names of the technologies will not be mentioned in the conversations. Students will have to infer the technologies based on the information in the conversations.
- Have students listen to all four conversations. Then have them listen again. Stop after each conversation to allow students to identify the technology. If necessary, allow students to listen again to confirm their answers.
- Bring the class together and go over the answers.

> **Language note:** Although *sketchy* is current slang, its use is not offensive. A *worrywart* is a person who worries too much. *Boonies* is a slang term for a rural area.

AUDIOSCRIPT

For audioscript, see page AS12.

B 🎧 Read the following idioms . . .

Suggested teaching time:	5–10 minutes	Your actual teaching time:	

- Call on volunteers to read the idioms. Ask *Which idioms have you heard before?*
- Then have students listen for each idiom in the conversations. Stop after each conversation and have students infer the meaning of the idiom. If necessary, have students listen to the conversations again.
- Bring the class together and have students share their interpretations of the idioms.

Option: [+5 minutes] Have pairs create short conversations using the idioms in this exercise. For example, A: *I think animal cloning should be banned. Nothing good can come of it.* B: *Actually, I'm still on the fence about cloning. I think there might be some benefits to it.* Have pairs read their conversations to a group of three or four pairs.

C Complete the paragraph . . .

Suggested teaching time:	5–10 minutes	Your actual teaching time:	

- Before students do the exercise, have them review the Vocabulary on page 104.
- As students complete the paragraph, tell them to note whether each noun is singular or plural and to make sure that the noun agrees with the verb in each sentence.
- Have pairs compare answers.

D Rewrite each of the following sentences . . .

Suggested teaching time:	5–10 minutes	Your actual teaching time:	

- After students rewrite the sentences, have them compare answers with a partner.
- Bring the class together and go over any outstanding queries. Then ask *In which sentences was the by phrase necessary? Why?*

EXTRAS (optional)

- **Workbook: Page 113**
- **Complete Assessment Package**

- **ActiveTeach:**
  Summit TV Video Program and Activity Worksheets
  Printable Audioscripts
  "Can-Do" Self-Assessment Charts
  Workbook Answer Key

- **MySummitLab:**
  Writing
  Summit TV Video Program and Activity Worksheets
  Achievement Test 9

Review

A 🎧 **Listening.** Listen to the conversations. Write the technologies the people are referring to.

5:15

1. _artificial intelligence_ 2. _remote surgery_ 3. _computer chip implant_ 4. _genetic engineering_

B 🎧 Read the following idioms from the conversations. Then listen again and infer their meanings from the context. Answers will vary, but may include:

5:16

1. "I find that a little sketchy." _That scares me a little._

2. "I think it's just pie in the sky." _I think it's impractical. OR I don't think it will ever happen._

3. "I'm still on the fence." _I'm not sure how I feel about it. OR I can't make up my mind about it._

4. "You know—you buy everything hook, line, and sinker!" _You're too gullible. OR You believe everything you hear._

C Complete the paragraph with words and phrases from the box. Make any necessary changes.

trend life expectancy mortality rate population growth statistics birthrate

Statistics indicate that there are over 6 billion people in the world, with an increase of
(1)

76,570,430 people each year. This _population growth_ is not a result of an increased _birthrate_. In fact,
(2)   (3)

there is actually a worldwide _trend_ for women to have fewer children. This increase in
(4)

population is mainly the result of a decrease in the child _mortality rate_, with more children living
(5)

to adulthood. People are living much longer lives. When the first humans walked the earth, the

average person lived only to the age of twenty. Today, the worldwide _life expectancy_ is 77.1.
(6)

D Rewrite each of the following sentences in the passive voice. Include a <u>by</u> phrase only if that information is necessary.

1. In two years, engineers will have designed a new factory. _In two years, a new factory will have been designed._

2. Engineers are going to equip the factory with filters. _The factory is going to be equipped with filters._

3. Workers will recycle paper, metal, and plastic. _Paper, metal, and plastic will be recycled._

4. They're going to treat waste before they dump it into rivers. _Waste is going to be treated before it is dumped into rivers._

5. New technologies are going to reduce energy demands by 50 percent. _Energy demands are going to be reduced by 50 percent by new technologies._

6. Pipes will collect rainwater, and they will transport it to tanks. Pipes will also carry excess heat from one building to another. _Rainwater will be collected and transported to tanks by pipes. Excess heat will also be carried from one building to another by pipes._

7. If engineers hadn't designed the factory to use solar energy, the national grid couldn't have met its demand for electricity. _If the factory had not been designed to use solar energy, the demand for electricity could not have been met by the national grid._

An interconnected world

GOALS After Unit 10, you will be able to:

1 Describe the cultural impact of foreign imports
2 React to news about global issues
3 Discuss the economic impact of globalization
4 Discuss the role of English in international communication

A **Topic Preview.** Read what these people say about globalization. Who seems enthusiastic about it? Who seems to be critical? Who seems neutral?

glob·al·i·za·tion /ˌgloʊbələˈzeɪʃən/ *n.* [U] the process of making something such as a business international, or the result of this: *the globalization of world markets* —**globalize** /ˈgloʊbəˌlaɪz/ *v.* [I,T]

Longman Advanced American Dictionary © 2007

"Globalization has changed us into a company that searches the world, not just to sell or to source, but to find intellectual capital—the world's best talents and best ideas."

Jack Welch, USA
former CEO General Electric

"This is a very exciting time in the world of information . . . The whole pace of business is moving faster. Globalization is forcing companies to do things in new ways."

Bill Gates, USA
CEO Microsoft

"[Globalization] increases to breakneck pace the speed of our transactions, financial or informational, but it also facilitates the spread of global plagues such as AIDS, social and ecological devastation, drugs, and international trafficking in arms or human beings."

Queen Noor, Jordan

"When protesters shout about the evils of globalization, most are not calling for a return to narrow nationalism but for the borders of globalization to be expanded, for trade to be linked to labor rights, environmental protection, and democracy."

Naomi Klein, Canada
activist and writer

"Across the world, as the 'free market' brazenly protects Western markets and forces developing countries to lift their trade barriers, the poor are getting poorer, and the rich richer."

Arundhati Roy, India
author and activist

"If we cannot make globalization work for all, in the end it will work for no one."

Kofi Annan, Ghana
former Secretary-General of the United Nations

"Globalization is not something we can hold off or turn off . . . It is the economic equivalent of a force of nature . . . like wind or water."

Bill Clinton, USA
former president

B **Express Your Ideas.** Which of the quotations come closest to *your* own views?

An interconnected world

A Topic Preview

Suggested teaching time:	15–20 minutes	Your actual teaching time:

- To introduce the topic, have a student read the title of the unit. Ask *How do you think the world is interconnected?* (Possible answers: via international companies; via the Internet)

- Ask a volunteer to read the definition of *globalization*. Then have students look at the photos and say which people they recognize or know something about. Ask *Do you think [name of person students know] is in favor of globalization?*

- Have students read the quotations. Then answer the Topic Preview questions as a class.

> **Language note:** *Brazenly* means shamelessly. *Source* means obtain something, such as materials, from another supplier. A *breakneck pace* is a dangerously fast pace. *Facilitate* means make easier.

> **Culture note:** <u>Bill Gates</u> (born in 1955); <u>Arundhati Roy</u> (born in 1961); <u>Jack Welch</u> (born in 1935); <u>Queen Noor</u> (born in 1951), fourth wife and widow of the late King Hussein of Jordan; <u>Kofi Annan</u> (born in 1938); <u>Naomi Klein</u> (born in 1970); <u>Bill Clinton</u> (born in 1946), 42nd president of the United States, 1993–2001.

B Express Your Ideas

Suggested teaching time:	5 minutes	Your actual teaching time:

- Discuss the question as a class. Encourage students to explain why they agree with the particular quotation they chose.

Option: [+10 minutes] Have students write a short statement about globalization that summarizes their opinion. Then bring the class together and have students share.

C 🎧 Sound Bites

Suggested teaching time:	10 minutes	Your actual teaching time:	

- Have students look at the photograph and read the signs. Ask:
  What does WTO stand for? (World Trade Organization)
  What do the signs say? (No Globalization without Representation; Labor says . . . WTO Ends Democracy)
  What do you think these signs mean?
  Do you think these demonstrators are for or against globalization?

- Then have students read and listen to the conversation.

- To check comprehension, ask:
  Which person is against globalization? (Eva)
  What is Craig's opinion of globalization? (He doesn't know what the big deal is.)
  What does Craig mean when he says, "Don't you think you're talking out of both sides of your mouth"? (He means that Eva is being hypocritical.)
  What do the Brazilian shoes, Chilean wine, and German car represent? (a positive aspect of globalization)

- Have students read and listen to the conversation again.

Culture note: Established in 1995, the World Trade Organization is an international organization that develops and enforces worldwide rules governing global trade. It is based in Geneva, Switzerland.

D Think and Explain

Suggested teaching time:	5–10 minutes	Your actual teaching time:	

- Have pairs discuss the questions. Then bring the class together and have students share answers using supporting information from Sound Bites. Point out that Eva's last line in Exercise C includes the word *benefits* as a verb. In Exercise D in item 2, *benefits* is a plural noun.

- To extend the discussion, ask:
  What are some other benefits of globalization? (Possible answers: Globalization creates more jobs. Barriers to trade are reduced.)
  What are some drawbacks of globalization? (Possible answer: The gap between the rich and the poor increases.)

Option: [+10 minutes] Ask a student to reread Naomi Klein's quotation about globalization on page 110. Ask *Do you agree with her statement? What other things do you think protestors "shout about" during anti-globalization demonstrations?*

STARTING **POINT**

Suggested teaching time:	10–15 minutes	Your actual teaching time:	

Support an Opinion

- Call on volunteers to read the situations. Then hold a class discussion. Encourage students to give reasons to support their answers.

Option: [+10 minutes] Have pairs think of an additional situation that illustrates the definition of globalization on page 110. Then have students read their situations to the class.

EXTRAS (optional)

- Workbook: Exercises 1–2
- MySummitLab: Preview

CN **Corpus Notes:** The expression *What is it with [someone or something]* is common in informal spoken English. Emphatic stress on *is* indicates disapproval.

C 🎧 5:17 **Sound Bites.** Read and listen to a conversation about globalization.

EVA: You may want to head home soon. They're closing off the streets for that antiglobalization demonstration. **CN**

CRAIG: Another one? What is it with these people? What's the big deal about globalization, anyway?

EVA: There are a lot of reasons to be against it. I think they have a point.

CRAIG: No offense, Eva, but don't you think you're talking out of both sides of your mouth? I mean, you've got your Brazilian shoes, your Chilean wine, your German car. How can you be against globalization?

EVA: OK, maybe I'm being a bit hypocritical. But not everyone benefits like we do. I still think we've got to stand up for what's right.

D **Think and Explain.** With a partner, discuss the questions and support your answers with information from Sound Bites.

1. Why does Craig think Eva is being hypocritical?

2. What benefits of globalization is Eva referring to?

3. Why does Eva think the demonstrators have a point?

1. Eva says she's against globalization, but she has shoes from Brazil, wine from Chile, and a car from Germany. 2. Economic benefits: Products from all over the world are available relatively inexpensively. 3. All countries of the world don't enjoy the economic benefits of globalization equally.

STARTING **POINT**

Support an Opinion. With a partner, decide which of the following you think are *not* examples of globalization. Explain your answers, according to the dictionary definition on page 110.
Not examples: a, d. Accept any answers students can support logically.

a Every year, New York City hosts a flamenco festival featuring artists from around the world who sing and dance in this traditional Spanish gypsy style.

d Canada charges that French and Russian fishing ships have violated its waters by fishing within the two-hundred-mile limit it claims along its Pacific and Atlantic coasts.

b At an international meeting in Porto Alegre, Brazil, participants from more than forty countries use English to communicate.

e Unemployed communications workers in Italy complain that their jobs are being taken by lower-paid workers in Sri Lanka.

c Nike, the U.S. sports apparel company, calls a news conference to answer further charges that workers in their factories in Southeast Asia are being paid poverty wages.

f Mexico, the United States, and Canada agree to eliminate trade barriers and permit sales of products from one country to the other without taxes.

111

D Grammar Practice

Suggested teaching time:	5–10 minutes	Your actual teaching time:	

- Before students do the exercise, have them skim the phrasal verbs and determine if they are separable or inseparable. (separable: 2, 3, 5, 6; inseparable: 1, 4) Remind students that with separable phrasal verbs, the direct object pronoun must come before the particle. Tell students to use the correct verb form in each sentence.

- Have students complete the exercise individually and then compare answers with a partner.

- Bring the class together and go over any questions.

NOW YOU CAN

Suggested teaching time:	15–20 minutes	Your actual teaching time:	

A Notepadding

- To introduce the topic, have students scan the photos and identify what they see. (a couple dancing; a Muslim woman in a store looking at a poster advertising jeans; a woman practicing yoga; an advertisement for Coca-Cola) Ask *Which of these things from foreign countries or cultures do you come across?*

- Then have students work individually to list examples on their notepad. Ask *Who included an Other category? What categories did you add?*

B Pair Work

- Have pairs discuss the statement and questions, referring to their notes.

- Then bring the class together and ask students to name products or traditions from their country that they think would have a positive impact on other countries.

C Use the Grammar

- Call on volunteers to read the statements about the future cultural impact of globalization. Then have students share their opinions about these statements. Encourage them to use phrasal verbs in their responses.

Project: Photocopy and distribute the following survey questions. Have pairs use them to find out more about the impact of foreign imports on their culture. Tell students to interview five people.

> What foreign imports play an important role in your life?
> What foreign imports do you think have a negative impact on this culture?
> What product or tradition from this country do you think would have a positive impact on other countries? Why?
> How could we try to market this product or tradition to other countries?

Then have pairs summarize the information in a presentation to the class.

EXTRAS (optional)

- **Grammar Booster**
- **Workbook: Exercises 3–5**
- **MySummitLab: Lesson 1**

D **Grammar Practice.** Complete each statement, using a form of the phrasal verb with the pronoun <u>it</u> or <u>them</u>. Pay attention to whether or not the phrasal verb is separable.

1. Although only a small minority of the population can read English, English words are visible everywhere. You often (come across) ___come across them___ on signs, product advertisements, and even clothing.

2. Tai chi has become really popular in this country. Even my eighty-year-old great-grandmother has (take up) ___taken it up___ !

3. For the governments of some countries, the benefits of globalization are not so clear. It may not be easy to (talk into) ___talk them into___ dropping trade tariffs.

4. Because many young adults have tremendous economic power, many fashion companies develop marketing campaigns that (go after) ___go after them___ exclusively.

5. A common marketing technique is to hand out free samples of new products at international trade fairs so people can (try out) ___try them out___ .

6. Many parents feel that certain songs express a negative social attitude and worry that their children will (pick up) ___pick it up___ just by listening to the songs.

NOW YOU CAN *Describe the cultural impact of foreign imports*

A **Notepadding.** On your notepad, list examples of things from foreign countries or cultures that you come across often.

Foods you eat:

Music you listen to:

Home furnishings:

Clothes and accessories you buy:

TV programs or movies you watch:

Other:

B **Pair Work.** Discuss whether the items you listed have had a positive or negative impact in your country. Of the things that are a part of your life, are there any that you would be willing to give up? Which products or traditions from *your* country do you think would have a positive impact on other countries?

C **Use the Grammar.** Do you agree with any of these statements about the future cultural impact of globalization? Explain. Try to use phrasal verbs when you can.

*"Globalization will lead to the creation of one global culture as people **give up** local traditions."*

*"Because of globalization, people will imitate the shallow, negative values they **pick up** from foreign movies, TV shows, and ads."*

*"Thanks to globalization, people around the world will **take up** the best aspects of each other's cultures while still retaining their own."*

GOAL
React to news about global issues

A 🎧 **5:19** **Conversation Snapshot.** Read and listen. Notice the conversation strategies.

To react positively

A: **Can you believe** how much money was donated for hunger relief?

B: It really makes you feel good, doesn't it?

A: I guess **it just goes to show you** what people can do when they put their minds to it. **CN**

To react negatively

A: **Can you believe** that no one's doing anything about global warming?

B: It's really mind-boggling, isn't it?

A: Yeah. **You'd think** in this day and age they could come up with a way to slow it down.

🎧 **5:20** **Rhythm and intonation practice**

> **5:21**
> 🎧 **Ways to react to world issues and news**
>
> It's really (mind-boggling / shocking / appalling), isn't it?
> It really makes you feel (angry / depressed / helpless), doesn't it?
> It's really (wonderful / heartwarming), isn't it?
> It really makes you feel (great / teary-eyed / fantastic), doesn't it?
> It's not really surprising, is it?
> It makes you feel kind of guilty, doesn't it?
> It really makes you stop and think, doesn't it?

Raising money in China for the World Food Program

CN **Corpus Notes:** *Put [your] mind to [something]* and *set [your] mind to [something]* have the same meaning, but *put [your] mind to [something]* occurs more frequently.

PRONUNCIATION BOOSTER ▸ p. P9
• Intonation in tag questions

B 🎧 **5:22** **Vocabulary. Phrasal Verbs to Discuss Global Issues.** Listen and practice.

lay off to stop employing a worker, especially for a period of time in which there is not much work to do
The company announced they were laying off two hundred employees.

put up with to accept a bad situation or person without complaining
For many years, the people in that village have put up with inadequate roads.

run out of use all of something and not have any left
If we're not careful, we'll run out of oil before alternative sources of energy have been found.

go without to live without something you need or usually have
No one should have to go without clean water to drink.

wipe out to remove or destroy
Illiteracy has been nearly wiped out there.

come up with to think of an idea, plan, reply, etc.
They need to come up with a new plan to shelter the homeless.

come down with to become sick with a particular illness
Since the flood, hundreds have come down with malaria.

carry out to do something that needs to be organized and planned
It's time the president carried out her plan to vaccinate all school-age children.

bring about to make something happen
We need to tell management our ideas if we expect to bring about any policy changes.

2

A 🎧 Conversation Snapshot

Suggested teaching time:	10 minutes	Your actual teaching time:	

These conversation strategies are implicit in the model:
- Use *Can you believe . . . ?* to indicate shock or disapproval.
- Use *It just goes to show you* to make a point.
- Begin a statement with *You'd think to* indicate dissatisfaction with a current situation.

- Direct students' attention to the photo. Have a volunteer read the caption. Then ask:
  What are the people doing? (putting money into a container)
  What do the words on the container say? (Walk World)
  What type of event is this? (probably a walk-a-thon)

- Have students read and listen to the conversations. Then ask:
  What is the first conversation about? (how much money was donated for hunger relief)
  Why does Student B react positively? (because a lot of money was donated)
  What is the second conversation about? (lack of efforts to stop global warming)
  Why does Student B react negatively? (because no one's doing anything about it)

- On the board, write *global warming, hunger.* Ask *What are some other global issues?* (Possible answer: AIDS)

- Finally, have students listen to Ways to react to world issues and news. With the class, determine which expressions are positive or negative and which expressions could be used to react either positively or negatively. See the Pronunciation Booster, pages P9 and P10, for intonation in tag questions to anticipate agreement or expect an answer.

- Ask students to find two of the ways to react in the Conversation Snapshot. (line 3: It really makes you feel good . . . ; line 8: It's really mind-boggling . . .) Ask volunteers to reread these lines, replacing the expressions with different ways to react from the box.

- Call students' attention to the conversation strategies highlighted in the model.

Language note: *Mind-boggling* means *hard to believe.* Something that makes you feel *teary-eyed* makes you feel emotional and ready to cry.

🎧 Rhythm and intonation practice

Suggested teaching time:	5 minutes	Your actual teaching time:	

- Have students repeat chorally. Make sure they:
  - use rising intonation for *Can you believe* in each conversation.
  - use falling intonation for *It really makes you feel good* and *It's really mind-boggling.*
  - use rising intonation for *doesn't it?* and *isn't it?*
  - use emphatic stress for <u>this</u> in *this day and age.*

B 🎧 Vocabulary

Suggested teaching time:	10 minutes	Your actual teaching time:	

- Have students skim the Vocabulary and note phrasal verbs they are less familiar with.

- After students listen and practice, bring the class together and answer any questions about the definitions. Point out that the following phrasal verbs are separable: *lay off, wipe out, carry out, bring about.* The rest of the phrasal verbs in the Vocabulary are inseparable. If necessary, refer students to the Appendices, pages A4 and A5, for complete lists of separable and inseparable phrasal verbs.

- Have pairs use the phrasal verbs to create additional sentences about global issues. Assist as needed.

- Have students listen and practice again.

ActiveTeach • **Vocabulary-Building Strategies**

C Vocabulary Practice

Suggested teaching time:	5–10 minutes	Your actual teaching time:

- Direct students' attention to the logo behind the text. Ask:

  What does this logo stand for? (the United Nations)
  What do you know about the United Nations?

  Then have a student read the title. Ask *What does UN stand for?* (the United Nations)

- Have students do the exercise individually. If necessary, refer them to the Vocabulary on page 114 to review phrasal verbs to discuss global issues. Then have students compare answers with a partner.

> **Culture note:** The United Nations (also called The UN) is a global organization that includes most of the countries in the world. Set up in 1945, following World War II, it promotes international peace and security as well as economic development. Its headquarters are in New York City.

Project: Have pairs look up the UN on the Internet and read about other projects that the organization is involved in, such as education, environment, health, human rights, or technology. Tell students to choose one project and write a paragraph about it, using phrasal verbs where appropriate. Have pairs share their paragraphs with the class.

D Vocabulary Practice

Suggested teaching time:	5–10 minutes	Your actual teaching time:

- Ask a volunteer to read the title. Clarify that *tap . . . rain forests* means make use of or take advantage of them. Ask *Why might a drug discovery plan tap rain forests?* (to look for new sources of drugs)

- Have students work individually to complete the sentences. Then have them compare answers with a partner. Circulate and assist as needed.

- Bring the class together and call on students to take turns reading the completed sentences.

NOW YOU CAN

Suggested teaching time:	10–15 minutes	Your actual teaching time:

- Have students read the newspaper clippings.

- Refer students to the Conversation Snapshot on page 114 to review reacting to news about global issues.

- Role-play a conversation with a more confident student. Play the role of Student A and react to an issue with the expression *Can you believe . . . ?* For example, *Can you believe the potential dangers of greenhouse emissions?* It is not necessary to have a complete conversation but only to get the activity going.

A Use the Conversation Strategies

- Then have pairs role-play their own conversations, alternating roles so that each student plays the role of Student A.

- Reinforce the use of the conversation strategies; for example, make sure students appropriately express shock or disapproval with *Can you believe . . . ?*

- Ask volunteers to present their role plays to the class. After each presentation, ask the class *Who has a different reaction to this issue? What is it?*

B Discussion

- Have students skim the list of world problems in the box. Then have the class brainstorm ways to address these problems. Encourage students to indicate as well what is already being done to deal with the problems.

- Then ask additional discussion questions:

  Which of these problems is common in this country?
  What is the country doing to resolve the problem?
  Why is it important for different countries to work together to resolve these problems?

ActiveTeach • Conversation Prompts

Option: [+10 minutes] For homework, have students skim an English-language newspaper, either in print or online, for articles that deal with world problems. Tell students to write down four or five article titles and share them in class. Hint: Tell students to reread the titles of the newspaper clippings for appropriate topic ideas.

Challenge: [+15 minutes] Have students read the list of world problems and then choose one that they feel particularly strongly about. Tell them to write one paragraph describing what countries should do on the national level to deal with the problem and one paragraph describing what countries should do on the international level. Have students share their ideas with the class.

EXTRAS (optional)

- **Pronunciation Booster**
- **Workbook:** Exercises 6–7
- **MySummitLab:** Lesson 2

C **Vocabulary Practice.** There are some errors with phrasal verbs in the article. Make corrections.

UN HUNGER RELIEF

In order to assist local hospitals in their battle against acute malnutrition, the UN World Food Program is carrying ~~through~~ operations out in the southern region, where thousands of children have been going ~~with~~ proper food or without sanitary conditions. The terrible hardship these children have had to put ~~on~~ up with is the result of extreme poverty brought ~~to~~ about by ongoing drought conditions and the increasing number of people who have been recently laid ~~away~~ off in the region because of factory closings. The poorest and most isolated families have run ~~away~~ out of money to buy the staples they need to feed their children. The program has come ~~down~~ up with a plan to provide emergency rations to these families.

D **Vocabulary Practice.** Fill in the blanks with appropriate forms of phrasal verbs from the Vocabulary on page 114.

Drug Discovery Plan to Tap and Help Rain Forests

In Madagascar, off the coast of Africa, as farmers **run out of** (1) usable land, they burn and destroy the rain forests to make more room for farming. If action is not taken, Madagascar's rain forests will soon be **wiped out** (2).

A team of international scientists have **come up with** (3) an interesting idea to help save the forests. Led by researcher Patricia Wright, they are currently negotiating agreements with local government officials to **carry out** (4) research in the area through a program called "The Drug Discovery and Biodiversity Program." The program will study local traditional healing methods from a scientific point of view. Researchers believe the rain forests of Madagascar may be home to sources of new drugs that will fight the numerous illnesses that millions of people **come down with** (5) each year, such as malaria, AIDS, and even the common cold. They are confident their plan will **bring about** (6) much needed economic growth in the area.

Information source: http://news.nationalgeographic.com

NOW YOU CAN   *React to news about global issues*

A **Use the Conversation Strategies.** Read and react to each newspaper clipping about global problems. Use the Conversation Snapshot as a guide. Start like this: "Can you believe …?"

Study Warns of Global Warming Threat
By 2050, more than a million species of animals and plants will have been wiped out because of rising temperatures caused by greenhouse emissions, according to a new study carried out by conservation biologist Chris Thomas.

Philippine Authorities Concerned about New Outbreaks
Hundreds of people have come down with malaria in Mindanao, causing authorities to increase their recent mosquito eradication campaign and further restrict travel there.

Scientists Concerned about South Asia Smog
A vast blanket of pollution stretching across South Asia, brought about by breakneck economic growth, is modifying rainfall patterns and putting the health of hundreds of thousands of people at risk.

Leaders Agree to Do More to Fight Poverty
World leaders gathered in Malta this week to come up with a plan to stamp out poverty by the end of the decade, while protesters fought with police outside.

Famine Sends Thousands into Refugee Camps
A catastrophic drought that has forced more than four million people to go without adequate food is filling United Nations refugee camps to capacity.

B **Discussion.** What do you think could be done to address some of the following world problems? Use phrasal verbs if you can.

hunger	pollution	war	destruction of the rain forests
poverty	illiteracy	disease	global warming

GOAL
Discuss the economic impact of globalization

A **Reading Warm-up.** Are people in your country generally advocates or critics of globalization? Why is that?

B 🎧 Reading. Read the article about economic globalization. Which view do you agree with?

GLOBALIZATION
Experts Debate Pros and Cons

Over the past few decades, more and more countries have opened up their markets, increasingly transforming the world economy into one free-flowing global market. The question is: Is economic globalization good for all?

According to the World Bank, one of its chief proponents, economic globalization has helped reduce poverty in a large number of developing countries. It cites one study that shows increased prosperity contributing to improved education and longer life expectancies in twenty-four developing countries as a result of integration of local economies into the world economy. Home to some three billion people, these twenty-four countries have seen incomes increase at an average rate of five percent—compared to two percent in developed countries.

Globalization advocates claim economies in developing countries will benefit from new opportunities for small and home-based businesses. For example, small farmers in Brazil who produce cashew nuts that would previously have sold only in local open-air markets can now promote their goods worldwide via the Internet.

Critics take a different view, believing that economic globalization is actually widening the gap between the rich and poor. A study carried out by the U.N.-sponsored World Commission on the Social Dimension of Globalization shows that only a few developing countries have actually benefited from integration into the world economy and that the poor, the illiterate, unskilled workers, and indigenous peoples have been left behind. Furthermore, they maintain that globalization may ultimately threaten emerging businesses. For example, Indian artisans who currently seem to benefit from globalization because they are able to export their products may soon face stiff competition that could put them out of business. When large-scale manufacturers start to produce the same goods, or when superstores like Wal-Mart move in, these small businesses will not be able to keep up and will be crowded out.

One thing is certain about globalization—there is no turning back. Advances in technology combined with more open policies have already created an interconnected world. The challenge now is finding a way to create a kind of globalization that works for the benefit of all.

Information sources: http://econ.worldbank.org and http://news.bbc.co.uk

On your ActiveBook disc: *Reading Glossary* and *Extra Reading Comprehension Questions*

The People Weigh In
The Pew Global Attitudes Project surveyed more than 38,000 people in forty-four countries. Majorities in all countries took a favorable view of growing international trade and business ties. Faster communication and travel, the growing availability of foreign culture, and the wide variety of products were cited as benefits.

Growing Trade and Business Ties

	SEE IT HAPPENING	THINK IT'S GOOD FOR THE COUNTRY
	%	%
Angola	79	89
Argentina	28	60
Bangladesh	31	84
Bolivia	65	77
Brazil	70	73
Bulgaria	42	89
Canada	59	85
China	53	90
Czech Republic	60	84
Egypt	55	67
France	50	88
Germany	58	91
Ghana	70	85
Great Britain	61	87
Guatemala	59	83
Honduras	70	93
India	65	69
Indonesia	73	87
Italy	71	79
Ivory Coast	48	96
Japan	74	72
Jordan	50	52
Kenya	67	90
Lebanon	74	83
Mali	79	95
Mexico	77	79
Nigeria	82	95
Pakistan	63	78
Peru	45	83
Philippines	78	83
Poland	76	78
Russia	75	88
Senegal	74	98
Slovak Republic	51	86
South Africa	69	88
South Korea	77	90
Tanzania	52	82
Turkey	51	82
Uganda	69	95
Ukraine	79	93
United States	67	78
Uzbekistan	84	97
Venezuela	45	86
Vietnam	92	98

Pew Research Center revises its country list each year.

C **Summarize Ideas.** Discuss these questions.

1. According to the article, what are the two opposing views of globalization? What examples are given to illustrate each view? Can you give other examples?

2. According to the survey, in which countries were people the most and least enthusiastic about globalization? What are the main reasons people felt positive about globalization in the survey?

D **Activate Prior Knowledge.** Take the survey and compare the responses in your class. What percentage of the students checked each box? Share your opinions and support your ideas with specific examples.

Do you see the following effects of globalization occurring in your country? Do you think they're beneficial?	I see it occurring.	I think it's beneficial.
1. Growing trade and business ties	☐	☐
2. Faster communication and travel	☐	☐
3. Growing availability of foreign culture	☐	☐
4. Wide variety of products from different parts of the world	☐	☐

3

A Reading Warm-up

Suggested teaching time:	5 minutes	Your actual teaching time:

- Before discussing the questions, make sure students understand that an *advocate* is a supporter. Call on different students to share their opinions. If there are disagreements, encourage students to further explain their points of view.

B 🎧 Reading

Suggested teaching time:	10 minutes	Your actual teaching time:

- Draw the following chart on the board:

Economic Globalization	
Pros	Cons

- To introduce the topic, invite students to predict the pros and cons of economic globalization that will be discussed in the article. Write these in the chart. You may also print out and distribute copies from *ActiveTeach* for students to fill out individually.

- Have students read and listen to the article. As they read, tell them to draw plus signs (+) next to the pros and minus signs (–) next to the cons.

- Have students look at the chart on the board to see if the class expressed any of the same pros and cons that were discussed in the article. Then have volunteers fill in the chart with any additional pros and cons from the article. (pros: Poverty has been reduced in a large number of developing countries. Prosperity has increased, contributing to improved education and longer life expectancies. Small and home-based businesses will benefit from new opportunities. cons: The gap between rich and poor has widened. The poor, the illiterate, unskilled workers, and indigenous peoples have been left behind. Emerging businesses may be threatened by stiff competition that could crowd them out.)

- Ask *According to the article, what is certain about globalization?* (There is no turning back—an interconnected world has already been created.) *What is the challenge?* (to find a way for everyone to benefit)

- For an explanation of a survey on attitudes toward growing international trade and business ties, have students read the box labeled The People Weigh In. Make sure students understand that the numbers in the survey are percentages of each country's population. Then tell students to find their country on the survey. Ask *Are you surprised by the percentages listed next to your country? Why? Why not?*

- Have students read and listen to the article again.

Challenge: [+10 minutes] Have students use the answers to the following questions as the basis for a class discussion: *Do you think that it is possible for everyone to benefit in the competitive global world? Why? Why not?* Then have students speculate about what can be done to ensure that globalization works for the benefit of the most people possible.

 • **Graphic Organizers**
- **Reading Strategies**
- **Reading Speed Calculator**
- **Extra Reading Comprehension Questions**
- **Reading Glossaries**

C Summarize Ideas

Suggested teaching time:	5–10 minutes	Your actual teaching time:

- Discuss the questions as a class. After students answer the questions in the second item, have them speculate about the countries in which people were least enthusiastic about globalization. Ask *Why do you think they were not enthusiastic?*

D Activate Prior Knowledge

Suggested teaching time:	5–10 minutes	Your actual teaching time:

- Have a volunteer read the items in the survey. Then have students take the survey individually.

- Bring the class together and have students share their opinions. Encourage them to support their ideas with examples.

- Then determine the percentage of students that checked each box.

Option: [+15 minutes] Have students ask five people the survey questions and bring the results to class. Then combine the results of all the respondents and calculate percentages. Ask *Are the percentages for the first question close to the percentages for your country in Exercise B? If not, why do you think the percentages differ?*

E 🎧 Vocabulary

Suggested teaching time:	5–10 minutes	Your actual teaching time:

- Have students skim the economic terms. Then have them listen and practice.

- Elicit example sentences for *employment rate, income,* and *imports*. Clarify meanings as needed.

- Then call on students to use the different economic terms to make statements about their country. For example, *The standard of living in this country is improving rapidly.*

- Then have students listen and practice again.

ActiveTeach • **Vocabulary-Building Strategies**

F 🎧 Listening

Suggested teaching time:	5 minutes	Your actual teaching time:

- Explain that each of the four conversations illustrates one of the economic terms from the Vocabulary.

- Have students listen to each conversation and then write the economic term from the Vocabulary. Have students listen again to check their work. Go over the answers as a class.

- Then ask pairs to create a statement summarizing the situation described in each conversation. Have pairs share their statements with the class. (Possible answers: 1. The unemployment rate has gone up since the factory closed. 2. The standard of living in the country they visited was very low. 3. Imports are cheaper than local products, but foreign beef treated with growth hormones may not be safe. 4. An investment in horse farms in Ireland can make a huge profit.)

Language note: Students should be able to complete the exercise without understanding every word. You may want to share the following definitions if students ask about specific expressions. *How come* is a question format that means *why*. *Stick with something* means *continue to support something*. *Go in on something* means *participate in something*.

Option: [+10 –15 minutes] Assign pairs one of the economic terms from the Vocabulary. Have them create a conversation illustrating the term, using the conversations in Exercise F as models. Remind students not to include the actual term in their conversation. The class will try to guess the terms when pairs present their conversations.

AUDIOSCRIPT

For audioscript, see page AS13.

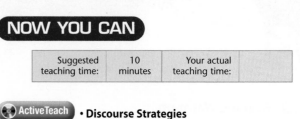

NOW YOU CAN

Suggested teaching time:	10 minutes	Your actual teaching time:

ActiveTeach • **Discourse Strategies**

A Notepadding

- Have a volunteer read the list of international companies. Ask *Are there any companies you've never heard of?* Have students explain what each company does.

- Then have students list three foreign companies that do business in their country—either companies on the list or their own examples. Have students list the company's products and then summarize the general response of the public to the companies or their products.

Culture note: BP is one of the top four oil companies in the world. Coca-Cola is a U.S. carbonated cola soft drink that has the most famous trademark in the world. Daewoo is a leading South Korean international trading company specializing in chemicals, textiles, metals, and steel. IKEA is a Swedish retailer that specializes in affordable home furnishings. Nestle, headquartered in Switzerland, is the world's largest food and beverage company. Sony is a Japanese electronics corporation, one of the world's largest producers of consumer electronics. Starbucks, headquartered in the United States, is a very popular chain of coffee shops. The Gap is a popular U.S. clothing store. Volkswagen is a German automobile manufacturer, one of the world's four largest car producers.

B Discussion

- Ask volunteers to read the statements. Then invite students to share the benefits or problems created by the foreign businesses or products they listed in Exercise A Notepadding.

- Take a poll. Ask *Do you think globalization is good or bad for your economy?* Then call on individual students to back up their point of view.

Challenge: [+15 –20 minutes] Have students think of the most popular foreign product or company in their country. Tell them to write a paragraph describing the impact it has had on the country's economy. Then have students read their paragraphs to the class. On the board, write the name of each product or company that students discuss. Encourage students to comment on each other's choices. Then take a vote to see which is truly the most popular product or company.

EXTRAS (optional)

- **Workbook:** Exercises 8–10
- **MySummitLab:** Lesson 3

CN Corpus Notes: *Make an investment* is a frequent collocation. For example, *You've made a wise investment.* The preposition *in* frequently follows *investment.* For example, *private investment in inner cities.*

E 🎧 **Vocabulary. Economic Terms.** Listen and practice.
⁵:²⁴

standard of living level of wealth, comfort, and access to goods
  Many hope globalization will raise the standard of living in developing countries.

CN **investment** money put into a company or business in order to make a profit and make a business successful
  The World Bank believes that foreign investment will benefit local economies.

employment rate the percentage of people who have jobs

unemployment rate the percentage of people who don't have jobs
  Advocates of globalization cite an increased employment rate in countries that have been integrated into the world economy. Critics, however, worry that the unemployment rate will, in fact, increase.

income money earned from work or investments

wages money paid according to the number of hours worked
  The World Bank reports that on average, incomes have improved in developing countries, but critics complain that inadequate wages are keeping the poorest people stuck in poverty.

imports products brought to one country from another to be sold

exports products sent from one country to another to be sold
  The promise of globalization is that old protective barriers against trade will give way to a freer flow of imports and exports.

F 🎧 **Listening. Listen to Activate Vocabulary.** Listen to the conversations. After each conversation, determine which economic term from the Vocabulary best describes the topic of the conversation. Listen again if necessary.
⁵:²⁵

Conversation 1: _unemployment rate_   **Conversation 3:** _imports (or exports)_

Conversation 2: _standard of living_   **Conversation 4:** _investment_

NOW YOU CAN *Discuss the economic impact of globalization*

A **Notepadding.** On your notepad, write the names of at least three foreign companies that do business in your country. What is the general response of the public to these companies or their products: positive, negative, or neutral?

Name of business / Product	General response of public

Some well-known international companies
BP (British Petroleum)
Coca-Cola
Daewoo
IKEA
Nestle
Sony
Starbucks
The Gap
Volkswagen

B **Discussion.** What benefits or problems have these businesses and products brought to your country? Overall, do you think globalization is good or bad for your economy? Explain. Use the terms from the Vocabulary in your discussion to clarify your ideas.

*"In my opinion, Starbucks hasn't had a particularly strong impact. The stores are small, so they haven't really reduced **unemployment**."*

*"Volkswagen's **investment** in local factories has been good for the country. It's provided **employment** for thousands, and it pays good **wages**. Its products are reliable and affordable, raising the **standard of living** for a lot of people."*

4

GOAL
Discuss the role of English in international communication

Answers will vary, but may include:

A **5:26 Listening. Listen to Summarize.** Listen to four people talking about their views on using English for international communication. Summarize each speaker's opinion.

Speaker 1	Knowing how to speak and understand English is enjoyable.
Speaker 2	English is a necessary tool for communicating with people from all over the world.
Speaker 3	English makes people more equal. It is the language of international business.
Speaker 4	English may not always be the number one international language in the world.

B **5:27 Listening. Draw Conclusions.** Now listen again. Write the number of the speaker you think would be most likely to make each statement. Explain why.

| 4 | "I'm willing to learn whatever language is needed for international communication." |

| 3 | "English makes international communication really fair." |

| 2 | "I really don't mind if I have an accent or make a few mistakes in English." |

| 1 | "There's no other language I'd rather learn than English." |

C **Word Skills. Using a Dictionary.** Use the Key to answer the following questions.

- Which of the verbs can be intransitive? dominate
- Which entries indicate that the word can be used as a part of speech other than a verb? dominate, maximize, neutralize, utilize
- Which two verbs are appropriate for formal use? surpass yourself, utilize
- Which entry includes an antonym (a word that means the opposite)? maximize

---

KEY

Grammar Codes
[C] countable
[U] uncountable
[I] intransitive
[T] transitive
[I,T] intransitive or transitive

Parts of Speech
adj. adjective
adv. adverb
n. noun
v. verb

dom·i·nate /ˈdɑmə͵neɪt/ *v.* [I,T] **1** to control someone or something, or to have more power or importance than them: *Movie directing is a profession dominated by men.* | *New Orleans dominated throughout the game.* **2** [I,T] to be the most important feature of something: *The murder trial has dominated the news this week.* **3** [T] to be larger or more noticeable than anything else in a place or situation: *A pair of red-and-gold boots dominated the display.* —**dominating** /ˈdɑmə͵neɪtɪŋ/ *adj.* —**domination** /͵dɑməˈneɪʃən/ *n.* [U]

max·i·mize /ˈmæksə͵maɪz/ *v.* [T] **1** to increase something as much as possible: *We need to look at how to maximize our cash flow.* | *Diamonds are cut to maximize the stone's beauty.* **2** to CLICK on a special part of a WINDOW on a computer screen so that it becomes as big as the screen —**maximization** /͵mæksəməˈzeɪʃən/ *n.* [U] —compare MINIMIZE

neu·tral·ize /ˈnutrə͵laɪz/ *v.* [T] **1** to prevent something from having any effect: *The Oilers managed to neutralize the other team's defenses.* **2** TECHNICAL to make a substance chemically NEUTRAL: *This fertilizer neutralizes the salts in the soil.* **3** a word meaning to kill someone, especially an enemy in a war, used when you do not want to say "kill" directly: *Government forces neutralized the rebels.* **4** to make a country or population NEUTRAL in war —**neutralization** /͵nutrələˈzeɪʃən/ *n.* [U]

sur·pass /sɚˈpæs/ *v.* [T] **1** to be even better or greater than someone or something else: *In 15 years, China will likely surpass the U.S. as the world's largest market.* | **surpass expectations/hopes/dreams** (=be better than you had expected, hoped etc.) **2 surpass yourself** FORMAL to do something even better than you have ever done before: *Stewart has surpassed himself with his latest novel.*

u·til·ize /ˈyuṭl͵aɪz/ *v.* [T] FORMAL to use something for a particular purpose: *The old fire station could be utilized as a theater.* —**utilizable** *adj.* —**utilization** /͵yuṭl-əˈzeɪʃən/ *n.* [U]

Excerpted from *Longman Advanced American Dictionary* © 2007

4

A 🎧 Listening

Suggested teaching time:	10 minutes	Your actual teaching time:

- To introduce the topic, ask:
  What is the top language for international communication today? (English)
  Do you know what used to be the top international language? (French)
  What language do you think will be the top international language in the future? (Possible answer: Chinese)
  Why do you think it's important to be able to communicate in the top international language?

- Have students listen to the four speakers. Then have students listen again. Stop after each speaker and have students summarize his or her opinion.

- Go over the answers as a class.

Option: [+10 minutes] Ask individual students *Why are you taking this English class?* Write their responses on the board and have students compare reasons. Then ask *Are you concerned about perfecting your accent in English? Why? Why not?*

AUDIOSCRIPT

For audioscript, see page AS13.

🔘 **ActiveTeach** • Listening Strategies

B 🎧 Listening

Suggested teaching time:	5–10 minutes	Your actual teaching time:

- Tell students to read the statements. Then have them listen again and match each speaker to the most appropriate statement.

- Have students compare answers with a partner. Then ask:
  Which of these statements might you make? Why?
  Which speaker do you disagree with most? Why?

C Word Skills

Suggested teaching time:	10 minutes	Your actual teaching time:

- Have students look at the Key. Review the different terms by asking the following questions:
  What are countable nouns? Give an example. (nouns that you can count: man, idea, machine)
  What are uncountable nouns? Give an example. (nouns that you cannot count: knowledge, furniture, water)
  What are transitive verbs? Give an example. (verbs that require a direct object to complete their meaning: hold, sell, write)
  What are intransitive verbs? Give an example. (verbs that do not require a direct object to complete their meaning: arrive, fall, sleep)
  What are some examples of verbs that can be transitive or intransitive? (leave, move, wash)

- Have students work individually to answer the bulleted questions. Then have them compare answers with a partner.

- Ask:
  Which entries include a noun form? (dominate—domination; maximize—maximization; neutralize—neutralization; utilize—utilization)
  Which nouns are countable and which are uncountable? (The nouns are all uncountable.)
  Which entries include an adjective form? (dominate—dominating; utilize—utilizable)

Option: [+10–15 minutes] Have pairs look in an English-language dictionary and find examples of entries that include the different items in the Key. Have students write down these examples or bookmark them in the dictionary to share with another pair.

Challenge: [+5–10 minutes] Have pairs write five sentences, using verb, noun, or adjective forms of the dictionary entries. Circulate and assist as needed.

D Word Skills Practice

Suggested teaching time:	5–10 minutes	Your actual teaching time:	

- Have students do the exercise individually. Tell them to refer to the dictionary entries in Exercise C to complete each sentence. Remind students to think carefully about the context to decide what part of speech is needed in each sentence.

- Tell pairs to compare answers. Then bring the class together and call on students to identify the part of speech of each word they wrote. (1. maximize—verb; 2. domination—noun; 3. utilize—verb; 4. surpass—verb; 5. neutralize—verb)

- Reread item 5 and then elicit names of countries where English is used because the populations speak different languages. If necessary, give as examples India and several countries in Africa, including Ghana, Nigeria, South Africa, and Zambia.

NOW YOU CAN

Suggested teaching time:	15–20 minutes	Your actual teaching time:	

A Frame Your Ideas

- Have a student read the items in the survey. Clarify meanings as needed. Elicit ideas for item 10, other English skills. For example, *reading original English-language literature.*

- After students complete the survey individually, have them compare answers with a partner and give reasons for their choices.

B Discussion

- Ask volunteers to read the statements. Encourage students to find the words from the dictionary entries in Exercise C. (statement 1: surpassed, statement 2: dominate, statement 3: neutralize)

- Invite students to respond to the statements. Ask for a show of hands to determine which statement most students agree with.

- Then have the class answer the question about the changing use of English.

C Express Your Ideas

- Have students read the questions and make some quick notes. Tell students to refer to the skills in Exercise A Frame Your Ideas and to think about the opinions presented in Exercise B on page 118 for ideas.

- Then have students write one to two paragraphs to answer the questions.

- If possible, have students read their paragraphs to the class. Otherwise, collect the papers and give students individual feedback.

Option: [+15 –20 minutes] Repeat the question from Exercise B Discussion: *How do you think the use of English as an international language will change over the next fifty years?* Have students write a paragraph answering the question. Encourage them to use the dictionary entries from Exercise C on page 118 where appropriate. Collect student writing and give individual feedback.

EXTRAS (optional)

- **Workbook: Exercises 11–13**
- **MySummitLab: Lesson 4**

D **Word Skills Practice.** Use the dictionary entries to find words to complete each sentence. Use the context of the sentence to determine the appropriate meaning and the correct part of speech.

1. The import-export company enrolls all new employees in an intensive English program designed to ____maximize____ the amount of time they are exposed to written and spoken English.

2. Some have argued that the ____domination____ of world communication by the English language has reduced the use of other languages.

3. Language experts point out that students of English are more likely to ____utilize____ their English skills to speak with other non-native speakers than with native speakers.

4. With approximately 100 million Chinese Internet users, it's not surprising that six of the world's top 20 most popular websites are in Chinese and that the number of websites in Chinese will soon ____surpass____ the number in English.

5. In some countries with populations who speak different languages, English is used to ____neutralize____ any arguments about which language to use in government and business transactions.

NOW YOU CAN *Discuss the role of English in international communication*

A **Frame Your Ideas.** Complete the survey. Rate how important each English skill is to you, with 1 being very important, 2 somewhat important, and 3 not important. Then compare and explain your answers with a partner.

English Skills	Importance		
1. understanding the customs of the U.S., Britain, Australia, or other English-speaking countries	1	2	3
2. sounding like a native speaker	1	2	3
3. watching movies or TV without subtitles in one's own language	1	2	3
4. being able to participate in business meetings and other business communication	1	2	3
5. reading academic journals and writing papers	1	2	3
6. functioning socially, such as meeting people or knowing how to be polite	1	2	3
7. expressing opinions precisely	1	2	3
8. being able to travel easily in English-speaking countries	1	2	3
9. teaching English to others	1	2	3
10. other	1	2	3

B **Discussion.** Do you agree with any of the statements below? How do you think the use of English as an international language will change over the next fifty years?

"English will soon be surpassed by another language as the number one international language in the world."

"The use of English as an international language is a reflection of how the United States and Britain dominate the world economically and culturally. If that changes, English will decline as an international language."

"Using English is actually an excellent way to neutralize any difficulties in international communication."

C **Express Your Ideas.** On a separate sheet of paper, write about the importance of learning English in your life. What role do you hope English will play in your life? What are your goals? What do you plan to do to achieve them? Then share your ideas with your classmates.

Stative verbs

amaze	contain	feel*	look*	please	smell*
appear*	cost	forget	look like	possess	sound
appreciate	desire	hate	love	prefer	suppose
astonish	dislike	have*	matter	realize	surprise
be*	doubt*	hear	mean	recognize	taste*
believe	envy	imagine	mind	remember*	think*
belong	equal	include*	need	resemble	understand
care	exist	know	owe	see*	want*
consist of	fear	like	own	seem	weigh*

* These verbs also have action meanings. Example: *I see a tree.* (non-action) *I'm seeing her tomorrow.* (action)

Transitive phrasal verbs

Some transitive phrasal verbs have more than one meaning. Not all are included here.

SEPARABLE

blow sth. **out**   stop a flame by blowing on it

blow sth. **up**   1 make sth. explode   2 fill sth. with air, e.g., a balloon   3 make sth. larger, e.g., a photo

bring sth. **about**   make sth. happen

bring sth. **back**   1 return sth. to a store   2 revive or renew sth., e.g., a custom or tradition

bring sth. **out**   1 introduce a new product   2 make a quality more noticeable

bring s.o. **up**   raise a child

bring sth. **up**   start to talk about an issue

burn sth. **down**   burn a structure completely

call s.o. **back**   return a phone call

call sth. **off**   cancel sth.

call s.o. **up**   call s.o. on the phone

carry sth. **out**   conduct a plan

check s.o./sth. **out**   look at s.o. or sth. more closely

cheer s.o. **up**   make s.o. feel happier

clean s.o./sth. **up**   clean s.o. or sth. completely

clear sth. **up**   clarify sth.

close sth. **down**   force a business or institution to close

cover sth. **up**   1 cover sth. completely   2 change facts to avoid responsibility

cross sth. **out**   draw a line through sth.

cut sth. **down**   make sth. fall by cutting, e.g., a tree

cut sth. **off**   1 remove sth. by cutting   2 stop the supply of sth.

cut s.o. **off**   interrupt s.o who is speaking

dream sth. **up**   invent or think of a new idea

drink sth. **up**   drink a beverage completely

drop s.o./sth. **off**   leave s.o. or sth. somewhere

empty sth. **out**   empty sth. completely

figure s.o./sth. **out**   understand s.o. or sth. after some thought

fill s.o. **in**   tell s.o. about recent events

fill sth. **out**   complete a form

fill sth. **up**   fill a container completely

find sth. **out**   learn new information

follow sth. **through**   do everything to complete a task

get sth. **across**   help s.o. understand an idea

give sth. **away**   give sth. you do not need or want

give sth. **back**   return sth. to its owner

give sth. **out**   distribute sth.

give sth. **up**   quit doing sth.

hand sth. **in**   submit work, e.g., to a boss or a teacher

hand sth. **out**   distribute sth.

hang sth. **up**   put sth. on a hanger or hook, e.g., clothes

help s.o. **out**   assist s.o.

keep s.o./sth. **away**   cause s.o. or sth. to stay at a distance

lay s.o. **off**   fire s.o. because of economic conditions

leave sth. **on**   1 not turn sth. off, e.g., an appliance   2 not remove sth. such as clothing or jewelry

leave sth. **out**   omit sth.

let s.o. **down**   disappoint s.o.

let s.o./sth. **in**   allow s.o. or sth. to enter

let s.o. **off**   allow s.o. to leave a bus, car, taxi, etc.

let s.o./sth. **out**   allow s.o. or sth. to leave

light sth. **up**   illuminate sth.

look s.o./sth. **over**   examine s.o. or sth.

look s.o./sth. **up**   1 try to find s.o.   2 try to find sth. in a book, the Internet, etc.

make sth. **up**   create a fictional story

pass sth. **out**   distribute sth.

pass sth. **up**   decide not to take an opportunity

pay s.o. **off**   bribe s.o.

pay sth. **off**   pay back money one owes

pick s.o./sth. **out**   identify or choose s.o. or sth.

pick s.o. **up**   stop a vehicle so s.o. can get in

pick s.o./sth. **up**   lift s.o. or sth.

pick sth. **up**   1 get or buy sth. from somewhere   2 learn sth. new   3 get an infectious disease

point s.o./sth. **out**   show s.o or sth. to another person

put sth. **away**   put sth. in its appropriate place

put sth. **back**   return sth. to its original place

put s.o./sth. **down**   1 stop holding or lifting s.o. or sth.   2 insult s.o.

put sth. **off**   delay or postpone sth.

put sth. **on**   get dressed or place sth. on one's body

put sth. **together**   1 put sth. on a wall   2 build sth.

put sth. **up**   build or erect sth.

set sth. **off**   cause sth. to explode

set sth. **up**   1 establish a new business, organization, etc.   2 prepare equipment for use

show s.o./sth. **off**   display the best qualities of s.o. or sth.

shut sth. **off**   stop a machine or supply

straighten sth. **up**   make sth. neat

switch sth. **on**   start a machine, turn on a light, etc.

take sth. **away**   remove sth.

take sth. **back**   1 return sth. to a store   2 accept sth. returned by another person

take sth. **down**   remove sth. that is hanging

take sth. **in**   1 notice and remember sth.   2 make a clothing item smaller

take sth. **off**   remove clothing, jewelry, etc.

take s.o. **on**   hire s.o.

take sth. **on**   agree to do a task

take s.o. **out**   invite s.o. somewhere and pay for his/her meal, show, etc.

take sth. **up**   start doing an activity habitually

talk sth. **over**   discuss sth.

tear sth. **down**   destroy sth.

tear sth. **up**   tear sth. into small pieces
think sth. **over**   consider sth.
think sth. **up**   invent or think of a new idea
throw sth. **away**   put sth. in the garbage
throw sth. **out**   put sth. in the garbage
touch sth. **up**   improve sth. with very small changes
try sth. **on**   try clothing to see if it fits
try sth. **out**   use sth. to see if one likes it or if it works
turn sth. **around**   **1** turn so the front is at the back   **2** cause things to get better
turn s.o./sth. **down**   reject s.o. or sth.
turn sth. **down**   lower the volume, heat, etc.

turn sth. **in**   submit a paper, application, etc.
turn sth. **off**   stop a machine, light, etc.
turn s.o. **off**   cause s.o. to lose interest (inf.)
turn sth. **on**   start a machine, light, etc.
turn sth. **out**   make or manufacture sth.
turn sth. **over**   turn sth. so the bottom is at the top
turn sth. **up**   raise the volume, heat, etc.
use sth. **up**   use sth. completely
wake s.o. **up**   cause s.o. to stop sleeping
wipe sth. **out**   remove or destroy sth.
work sth. **out**   **1** resolve a problem   **2** calculate a math problem
write sth. **down**   write sth. to have a record of it

ALWAYS SEPARATED

ask s.o. **over**   invite s.o. to one's home
bring s.o./sth. **down**   remove a ruler or government from power
do sth. **over**   do sth. again
keep sth. **on**   not remove sth. such as clothing or jewelry

see sth. **through**   complete a task
start sth. **over**   begin sth. again
talk s.o. **into** sth.   persuade s.o. to do sth.

INSEPARABLE

cater to s.o.   provide what s.o. wants or needs
carry on sth.   continue sth. another person has started
come across s.o./sth.   find s.o. or sth. unexpectedly
count on s.o./sth.   depend on s.o. or sth.
do without s.o./sth.   live without s.o. or sth. one needs or wants
go after s.o./sth.   pursue s.o. or sth.

go over sth.   examine sth. carefully
go without sth.   live without sth. one needs or wants
run into s.o.   meet s.o. unexpectedly
run into sth.   accidentally hit or crash into sth.
stick with s.o.   stay close to s.o.
stick with sth.   continue doing sth. as before

Intransitive phrasal verbs

Some intransitive phrasal verbs have more than one meaning. Not all are included here.

blow up   **1** explode   **2** suddenly become very angry
break down   stop functioning
break out   start suddenly, e.g., a war, disease, or fire
burn down   burn completely
call back   return a phone call
carry on   **1** continue doing sth.   **2** behave in a silly or emotional way
catch on   become popular
check in   report one's arrival at an airport or hotel
check out   pay one's bill and leave a hotel
cheer up   become happier
clear up   become better, e.g., a rash or the weather
close down   stop operating, e.g., a factory or a school
come along   accompany s.o.
come back   return
come in   enter
come off   become unattached
come out   **1** appear, e.g., the sun   **2** be removed, e.g., a stain
dress up   wear more formal clothes or a costume
drop in   visit unexpectedly
drop out   quit a class, school, or program
eat out   eat in a restaurant
empty out   empty completely
fall off   become unattached
fill out   become bigger
fill up   become completely full
find out   learn new information
follow through   continue working on sth. until it is completed
fool around   have fun or not be serious
get ahead   make progress or succeed
get along   to not argue
get back   return from a place
get together   meet somewhere with a friend or acquaintance
get up   get out of bed
give up   quit
go along   **1** accompany s.o.   **2** agree
go back   return

go off   explode; make a sudden noise
go on   continue to talk about or describe sth.
go out   **1** leave a building   **2** leave one's home to meet people, enjoy entertainment, etc.
go up   be built
grow up   become an adult
help out   do sth. helpful
hang up   end a phone call
hold on   wait during a phone call
keep away   stay at a distance
keep on   continue
keep up   go or think as fast as another person
lie down   rest on a bed
light up   **1** begin to shine brightly   **2** look pleased or happy
make up   end an argument and reestablish a friendly relationship
pass out   become unconscious
pay off   be worthwhile
pick up   improve, e.g., the economy
play around   have fun or not be serious
run out   no longer in supply
show up   appear
sign up   register
sit down   sit
slip up   make a mistake
stand up   rise to one's feet
start over   begin again
stay up   not go to bed
straighten up   make neat
take off   depart by plane
turn in   go to bed (inf.)
turn out   have a particular result
turn up   appear
wake up   stop sleeping
watch out   be careful
work out   **1** exercise   **2** be resolved; end successfully

Three-word phrasal verbs

Some three-word phrasal verbs have more than one meaning. Not all are included here.

catch up on sth. **1** do sth. one didn't have time to do earlier
2 get the most recent information
catch up with s.o.   exchange information about recent activities
check up on s.o.   make sure s.o. is OK
come away with sth.   learn sth. useful from s.o. or sth.
come down to sth.   be the most important point or idea
come down with sth.   get an illness
come up against s.o./sth.   be faced with a difficult person or
situation
come up with sth.   think of an idea, plan, or solution
face up to sth.   accept an unpleasant truth
fall back on sth.   use an old idea because new ideas have failed
follow through on sth.   continue doing sth. until it is completed
get around to sth.   finally do sth.
get away with sth.   avoid the consequences of a wrong act
get back at s.o.   harm s.o. because he / she harmed you
give up on s.o.   stop hoping that s.o. will change

give up on sth.   stop trying to make sth. happen
go along with sth.   agree to do sth.
go through with sth.   do sth. difficult or painful
grow out of sth.   stop doing sth. as one becomes an adult
keep up with s.o.   stay in regular contact
look down on s.o.   think one is better than another person
look out for s.o.   protect s.o.
look up to s.o.   admire or respect s.o.
make up for sth.   do sth. to apologize
put up with s.o./sth.   accept s.o. or sth. without complaining
run out of sth.   no longer have enough of sth.
stand up for sth.   support an idea or a principle
stand up to s.o.   refuse to let s.o. treat anyone badly
team up with s.o.   do a task together
think back on s.o./sth.   think about and remember s.o. or sth.
walk out on s.o.   end a relationship with a wife, boyfriend, etc.
watch out for s.o./sth.   protect s.o. or sth.

Verb forms: overview

Summary of verb forms

	Present time	Past time	Future time
Simple	**Simple present** walk / walks	**Simple past** walked	**Simple future** will walk
Continuous	**Present continuous** am walking / is walking / are walking	**Past continuous** was walking / were walking	**Future continuous** will be walking
Perfect	**Present perfect** have walked / has walked	**Past perfect** had walked	**Future perfect** will have walked
Perfect continuous	**Present perfect continuous** have been walking / has been walking	**Past perfect continuous** had been walking	**Future perfect continuous** will have been walking

Simple verb forms: usage

	Present time	Past time	Future time
Simple verb forms describe habitual actions or events that occur at a definite time.	**Simple present**[1] **Habitual action** *The department **meets** once a month to review the status of projects.*	**Simple past** **Completed action that occurred at a definite time in the past** *Last year researchers **discovered** a new cancer treatment.*	**Simple future**[3] **Action that will occur at a definite time in the future** *Next year they **will offer** a course on global trade.*
	Facts and generalizations *The Earth **rotates** around the sun every 365 days.*	**Habitual action in the past**[2] *When I was young we **visited** my grandparents every week.*	**Habitual action in the future** *Next month I**'ll go** to the gym three times a week.*

[1] The simple present can also express a future action: *Her flight arrives this evening at eight.*

[2] <u>Used to</u> and <u>would</u> also express habitual actions in the past: *When I was a child, we used to spend the summer in the mountains. In the mornings we would go hiking and in the afternoons we would swim in a nearby lake.*

[3] <u>Be going to</u> can also express a future action: *Next year they are going to offer a course on global trade.*

Continuous verb forms: usage

	Present time	Past time	Future time
Continuous verb forms describe continuous actions or events that occur at a definite time.	**Present continuous**[*] **Action in progress now** *The business managers are discussing next year's budget right now.*	**Past continuous** **Action in progress at a definite time in the past** *None of the computers were working when I came in this morning.*	**Future continuous** **Action that will be in progress during a definite time in the future** *We'll be listening to the speech when you arrive.*

[*]The present continuous can also express a future plan: *They're getting married next month.*

Perfect verb forms: usage

	Present time	Past time	Future time
Perfect verb forms describe actions or events in relation to other time frames.	**Present perfect**[*] **Completed action that occurred at an indefinite time before the present** *She has made many contributions to the field.* **Recently completed action** *He has just published an article about his findings.* **Uncompleted action (action that began in the past, continues into the present, and may continue into the future)** *They have studied ancient cultures for many years.*	**Past perfect** **Action that occurred at some point before a definite time in the past** *By 2002, he had started a new business.* **Action that occurred before another past action** *They had already finished medical school when the war broke out.*	**Future perfect** **Action that will be completed by some point at a definite time in the future** *By this time next year, I will have completed my research.*

[*]Many statements in the present perfect can also be stated correctly using the simple past, depending on the speaker's perspective: *She made many contributions to the field.*

Perfect continuous verb forms: usage

	Present time	Past time	Future time
Perfect continuous verb forms describe continuous actions or events in relation to other time frames.	**Present perfect continuous** **Uncompleted continuous action (action that began in the past, continues into the present, and may continue into the future)** *She has been lecturing about that topic since 2001.* **Very recently completed action** *The workers have been protesting. They're finished now.*	**Past perfect continuous** **Continuous action that occurred before another past action or time** *By 2005, researchers had been seeking a cure for AIDS for more than twenty years.*	**Future perfect continuous** **Continuous action that occurred before another action or time in the future** *When the new director takes over, I will have been working at this company for ten years.*

Pronunciation table

These are the pronunciation symbols used in *Summit 2*.

	Vowels					Consonants			
symbol	key word		symbol	key word	symbol	key word		symbol	key word
i	beat, feed		ə	banana, among	p	pack, happy		z	zip, please, goes
ɪ	bit, did		ɚ	shirt, murder	b	back, rubber		ʃ	ship, machine,
eɪ	date, paid		aɪ	bite, cry, buy, eye	t	tie			station, special,
ɛ	bet, bed		aʊ	about, how	d	die			discussion
æ	bat, bad		ɔɪ	voice, boy	k	came, key, quick		ʒ	measure, vision
ɑ	box, odd, father		ɪr	beer	g	game, guest		h	hot, who
ɔ	bought, dog		ɛr	bare	ʧ	church, nature,		m	men, some
oʊ	boat, road		ɑr	bar		watch		n	sun, know,
ʊ	book, good		ɔr	door	ʤ	judge, general,			pneumonia
u	boot, food, student		ʊr	tour		major		ŋ	sung, ringing
ʌ	but, mud, mother				f	fan, photograph		w	wet, white
					v	van		l	light, long
					θ	thing, breath		r	right, wrong
					ð	then, breathe		y	yes, use, music
					s	sip, city,		t̬	butter, bottle
						psychology		t̚	button

Pronunciation Booster

The *Pronunciation Booster* is optional. It provides more information about pronunciation as well as additional practice.

Unit 1

Sentence stress and intonation: review

Sentence stress
Remember: Content words are generally stressed in a sentence.

I've **ALWAYS DREAMED** about **BEING** a **PHOTOGRAPHER**.
You've been **TALKING** about **DOING** that for **YEARS**!
Have you **EVER THOUGHT** about a **CAREER** in **LAW**?

Content words

nouns	photographer, Robert, career
verbs	think, study, discuss
adjectives	important, young, successful
adverbs	carefully, ever, recently
possessive pronouns	ours, yours, theirs
demonstrative pronouns	this, that, these
reflexive pronouns	myself, yourself, ourselves
interrogative pronouns	who, what, why

In compound nouns, stress only the first word.

She has just been accepted to a top **BUSINESS** school.

Have you made any progress with your **JOB** search?

Intonation
Lower pitch after the stressed syllable in the last stressed word in statements, commands, and information questions. Raise pitch after the last stressed syllable in <u>yes</u>/<u>no</u> questions.

I love the outdoors, so I've decided to become a naturalist.

What's stopping you?

Tell me something about your experience.

Have you made plans to get married?

If the last syllable in the sentence is stressed, lengthen the vowel and lower pitch. In <u>yes</u>/<u>no</u> questions, lengthen the vowel and raise pitch.

I just gave notice at the bank.

Have you decided on a career?

A 🎧 6:02 Listen and practice.

1. I've always dreamed about being a photographer.
2. You've been talking about doing that for years!
3. Have you ever thought about a career in law?

Pronunciation Booster

Note about the Pronunciation Booster

Many will elect to do the Pronunciation Booster as self-study. If you choose to use the Pronunciation Booster as a classroom activity instead, included in these pages are teaching notes for the pronunciation presentations and exercises.

Unit 1

Sentence stress and intonation: review

• Have a student read the title of the box. Remind students that sentence stress refers to the words that are emphasized in a sentence. Intonation refers to the rising or falling tone the speaker uses.

Sentence stress

• Read aloud the first explanation about content words. Review that content words are words that carry the basic meaning of a sentence. Point out that capital letters are used to show which words are stressed.

• Have students read the categories and examples of content words in the Content words note. For further review, have students suggest additional words for each category.

• Read the first example sentence, putting stress on the capitalized content words, and have students repeat. Then ask volunteers to read the next two example sentences. Make necessary corrections, and have students repeat.

• Focus on the note about compound nouns. Make sure students understand that a compound noun is made up of two or more words. Have students read aloud the example sentences in the note, putting appropriate stress on the first word. Point out that the large dot above a capitalized word shows which syllable gets the most stress.

• Elicit additional compound nouns and write them on the board. (Possible answers: dream job, traffic jam, cell phone) Have volunteers say the compound nouns aloud, putting appropriate stress on the first word of each compound noun.

Intonation

• Have students read the first explanation. If necessary, review that pitch refers to how high or low a sound is.

• Point out that the last stressed word in a sentence is usually the last content word. Have students study the example sentences. Explain that a falling line indicates lower pitch. A rising line indicates higher pitch. Ask:

> *What is the last stressed word in each sentence?*
> (naturalist, experience, stopping, married)
>
> *What type of sentence is each example?*
> (statement, command, information question, <u>yes</u> / <u>no</u> question)

• Summarize on the board:

> statements
> commands } lower pitch falls after last
> information   stressed syllable
> questions
>
> <u>yes</u> / <u>no</u> questions   raise pitch after last stressed
>   syllable

Call on volunteers to read each example sentence, using the correct intonation.

• Have students read the second explanation to themselves. Explain that an arrow pointing downward indicates a lengthened vowel and lowered pitch. An arrow pointing upward indicates a lengthened vowel and rising pitch.

• Call on volunteers to read the example sentences. Offer corrections as needed, and have students repeat. Make sure students hear how the last syllable is stressed in each of the sentences.

A 🎧 Listen and practice.

• First listening: Have students listen and study the examples.

• Second listening: Have students listen and repeat chorally.

Note: This procedure for first and second listening is repeated in each unit.

Unit 4

Shifting emphatic stress

- Ask a volunteer to read the explanation. Point out that the focus of a sentence can change depending on the emphatic stress you use.

- Invite a volunteer to read the first conversation with you. Have the student read Student A's line, and you read Student B's. Then have students repeat B's line chorally.

- Have pairs read the remaining conversations, alternating parts. Circulate and offer corrections as needed.

- Bring the class together and discuss the emphatic stress and its meaning in each conversation. (Conversations 1 and 2 focus on the adverbs *enough* and *too* to show how critical each person is of other people. Conversation 3 focuses on the pronoun *I'm* to emphasize which speaker is too critical. Conversation 4 focuses on the verb *think* to show that the person isn't sure whether he or she is too critical.)

A ∩ **Listen and practice.**

- Refer to the procedure for Exercise A on page TP2.

B **Study each conversation ...**

- Instruct pairs to read the conversations, alternating parts. Tell them to use emphatic stress as shown.

∩ **Now practice reading ...**

- Have students read each response aloud and then listen for confirmation.

- For further practice, call on volunteers to read the conversations again, placing emphatic stress on different key words. Discuss how the focus of a sentence shifts when the emphatic stress is changed.

∩ **Option:** To provide more practice, refer students to the Conversation Snapshot on page 40. Have pairs read the conversation aloud, placing emphatic stress on key words. Tell students to underline the words they put stress on. Then have them listen to the Conversation Snapshot to compare their reading. (CD 2, Track 15)

 • **Pronunciation Activities**

Unit 5

Linking sounds

- On the board, write /z/, /s/, and /ɪz/. Elicit or produce the sound of each symbol. Then call on volunteers to read the words in each column of the Remember note. Correct pronunciation as needed. If necessary, have students repeat the final sound in each word to hear the difference in the endings. Then read the explanation in the Remember note aloud.

- Have students study the first explanation and the example sentences. Read each sentence aloud, and have students repeat chorally.

- Tell students to study the second explanation and the example sentences. Read each sentence aloud, and have students repeat chorally.

Option: For additional practice in linking the /z/ sound to the first sound in the word that follows, write on the board:

> Superstitions‿about animals are popular in this country.
> I recycled the bottles‿last night.

Have students repeat. For additional practice in linking the /s/ and /ɪz/ sounds to the first sound in the word that follows, write on the board:

> The dog sleeps‿on the kitchen floor.
> My shirt matches‿my shoes.

Have students repeat.

A ∩ **Listen and practice.**

- Refer to the procedure for Exercise A on page TP2.

Unit 4

Shifting emphatic stress

You can shift stress within a sentence to change emphasis. Place emphatic stress on key words to get your meaning across.

A: I think I'm too critical of other people.
B: Really? I don't think I'm critical **ENOUGH**.

A: I don't think I'm critical enough.
B: Really? I think I'm **TOO** critical.

A: I think I'm too critical of other people.
B: I don't see you that way at all. **I'M** too critical.

A: I think I'm too critical of other people.
B: Really? Not me . . . At least I don't **THINK** I'm too critical.

A 🎧 6:10 Listen and practice.

1. I don't think I'm critical **ENOUGH**.
2. I think I'm **TOO** critical.
3. **I'M** too critical.
4. I don't **THINK** I'm too critical.

B Study each conversation, paying attention to emphatic stress.

1. "You know what my problem is? I'm a perfectionist."
   RESPONSE: Well, **I'M** just the opposite.

2. "You know what my problem is? I'm a perfectionist."
   RESPONSE: Not me. I'm just the **OPPOSITE**.

3. "There goes Carla again—yelling at Phil."
   RESPONSE: I'm not surprised. She's **ALWAYS** angry about **SOMETHING**.

4. "Why is Carla yelling at Phil?"
   RESPONSE: It's just the way she is. She's always **ANGRY** about something.

5. "Why was John so angry this morning?"
   RESPONSE: I don't know. I've **NEVER** seen him lose his temper like that.

6. "Can you believe how angry John was this morning?"
   RESPONSE: Not really. I've never seen him lose his temper like **THAT**.

🎧 6:11 Now practice reading each response aloud, using emphatic stress as shown. Listen to compare.*

Unit 5

Linking sounds

Link plural noun endings to the first sound in the word that follows.
Diamonds are very expensive. /daɪməndzɑr/
Diamonds make great gifts. /daɪməndzmeɪk/

Link third-person singular endings to the first sound in the word that follows.
It makes an impressive gift. /meɪksən/
The company promises to give you a diamond. /prɑməsɪztə/

Remember: There are three different sounds for the endings of plural nouns and third-person singular verbs.

/z/	/s/	/ɪz/
diamonds	results	promises
superstitions	sharks	noises
bottles	types	matches
believes	beliefs	wishes
dreams	sleeps	judges

A 🎧 6:12 Listen and practice.

1. Diamonds are very expensive.
2. Diamonds make great gifts.
3. It makes an impressive gift.
4. The company promises to give you a diamond.

B 🎧 **Listen and practice.**

• Refer to the procedure for Exercise A on page TP2.

C **Circle the correct pronunciation . . .**

• First have students focus on the sound at the end of each base form. Then have them circle the correct pronunciation of the *-ed* ending.

• After pairs practice saying each word, bring the class together and answer any questions. If necessary, refer students to the box on page P6 to review the pronunciation of the *-ed* ending following the sounds /t/ and /d/ and voiced and voiceless sounds.

🎧 **Now practice saying . . .**

• Have students say each word aloud and then listen for confirmation.

D 🎧 **Practice saying each sentence . . .**

• Have students scan the sentences and underline the perfect modals. (1. wouldn't have; 2. might have; 3. could have; 4. wouldn't have; 5. might not have) Then have them look at the past participle that follows each perfect modal and circle the past participles that end in *-ed*. (2. avoided, 4. missed)

• Tell pairs to practice saying the sentences aloud, paying attention to the reductions and the pronunciation of the *-ed* endings.

• Have students read each sentence aloud and then listen for confirmation.

 • **Pronunciation Activities**

Unit 7

Intonation of sentences . . .

• Tell students to study the explanation and the example statements. (The word *statement* is used because these intonation patterns do not include questions.) Then have pairs practice reading the two statements to each other, using correct intonation. Explain that the rising arrow indicates rising intonation, and the falling arrow indicates falling intonation. Remind students to pause slightly between clauses.

• Bring the class together, and have volunteers read the statements. Make any necessary corrections, and ask the class to repeat chorally.

• Elicit additional statements with subordinating conjunctions and write them on the board. (Possible answers: Because she has a knack for languages, she became a translator. Unless you have an ear for music, I don't think you'll enjoy tonight's concert.) Have students practice reading the statements, using correct intonation.

Intonation of sentences with transitions

• Have students study the explanation and the example statements. Then have pairs practice reading the two statements to each other, using correct pitch and intonation. Remind students that the falling line indicates lower pitch.

• Bring the class together, and have volunteers read the statements. Make any necessary corrections, and ask the class to repeat chorally.

Challenge: Write the following transitions on the board:

consequently	otherwise
therefore	nonetheless
nevertheless	however

Have pairs create statements that include these transitions. Then have volunteers write their statements on the board for the class to read. Make corrections as needed, and have students repeat.

B 🎧 6:15 Listen and practice.

   1. If I'd looked at the expiration date, I would have renewed my passport.

   2. If I weren't Japanese, I might have needed a visa to enter the country.

   3. If we'd left on time, we wouldn't have missed our flight.

C Circle the correct pronunciation of each _–ed_ ending.

1. avoided	(/ɪd/)	/t/	/d/		**9.** promised	/ɪd/	(/t/)	/d/
2. looked	/ɪd/	(/t/)	/d/		**10.** covered	/ɪd/	/t/	(/d/)
3. summarized	/ɪd/	/t/	(/d/)		**11.** added	(/ɪd/)	/t/	/d/
4. arrived	/ɪd/	/t/	(/d/)		**12.** changed	/ɪd/	/t/	(/d/)
5. owed	/ɪd/	/t/	(/d/)		**13.** reported	(/ɪd/)	/t/	/d/
6. ruined	/ɪd/	/t/	(/d/)		**14.** discussed	/ɪd/	(/t/)	/d/
7. kicked	/ɪd/	(/t/)	/d/		**15.** investigated	(/ɪd/)	/t/	/d/
8. refunded	(/ɪd/)	/t/	/d/		**16.** enjoyed	/ɪd/	/t/	(/d/)

🎧 6:16 Now practice saying each word aloud and listen to check.*

D 🎧 6:17 Practice saying each sentence aloud, paying attention to reductions. Listen to compare.*

   1. If I'd put the film in my carry-on, it wouldn't have gotten damaged.

   2. If you'd checked the luggage limits, you might have avoided extra charges.

   3. If my friend's luggage hadn't gotten stolen, he could have gone on the sightseeing tour.

   4. I probably wouldn't have missed my flight if I had come on time.

   5. If they'd taken a few simple precautions, their luggage might not have gotten stolen.

Unit 7

Intonation of sentences with subordinating conjunctions

In statements with subordinating conjunctions, it is common to use rising intonation in the first clause and falling intonation in the second clause. Pause slightly between clauses.

One's EQ can be high   even if one's IQ is low.

Even if one's IQ is low,   one's EQ can be high.

Intonation of sentences with transitions

In statements with transitions, it is common to lower pitch after the last stressed syllable of the transition word and pause after it. Use falling intonation in the rest of the sentence.

He must have a high IQ. Otherwise, he wouldn't have gotten that job.

She achieved success. However, she doesn't do well on EQ tests.

A 🎧 6:18 Listen and practice.

1. One's EQ can be high even if one's IQ is low.
2. Even if one's IQ is low, one's EQ can be high.
3. He must have a high IQ. Otherwise, he wouldn't have gotten that job.
4. She achieved success. However, she doesn't do well on EQ tests.

B 🎧 6:19 Practice reading each sentence aloud, using the intonation you learned for sentences with subordinating conjunctions. Listen to compare. *

1. You'll be given an interview as long as you get a high score on the test.
2. Unless a new theory emerges, our abilities will continue to be measured with IQ and EQ tests.
3. The IQ test can be an accurate measure of intelligence only if there is such a thing as general intelligence.
4. Because the science of investigating the brain is quite new, no theory of intelligence has yet been proved.
5. Some people have achieved extraordinary successes, although they didn't have high IQs.
6. Intelligence is not easy to measure since there isn't just one kind of intelligence.
7. Although good memory and creativity show intelligence, common sense is important, too.

C 🎧 6:20 Practice reading each sentence aloud, using the intonation you learned for sentences with transitions. Listen to compare.*

1. No theory of intelligence has yet been proved. Nevertheless, many people believe success depends on high IQs.
2. She has a low IQ score. However, her EQ could be high.
3. The science of investigating the brain is quite new. Consequently, no theory of intelligence has yet been proved.
4. He has a high IQ score. Nonetheless, he didn't get the job.
5. There isn't just one kind of intelligence. Therefore, intelligence is not easy to measure.
6. Good memory and creativity show intelligence. However, common sense is important, too.

Unit 8

Intonation of sarcasm

Saying the opposite of what you mean in order to show that you don't think a joke is funny is a type of sarcasm. When someone thinks a joke is funny, the response is usually said with raised pitch. The same response can convey sarcasm if it is said with flattened pitch and at a slower pace.

Pleasure	Sarcasm
What a riot! (= It's funny.)	What a riot. (= It's not funny.)
That cracked me up! (= It's funny.)	That cracked me up. (= It's not funny.)
That's terrific! (= It's great.)	That's terrific. (= It's not great.)
I love it! (= It's great.)	I love it. (= It's not great.)

A 🎧 6:21 Listen and practice.

1. What a riot! / What a riot.
2. That cracked me up! / That cracked me up.
3. That's terrific! / That's terrific.
4. I love it! / I love it.

A 🎧 Listen and practice.

• Refer to the procedure for Exercise A on page TP2.

B 🎧 Practice reading each sentence ...

• First have students circle the subordinating conjunction in each sentence. (1. as long as; 2. Unless; 3. only if; 4. Because; 5. although; 6. since; 7. Although)

• Then have pairs practice reading the sentences, using correct intonation. Remind them to pause slightly between clauses.

• Have students read each sentence aloud and then listen for confirmation.

Option: For further practice, have pairs read each sentence again, reversing the subordinate clause and the main clause.

C 🎧 Practice reading each sentence ...

• First have students circle the transition in each sentence. (1. Nevertheless, 2. However, 3. Consequently, 4. Nonetheless, 5. Therefore, 6. However)

• Then have pairs practice reading the sentences, using correct pitch and intonation.

• Have students read each sentence aloud and then listen for confirmation.

 • **Pronunciation Activities**

Unit 8

Intonation of sarcasm

• On the board, write *sarcasm*. Ask *What is the meaning of* sarcasm? (saying the opposite of what you mean)

• Write on the board *Nice shirt*. Read it aloud two ways, first with raised pitch to convey pleasure and then with flattened pitch and at a slower pace to convey sarcasm. Ask *How can you tell if a comment is sarcastic?* (Flattened pitch and a slower pace convey sarcasm.)

• Have a volunteer read the explanation aloud. Then have pairs practice reading the sets of example sentences, contrasting their pitch and pace to convey pleasure and sarcasm. Circulate and offer suggestions if students have difficulty.

• Ask pairs of volunteers to read their contrasting sentences to the class.

Language note: Point out that, while there are tips for the intonation of sarcasm, there is no one correct way to communicate a sarcastic remark. While one person may be overtly sarcastic, another may be much more subtle, possibly to the point of leaving the listener uncertain whether or not the speaker is being serious.

Culture note: Body language such as rolling one's eyes or making a facial expression may also accompany a sarcastic remark. In addition to pitch, body language helps the listener interpret sarcasm.

A 🎧 Listen and practice.

• Refer to the procedure for Exercise A on page TP2.

B 🎧 **Practice saying each statement . . .**

- Have partners practice reading the pairs of statements, using the appropriate intonation for pleasure and for sarcasm.

- Have students read each pair of statements aloud and then listen for confirmation.

Option: For more practice, have pairs tell each other jokes. Students can tell their own jokes or the joke in Exercise A on page 90, or the jokes in Exercise D on page 93. Have students respond with one of the sentences from Exercise B. The intonation of the response should indicate whether the listener thought the joke was funny or not.

Challenge: Have pairs create short conversations using the intonation of sarcasm. For example,

> A: *Nice job on that presentation.* [sarcastic tone]
>
> B: *I know. It was horrible, wasn't it? I really had no time to prepare.*

Invite pairs to present their conversations to the class. After each presentation, ask students to use a different intonation to make the sarcastic remark express pleasure.

🔘 **ActiveTeach** • **Pronunciation Activities**

Unit 9

Formal pronunciation, rhythm, . . .

- To introduce the topic, ask:
  What's the difference between reading aloud to an audience and reading to oneself? (Possible answer: When you read to yourself, you focus on understanding the text rather than on making sure others understand it.)
  Do you prefer to read or listen to someone read? Why?

- Read the explanation to the class. Then have students read it to themselves. Ask *Did you understand more when you read the explanation to yourselves or when I read it to you? Why do you think that is?*

- Have pairs practice reading the example selection to each other, using a regular rhythm, making fewer reductions, pausing at all punctuation, and separating thought groups. Point out that the single slash (/) in the selection indicates a pause within a sentence or between sentences.

- Bring the class together, and invite a volunteer to read the selection. Ask students to give feedback on the clarity of the reading. Suggest corrections, and have students repeat after you.

A 🎧 **Listen to the selection . . .**

- After listening to the selection, have pairs practice reading it to each other.

B 🎧 **Practice reading each selection . . .**

- First have students use single slashes (/) to mark necessary pauses in the selections, following the example in the box.

- Then have pairs practice reading the selections to each other. Remind students to use a regular rhythm and to make appropriate pauses.

- Have students read the first selection aloud. Then play the selection so students can listen for confirmation. Repeat with the second selection.

🎧 **Challenge:** For more practice reading aloud, have pairs choose either the reading on Jules Verne on page 100 or "World's First 'Green' Dealership" on page 106. Tell pairs to read the article aloud to each other, pausing at all punctuation and between thought groups. Remind students to state the title separately with falling intonation. Circulate and assist as needed. Then have students listen to each article, to compare with their reading. (CD5, Tracks 3, 14) If there is time, create groups of four and have pairs read their articles to each other.

🔘 **ActiveTeach** • **Pronunciation Activities**

Unit 10

Intonation in tag questions

- Tell students to study the explanation and example sentences at the bottom of the page. Then have pairs practice reading the sentences to each other, using correct intonation. Explain that the falling arrow indicates falling intonation. Circulate and offer feedback as needed.

Note: The chart continues on page P10.

🎧 Practice saying each statement two ways, first with intonation showing pleasure and then sarcasm. Listen to compare after you say the statement each way.* (Note that your choices may differ from what you hear on the audio.)

1. That's hysterical! / That's hysterical.
2. That's so funny! / That's so funny.
3. What a scream! / What a scream.
4. What a hoot! / What a hoot.

5. That's hilarious! / That's hilarious.
6. That's too much! / That's too much.
7. That really tickled me! / That really tickled me.

Unit 9

Formal pronunciation, rhythm, and intonation for reading aloud

Because it's more difficult to understand language when it is read rather than spoken in conversation, read with a regular rhythm and use fewer reductions. If there's a title, state it separately with falling intonation. Pause at all punctuation, and separate sentences into thought groups.

Rocket-delivered mail
On June 8, / 1959, / a rocket / carrying three thousand letters / was launched from a submarine in the ocean / and delivered to a U.S. naval station in Florida. / Some people believed / the age of rocket-delivered mail had begun. / But rocket-delivered mail / was a bust.

A ^{6:23} 🎧 Listen to the selection. Then practice reading it aloud.

Rocket-delivered mail

On June 8, 1959, a rocket carrying three thousand letters was launched from a submarine in the ocean and delivered to a U.S. naval station in Florida. Some people believed the age of rocket-delivered mail had begun. But rocket-delivered mail was a bust.

B ^{6:24} 🎧 Practice reading each selection aloud. Then listen to compare. (Note that your choices may differ from what you hear on the audio.)

1. Smell-O-Vision

In 1960, the movie *Scent of Mystery* combined visual images with releases of odors into the theater. The movie-maker predicted this technology would be used in all movies of the future. Smell-O-Vision was a flop.

2. Cryonics for immortality

In the 1960s, Robert Ettinger's book *The Prospect of Immortality* argued that people with fatal illnesses could have their bodies frozen before death and, once a cure for the illness was found, could then be thawed and cured. This would permit us to live beyond our natural life. This technology never took off.

Unit 10

Intonation in tag questions

When a tag question follows a statement to which a speaker anticipates agreement, both the statement and the tag question are said with falling intonation. The main stress in the tag question falls on the auxiliary verb and not on the pronoun. Note that there is generally no pause at the comma.

It's really shocking, isn't it?

It's not really surprising, is it?

It really makes you feel angry, doesn't it?

They'll come up with a solution, won't they?

She didn't speak out against that project, did she?

When the tag question represents a genuine question to which the speaker expects an answer, the statement is said with falling intonation, but the tag question is said with rising intonation.

It's really shocking, isn't it?

They'll come up with a solution, won't they?

It's not really surprising, is it?

She didn't speak out against that project, did she?

It really makes you feel angry, doesn't it?

A Listen and practice. (Each sentence is said two ways.)

1. It's really shocking, isn't it?
2. It's not really surprising, is it?
3. It really makes you feel angry, doesn't it?
4. They'll come up with a solution, won't they?
5. She didn't speak out against that project, did she?

B Listen to the following tag questions. Check to indicate if each one anticipates agreement or expects an answer.

	Anticipates agreement	Expects an answer
1. That's really appalling, isn't it?	☑	☐
2. He's worried about his children, isn't he?	☑	☐
3. It really makes you feel good, doesn't it?	☑	☐
4. It wasn't really true, was it?	☐	☑
5. They're going to do something about that problem, aren't they?	☐	☑
6. It's not really important, is it?	☑	☐
7. You heard that on TV, didn't you?	☐	☑
8. You'll support us, won't you?	☐	☑

Now practice saying each tag question aloud and listen to compare.*

C Practice saying each tag question two ways, first to express anticipated agreement and then to express a genuine question. Listen to compare after you say each pair of questions.*

1. It really makes you stop and think, doesn't it?
2. They're concerned about global warming, aren't they?
3. It won't be easy to talk them into dropping trade tariffs, will it?
4. The president's economic policy is effective, isn't it?
5. The benefits of globalization are very clear, aren't they?
6. The benefits of globalization aren't very clear, are they?
7. There's no turning back, is there?

- Have students study the explanation and example sentences at the top of the page. Then have pairs practice reading the sentences to each other, using correct intonation. Explain that the rising arrow indicates rising intonation. Circulate and offer feedback as needed.

- Write the following sentence on the board:

  That's really wonderful, isn't it?

  Read the sentence two ways: First say both the statement and tag question with falling intonation, and then say the statement with falling intonation and the tag question with rising intonation. Ask *What does each intonation convey?* (The first intonation pattern anticipates agreement, and the second expects an answer.)

- To check understanding, read the example sentences to the class, varying intonation for anticipated agreement and for an expected answer. Have students identify the meaning each intonation expresses.

A 🎧 Listen and practice.

- Refer to the procedure for Exercise A on page TP2.

B 🎧 Listen to the following tag questions ...

- To review, ask:

  What intonation do you use in a tag question to anticipate agreement? (Both statement and tag question are said with falling intonation.)

  What intonation do you use when you expect an answer to a tag question? (The statement is said with falling intonation, and the tag question is said with rising intonation.)

- Before students listen, have them read the items and note the check boxes.

- Then have students listen to the tag questions and check the correct boxes.

- Tell students to compare answers with a partner. Then go over the answers as a class.

🎧 Now practice saying ...

- Have students say each tag question aloud and then listen for confirmation.

C 🎧 Practice saying each tag question ...

- Have pairs practice saying each tag question two ways, using appropriate intonation.

- Then have students read each tag question aloud two ways and then listen for confirmation.

🎧 **Option:** Refer students to the Conversation Snapshot on page 114. Have them read the two conversations and decide what type of intonation is necessary for each tag question. (In both cases the speaker anticipates agreement, so both the statement and the tag question should be read with falling intonation.) Then have pairs practice reading the conversations together. Have students listen to compare their intonation with the Conversation Snapshot. (CD 5, Track 19)

Challenge: Have pairs create short conversations using Ways to react to world issues and news on page 114. Tell students to use intonation in two ways, both to show that the speaker anticipates agreement and to represent a question to which the speaker expects an answer. Invite pairs to read their conversations to the class. Have students decide from the intonation whether the speaker anticipates agreement or expects an answer.

 • **Pronunciation Activities**

Grammar Booster

Unit 1

Stative verbs

• On the board, write *1. I love chocolate! 2. I am loving chocolate!* To check student knowledge, ask *Which sentence is preferred? (1) Why?* (*Love* is a stative or non-action verb and is not usually used in the continuous.)

• Have a volunteer read the first explanation and example sentences in the Grammar box. Write on the board *believe, understand.* Ask *What does each stative verb express?* (They both express a mental state.) Then elicit additional stative verbs and what they express. (Possible answers: **amaze:** emotion or mental state; **exist:** description; **please:** emotion or mental state; **suppose:** mental state)

• Call on a student to read the second explanation. Then have pairs take turns reading the sets of example sentences with Non-action and Action meanings.

• Read the Note, and call on volunteers to read the example sentences. Stress that continuous forms of certain stative verbs are common in spoken English but should not be used in formal writing.

Option: Write the following sentences on the board, or photocopy and distribute them. Tell pairs to decide if the stative verb in each sentence shows a non-action or an action meaning.
1. I <u>have been seeing</u> John for over a year now.
2. We <u>have</u> a problem with flooding in our basement.
3. This material <u>feels</u> nice and soft.
4. You <u>look</u> really good in that jacket.
5. Kerry <u>is appearing</u> in a new feature film.
6. The kids <u>are looking</u> at the elephants in the zoo.

(Answers: 1. action, 2. non-action, 3. non-action, 4. non-action, 5. action, 6. action)

Then have students use the verbs to write sentences that depict the alternate meaning. Have students share their sentences with the class. (Possible answers: 1. I saw John yesterday. 2. They're having a discussion about which course to sign up for. 3. I'm feeling the sweater to see if it's dry. 4. She was looking for a way to realize her childhood dream. 5. Jim's long-term goal appeared difficult to achieve. 6. The weather for tomorrow looks cold and windy.)

Challenge: Have students reread the second explanation. Then refer students to the list of stative verbs in the Appendices, page A4, and have them choose three starred verbs. Have students work together to write three pairs of sentences — one using the verb with a non-action meaning and one using the verb with an action meaning. Circulate and assist as needed.

A Decide if each stative verb . . .

• Have students check the correct boxes and complete the sentences individually.

• Then have students compare answers with a partner.

• Bring the class together and ask:
  Which non-action verbs express a mental state?
    (1. doubts, 6. doesn't remember)
  What does the non-action verb costs *express?*
    (measurement)
  Which non-action verb expresses possession? (2. has)

• Go over any questions.

Note: If students are unsure which stative verbs have an action meaning, have them consult the list in the Appendices, page A4.

Challenge: Have students use the stative verbs in items 1–3 and 5–8 to create sentences with the alternate action or non-action meaning. (Note that *cost*, item 4, does not have an active meaning.) Have students share sentences with a partner. (Possible answers: 1. We were doubting her ability to get the job done on time. 2. They're not having lunch at home today. 3. Philip thinks the rule will be hard to enforce. 5. The bookstore has two copies of the book you ordered. 6. I was remembering the old songs I used to sing as a child. 7. I included my cell phone number on the application. 8. Ellen saw immediately how the movie would end.)

Grammar Booster

The *Grammar Booster* is optional. It provides more explanation and practice, as well as additional grammar concepts and review.

Unit 1

Stative verbs

Stative (non-action) verbs express mental states, emotions, perceptions, descriptions, relationships, possession, measurements, and other conditions, rather than actions. They are not usually used in the continuous or perfect continuous, even when they describe a situation that is in progress.

Many people **believe** the environment should be the government's top priority.
NOT Many people ~~are believing~~ the environment should be the government's top priority.
She **has** always **understood** that job satisfaction was important to the employees.
NOT She ~~has always been understanding~~ that job satisfaction was important to the employees.

Some stative verbs have both non-action and action meanings. A stative verb that has an action meaning may be used in the continuous.

Non-action meaning	Action meaning
That's **ridiculous**! (description)	You're **being** ridiculous! (act in a ridiculous way)
She **has** two children. (possession)	She's **having** another baby soon. (act of giving birth)
Do they **have** any fish? (possession)	What are we **having** for dinner? (act of eating)
We **think** these laws are unfair. (mental state: opinion)	We're **thinking** of organizing a protest. (act of planning)
That perfume **smells** beautiful! (perception)	The customer **is smelling** the perfumes. (act of smelling)
How does the soup **taste**? (perception)	I'm **tasting** the soup to see if it needs salt. (act of tasting)
This garden **looks** neglected. (description)	The child **is looking** at the flowers. (act of looking)
He's very thin. How much does he **weigh**? (measurement)	The nurse **is weighing** the patient. (act of weighing)

NOTE: In informal spoken English, certain stative verbs, especially <u>want</u>, <u>need</u>, and <u>have to</u>, are becoming common in the continuous:

I'm really **wanting** a cup of good coffee. Let's go into that coffee bar.
John called. He says he's **needing** to talk to you. Please give him a call.
We're so busy! We're **having** to rewrite all these reports before tomorrow.

For a complete list of stative verbs, see the Appendices, page A4.

A Decide if each stative verb in parentheses has an action or a non-action meaning. Then complete each sentence with the simple present tense or the present continuous.

     action   **non-action**

1. ☐   ☑   Sara _____doubts_____ (doubt) that she'll get a promotion since she's been here less than a year.

2. ☐   ☑   Ms. Linder's skills are excellent, and she _____has_____ (have) experience working in the field.

3. ☑   ☐   Philip _____is thinking_____ (think) about moving abroad to teach for a year.

4. ☐   ☑   The training she needs to achieve her goal _____costs_____ (cost) more than she was planning to spend.

5. ☑   ☐   We _____'re having_____ (have) dinner at 6:00 today so we can go to Jane Goodall's lecture on changes at Gombe.

6. ☐   ☑   Michael _____doesn't remember_____ (not remember) where the meeting will take place.

7. ☑   ☐   I _____'m including_____ (include) some diagrams with my paper to explain my theory.

8. ☑   ☐   The doctor _____is seeing_____ (see) another patient now.

Unit 2

Adjective clauses: overview

Adjective clauses	Examples
to identify or give additional information about a person • relative pronoun can be subject or object of clause	The physicist { who / that } **made that discovery** } teaches at my university. The psychologist { whom / that / who } **he interviewed** } did a study about lying.
to identify or give additional information about a place or thing • relative pronoun can be subject or object of clause	The building { that / which } **is on your left** } was formerly a private palace. The article { (that) / (which) } **I read yesterday** } is fascinating.
to show possession	The woman **whose house you admired** is a famous author. Paris, **whose museums hold so many treasures**, is a favorite destination for tourists. The precious stone, **whose origin is unknown**, was stolen from the gallery.
to modify a noun of place	The town { where they live / in which they live / which they live in / that they live in } has many beautiful parks and squares.
to modify a noun of time	I can't remember the year { (when) / (that) / (in which) } **we visited them for the first time.**

NOTE: Words in parentheses may be omitted.

A Underline the best word or words to complete each sentence.

1. Parents (<u>who</u> / which) spend time with their children give them a sense of security.
2. The city (that / <u>in which</u>) my father grew up was destroyed during the war.
3. The Miller family, (<u>whose</u> / who) house is for sale, hopes to find a buyer soon.
4. I want to buy a cell phone (who / <u>that</u>) has a digital camera function.
5. The star of the film, (<u>whom</u> / which) we had hoped to meet, didn't come to the reception.
6. I will never forget the time (<u>when</u> / who) I told the truth and was punished for it.
7. The woman (<u>who</u> / which) used to teach English at my school is now the director there.
8. The *Sun Times*, (whose / <u>which</u>) is the best newspaper in town, recently published an article about the social uses of lying.

Adjective clauses with quantifiers

Some adjective clauses may include a quantifier that refers to a previously mentioned noun or noun phrase. These clauses are constructed as follows: quantifier + <u>of</u> + relative pronoun (<u>whom</u>, <u>which</u>, or <u>whose</u>).

He consulted three doctors, **all of whom** confirmed the original diagnosis.
I can think of several possible explanations, **none of which** justifies their behavior.
The reporters questioned the president, **one of whose** strengths is his ability to remain calm under pressure.

Adjective clauses that include quantifiers appear more often in written than spoken English.

Some expressions of quantity used with <u>of</u>
a few of
all of
a number of
both of
each of
half of
little of
many of
most of
neither of
none of
one of
several of
some of

Unit 2

Adjective clauses: overview

• Have students skim the information in the first column of the chart to review the uses of adjective clauses.

• Focus on each horizontal section of the chart. Have volunteers read the example sentences. If appropriate, elicit additional example sentences for each section.

• After the class has gone through each section, point out that adjective clauses can be divided into restrictive and non-restrictive clauses. (Note that restrictive and non-restrictive clauses are taught on the Writing page.) Ask:

  What does a restrictive clause do? (It gives information that is needed to identify the noun or pronoun it modifies.)
  What does a non-restrictive clause do? (It gives additional information that is not necessary to identify the noun or pronoun it modifies.)
  Which of the two types of clauses can be omitted from a sentence without affecting its meaning? (a non-restrictive clause)

• Have students skim the example sentences in the chart and note the restrictive clauses and non-restrictive clauses. (Only the example sentences in section 3 — to show possession — that begin *Paris . . .* and *The precious stone . . .* are non-restrictive.)

• Tell students that the relative pronoun *that* cannot be used with non-restrictive clause. Also remind students that a non-restrictive clause requires a comma before and after (or a comma before and a period after when the clause comes at the end of the sentence).

• Write the following on the board and have students note the commas in sentence 1 and the comma and period in sentence 2:

  1. *Tom, who has worked for our company for eight years, lied to his boss.*
  2. *Tom lied to his boss, which was a serious mistake.*

Option: Write the following sentences on the board. Call on students to add commas to the sentences where they are necessary.

  1. *The person that we are talking about is standing over there.*
  2. *My mother who had never used a computer learned to surf the Internet.*
  3. *The bench that is in front of the library was donated by the class of 1987.*
  4. *Tabor whose town square is 100 years old is a popular tourist destination.*
  5. *This summer we are going to Vienna which is where my husband was born.*

(Answers: 2. My mother, who had never used a computer, learned to surf the Internet. 4. Tabor, whose town square is 100 years old, is a popular tourist destination. 5. This summer we are going to Vienna, which is where my husband was born.)

Challenge: Have pairs write five sentences with adjective clauses, one for each category in the chart. Tell students to include both restrictive and non-restrictive clauses. Circulate and check as students work. Then have pairs swap sentences and identify the restrictive and non-restrictive clauses.

A Underline the best word . . .

• Have students look at the noun before each parenthetical choice of words. Have pairs decide whether the noun is a person, place, or thing. (1. person, 2. place, 3. person, 4. thing, 5. person, 6. thing [time], 7. person, 8. thing) Ask:
  Which words introduce an adjective clause about people? (who, whom, that, whose)
  Which words introduce an adjective clause about place? (which, that, where, in which)
  Which words introduce an adjective clause about things? (which, that)
  Which words introduce an adjective clause about time? (when, that, in which)

• Have students complete the exercise individually and then compare answers with a partner.

• Bring the class together and go over any questions. Then ask:
  How is the adjective clause used in each sentence? (1. to identify people; 2. to identify a place; 3. to give additional information about people; 4. to give additional information about a thing; 5. to give additional information about a person; 6. to identify a time; 7. to identify a person; 8. to give additional information about a thing)

Adjective clauses with quantifiers

• Have a volunteer read the explanation in the Grammar box. Then have students read the example sentences to themselves. Ask:
  In the first sentence, what does all of whom *refer to?* (three doctors)
  In the second sentence, what does none of which *refer to?* (several possible explanations)
  In the third sentence, what does one of whose *refer to?* (the president)

• Ask *Are the adjective clauses in these sentences restrictive or non-restrictive?* (non-restrictive) Point out that quantifiers can be used only with non-restrictive clauses.

• Have students skim Some expressions of quantity used with *of*. Elicit additional example sentences. (Possible answer: I spoke to both managers, *neither of whom* was willing to take responsibility for the mistake.)

• Read aloud the last explanation about adjective clauses with quantifiers. Add that students might also hear quantifiers used in formal spoken contexts.

B Complete each sentence . . .

- Have students decide whether each adjective clause refers to a person or a thing. (1. thing: products; 2. person: children; 3. person: students; 4. thing: articles; 5. person: parents) Review the construction quantifier + of + *whom, which,* or *whose.* Then ask:
  Which relative pronoun can you use with a quantifier that refers to things? (which)
  Which relative pronouns can you use with a quantifier that refers to people? (whom, whose)

- Have students do the exercise in pairs. Circulate and assist as needed. If students have difficulty, tell them to make sure the verb in the sentence agrees with the quantifier. Explain that *both of* and *neither of* are used when talking about two people or things.

- Bring the class together and go over the answers.

Challenge: Have pairs rewrite items 1, 2, and 4, using different expressions of quantity from the list on page G2. (In items 3 and 5, no other quantifier retains the same meaning.) Tell students to make any necessary changes. Ask volunteers to read their sentences to the class. (Possible answers: 1. . . . only some of / half of which work. 2. . . . all of / some of whom always make . . . 4. . . . each of which deals . . .)

Grammar for Writing: adjective clauses . . .

- Read the first explanation in the Grammar box. Then have students review the definitions of a clause and a phrase in the Remember note. Focus on the example sentences. Ask:
  In the clause in the first sentence, what is the subject? What is the verb? (The subject is the relative pronoun *which.* The verb is *is.*)
  Does the phrase in the second sentence have a subject and a verb? (No. A phrase doesn't have both a subject and a verb.)

- Tell students that there are two ways to reduce an adjective clause to an adjective phrase. Ask a volunteer to read the first way. Then have students look at the example sentences and notice that the relative pronoun *who* and the verb *was* were dropped. Tell students that this kind of adjective phrase can also start a sentence: <u>The first Greek historian,</u> *Herodotus wrote about the wars between ancient Greece and Persia.*

- Write on the board *Rome, which is the capital of Italy, is one of the world's oldest cities.* Have students identify the adjective clause. (which is the capital of Italy) Tell the class to rewrite the sentence, changing the clause to a phrase. (Rome, the capital of Italy, is one of the world's oldest cities.) Write the sentence on the board for confirmation.

- Ask a volunteer to read the second way to reduce an adjective clause to an adjective phrase. Review that a present participle is the base form of a verb + *-ing.* Have students study the two pairs of sentences and notice that the relative pronouns (which, who) and verbs (contains, tamper) were replaced by present participles (containing, tampering). Tell students that this type of adjective clause can be placed at the beginning or end of a sentence as well as in the middle: <u>Containing 206 separate bones,</u> *the human skeleton is a strong and flexible structure. The human skeleton is a strong and flexible structure,* <u>containing 206 separate bones.</u>

- Ask a volunteer to read the last explanation in the Grammar box. Point out that when an adjective phrase such as *a very practical and hardworking woman* appears in the middle of the sentence, it must follow the noun or pronoun it gives additional information about—in this case, *My grandmother.*

- Call on volunteers to change each adjective phrase in the examples to a clause. (My grandmother, who is a very practical and hardworking woman, . . . ; Istanbul, which is the largest city in Turkey, . . . ; . . . a quiet place to live, preferably one that is in the suburbs; Chanterelles, which are a type of edible mushroom with a rich yellow color, . . . ; These plants are in the cactus family, which is the kind of vegetation . . .)

C Reduce the adjective clause . . .

- To introduce the exercise, ask:
  In which sentences does the adjective clause include a relative pronoun and a form of the verb be? (1. who is; 2. which are; 5. which is)
  How can these adjective clauses be reduced to adjective phrases? (Drop the relative pronoun and the verb *be.*)
  How can the adjective clauses in the other sentences be reduced to adjective phrases? (Drop the relative pronoun and use the present participle of the verb.)

- After students complete the exercise individually, have them compare answers with a partner.

Option: To provide more practice reducing adjective clauses to adjective phrases, write the following sentences on the board, or photocopy and distribute them. Have pairs reduce the adjective clauses to adjective phrases.
  1. Tucker College, which is famous for its football team, has 5,000 students.
  2. Yoga, which reduces stress for many people, is a popular form of exercise.
  3. Versace, who is a well-known Italian clothing designer, often lends clothing to celebrities.
  4. The Internet, which allows people to send each other messages instantaneously, has changed the way we communicate.

(Answers: 1. Tucker College, famous for its football team, . . . ; 2. Yoga, reducing stress for many people, . . . ; 3. Versace, a well-known Italian clothing designer, . . . ; 4. The Internet, allowing people to send each other messages instantaneously, . . .)

B Complete each sentence with a quantifier from the box and the correct relative pronoun. Use each quantifier only once.

> all of   each of   neither of   one of   both of

1. I know many commercials make false claims because I've bought many advertised products, only _____one of which_____ works.

2. He's upset with his three children, _____each of whom_____ always makes up a different excuse to avoid sharing chores at home.

3. The teacher punished the six students, _____all of whom_____ were caught cheating on the same exam.

4. These two articles, _____both of which_____ deal with the issue of honesty in the workplace, should be required reading for everyone in the company.

5. My parents, _____neither of whom_____ has ever told a lie, are the most honest people I know.

Grammar for Writing: adjective clauses reduced to adjective phrases

Adjective clauses can be reduced to adjective phrases.

clause: Hawaii, **which is known for its beautiful topography and climate**, lies in the middle of the Pacific Ocean.

phrase: Hawaii, **known for its beautiful topography and climate**, lies in the middle of the Pacific Ocean.

> **REMEMBER**
>
> A <u>clause</u> is a group of words that has both a subject and a verb.
> A <u>phrase</u> is a group of words that doesn't have both a subject and a verb.

There are two ways to reduce an adjective clause to an adjective phrase:

1. **When the adjective clause contains a form of the verb <u>be</u>, drop the relative pronoun and the verb <u>be</u>.**
   Herodotus, **who was the first Greek historian**, wrote about the wars between ancient Greece and Persia. →
   Herodotus, **the first Greek historian**, wrote about the wars between ancient Greece and Persia.

2. **When the adjective clause does not contain a form of the verb <u>be</u>, drop the relative pronoun and use the present participle of the verb.**
   The human skeleton, **which contains** 206 separate bones, is a strong and flexible structure. →
   The human skeleton, **containing** 206 separate bones, is a strong and flexible structure.

   Those **who tamper** with the smoke detector will be prosecuted. →
   Those **tampering** with the smoke detector will be prosecuted.

Adjective phrases are common in writing. They often begin with an article or with words and expressions like <u>one</u>, <u>a type of</u>, <u>the kind of</u>.
   My grandmother, **a very practical and hardworking woman**, made clothes for the entire family.
   The **largest city in Turkey**, Istanbul is at the point where Europe joins Asia.
   They're looking for a quiet place to live, preferably **one in the suburbs**.
   Chanterelles, **a type of edible mushroom with a rich yellow color**, are very expensive.
   These plants are in the cactus family, **the kind of vegetation with the most tolerance for a hot, dry climate**.

C Reduce the adjective clause in each sentence to an adjective phrase.

1. James Bond, ~~who is~~ one of the best-known movie characters, often uses a fake identity when he is on a mission.

2. LaFontaine's *Fables*, ~~which are~~ short tales of animals behaving like people, comment on human nature.

3. Executives ~~who fail~~ᶠᵃⁱˡⁱⁿᵍ to accept responsibility for their mistakes often lose the trust of their employees.

4. "The Boy Who Cried Wolf," ~~which teaches~~ᵗᵉᵃᶜʰⁱⁿᵍ the moral that liars are never believed even when they tell the truth, is a fable by Aesop.

5. Compassion, ~~which is~~ believed to be the source of moral behavior, develops in children at a very young age.

D On a separate sheet of paper, combine each pair of sentences. Use the second sentence as an adjective phrase.

1. Aesop wrote a lot of fables using animal characters.
   (Aesop was a Greek writer living in the sixth century B.C.)

   > *Aesop, a Greek writer living in the sixth century B.C., wrote a lot of fables using animal characters.*

2. My nephew Brian enjoys volunteering in a local hospital.
   (My nephew Brian is a man of great compassion and integrity.)

   My nephew Brian, a man of great compassion and integrity, enjoys volunteering in a local hospital.

3. Margo Farmer is an honest and independent legislator.
   (Margo Farmer is one legislator never influenced by any special interest groups.)

   Margo Farmer, one legislator never influenced by any special interest groups, is an honest and independent legislator.

4. The morality play offers moral instructions by presenting good and evil as human characters.
   (The morality play is a type of play once popular in the fifteenth and sixteenth centuries.) (See below for answers to items 4, 5, and 6.)

5. Making up an excuse for being late can get a person into trouble.
   (Making up an excuse for being late is the kind of mistake most common among office workers.)

6. A lot of money was raised at last night's concert.
   (Last night's concert was the biggest charity event of the year.)

Unit 3

Describing past actions and events: review

The past of be and the simple past tense
Use for completed actions and states and for those that occurred at a specific time in the past.
   He **was** here at 10:00 and **left** this message.

The past continuous
Use for one or more actions in progress at a specific time in the past.
   The baby **was sleeping** and the older children **were eating** dinner when we arrived.

The present perfect
Use for actions completed at an unspecified time in the past.
   She **has** already **informed** her manager about the problem.
   I've stayed at that hotel three times.

The past perfect
Use for an action that occurred before another past action.
   They **had** already **made** a decision when we called to discuss the matter.

The past perfect continuous
Use for a continuous action that had occurred before another past action.
   We **had been working** in the garden for two hours when the storm began.

Used to / would
Use used to for past situations and habits that no longer exist. Use would or used to for actions that were repeated regularly in the past.
   When she was younger, she never **used to** be afraid of anything.
   In those days, we **would take** a long walk every evening after supper.

The future as seen from the past
Use was / were going to + the base form of a verb to express future plans someone had in the past.
   He **was going to start** his own business, but he couldn't get a loan.

Would + the base form of the verb can also express the future as seen from the past, but only after statements of knowledge or belief.
   We always thought that she **would become** an actress, but she decided to study law.

Answers for Exercise D, continued:
4. The morality play, a type of play once popular in the fifteenth and sixteenth centuries, offers moral instructions by presenting good and evil as human characters. 5. Making up an excuse for being late, the kind of mistake most common among office workers, can get a person into trouble. 6. A lot of money was raised at last night's concert, the biggest charity event of the year.

D **On a separate sheet of paper, . . .**

• Have students scan the pairs of sentences. Tell them to note the noun phrase that each adjective phrase will modify. (1. Aesop; 2. My nephew Brian; 3. Margo Farmer; 4. The morality play; 5. Making up an excuse for being late; 6. last night's concert)

• Have students do the exercise in pairs. Then go over any questions as a class.

Option: Have pairs take turns reading the sentences, changing the adjective phrases to adjective clauses. Remind students to choose the correct relative pronoun. (1. Aesop, who was a Greek writer . . . ; 2. My nephew Brian, who is a man . . . ; 3. Margo Farmer, who is one legislator . . . ; 4. The morality play, which is a type . . . ; 5. Making up an excuse for being late, which is the kind . . . ; 6. . . . last night's concert, which was the biggest charity event . . .)

Unit 3

Describing past actions and events: review

• Give students a few minutes to read the seven headings and explanations in the review. Point out that most of the material reviews the grammar points covered in units 1 and 3.

• Focus on *used to* and *would*. Explain that it is common in writing to use *used to* at the beginning of a paragraph and then continue with *would* in the following sentences that provide further details. Write the first sentence on the board *When I was younger, I used to exercise a lot*—and have students suggest additional details. (Possible answers: I would take an aerobics classes every morning. I would go dancing a couple of times a week. I would also play volleyball with friends on the weekend.)

• Call on a volunteer to read the first explanation and example sentence under The future as seen from the past. Have students suggest additional sentences describing things they had planned to do but didn't for some reason. (Possible answer: I was going to take a translating course, but it wasn't offered in the spring.)

• Have a student read the second explanation and example sentence. Point out that the future as seen from the past is also used after such verbs as *understood, believed*, and *claimed*. Write these verbs on the board for reference, and have students suggest sentences using them. (Possible answer: She claimed that she would learn how to drive, but she never did.)

Challenge: Have students write a paragraph describing five activities they used to do regularly. Instruct students to use *used to* and *would* appropriately in their paragraph. Collect the papers and give feedback.

A Correct the errors . . .

- Have students do the exercise individually. Refer them to the review of past actions and events on page G4 if they need help.
- Bring the class together and go over the answers. Call on students to explain each error and the best way to correct it. Note that for item 2 there are two possible corrections.

Unit 4

Infinitive and gerund phrases . . .

- Have students read the first explanation in the Grammar box and the example sentences. Ask:
    Which sentence includes the subjunctive form? (the first one)
    What is the expression of urgency, obligation, or advisability? (It is essential)
    What is the verb? (find)
    What is the infinitive phrase in the second sentence? (to find)
- Write the following sentences on the board. Have students rewrite them, using an infinitive phrase instead of the subjunctive.
    1. It is crucial that Sarah not forget the concert tickets.
    2. It is necessary that we arrive at the airport two hours before our flight.
    3. It is desirable that you bring a gift to the party.

(Answers: 1. It is crucial for Sarah not to forget . . . ; 2. It is necessary for us to arrive . . . ; 3. It is desirable for you to bring . . .)

- Have students read the second explanation and the example sentences. Ask:
    Which sentence includes the subjunctive form? (the first one)
    What is the expression of urgency, obligation, or advisability? (Dr. Sharpe recommends)
    What is the verb? (spend)
    What is the gerund phrase in the second sentence? (spending)
- Write the following sentences on the board. Have students rewrite them, using a gerund phrase instead of the subjunctive.
    1. The directors proposed that the city build a new stadium.
    2. The professor suggests that students not postpone studying for the exam.
    3. He recommends that you meditate at least four hours a week.

(Answers: 1. The directors proposed building . . . ; 2. The professor suggests not postponing . . . ; 3. He recommends meditating . . .)

- Read aloud the final explanation, and have students skim the example sentences.

A On a separate sheet of paper, . . .

- Have students scan the verbs and adjectives of urgency, obligation, and advisability and determine which ones will be followed by a gerund and which will be followed by an infinitive. (1. infinitive, 2. gerund, 3. gerund, 4. infinitive, 5. object before an infinitive OR gerund, 6. infinitive) If necessary, refer students to page A3 in the Appendices to review which verbs can be followed by a gerund or an infinitive.
- Then have students rewrite the sentences. Have students focus on items 4 and 6, and remind the class to change the pronoun as appropriate. (4. for us; 6. for her)
- Go over the answers as a class. Point out that items 1, 4, and 6 can be rewritten both with and without a pronoun. Remind students that infinitive or gerund phrases used without a pronoun refer to people in general. Note that it is also correct to use a possessive pronoun before a gerund phrase. See items 2, 3, and 5.

Unit 5

More phrases that make non-count nouns . . .

- Have students read the heads in the chart and skim the phrases. Divide the class into four groups and assign a category to each group. Tell students to create pairs of sentences—one sentence using a phrase + non-count noun, and another sentence using just the non-count noun. For example, *I would like to order a cup of coffee. If I drink coffee after dinner, I can't sleep.* Have groups share their sentences.

Note: The chart continues on page G6.

A Correct the errors with past forms.

1. Florence ~~has~~ *had* been walking for several hours before she realized that her wallet was missing.
2. As a child, he ~~was practicing~~ *used to practice OR would practice* the piano for hours every day. Then he stopped taking lessons.
3. Eleanor's neighbor was here at noon and ~~had~~ left some flowers for her.
4. "I ~~have seen~~ *saw* that movie last year, and I thought it was great," Frank exclaimed.
5. When the power went off, I ~~read~~ *was reading* an article in this morning's paper.
6. Before this morning, I ~~never took~~ *had never taken* a yoga class.
7. I ~~am~~ *was* going to travel to Venice this summer, but I can't take time off from work.
8. He ~~was~~ *had been* working on the problem all morning when he finally found the solution.

Unit 4

Infinitive and gerund phrases in place of the subjunctive

It is often possible to use an infinitive phrase after adjectives of urgency, obligation, or advisability with almost the same meaning as the subjunctive.
It is essential that John **find** the time each day to relax. = It is essential for John **to find** the time each day to relax.

It is also often possible to use a gerund phrase after verbs of urgency, obligation, or advisability with almost the same meaning as the subjunctive.
Dr. Sharpe recommends (that) you **spend** a few moments relaxing. = Dr. Sharpe recommends **spending** a few moments relaxing.

Note that when an infinitive or gerund phrase is used without a pronoun, it usually refers to people in general.
It is essential **to find** the time each day to relax.
Dr. Sharpe recommends **spending** a few moments relaxing.

A On a separate sheet of paper, rewrite each sentence with an infinitive or a gerund phrase. Make any necessary changes.

1. It is crucial that you practice feng shui. It is crucial to practice . . . OR It is crucial for you to practice . . .
2. The article suggests that you carry several lucky charms. The article suggests carrying . . . OR The article suggests your carrying . . .
3. The manager recommended that they finish the project before the holiday. The manager recommended finishing . . . OR The manager recommended their finishing . . .
4. It is important that we get enough sleep every night. It is important to get . . . OR It is important for us to get . . .
5. The directions advise that you throw salt over your shoulder. The directions advise throwing . . . OR The directions advise your throwing . . . OR The directions advise you to throw . . .
6. It is necessary that she arrive at the theater by 4:00 PM. It is necessary to arrive . . . OR It is necessary for her to arrive . . .

Unit 5

More phrases that make non-count nouns countable

Natural phenomena	Foods	Drinks and liquids	Household products
a bolt of lightning	**a bar of** chocolate	**a bottle of** water	**a bar of** soap
a breath of air	**a clove of** garlic	**a carton of** milk	**a tube of** toothpaste
a clap of thunder	**a cup of** sugar	**a cup of** coffee	**a box of** detergent
a cloud of smoke	**a teaspoon of** salt	**a glass of** juice	**a can of** cleanser
a drop of rain	**a loaf of** bread	**a liter of** gasoline	
a gust of wind			
a ray of sun			

Here are four common phrases that are used to make a number of non-count nouns countable.

a piece of	advice equipment furniture gossip information news paper	a sense of	achievement community confidence control humor identity	an act of	anger insanity justice defiance kindness generosity heroism	a state of	confusion disrepair emergency war mind

A Choose the best word from the box to complete each sentence.

| act |
| bar |
| cloud |
| glass |
| piece |
| sense |
| state |

1. The group's donation was a true __act__ of generosity
2. My sister has an amazing __sense__ of humor.
3. The room was filled with a __cloud__ of smoke.
4. The woman slipped on a __bar__ of soap in the shower.
5. Our town has been in a __state__ of emergency since the hurricane.
6. The park just installed a new __piece__ of equipment in the playground.
7. I asked the waitress for a __glass__ of orange juice.

More non-count nouns with both a countable and an uncountable sense

With some non-count nouns, the change in meaning is subtle: the countable meaning refers to something specific and the uncountable meaning refers to something general.

a fear = the anticipation of a specific danger; a phobia *He had **a fear** of heights.*	**fear** = a general anticipation of danger *Irrational **fear** can lead to anxiety.*
a victory = a specific event in which mastery or success is achieved *The battle of Waterloo was **a great victory** for the English.*	**victory** = the phenomenon of winning *She led her party to **victory**.*
a time = a specific moment in the past or future; a specific occasion *There was **a time** when food was much cheaper.* *How **many times** did you read it?*	**time** = the general concept; clock time ***Time** passes so quickly!* *What **time** did you arrange to meet?*
a superstition = a specific belief or practice *A common American **superstition** is that Friday the 13th brings bad luck.*	**superstition** = a general attitude *The prevalence of **superstition** among educated people is surprising.*

B Complete each pair of sentences. Write <u>a</u> before a noun where necessary. Write <u>X</u> if a noun should not have an article.

1. **a.** Will people ever learn to control their phobias? Only __X__ time can tell.
   b. There has never been __a__ time when people didn't try to interpret their dreams.

2. **a.** If you have __a__ fear of flying, you shouldn't take a job that requires overseas travel.
   b. Psychologists agree that __X__ fear is a universal emotion.

3. **a.** Ignorance and fear may sometimes lead to __X__ superstition.
   b. There is __a__ widely held superstition that knocking on wood brings good luck.

4. **a.** The coach's tactics helped the team win __a__ major victory in last night's game.
   b. Everyone cannot always experience the joy of __X__ victory; someone has to lose.

- Read the explanation in the Grammar box. Have students skim the phrases and nouns. Elicit an example sentence for each phrase and write them on the board. (Possible answers: He gave his son a piece of advice about paying his bills on time. I think it's important to have a sense of humor, don't you? His offer was an act of kindness. The country is in a state of confusion.)

- Have students suggest sentences using the same noun in an uncountable sense. Write them on the board to compare. (Possible answers: It's easy to give advice and hard to follow. Humor has health benefits. The whole town talks about his kindness. The doctor said I might experience confusion after taking the medication.)

Option: Tell students to keep their books closed. Divide the class into two teams. Alternate giving teams a non-count noun from one of the charts. Have students use the noun with a phrase to make it countable. (Possible answer: sugar; a box of sugar) Use a selection of 15 to 25 nouns, depending on available time. Give one point for each correct phrase + noun. The team with the most points wins.

A Choose the best word . . .

- Have students cover the sentences with a piece of paper and scan the list of words in the box. Ask *Which non-count nouns might these words be combined with?* (Possible answers: an act of insanity; a bar of chocolate; a cloud of dust; a glass of water; a piece of candy; a sense of danger; a state of innocence)

- Then have students complete the exercise individually. Have them compare answers with a partner.

Challenge: Elicit sentences using the phrases from the exercise with other nouns. (Possible answer: The house was surrounded by a cloud of dust.)

More non-count nouns with both a countable . . .

- Read the explanation in the Grammar box aloud. Then have partners take turns reading the pairs of example sentences.

- Elicit other non-count nouns that have both a countable and an uncountable sense, such as *noise, room,* and *work.* Ask partners to create sentences for each sense. (Possible answers: 1. A noise from the kitchen interrupted my studying. Too much noise can lead to hearing damage. 2. It's relaxing to sit in a room with a view of the ocean. There's no more room in this closet. 3. The museum has many works of art. Work takes up most of my day.)

- Bring the class together and have students share their sentences.

Option: Write these sentences on the board, and have students indicate whether the underlined non-count noun has a countable or an uncountable sense.

> *1. The team celebrated victory over its opponents.*
> *2. I remember a time when I had fewer worries.*
> *3. It's very difficult to overcome fear.*
> *4. A college education was once more affordable.*
> *5. Superstition used to be more common.*

(Answers: 1. uncountable, 2. countable, 3. uncountable, 4. countable, 5. uncountable)

B Complete each pair of sentences . . .

- After students complete the exercise individually, have them compare answers with a partner.

- Bring the class together and go over any questions.

Challenge: For more practice, have pairs write one sentence for each non-count noun in the Grammar box. Have them use either a countable or an uncountable sense and leave a space before the noun. Then have pairs swap papers and add articles where needed. Circulate and assist as needed.

Article usage: overview

- Before students open their books, ask:
  What is the definite article? (the)
  What are the indefinite articles? (a, an)

- Focus on the use of articles in general statements. Call on a volunteer to read the explanation and example sentence under the heading Indefinite article. Then have another student read the explanations and the example sentences under the heading Definite article. Point out that, unlike the indefinite article, the definite article can be used with both count and non-count nouns. Finally, read aloud the explanations and example sentences under the heading No article.

- Have students look at the second row of the chart. Then ask *Would you use the indefinite article, the definite article, or no article for the first mention of a noun?* (the indefinite article or no article)

- On the board, create a chart like the one following. Have a student read aloud the explanations and example sentences, and write the example sentences in the first row on the board.

Singular count nouns	Plural count nouns	Non-count nouns
I found a lucky charm.	*I have lucky charms.*	*I bought shampoo.*
The lucky charm was in a box.	*The lucky charms are in a box.*	*The shampoo is in the closet.*

- Have students look at the third row of the chart in their book. Then ask *Would you use the indefinite article, the definite article, or no article for the second mention of a noun?* (the definite article) Ask a student to read the explanations and example sentences aloud, and write the example sentences in the second row on the board.

- Pointing to the chart on the board, review that singular count nouns use *a* for the first mention and *the* for the second mention. Plural count nouns use no article for the first mention and *the* for the second mention. Non-count nouns use no article for the first mention and *the* for the second mention.

Challenge: Bring English-language magazines to class (or print out appropriate materials from the Internet) and have pairs choose one article to focus on. Tell students to find examples of the article usage outlined in the chart. Have them highlight the examples and then share them with the class.

C Read the paragraph . . .

- Tell students to read the paragraph through once before making the corrections. Then have students compare answers with a partner.

- Bring the class together, and have students explain the reasons for the corrections. (*Homes*: no article, general statement, plural count noun; *a small house*: article *a*, first mention, singular count noun; *The house*: article *the*, second mention, singular count noun; *a large kitchen, a living room*: article *a*, first mention, singular count nouns; *the living room*: article *the*, second mention, singular count noun; *The bedrooms*: article *the*, second mention, plural count noun; *help*: no article, general statement, non-count noun; *a party*: article *a*, first mention, singular count noun; *the house*: article *the*, second mention, singular count noun; *furniture*: no article, general statement, non-count noun)

Definite article: additional uses

- Have pairs read through the chart of additional uses of the definite article and the example sentences. Circulate and answer questions as needed.

- Then bring the class together. Elicit examples as follows:
  Give some other examples of a noun that represents a unique thing. (Possible answers: the equator; the universe; the sky; the president)
  Give some other examples of a superlative adjective that makes a noun unique. (Possible answers: the funniest joke; the oldest person; the most advanced computer)
  Give some other examples of a context that makes a noun specific. (Possible answers: the ideas in this essay; the food on this table)

Note: The chart continues on page G8.

Article usage: overview

Note where indefinite or definite articles are used or omitted.

	Indefinite article	Definite article	No article
General statement	Use with singular count nouns: *A cat* *may symbolize good or bad fortune.*	Use with singular count nouns: *The cat* *may symbolize good or bad fortune.* *The telephone* *was invented by Bell.* *The guitar* *is a string instrument.* Use with non-count nouns: *Freud called attention to **the importance** of dreams.*	With plural count nouns: *Cats* *may symbolize good or bad fortune.* With non-count nouns: *Misfortune* *may strike at any time.*
First mention	Use with singular count nouns: *I found **a lucky charm**.*		With plural count nouns: *I have (some) lucky **charms**.* With non-count nouns: *I bought (some) **shampoo**.*
Second mention		Use with singular count nouns: *The lucky **charm** was in a box.* Use with plural count nouns: *The lucky **charms** were in a box.* Use with non-count nouns: *The **shampoo** is in the closet.*	

C Read the paragraph. Then correct eleven errors in article usage. Make any necessary changes.

~~The~~ H homes are expensive these days, but Peter got lucky and bought ∧a small house last week. ~~A~~ The
house has two bedrooms and one bathroom. It also has ∧a large kitchen and ~~the~~ ∧a living room. Peter
will use ∧the living room as his home office. ∧The bBedrooms are in bad condition, and Peter will need ✗
help painting them. Then he wants to have ~~the~~ ∧a party so his friends can admire ∧the ahouse. Later
Peter will buy ✗ furniture—when he saves some money!

Definite article: additional uses

	Definite article
When a noun represents a unique thing	Use with singular count nouns: *The sun* *rises in the east.*
With a comparative or superlative adjective to make a noun unique (or with <u>right</u>, <u>wrong</u>, <u>first</u>, <u>only</u>, <u>same</u>)	Use with singular count nouns: *Telling the truth is **the best course** of action. It's always **the right thing** to do.* *The robin is **the first sign** of spring.* Use with plural count nouns: *People in different places often have **the same superstitions**.* Use with non-count nouns: *That's **the only information** I was able to find on the Internet.*
When context makes a noun specific	Use with singular count nouns: *The hospital* *in this town has an excellent emergency room.* Use with plural count nouns: *The buildings* *in this town are no higher than ten stories.* Use with non-count nouns: *The air* *in this city is polluted.*

	Definite article
When an adjective clause makes a noun specific	Use with singular count nouns: ***The mirror that you broke*** *will bring you bad luck.* Use with plural count nouns: ***The mirrors that you broke*** *will bring you bad luck.* Use with non-count nouns: ***The progress that she made*** *was due not to good luck but to hard work.*
When an adjective represents a certain group of people	Use with a noun derived from an adjective, such as the blind / the deaf / the dead / the living / the young / the old / the poor / the rich / the unemployed / the privileged / the underprivileged: ***The unemployed*** *must often learn new job skills.*

D   Complete the paragraphs with words from the box. Use a definite article when appropriate.

tourists	gasoline	view	world
wealthy	sky	ballooning	first men

On March 20, 1999, Bertrand Piccard of Switzerland and Brian Jones of Britain were ___the first men___
(1)
to travel around ___the world___ in a balloon. The numerous balloonists who had been attempting this
(2)
journey for decades beforehand ran into various problems with weather and equipment.

In the past several years, ___ballooning___ has become a popular adventure sport. Due to the
(3)
high cost of balloons and ___gasoline___ , however, it is a sport reserved for ___the wealthy___ .
(4)   (5)
___Tourists___ can get a taste of ballooning during their travels. ___The view___ of a city or
(6)   (7)
landscape from ___the sky___ is always breathtaking.
(8)

Unit 6

The conditional: overview

Type	Use	If clause (states the condition)	Result clause (states the result)	Examples
Factual conditional	To express a general or scientific fact	**simple present** Note: In this type of conditional, if can be replaced by <u>when</u> or <u>whenever</u>.	**simple present**	*If it **rains**, the gardens **close** early.* *Water **freezes** if the temperature **falls** below zero degrees Celsius.*
	To talk about what will happen in the future under certain conditions	**simple present** Note: Don't use a future form in the <u>if</u> clause.	**<u>will</u> / <u>be going to</u> + base form of the verb** Note: Use <u>can</u>, <u>may</u>, <u>might</u>, <u>should</u> if the result is not certain.	*If you **plan** your trip carefully, things **will go** smoothly.* *If we arrive late, they**'re going to start** without us.* *If we **hurry**, we **may be able to catch** the train.*
Present unreal conditional	To talk about present unreal or untrue conditions	**simple past or <u>were</u>** Note: Don't use <u>would</u> in the <u>if</u> clause.	**<u>would</u> + base form of the verb** Note: Use <u>could</u> or <u>might</u> if the result is not certain.	*If I **had** the time, I **would explain** the problem to you.* *If he **were** here, he **might make** a lot of changes.*

- Continue eliciting examples from the class, as follows:

  Give some other examples in which an adjective clause makes a noun specific. (Possible answers: the report that's on the copier; the woman who came to the door)

- Have students suggest example sentences for the adjectives in the chart that represent a certain group of people. Remind them to use the definite article. (Possible answer: The unemployed in this city are eligible for food stamps.)

D Complete the paragraphs . . .

- After students complete the exercise individually, have them compare answers with a partner.

- Then bring the class together and go over the uses of the definite article. (1. the first men: adjective makes a noun unique; 2. the world: unique thing; 5. the wealthy: adjective represents a certain group of people; 7. The view: context makes the noun specific; 8. the sky: unique thing)

Unit 6

The conditional: overview

- Have students scan the first column to review the different types of conditionals. Note that the chart continues on page G9 with the past unreal conditional and the mixed conditional.

- Focus on the factual conditional. Tell students to read the explanation about factual conditions that express a general or scientific fact. Elicit additional examples. (Possible answers: Classes are canceled if it snows heavily. If a pot is made of aluminum, a magnet doesn't stick to its surface.) Check that students use the simple present in both the if clause and the result clause. Then have students restate these sentences, replacing *if* with *when* or *whenever*. (. . . when OR whenever it snows heavily. When OR Whenever a pot is made . . .)

- Have a volunteer read the explanation for the second use of the factual conditional. On the board, write *If you will help me study, I will pass the exam.* Ask *Is this sentence correct?* (no) Have students correct the mistake. (If you help me study . . .) Point out that you cannot use a future form in the <u>if</u> clause.

- Next write on the board:

  If I knew the answer, I would help you.
  If I had known the answer, I would have helped you.

  Ask:

  Are these sentences examples of the factual or the unreal conditional? (unreal)
  Which sentence contains the present unreal conditional? (the first one)

  Keep the sentences on the board for use with discussion of the past unreal conditional on page TG9.

- Tell students to read the explanation and example sentences for the present unreal conditional. Refer students to the first example sentence and ask:

  Do I have the time to explain the problem to you? (no)
  Under what condition would I explain the problem to you? (if I had the time)

Note: The chart continues on page G9.

- Continue referring to the two sentences on the board. Ask *Which sentence contains the past unreal conditional?* (the second one)

- Tell students to read the explanation and example sentences for the past unreal conditional.

  Refer students to the first example sentence and ask:
  Did they know about the storm? (no)
  Under what condition would they have taken a different flight? (if they had known about the storm)

- Finally, have students read the explanations for the mixed conditional. Ask students to create statements using the mixed conditional in relation to the present or to the past. (Possible answers: If I had understood the directions, I wouldn't get lost. If I knew how to repair my car, I wouldn't have called the service station.)

- Focus on the Special cases. Ask a student to read the first explanation. On the board, write *If Natalie calls, tell her the good news.* Have volunteers restate the if clause three different ways. (If Natalie should call; If Natalie happens to call; If Natalie should happen to call)

- Ask a volunteer to read the second explanation and example sentences. Ask *Which sentence expresses regret and which one expresses relief?* (The first expresses regret and the second expresses relief.) Elicit additional sentences following the models. (Possible answers: If it weren't for rain, we would be able to take a walk. If it hadn't been for my lucky charm, I wouldn't have won the contest.)

- Read the third explanation and example sentences to the class. Make sure students understand that inferences are deductions. Discuss the context of each situation. (Possible answers: Julie probably went to the party, so she saw what happened. Since you don't know the answer, I can tell you didn't do the homework. The results didn't come out yesterday, so they'll come out today. Since you haven't finished packing, you're going to miss your flight.)

Option: Write the following if clauses on the board. To review the factual, present unreal, and past unreal conditional, have students write a result clause for each clause. Then have them identify the type of conditional.

> 1. *If Phil leaves at 11:00. . . .*
> 2. *If I were you. . . .*
> 3. *If you put sugar in water. . . .*
> 4. *If they had called us. . . . .*

(Possible answers: 1. he will come to class on time—factual; 2. I wouldn't buy that coat—present unreal; 3. the sugar melts—factual; 4. we would have picked them up—past unreal)

A Underline the correct word . . .

- Have students scan the if clauses and think about the possible verb forms that could be used in the result clauses. Then have students complete the exercise individually. Refer them to the chart if they have difficulty.

- Have students compare answers with a partner. Bring the class together and have students identify each type of conditional sentence. (1. factual; 2. factual—scientific fact; 3. factual—the condition is less likely; 4. past unreal—to express relief; 5. past unreal; 6. conditional expressing inference; 7. present unreal; 8. mixed)

Challenge: For more practice, have pairs make up different result clauses for the if clauses in the exercise, and different if clauses for the result clauses. Have students share their sentences with the class.

Type	Use	If clause (states the condition)	Result clause (states the result)	Examples
Past unreal conditional	To talk about past unreal or untrue conditions	**past perfect** Note: Don't use <u>would have</u> in the <u>if</u> clause.	<u>**would have**</u> + **past participle** Note: Use <u>could have</u> or <u>might have</u> if the result is not certain.	*If they **had known** about the storm, they **would have taken** a different flight.* *If you **had told** us about the delay, we **could have made** other arrangements.*
Mixed conditional	To talk about past unreal or untrue conditions in relation to the present	**past perfect** Note: Don't use <u>would</u> in the <u>if</u> clause.	<u>**would**</u> + **base form of the verb** Note: Use <u>could</u> or <u>might</u> if the result is not certain.	*If I **had prepared** for the interview, I **wouldn't be** so nervous.* *If we **had left** earlier, we **might be** on time now.*
	To talk about present unreal or untrue conditions in relation to the past	**simple past or <u>were</u>** Note: Don't use <u>would have</u> in the <u>if</u> clause.	<u>**would have**</u> + **past participle** Note: Use <u>could have</u> or <u>might have</u> if the result is not certain.	*If she **were** honest, she **would have told** us the truth.* *If I **spoke** Russian, I **might have understood** the guide.*

Special cases

1. Use <u>should</u>, <u>happen to</u>, or <u>should happen to</u> in the <u>if</u> clause in factual conditionals when the condition is less likely.

   If you { should / happen to / should happen to } see Peter, tell him to call me.

2. Use **If it weren't for . . .** / **If it hadn't been for . . .** in the <u>if</u> clause in unreal conditionals to express regret or relief.
   If it weren't for the traffic, we would be at the airport by now.
   (= Without the traffic, we would be at the airport by now.)
   If it hadn't been for your help this morning, we wouldn't have been able to meet the deadline.
   (= Without your help this morning, we wouldn't have been able to meet the deadline.)

3. **To express inferences in conditional sentences, different combinations of tenses can be used.**
   If Julie **went** to the party last night, she definitely **saw** what happened.
   If you **don't know** the answer to this question, you **didn't do** your homework.
   If the results **didn't come out** yesterday, they'**ll** definitely **come out** today.
   If you still **haven't finished** packing by now, you'**re not going to catch** your flight.

A Underline the correct word or words to complete each sentence.

1. If Sam (<u>does</u> / will do) well this year, he will apply to medical school.

2. Water (<u>boils</u> / is going to boil) when the temperature reaches 100° Celsius.

3. If you (will / <u>should</u>) find my scarf, please hold it for me.

4. If it (wouldn't have been / <u>hadn't been</u>) for her savings, Anna wouldn't have been able to attend university.

5. If we (would have known / <u>had known</u>) that car insurance was so expensive, we would not have bought a car.

6. If you didn't get a reply today, you (would definitely hear / <u>will definitely hear</u>) from us tomorrow.

7. If I (<u>had</u> / would have) a garden, I would grow several types of flowers.

8. If I (would have practiced / <u>had practiced</u>) my speech a bit more, I might not be so worried now.

Unit 7

REMEMBER
- A <u>coordinating conjunction</u> links two independent clauses in a sentence. It is preceded by a comma.
- A <u>subordinating conjunction</u> introduces a dependent clause in a sentence. When a dependent clause starts a sentence, the clause is followed by a comma.
- A <u>transition</u> links ideas between sentences or paragraphs. It is followed by a comma. A transition can be preceded by a semicolon.

Grammar for Writing: more conjunctions and transitions

Purpose	Coordinating conjunctions	Subordinating conjunctions	Transitions
To add information *Marc is working as a photographer, **and** he has experience in graphic design.* ***In addition to** working as a photographer, Marc has experience in graphic design.*	and	in addition to besides	in addition furthermore moreover besides
To clarify information *Smaller cars are more efficient; **in other words**, they use less fuel.*			that is in other words in fact
To illustrate or exemplify information *Many European cities are found along waterways.* ***For example,** London, Paris, Vienna, and Budapest all lie on major rivers.*			for instance for example to illustrate
To show contrast *Meg does not usually perform well under pressure, **but** she gave a brilliant recital.* *Meg does not usually perform well under pressure.* ***Despite this,** she gave a brilliant recital.*	but yet	even though although though while whereas	however nevertheless nonetheless in contrast even so still despite this / that
To express cause or result *They have a new baby, **so** they rarely get a good night's sleep!* ***Now that** they have a new baby, they rarely get a good night's sleep!*	so for	because since due to the fact that now that so that	therefore consequently accordingly as a result
To express a condition *Pollution can be reduced **provided that** car manufacturers mass-produce cars with greater fuel efficiency.* *Car manufacturers should mass-produce cars with greater fuel efficiency. **Otherwise,** pollution will not be reduced.*	or (else)	(only) if provided that as long as unless even if whether (or not)	otherwise
To show similarity *Water is necessary for life. **Similarly,** oxygen is required by all living things.*			similarly likewise

Unit 7

Grammar for Writing: more conjunctions . . .

- Have students read the Remember note to review the uses and punctuation of coordinating conjunctions, subordinating conjunctions, and transitions. Have students scan the chart vertically to see examples of each conjunction or transition.

- Then tell pairs to read through the chart horizontally and create example sentences with the conjunctions and transitions that are not already used in the examples in the chart or on pages 78 and 84. If students have difficulty, write one or more of the following example sentences on the board for reference.

Note: In the following example sentences, SC stands for subordinating conjunctions, T stands for transitions, and CC stands for coordinating conjunctions.

To add information:
SC   <u>Besides</u> working from 9:00 to 5:00, the job requires a lot of travel.
T   The new cafeteria has a wonderful menu; <u>in addition</u>, it's right around the corner.
The project still requires a lot of research. <u>Furthermore</u>, we need more funding.
Public School 67 desperately needs more textbooks and school supplies. <u>Moreover</u>, we need volunteers to help run the lunch program.
I really don't want to go skiing this weekend; <u>besides</u>, it's supposed to rain on Saturday.

To clarify information:
T   I will be doing research on my paper all day today; <u>that is</u>, if the library is open.
The job fair is open to all students at this university. <u>In fact</u>, we hope all students will participate.

To illustrate or exemplify information:
T   We're having serious problems with the car. <u>For instance</u>, when I try to start it, it makes a coughing noise.
This is a good neighborhood for young families. <u>To illustrate</u>, there are many parks, and the school system is excellent.

To show contrast:
CC   She had followed all the instructions, <u>yet</u> she couldn't get the camera to work.
SC   <u>Though</u> the location of the apartment is convenient, the rent is too high.
<u>While</u> King Food is closer to our home, the groceries are much more expensive than at Shop Cheap.
<u>Whereas</u> I had hoped to make more money at this job, I didn't expect to work every weekend.
T   My old MP3 player can hold only 50 songs; <u>in contrast</u>, my new one can hold 200!
I left for the airport late. <u>Even so</u>, I was on time for my flight.
Train tickets have increased in price by 25 percent. <u>Still</u>, train travel is cheaper than flying.

To express cause or result:
CC   Spring must be approaching, <u>for</u> the days are getting longer.
SC   I'm giving you this calendar <u>so that</u> you don't keep forgetting everyone's birthday.
T   There has been a problem with theft at the office; <u>accordingly</u>, security cameras have been installed.

- Note that the use of the coordinating conjunction *for* often requires a shift in word order. *They have a new baby, <u>so</u> they rarely get a good night's sleep! They rarely get a good night's sleep, <u>for</u> they have a new baby!*

To express a condition:
CC   Be on time, <u>or else</u> Richard will be very angry.
SC   <u>Whether or not</u> the plane leaves on time, it will arrive late because of the weather.

To show similarity:
T   Angela has a degree in fine arts; <u>likewise</u>, her sister hopes to become an artist.

A On a separate sheet of paper, ...

- Have students scan the connecting words in the exercise and identify which are subordinating conjunctions and which are transitions. (1. while: SC, in contrast: T; 2. although: SC, despite that: T; 3. in addition to: SC, furthermore: T; 4. unless: SC, otherwise: T; 5. now that: SC, as a result: T)

- To review, ask:
  What punctuation is used with subordinating conjunctions? (When a subordinating conjunction introduces a dependent clause that starts a sentence, the clause is followed by a comma.)
  What punctuation is used with transitions? (A transition is followed by a comma. It can be preceded by a semicolon.)

- Have students rewrite the sentences individually. Then have them compare answers with a partner.

Answers for Exercise A
1. a. While the ability to think logically is essential for making plans, the ability to think creatively is important for brainstorming new ideas. OR While the ability to think creatively is important for brainstorming new ideas, the ability to think logically is essential for making plans.
b. The ability to think logically is essential for making plans; in contrast, the ability to think creatively is important for brainstorming new ideas. OR The ability to think creatively is important for brainstorming new ideas; in contrast, the ability to think logically is essential for making plans.
2. a. Although Nicole has been under a lot of pressure lately, she still manages to stay calm and pleasant. OR Although Nicole still manages to stay calm and pleasant, she has been under a lot of pressure lately. b. Nicole has been under a lot of pressure lately; despite that, she still manages to stay calm and pleasant.
3. a. In addition to needing to know the products very well, salespeople need to have strong interpersonal skills. OR In addition to needing to have strong interpersonal skills, salespeople need to know the products very well.
b. Salespeople need to know the products very well; furthermore, they need to have strong interpersonal skills. OR Salespeople need to have strong interpersonal skills; furthermore, they need to know the products very well.
4. a. Unless we stay focused on the roots of the problems, we can't come up with effective solutions. OR We can't come up with effective solutions unless we stay focused on the roots of the problems. b. We have to stay focused on the roots of the problems; otherwise, we can't come up with effective solutions.
5. a. Now that Charlie realizes that he is mechanically inclined, he wants to become a mechanical engineer.
b. Charlie realized that he is mechanically inclined; as a result, he wants to become a mechanical engineer.

Unit 8

Indirect speech: review

Optional tense changes

- Read aloud the statement about backshifting, the first numbered explanation, and the example sentences. Have pairs take turns creating statements such as *I know a great joke.* Then bring the class together and have students tell what their partner just said: *Hanna said that she knows a great joke.*

- Ask a student to read the second numbered explanation and the example sentences. Again, have pairs take turns creating statements that are still true,

such as *I need a new jacket.* Then bring the class together and have students tell what their partner just said: *John said that he needs a new jacket.*

- Finally, ask a volunteer to read the third numbered explanation and the example sentences. Elicit additional factual statements such as *There are 24 hours in a day.* After each statement, call on another student to retell the fact: *Wendy said that there are 24 hours in a day.*

- Then read the Be Careful! note to the class.

Changes in pronouns and possessives

- Have students read the explanation and then study the pairs of sentences, focusing on the pronouns.

- Write the following chart and sentences on the board:

Direct speech	Indirect speech
1. *Nancy said, "I'm never too busy to complain to you about how busy I am."*	
2.	*He said he hoped I understood and that he didn't want to repeat the assignment.*

Have students change the first sentence from direct to indirect speech, and the second from indirect to direct speech. (1. Nancy said <u>she</u>'s never too busy to complain to <u>me</u> about how busy <u>she</u> is. 2. He said, "<u>I</u> hope <u>you</u> understand. <u>I</u> don't want to repeat the assignment.")

Questions in indirect speech

- Tell students to keep their books closed. To check their knowledge, write on the board "*Did you read Cousins's book?*" Write the beginning of the sentence on the board: *The teacher asked me ....,* and ask a volunteer to write the question in indirect speech. (The teacher asked me if / whether / whether or not I had read Cousins's book.) Then write on the board "*What day of the week is it?*" Call on a volunteer to write the question in indirect speech, beginning with *The teacher asked me ...* (The teacher asked me what day of the week it is / was.) Leave both indirect questions on the board.

- Read the explanation in the Grammar box aloud. Point out how each indirect question on the board follows statement word order, not inverted word order.

- Have students study the example sentences in the book. Tell them to note the changes in verb forms and the statement word order. Point out the use of *if* or *whether (or not)* in the first sentence.

- Finally, call on a student to read aloud the information in the Remember note.

Imperatives in indirect speech

- Have a volunteer read the explanation. Then have pairs take turns reading each example, first in direct speech and then in indirect speech.

A On a separate sheet of paper, combine each pair of sentences two ways, once with the connecting word(s) in **a** and once with the connecting words in **b**. Use a semicolon before a transition. Change the wording as necessary to retain the meaning. (See page TG11 for answers.)

1. The ability to think logically is essential for making plans. The ability to think creatively is important for brainstorming new ideas. (**a.** while **b.** in contrast)

2. Nicole has been under a lot of pressure lately. Nicole still manages to stay calm and pleasant. (**a.** although **b.** despite that)

3. Salespeople need to know the products very well. Salespeople need to have strong interpersonal skills. (**a.** in addition to **b.** furthermore)

4. We have to stay focused on the roots of the problems. We can't come up with effective solutions. (**a.** unless **b.** otherwise)

5. Charlie realized that he is mechanically inclined. Charlie wants to become a mechanical engineer. (**a.** now that **b.** as a result)

Unit 8

Indirect speech: review

Optional tense changes
When a reporting verb is in the simple past tense, backshifting is optional when:

1. **the statement refers to something JUST said:**
   Tom just called. He said that the director is leaving.
   OR Tom just called. He said that the director was leaving.

2. **the direct speech refers to something that's still true:**
   Ann mentioned that she needs to renew her passport.
   OR Ann mentioned that she needed to renew her passport.

3. **the direct speech refers to a scientific or general truth:**
   He noted that the Earth is the fifth largest planet in the solar system.
   OR He noted that the Earth was the fifth largest planet in the solar system.

> **BE CAREFUL!** Remember that when the reporting verb is in the present tense, the verb tense in indirect speech does not change.
>
> They say an exceptionally cold winter is expected this year. NOT They say an exceptionally cold winter was . . .

Changes in pronouns and possessives
In indirect speech, pronouns and possessives change to reflect the point of view of the reporter rather than the speaker.
My manager said, "You have to finish your report and give it to me as soon as possible." →
My manager said (that) I had to finish my report and give it to her as soon as possible.

I told her, "You'll have it on your desk by noon." →
I told her (that) she would have it on her desk by noon.

Questions in indirect speech
Indirect questions are a kind of embedded question—a question that is included in another sentence. Indirect <u>yes</u> / <u>no</u> questions begin with <u>if, whether</u>, or <u>whether or not</u>. Indirect information questions begin with a question word. All indirect questions follow statement (not inverted) word order and do not usually use <u>do, does</u>, or <u>did</u>.
He asked, "Did you see the movie?" → He asked if I had seen the movie. OR He asked whether (or not) I had seen the movie.
She asked, "When are you planning to go?" → She asked when I was planning to go.

> **REMEMBER**
>
> Indirect questions end with a period, not a question mark. The verbs in indirect questions follow the same changes as the verbs in indirect statements.

Imperatives in indirect speech
When imperatives are used to report commands, requests, instructions, and invitations, the imperative form changes to the infinitive. The negative infinitive is used for negative commands, requests, and instructions.

Direct speech	Indirect speech
"Could you please go to the store?"	She asked me to go to the store.
The chef said, "Add two eggs and stir the mixture."	The chef said to add two eggs and stir the mixture.
"Please have dinner with us," he said.	He invited me to have dinner with them.
She told the child, "Don't cross the street."	She told the child not to cross the street.

A On a separate sheet of paper, write the sentences in indirect speech. If a sentence can be written both with and without backshifting, write it both ways.

1. Zachary mentioned, "I need a new suit, but I really want a new jacket." Zachary mentioned (that) he needs / needed a new suit, but (that) he really wants / wanted a new jacket. **Note:** If students use *that*, they should delete the comma before *but*.
2. Kate just called. She asked, "Did you enjoy your vacation?"
   Kate just called. She asked if / whether / whether or not we enjoyed / had enjoyed our vacation.
3. In his lecture, Dr. Taylor stated, "The Earth rotates around the sun."
   In his lecture, Dr. Taylor stated (that) the Earth rotates / rotated around the sun.
4. Georgia says, "I've never seen such exciting paintings before."
   Georgia says (that) she's never seen such exciting paintings before.
5. The professor explained, "I want you to finish your essays for the next class."
   The professor explained (that) he / she wanted us to finish our essays for the next class.

B On a separate sheet of paper, write these conversations in indirect speech, using correct pronouns and possessives.

1. **MARIA:** Your cartoon is really good. Your drawing of the penguin is a hoot.
   JACK: Yours is hilarious, too! It really cracked me up! Maria told Jack (that) his cartoon was really good, and (that) his drawing of the penguin was a hoot. Jack said / answered (that) hers was hilarious too, and (that) it really cracked him up.
2. **RICHARD:** My paper on the health benefits of humor has just been published in a medical journal.
   ME: I'm happy for you! I'd appreciate it if you could give me a copy. Richard told me (that) his paper on the health benefits of humor had just been published in a medical journal. I said / answered (that) I was happy for him, and (that)
3. **KIM:** I bought a new MP3 player last week.
   BEN: I know. I saw it on your desk. It looks much better than your old one. Kim told Ben (that) she had bought a new MP3 player last week / the week before. Ben said / answered (that) he knew. He said (that) he had seen it on her desk, and (that) it looked much better than her old one.
   Note: If students use *that* in items 1–3, they should delete commas before *and*.

C On a separate sheet of paper, rewrite each of the following in indirect speech.

1. The teacher asked his students, "Can you tell me what the joke is about?"
   The teacher asked his students if / whether / whether or not they could tell him what the joke was about.
2. Don asked his wife, "Have you finished reading the book on humor?"
   Don asked his wife if / whether / whether or not she had finished reading the book on humor.
3. Lisa asked her boyfriend, "Why did you have to tell an ethnic joke at my father's birthday party last night?"
   Lisa asked her boyfriend why he had to tell an ethnic joke at her father's birthday party last night / the night before.
4. Barry sometimes wonders, "How would I react if someone made me the butt of a joke?"
   Barry sometimes wonders how he would react if someone made him the butt of a joke.
5. Vivian wondered, "When is the best time to tell a joke?"
   Vivian wondered when is / was the best time to tell a joke.

D On a separate sheet of paper, write the conversation in indirect speech. Begin like this: Harry asked me . . . (See page TG12 for answers.)

HARRY: Can I borrow your car on Saturday?
ME: Yes, you can. But you'll have to return it to me by 7:00 PM.
HARRY: Do you really need your car by 7:00? Could I bring it back by 9:00 PM instead?
ME: I'm sorry, but I promised to take my nephew to the movies.
HARRY: Oh, I understand. I'll return it to you by 7:00.

E On a separate sheet of paper, write each sentence in indirect speech. (See page TG12 for answers.)

1. The patient asked the nurse, "Could you please bring me a funny movie?"

2. Dr. Baker advised, "Don't let emotional tension make you sick."

3. She told me, "Be a good sport and laugh about it."

4. "Don't laugh at that joke," Fred instructed his son. "It's disgusting," he said.

5. "Laugh first, cry later," an old saying advises us.

6. Lucas told us, "Never touch the green button on the printer."

7. "Take the penguin to the zoo tomorrow," Mr. Franklin's neighbor told him.

8. Nick said, "Please don't ask how the meeting went."

A On a separate sheet of paper, . . .

- After students do the exercise individually, have them compare answers with a partner.

- Then bring the class together and discuss which sentences can be written without backshifting, and why. (1. The direct speech refers to something that is still true. 2. The statement refers to something just said. 3. The direct speech refers to a scientific truth. 4. The reporting verb is in the present tense.)

- Point out that answers written without *that* generally use a comma before *but* and *and*: *Zachary mentioned he needs a new suit, but he really wants a new jacket.* Answers written with *that* should not have a comma before *but* or *and*: *Zachary mentioned that he needs a new suit but that he really wants a new jacket.*

B On a separate sheet of paper, . . .

- Have volunteers read the conversations. Ask *What changes will you need to make when you write these conversations in indirect speech?* (There will be changes in verb forms, pronouns, and possessives.)

- Have students rewrite the conversations individually. Then have students compare answers with a partner.

- Bring the class together and go over any questions.

Challenge: Have pairs write their own short conversations. Then combine pairs into groups of four and have each pair read their conversation. Have the pair that is listening restate what the other pair said to each other.

Option: Have students write five questions in direct speech on a piece of paper. Then have students exchange papers with a partner and rewrite the questions in indirect speech. (Possible answer: Ingrid asked, "Where did you put the computer paper?" Ingrid asked where I had put the computer paper.)

C On a separate sheet of paper, . . .

- Have students scan the questions in quotes. Ask: *Which questions are yes / no questions?* (1 and 2) *Which questions are information questions?* (3, 4, and 5)

- After students rewrite the questions in indirect speech, bring the class together and go over the answers.

D On a separate sheet of paper, . . .

- Ask two volunteers to read the conversation. Ask *What changes will you need to make when you write this conversation in indirect speech?* (There will be changes in verb forms, pronouns, and possessives.)

- Working in pairs, have students rewrite every other line in the conversation. Then have them work with new partners and rewrite the remaining lines.

- Bring the class together and go over any questions.

Challenge: Have students change *me* in the conversation to *Carol*. In addition, tell students to play the role of Harry and to rewrite the conversation from his perspective. (I asked Carol if I could borrow her car on Saturday. She said that I could but that I would have to return it to her by 7:00 P.M. I asked if she really needed her car by 7:00 and if I could bring it back by 9:00 P.M. instead. She said that she was sorry but that she had promised to take her nephew to the movies. I said that I understood and would return it to her by 7:00.)

Answers for Exercise D
Harry asked me if / whether / whether or not he could borrow my car on Saturday.
I said / answered (that) he could, but (that) he'd have to return it to me by 7:00 PM.
He asked me if / whether / whether or not I really needed my car by 7:00 and if / whether / whether or not he could bring it back by 9:00 PM instead.
I said / answered (that) I was sorry, but (that) I had promised to take my nephew to the movies.
Harry said / answered that he understood, and (that) he would return it to me by 7:00.
Note: If students use *that*, they should delete the comma before *but* and *and*.

E On a separate sheet of paper, . . .

- Remind students to make any necessary changes in pronouns when they rewrite the sentences in indirect speech.

- After students complete the exercise individually, have them compare answers with a partner. Then bring the class together and go over any questions.

Answers for Exercise E
1. The patient asked the nurse if / whether / whether or not he / she could bring him / her a funny movie.
2. Dr. Baker advised (me) not to let emotional tension make me sick.
3. She told me to be a good sport and (to) laugh about it.
4. Fred instructed his son not to laugh at that joke. He said (that) it was disgusting.
5. An old saying advises us to laugh first and to cry later.
6. Lucas told us never to touch the green button on the printer.
7. Mr. Franklin's neighbor told him to take the penguin to the zoo tomorrow / the next day.
8. Nick said not to ask how the meeting went / had gone.

Unit 9

Grammar for Writing: when to use . . .

- Read the introduction in the Grammar box. Then divide the class into five groups. Assign each group one of the first five situations. Have groups read the situations in which the passive voice is preferred and the example(s).

- Invite groups to present their situation and the example(s) to the rest of the class.

- Finally, read the last situation and example to the class. Write two more example sentences on the board.

  1. Harriet King, who has also published four books on nutrition, wrote the article "Eating Less."

  2. The dealership, which has been getting numerous complaints about faulty seatbelts, recalled the new SUV model.

Ask students to change the sentences to the passive voice to avoid clumsy sentence constructions. (1. The article "Eating Less" was written by Harriet King, who has also published four books on nutrition. 2. The new SUV model was recalled by the dealership, which has been getting numerous complaints about faulty seatbelts.)

Option: Have students look for examples of the passive voice in English-language magazines and newspapers or in Internet articles. Tell students to copy down or bring to class three examples and to note the situation in which the passive voice is used. (Possible answer: The museum tour has been canceled and rescheduled for next week. Situation 3)

A On a separate sheet of paper, . . .

- Have students underline the agent in each sentence. (1. Construction workers; 2. People; 3. The company, They; 4. engineers, workers, engineers, engineers, factory; 5. We; 6. The reporter) Remind students that the agent is often unknown or unimportant. In these cases, it is not necessary to include the agent in the sentence in the passive voice.

- After students complete the exercise, bring the class together and call on volunteers for answers. Ask *In which sentence is an agent necessary? Why?* (Sentence 6 is the only sentence in which the agent is necessary. It is necessary because the agent has a long modifier: *whose investigation uncovered many shocking facts and a pattern of corrupt behavior.*)

- Ask pairs to skim the situations again and match each sentence in the exercise to the appropriate situation. (sentence 1: situation 1; sentence 2: situation 5; sentence 3: situation 4; sentence 4: situation 2; sentence 5: situation 3; sentence 6: situation 6) Go over the answers as a class and review as necessary.

Grammar for Writing: when to use the passive voice

Sentences in the passive voice can have the same meaning as those in the active voice. However, the word order in passive sentences gives a different emphasis to the information. Passive sentences focus the reader's (or listener's) attention on the result of the action rather than on the performer of the action (the agent). Writers prefer the passive voice in the following situations:

1. **To emphasize the result of an action, or if the agent is unimportant or unknown. This use is common in academic writing, scientific articles, and news reports.**
   A number of sophisticated treatments for heart disease **have been developed** in the last decade. (The writer emphasizes the treatments rather than the people who developed them.)
   Hundreds of people **were made** homeless by yesterday's floods. (The writer emphasizes the result of the floods rather than the floods themselves.)
   The Parthenon **was built** in the fifth century BC. (The builder is unknown or unimportant.)

2. **To describe a process. This use is found in technical and scientific writing.**
   There are four basic steps in the production of juice. First the oranges **are unloaded** from the trucks and **placed** on a conveyor belt. Then they **are washed** and **sorted**. Next they **are put** into machines that remove the juice and put it into cartons. Finally the juice **is distributed** all over the world.

3. **To use an impersonal or indirect tone, which suggests formality, impartiality, or objectivity. This use is favored in official documents, formal announcements, and signs, or to avoid placing blame.**
   Their wedding **will be celebrated** in June.
   Walking on the grass **is prohibited**.
   A mistake **has been made** in your account. It **will be corrected** on next month's statement. (The writer avoids mentioning who made the mistake and emphasizes the fact that it will be corrected, rather than who will do the correcting.)

4. **To keep the reader's attention focused on a previously mentioned noun, because it is the central topic of the paragraph.**
   They caught the thief later that evening. He **was placed** in jail and **was allowed** to call a lawyer. (The topic of the paragraph is the thief. By using the passive voice in the second sentence, the writer keeps the reader's attention focused on the thief.)

5. **To avoid using a general subject, which is considered weak. General subjects include the impersonal <u>you</u>, <u>we</u>, and <u>they</u>; <u>people</u>; <u>one</u>; <u>someone</u> / <u>somebody</u>; <u>anyone</u> / <u>anybody</u>. This use is common in formal documents, in official signs, and in newspaper editorials and other texts that express an opinion.**
   People must show their IDs before boarding. PREFERRED: IDs **must be shown** before boarding.
   We have cut prices on all merchandise. PREFERRED: Prices on all merchandise **have been cut**.
   Someone should inform voters of their rights. PREFERRED: Voters **should be informed** of their rights.

6. **To avoid clumsy sentence constructions. This is a common solution when the agent has a long or complex modifier.**
   The Tigers, whose new strategy of offense and defense seemed to be working, defeated the Lions.
   PREFERRED: The Lions **were defeated** by the Tigers, whose new strategy of offense and defense seemed to be working.

A On a separate sheet of paper, write each sentence in the passive voice.

1. Construction workers built the museum in less than six months.

2. People must present their passports at the border.

3. The company hired Ben Jones to replace the executive director. They gave Jones the corner office and offered him a very generous salary.

4. First engineers perfect the design for the new product. Then workers build a prototype. Next engineers test the prototype. After engineers approve the design, the factory begins production.

5. We have credited the sum of eighty-five dollars to your VISTA account.

6. The reporter, whose investigation uncovered many shocking facts and a pattern of corrupt behavior, exposed the official for taking bribes.

1.The museum was built in less than six months. 2. Passports must be presented at the border. 3. Ben Jones was hired to replace the executive director. Jones was given the corner office and offered a very generous salary. 4. First the design for a new product is perfected. Then a prototype is built. Next the prototype is tested. After the design is approved, production is begun. 5. The sum of eighty-five dollars has been credited to your VISTA account. 6. The official was exposed for taking bribes by the reporter, whose investigation uncovered many shocking facts and a pattern of corrupt behavior.

Unit 10

REMEMBER

Intransitive phrasal verbs are always inseparable. They can't be used in the passive voice since they don't have direct objects.

Phrasal verbs: expansion

The passive form of phrasal verbs

Transitive phrasal verbs are always inseparable in the passive voice, even when they are separable or always separated in the active voice.

> The TV couldn't be **turned on** this morning. (I couldn't **turn** the TV **on** this morning.)
> The empty lot has been **turned into** a beautiful garden. (They **turned** the empty lot **into** a beautiful garden.)

Transitive and intransitive meanings

Some phrasal verbs have both a transitive and an intransitive meaning.

> He went to bed without **taking off** his clothes. (transitive meaning: remove)
> What time does your plane **take off**? (intransitive meaning: leave)

> Thieves **broke in** and stole her jewelry. (transitive meaning: enter by force)
> She **broke in** the new employees by showing them the procedures. (intransitive meaning: train someone)

For a complete list of transitive and intransitive phrasal verbs, see the Appendices, pages A4–A5.

Three-word phrasal verbs

A three-word phrasal verb consists of a verb, a particle, and a preposition that together have a specific meaning. The verb and the particle in three-word phrasal verbs are inseparable.

> As a result of his controversial ideas, the senator **came up against** members of his own party, who opposed him vigorously.
> Does society have an obligation to **look out for** people who are disadvantaged?
> Temper tantrums are not uncommon in young children. As they mature, they **grow out of** this behavior.
> I'm going to close my door and not take any calls today; I've just got to **catch up on** my work.

For a complete list of three-word phrasal verbs, see the Appendices, page A6.

A On a separate sheet of paper, write each sentence in the passive voice. Use a <u>by</u> phrase, if necessary.

1. We have to call the meeting off. The meeting has to be called off.

2. He talked the client into a better deal. The client was talked into a better deal.

3. The president covered the mistake up. The mistake was covered up by the president.

4. She dropped the children off in front of the school. The children were dropped off in front of the school.

5. One of the applicants filled the form out incorrectly. The form was filled out incorrectly by one of the applicants.

6. I paid the balance off last month. The balance was paid off last month.

7. Someone threw the document away by mistake. The document was thrown away by mistake.

8. The speaker handed pamphlets out at the end of the presentation.
   Pamphlets were handed out by the speaker at the end of the presentation.

B Underline the phrasal verb in each sentence. Then decide if it has a transitive or an intransitive meaning.

	transitive	intransitive	
1.	☑	☐	The photographer <u>blew up</u> the photo 200 percent so we could use it for the poster.
2.	☐	☑	The plane <u>blew up</u> shortly before it was supposed to land.
3.	☐	☑	The workers won't <u>give up</u> until they're paid fair wages.
4.	☑	☐	She has tried to <u>give up</u> smoking several times, without success.
5.	☐	☑	Phil has to <u>wake up</u> at 5:00 AM every morning to get to work on time.
6.	☑	☐	The children played quietly in order not to <u>wake up</u> their parents.
7.	☐	☑	He <u>works out</u> three or four times a week in order to keep in shape.
8.	☑	☐	World leaders are meeting to <u>work out</u> a plan to eradicate poverty.

Unit 10

Phrasal verbs: expansion

The passive form of phrasal verbs

• Review that a transitive verb is a verb that needs a direct object to complete its meaning. Ask a student to read the explanation in the Grammar box. Have students read the Remember note and study the pairs of example sentences.

• Write the following phrasal verbs on the board: *throw away, hand out, talk into, do over, cater to, count on.* Ask *Which phrasal verbs are separable?* (throw away, hand out) *Which phrasal verbs are always separated?* (talk into, do over) *Which phrasal verbs are inseparable?* (cater to, count on) If necessary, refer students to the lists of transitive phrasal verbs on pages A4–A5 in the Appendices.

• Have pairs use the phrasal verbs on the board in sentences in the passive voice. (Possible answers: The leftovers had to be <u>thrown away</u> because we forgot to put them in the fridge. Samples were <u>handed out</u> at the beginning of the presentation. I was <u>talked into</u> buying the product even though I didn't want it. The report had to be <u>done over</u> because the client was unhappy with it. The guests were <u>catered to</u> with great speed and care. I promised my employer that I could be <u>counted on</u> to complete the project on time.)

• Bring the class together and have pairs share sentences.

Transitive and intransitive meanings

• Review that while a transitive verb needs a direct object to complete its meaning, an intransitive verb does *not* need a direct object.

• Have students read the explanation and the pairs of example sentences independently.

• On the board, write the phrasal verb *turn in*, and elicit sentences that show its transitive and intransitive meaning. (Possible answer: I <u>turned in</u> the application yesterday. Transitive meaning: submit. We're really tired, so we're going to <u>turn in</u> early. Intransitive meaning: go to bed.) If necessary, refer students to the lists of transitive and intransitive phrasal verbs on pages A4–A5 in the Appendices.

Challenge: For more practice, write the following phrasal verbs on the board: *1. give up. 2. work out. 3. make up.* Have partners write pairs of sentences to illustrate the transitive and intransitive meaning. (Possible answers: 1. Tanya <u>gave up</u> eating chocolate as part of her diet. Transitive meaning: quit doing something. I <u>give up</u>! Intransitive meaning: quit. 2. I can't <u>work out</u> this problem. Transitive meaning: resolve a problem. Peter <u>works out</u> every day. Transitive meaning: exercise. 3. Even though they fight a lot, they <u>make up</u> quickly. Intransitive meaning: end an argument and reestablish a friendly relationship. I <u>made up</u> an excuse about being stuck in traffic. Transitive meaning: create a fictional story.) Have students share their sentences with the class.

Three-word phrasal verbs

• Ask a volunteer to read the explanation and have students study the example sentences. Have students name the direct object in each example. (1. members, 2. people, 3. this behavior, 4. my work)

Option: Have pairs look at the list of three-word phrasal verbs on page A6 in the Appendices and write two example sentences. Then have them share the sentences with the class. (Possible answers: Every evening, I sit down with the newspaper and try to <u>catch up on</u> the news. E-mail has made it easier to <u>keep up with</u> friends.)

On a separate sheet of paper . . .

• Have students underline the phrasal verb in each sentence. (1. call off; 2. talked into; 3. covered up; 4. dropped off; 5. filled out; 6. paid off; 7. threw away; 8. handed out)

• Before students complete the exercise, remind them that transitive phrasal verbs are always inseparable in the passive voice.

• Go over the answers as a class. Point out that only sentence 5 requires an agent. Tell students that sentences 3 and 8 are correct with or without an agent. In these two cases, the agent provides additional and more precise information.

Option: Have students look at the phrasal verbs they underlined in the exercise. Ask *Which phrasal verb is always separable?* (2. <u>talk</u> someone <u>into</u>) Call on volunteers to restate all the sentences except 2 with the phrasal verbs *not* separated. (1. We have to <u>call off</u> the meeting. 3. The president <u>covered up</u> the mistake. 4. She <u>dropped off</u> the children in front of the school. 5. One of the applicants <u>filled out</u> the form incorrectly. 6. I <u>paid off</u> the balance last month. 7. Someone <u>threw away</u> the document by mistake. 8. The speaker <u>handed out</u> pamphlets at the end of the presentation.)

Underline the phrasal verb . . .

• After students do the exercise, bring the class together and elicit the direct object for each phrasal verb with a transitive meaning. (1. the photo, 4. smoking, 6. their parents, 8. a plan)

• Go over any questions.

Audioscript

Note: Printable unit audioscripts are also available on ActiveTeach.

UNIT 1

Page 4. Exercise C.

Conversation 1

F*: What are Jan's plans for next year? I'll bet she'll be doing something with math—she's such a whiz.

M: As a matter of fact, she's starting engineering school in September.

F: No surprise there.

M: And three schools have already accepted her!

F: That's great.

Conversation 2 [F = French]

M: So, have you made up your mind about a career yet?

F: Pretty much. It's going to be something with either singing or dance. I'm really serious about a career in music.

M: Makes sense to me. You've always been the musical type.

Conversation 3

M1: Bob seems a lot calmer than he used to. What's come over him?

M2: I know—I've noticed it, too. I guess those meditation classes have really taught him how to relax.

M1: So that's it.

Conversation 4

F1: What's with Nina? Someone started talking about where we'd all be a year from now, and she just got up and walked out of the room.

F2: Oh, she's a bit disappointed. She just heard from two of the three graduate programs she applied to. And she didn't get into either of them.

F1: Wow. That's too bad.

F2: Well, you can't blame her for feeling down.

F1: Nope.

Conversation 5 [M = Australian English]

M: Did you hear about Tom? He just quit his job in accounting and accepted a position teaching math at the university.

F: That's quite a career change!

M: No kidding. But you know, I never thought he was really well suited for the business world.

F: Me neither … I think he'll make a great teacher, though.

M: Me too.

Conversation 6 [F = Japanese]

M: I hear you want to do something in medical research.

F: That's right.

M: Well, have you gone on any interviews yet?

F: Not yet. But I found out that MediLabs has an opening for a junior lab specialist.

---

*F refers to a female speaker, and M refers to a male speaker.

M: Oh, great.

F: So I filled out an application and I'm going for an interview on Monday.

Page 10. Exercise C.

[L = Linda Foster, interviewer; M = Spanish]

L: Mr. Ferrante?

M: Yes. Hi. Marcos Ferrante.

L: I'm Linda Foster. Nice to meet you.

M: Hi. Nice to meet you, too.

L: I was very interested to read your application—I see you have some experience in the tourism industry. In hotels, right?

M: That's right. I've been working as an assistant hotel manager for two years now.

L: And why are you looking for a change? Aren't you happy at your current job?

M: Oh, I am. Yes. The thing is, I've always dreamed about working on a cruise ship.

L: Ah, so this is a step toward fulfilling your dream. That's very nice!

M: Uh-huh.

L: So, working in a hotel, you must have gotten some good experience with people—you must have to deal with all kinds of personalities, right?

M: Definitely. I find it very rewarding. I actually enjoy helping people work out their problems and helping them get what they need to make their stay at the hotel enjoyable.

L: Great … Mr. Ferrante, at the hotel, I imagine you're basically working with people on a one-on-one basis. Why do you think you have the right qualities to manage groups of people?

M: Well, I'm basically a real people person. I'm very friendly … I think people warm up to me easily. I find it pretty easy to win people over. By the way, please call me Marcos.

L: OK, Marcos. So, how do you do that? Win them over, I mean.

M: Well, for starters, I try to get to know them right away— what they like, what they don't like—and try to make them feel at home.

L: Interesting … Would you describe yourself as organized?

M: Very. As an assistant manager, you have to be. You've got reservation details to work out, transportation arrangements, people to please … If you're not organized, you're in big trouble.

L: I see.

M: And you always have to be ready for the unexpected— guests who don't show up, two guests assigned to the same room … no electricity. I'm very flexible in those situations, and I'm able to make quick decisions—to handle any problem that might come up.

L: What about training in emergency procedures? Did you get any of that in your current position?

M: You mean like a class or something like that? Because we are expected to know the general procedures for fire, or …

L: Not necessarily a class. Just tell me what training you've gotten.

M: Well, as soon as you start at the hotel, you're instructed in the hotel's procedures—to call the fire department as soon as an alarm goes off. And we have practice drills about twice a year.

L: That's great. Marcos, do you see yourself continuing to work in the travel business in the future?

M: Well, my short-term goal is to get experience working on a cruise ship where I can work with people and make a contribution. But my long-term goal is to start my own travel agency.

L: You seem to really know what you want to do.

M: I guess that's pretty true.

Page 13. Exercise A.

Conversation 1 [M = Chinese (Mandarin)]

F: That's quite a stamp collection!

M: I guess. I've been collecting for over 30 years now.

F: Really? You must have started when you were really young.

M: When I was five, actually. And after all these years, I still dream about having the biggest collection in the world.

F: And do you think you ever will?

M: It's hard to tell. Some people have huge collections. To be honest, though, I don't think I'll ever really be able to outdo them.

Conversation 2

F: Have you found a house yet?

M: Nope. I've been looking for a year now, but no luck. Not even close. I'm starting to feel like maybe it's time to just give up.

F: What? Don't give up now! I'm sure something will turn up.

M: The thing is, I'm looking and looking and prices just keep going up. I'm really not sure I'll ever have a house of my own.

F: Look. Just be patient. Who ever said finding a house was going to be easy?

Conversation 3

F: I'm really fed up with working for a large corporation.

M: Huh? What are you all ticked off about?

F: I'm just tired of having to do what other people tell me to do. I want to be able to make my own decisions for a change.

M: OK … So, like, what are you going to do about it?

F: Start my own business.

M: Start your own business? … You're dead serious, aren't you!

F: You bet I am. Don't tell anyone, but I've already applied for a loan.

M: Good for you!

Conversation 4 [F = Italian]

F: You know, I've always dreamed about being a flight attendant. I love traveling and meeting new people.

M: Why don't you apply for a job, then?

F: Well, I just don't think I have the right qualifications.

M: What do you mean? You speak three languages … and you've got some experience in the travel industry.

F: You mean the job I had as a tour guide?

M: That's right. I think they'd consider that to be related experience. Your qualifications are fine.

F: You're probably right.

UNIT 2

Page 18. Exercise C.

Conversation 1 [F = Portuguese]

F: I don't know how to tell you this, but I had a little accident with your bike.

M: Oh, no! Are you OK?

F: I'm fine. I'm fine.

M: Thank goodness.

F: But I'm afraid the bike got pretty badly damaged. Don't worry, though. The repair shop says they can fix it … and I will pay for the damage, of course.

Conversation 2

F: Uh, what happened to this suitcase? When I loaned it to you, it had two wheels.

M: Uh-oh. I guess they broke off when they were unloading the luggage. Those baggage guys are way too rough with people's bags.

F: Well, it's not going to be much use to me this way. Do you think you could get it repaired?

M: You know, it wasn't really my fault. Why don't you just call the airline and see if they'll take care of it?

Conversation 3

F: Frank! Why didn't you slow down? We could have been killed!

M: Didn't you see? That guy just cut me off!

F: What are you talking about? It was your fault. You were going too fast.

M: No way. If it hadn't been for him, we'd be fine.

Conversation 4

M: Pat, I was looking at this contract you completed. It's got June first as the due date. I'm sure it was supposed to be May first. I hope you didn't send it out like this.

F: I don't believe I missed that … I'm sorry. I just sent it out in the morning mail.

M: Well, we've got to do something about it.

F: I know. Look, it was totally my fault. I'll send out a revised contract right away.

Conversation 5

M: So, how'd the meeting go?

F: Not good. I was an hour late.

M: Uh-oh. They must have been pretty annoyed.

F: Well, I just told them the traffic was terrible.

M: Did they buy it?

F: Not really. I looked pretty bad.

Conversation 6 [F1 = Slovak]

F1: Laura, this is for you.

F2: What's this? My birthday isn't till next month!

F1: Well, you know that scarf you loaned me? I'm afraid I lost it. Uh, I feel just terrible about it … So I got you this to replace it.

F2: You didn't have to do that!

F1: No, really. I want to do the right thing.

Page 20. Exercise C.

[C = Claire Whitney, British English; V = Vivian Bridge; J = James Duncan]

C: Good morning. Welcome to "A World of Difference." I'm Claire Whitney. Most of us never know about the good deeds done by ordinary people, but their quiet actions can make a world of difference to many. Today we're privileged to have as our guests Vivian Bridge and James Duncan—two ordinary people who have done some extraordinary things to help out those in need. Vivian, let's start with you. I understand you're involved in a very interesting program.

V: That's right. The program I'm involved in is called Reach Out, and it focuses on helping elderly people who are confined to nursing homes.

C: And what kind of work do you do with this program?

V: Well, twice a week I visit a nursing home where I spend time with the people who live there. We talk, play cards—anything to help make them feel connected. Sometimes I run errands for them—even little things mean a lot to people who can't get out. I also helped create a small library in the corner of the cafeteria where people can sit and read together.

C: Hmm, and could you tell us a little bit about how you decided to get involved in this program?

V: Sure. Uh, actually, I just followed the example set by my mother. When I was a child, she used to visit a children's hospital to bring toys and play with the kids. Sometimes she took me along. I can still remember her saying how good it made her feel to be able to help, and I guess the feeling just rubbed off on me.

C: What a great role model!

V: I'm really proud of her. She felt really sorry for children who couldn't go out and play like I could. You know, I'll always be thankful to my mother for having taught me how to be generous without expecting anything in return. I look up to her a lot.

C: Your mother sounds like a really special person. James, what about you? Tell us something about the program you're currently involved in.

J: Certainly. I've founded a program called All Kids Count that tutors kids who are having trouble in school, especially in math. We have a drop-in center at the public library where students from the ages of about nine to eleven can come in once a week and get help with their math homework.

C: For free?

J: Uh-huh. All Kids Count is completely free and run entirely by unpaid volunteers—most of them retired schoolteachers. We provide some healthy snacks—crackers, fruit, and fruit juice—and a comfortable spot where students can work. For me, I've always found it really touching to see how many people are willing to volunteer for this program.

C: And what made you decide to start the program?

J: Well, the truth is I actually had trouble with math myself when I was in school. I was lucky enough to get help from a retired schoolteacher who lived on my street. So I have a lot of compassion for any kid having trouble in school, and I just thought I'd like to do something about it myself.

C: What a story!

J: Well, maybe it's because of my own memories of struggling in school, or maybe it's because the program has been so successful, but All Kids Count has turned out to be tremendously rewarding for me. I even tutor the kids myself!

C: Is there one particular success story you can tell us about?

J: Hmm … Oh, I know one. About a year ago, one of the kids who had come in for tutoring years before showed up. She had just graduated from college and said she wanted to volunteer in the program. Well, I was floored. Talk about "One good turn deserves another"!

C: Oh, that must have made you feel really good.

J: Oh, it did.

C: Well, I'm afraid our time's up. Thank you, James Duncan—and thank you, Vivian Bridge—for being with us today and sharing your inspiring stories. If our listeners would like more information about these programs or other programs they might want to get involved in, visit our website at www.aworldofdifference.com.

Page 25. Exercise A.

Conversation 1 [M = Spanish]

M: You know Allan, that new guy at the office I was telling you about?

F: I think so. What about him?

M: Well, I hate to complain, but … he's always borrowing money from me.

F: You mean he doesn't pay you back?

M: No … no. He always pays me back. But the truth is, I really don't like being put in the position of lending people money. I don't even like borrowing money myself.

F: Oh, I see.

M: I'm wondering if maybe I should just tell him the truth next time he tries to borrow money from me.

F: Hmmm. Tough call. Why don't you just tell him you're short of cash?

M: I don't know … I really hate to tell lies.

F: Yeah, but you also don't want to offend him, right?

M: I suppose. Maybe I'll try that next time he asks.

Conversation 2 [F = Chinese (Mandarin)]

F: I'm in an embarrassing situation.

M: What happened?

F: Well, last week I borrowed this beautiful silk jacket from Mary.

M: So?

F: I lost it.

M: Uh-oh. Not good.

F: I know. I feel just terrible. I think I left it on the train.

M: Did you check the lost-and-found?

F: Of course. Twice. But no one's returned it.

M: Yikes. So what are you going to do now?

F: Well, I can't shift the blame to anyone else. It was my fault.

M: Why don't you just get her a new one?

F: I would, but the thing is, she bought it in one of those out-of-the-way places she always goes to on vacation.

M: So much for buying a new one, I guess.

F: I'm just going to have to tell her what happened. Since I can't replace the jacket, I'll just ask her what she'd like me to buy her instead.

Conversation 3

M: Did you happen to listen to "A World of Difference" last night on the radio?

F: No, I missed it. Was it good?

M: Interesting. They were talking about how community programs aren't getting enough volunteers to help out with the work they need to do.

F: Really? That's too bad.

M: Well, most people really don't have the time to get involved, you know?

F: I guess. But I imagine most of those programs can't survive without volunteers.

M: Probably not.

F: Hmmm. It makes you think, though, doesn't it? Maybe I'll get involved in some volunteer work.

M: Well, uh, I'm sure it would be really rewarding.

F: You know, Bill was telling me about a local program that raises money for schools. And sometimes they actually roll up their sleeves and do some of the work themselves—painting classrooms and things like that.

M: Oh, yeah?

F: I think I'll give Bill a call and find out more about it. What do you think? Want to give it a go?

M: Sure. Why not? Might actually be fun.

UNIT 3

Page 31. Exercise E.

Conversation 1

M: So, how are things?

F: Not bad. But I'm a little worried about my twelve-year-old. He's causing problems at school.

M: Tom? But he's never given you any problems before.

F: I know. We're hoping he's just going through a stage.

M: Well, I wouldn't worry too much about it. I'm sure when he's a little older, it'll work out fine.

Conversation 2 [M = Japanese]

M: I don't know how I'm going to get all this work done with the monthly report due on Friday.

F: But you've got two more days to finish it.

M: I know. If I didn't have all this other work, I'd be fine. But I don't think I can do it all alone.

F: So I'll give you some help, OK?

M: Are you sure?

F: It's no problem.

Conversation 3

M: My sister has really gone over the edge now. She says she wants to take up parachute jumping. Can you believe that?

F: What? You've got to be kidding.

M: I'm not. She's dead serious.

F: Well, you've got to talk her out of it. It's really a dangerous sport.

Conversation 4

F1: I haven't seen either of your kids in ages. How are they doing?

F2: Funny you should ask. The older one just announced he wants to be an actor.

F1: Really! That's great!

F2: What's so great about it? We were hoping he'd go to medical school like his father.

F1: I know you don't want my opinion, but if that's what he really wants, I'd suggest you encourage him. I wish my kids knew what they wanted to do.

Page 34. Exercise B.

F: You're watching "30 Minutes." And I'm Katie Fleming. And do we have a story for you tonight—a terrible tragedy and an amazing heroic act.

The desire to save one's own life is an extremely powerful instinct in all of us. It takes tremendous courage to be able to act against such a powerful instinct, to risk one's own life to save the life of another person.

Twenty-five-year-old tour guide Seol Ik Soo was returning home with a group of South Korean tourists from a trip to Beijing, China. As the plane prepared to land at Kimhae Airport in South Korea, Seol was thinking about his wife. They'd been married one month earlier, and it was their first time apart. Suddenly the airplane started shaking and he heard a crashing sound. The lights went out and a ball of fire ran up and down the cabin. The plane crashed into a mountaintop, killing more than a hundred twenty of the passengers on board.

Somehow Seol managed to crawl through a hole in the side of the plane and escape.

Seol feared an explosion, so his first thought was to run to save his own life. But he could hear the other passengers inside the plane calling for help. He went back and lifted a survivor onto his back, carrying him away from the plane to safety. Seol remembers carrying at least three or four injured people from the plane—but in fact there may have been as many as ten. When asked about it later, he said, "I don't know where the energy came from. It felt like I wasn't carrying anything at all."

Seol tore his shirt into bandages for the wounded and used his belt to bind up a man's badly bleeding leg. It wasn't until he stopped and sat down to smoke a cigarette that he realized his own face was covered in blood. When asked how he managed to perform so heroically, Seol replied, "I couldn't have done it in my right mind."

Everyone who knows Seol describes him as an ordinary guy. His boss describes him this way: "I know Seol as cheerful and hardworking, but just a normal young man. Now I have a new view of him. He's a remarkable person. We're all very proud."

Where does this kind of courage come from? How does a normal person manage to act so fearlessly? Seol says, "My parents always brought me up to believe people and life are very precious." It was this belief that enabled Seol, an ordinary person, to do something truly extraordinary and heroic.

Page 37. Exercise A.

1.

F: Felix Tan is putting in very long hours on a big project he's been assigned at work. Felix has been working nights and weekends to finish the project on time, but it doesn't look like he'll make it. He has been telling his boss that he needs help in order to meet the project deadline, but his boss ignores his requests.

2.

F: Robert Reston has been struggling with high blood pressure since he was a child. His doctors have tried everything they can to help him lower it, from diet to exercise and now drugs, but his blood pressure just doesn't come down.

3.

M: Eva Garcia's husband is turning 30 next week, and Eva would like to get him something special to mark the occasion. She's spent a lot of time and energy going from store to store in her search for the "perfect" gift, but she just can't find the right thing.

UNIT 4

Page 40. Exercise C.

F: Good morning. I'm Rosanna MacKenzie from the Executive Training Center, and I'd like to tell you about some exciting morning workshops we offer that will begin next week. These professional-development workshops will help you be a more successful manager. And they will provide you with useful skills that will add value to your life outside of work. Each one-hour workshop begins at 7:00 A.M. And since we know how busy you are, a continental breakfast will always be available. Now to the workshops.

On Monday, join motivational psychologist Dr. Margaret Smith to learn how to stop putting off until tomorrow what you can do today. Dr. Smith is a lively and entertaining presenter, and you can expect lots of audience participation.

Are you the kind of person who finds it impossible to live with imperfections of any kind? If even small mistakes drive you crazy, then Tuesday's workshop may be just what you need. CEO Steven Cobb shows you when and how to lower your standards and accept less than the best. You can learn to work and live happily in an imperfect world!

Wednesday's workshop is for those of you who always try to do too much. If you're constantly accepting assignments from other people and then finding you're overwhelmed and unable to meet your deadlines, then this is for you. With the help of Dr. John Hill, you'll learn to live with your own limitations and avoid taking on more than you can handle.

On Thursday, psychologist Dr. Anne Hammond shows you how to keep your cool under trying circumstances. Learn how get your emotions under control and face everyday problems calmly and confidently. You'll be better equipped to cope with anything and everything after Dr. Hammond's class. We promise!

And on Friday, a special workshop for negative people who just can't seem to see the sunny side of things. A simple, five-step program will show you how to focus on the positive and enjoy success in your work and happiness in your relationships.

Page 44. Exercise C.

[I = interviewer; MC = Michael Chen, Chinese (Mandarin)]

I: I'm here with Michael Chen, who is from Taiwan. And we're discussing cultural differences in the way people express anger. Michael, is there any way to generalize about people in Taiwan? I mean, are there strong cultural traditions about expressing anger? I've actually heard that it's unacceptable to show anger there. Is that true?

MC: Well, generally, I think it's very unusual for someone to express anger toward an authority figure … say a parent, or a superior at work. That's just not considered appropriate. Speaking for myself, if I got mad at my boss, I certainly wouldn't lose my temper. As a matter of fact, I probably wouldn't even raise my voice. I might let off a little steam by talking with a colleague about what happened, but I'd try not to let anything show—to my boss, I mean. I'd definitely keep it in.

I: What about with friends and colleagues? Are people in Taiwan always so controlled about their anger?

MC: Of course not. I wouldn't want to suggest that everyone is the same, but I think we are a little slower to anger than people in many other places. We tend to let things go for a while. You really have to be provoked before you show it. Let's say you're meeting a friend for lunch and he's late. You probably wouldn't say anything. But if it happened all the time, well, eventually, you wouldn't be able to hold it back. You'd have to say what's on your mind.

I: So, in other words, you're less likely to make an issue out of something.

MC: Right.

I: Things have to be very bad before you'll have it out with someone, right?

MC: Right. But even then, you wouldn't really explode. I think that kind of thing is very rare among people who know each other. People are more subdued in expressing their anger: You'd raise your voice, sure—but not as much. You'd say what's on your mind—but really tell someone off? No, I can't imagine someone doing that.

I: What about when people don't know each other, like with complete strangers? For example, when someone cuts you off while you're driving?

MC: Ah, road rage—that's one situation where you might not hold back! When it comes to nasty drivers, it's no different in Taiwan than anywhere else in the world: Some people become enraged, and they show it, no holds barred!

I: But what about you?

MC: Me? I might get mad, but I wouldn't do anything about it.

Page 49. Exercise A.

Speaker 1 [M = Portuguese]

M: There are so many sources of stress in my work that I don't even know where to begin. Forget about avoiding it. That would be impossible. But there is one technique I learned—in a workshop the company gave—that actually has helped a bit. When the stress really starts getting to me, I take a five- or ten-minute walk at lunchtime. That really helps me loosen up and get away from things for a moment. It makes a big difference, believe me.

Speaker 2

F: Sometimes I feel totally burned out. I mean, I know what's causing it. I'm always taking on more than I can handle. But I still haven't been able to figure out a solution. Last month I decided to start asking other people to give me a hand. It worked pretty well for the first two or three days, but little by little I began taking on more and more work and before I knew it, I was overwhelmed again. I guess it's my nature. I don't think I have a cure for it.

Speaker 3 [F = U.S. regional]

F: It's a little embarrassing to admit, but I have a bit of a problem with my temper. I mean, at work, I never show my feelings. If someone makes me angry, I usually just hold it in. But when I get home, that's another story. My kids are great kids, but when they do something wrong, I sometimes completely lose my temper and start yelling at them. The thing is, I know it's really about what happened at work. I'm just taking it out on them. Anyway, I wasn't happy about my behavior with my kids, so I went to a workshop on anger management—not that long ago, actually. I think it really helped. They suggested finding a way to let off a little steam when I'm angry. So I've taken up aerobics three times a week. It helps me think through what's been bugging me—and then I can just let it go. By the time I'm with my kids again, I have a whole new perspective on things.

Unit 5

Page 58. Exercises C and D.

[A = female announcer; M = Margo Edmonds;
W = Dr. Max Walker; S = Simon Grant, Australian English]

A: Good morning, and welcome to "Psychology and You." Today we're here with Dr. Max Walker of the Chapman Institute to talk about dreams. What do your dreams mean? What can they tell us? Call us if you've got a dream to share, at 555-8787. Thank you for being with us today, Dr. Walker.

W: My pleasure.

A: Our first caller is Margo Edmonds. Go ahead, Margo.

M: Good morning, Dr. Walker.

W: Hello, Margo. So you've got a dream to tell us about?

M: Yes, I do ... Well, for about two weeks, I've been having this dream that I'm falling.

W: Mm-hmm.

M: Night after night, it's the same thing: I'm falling into a dark, endless tunnel.

W: I see.

M: There's absolutely nothing I can do to stop falling. I feel so helpless—it's really terrifying.

W: Of course.

M: When I wake up, my heart is pounding. The dream always shakes me up. I mean, I have this nervous, worried feeling for the rest of the day—as if something terrible is about to happen.

W: Is there something in particular, Margo, that you've been worried about in the last month or so?

M: Well, I'm not really sure ... Well ... come to think of it, ... yes. I have exams coming up, and ... I guess I'm really nervous that I won't pass them.

W: Well, Margo, it's possible that your dream expresses your fear of failure and your insecurity about the exams.

M: Are you sure? I think the dream is telling me that I'm going to fail the exams.

W: No, not at all. Don't ever take a dream as a sign that something bad or good is about to happen. It's just a dream. However, it could mean that you're afraid that something terrible will happen. Our dreams just reflect what is going on inside us.

M: Well, that's a relief. Thank you, Dr. Walker.

A: Good luck on your exams, Margo! Our next caller is Simon Grant.

S: Hello, Dr. Walker.

W: Hi, Simon. How are you?

S: Doing very well. Thanks.

W: So, Simon, you've got a dream you want to tell us about?

S: I sure do. Last night I had this incredible dream. I was flying like a bird.

W: Wow! That's great.

S: I have no idea where I was, but the view was absolutely fantastic.

W: I'll bet.

S: And the higher I flew, the more beautiful it was. It put me in a great mood.

W: Nice!

S: When I woke up, I felt really optimistic! Anyway, I can't help thinking it's a sign that something good is going to happen.

W: Whoa! I don't want to disappoint you, Simon. That was a terrific dream, but just as I told Margo, dreams don't predict the future.

S: Oh.

W: However, they can reflect how we're feeling about things at the moment. Have you experienced something recently that you really feel good about?

S: Well ... as a matter of fact, I got a big promotion at work last week.

W: Aha!

S: I can't wait to get started.

W: Well, Simon, that might explain your dream.

S: How's that?

W: You're happy about your success and excited about your new responsibilities. Your dream may just be an expression of how you feel about your life right now.

S: Oh, that makes sense. Thanks, Dr. Walker. That's very interesting.

A: Well, that's about all the time we have this week. Thanks, Dr. Walker.

W: Thank you.

Page 61. Exercise A.

Conversation 1

M: Listen to this—a way to make big money in just two weeks.

F: Uh ... That sounds too good to be true.

M: No, really. They send you a list of names and addresses. You just send the last person on the list ten dollars and then add your name to the list.

F: And ...

M: ... And then someone gets your list and the money starts rolling in.

F: That's such an obvious get-rich-quick scam. You're not going to fall for that, are you?

M: Well, I suppose you're right—it's just wishful thinking on my part.

Conversation 2 [F = Portuguese]

F: Honestly, they must think people will believe anything!

M: What are you talking about?

F: This company has a method for learning a language while you sleep. That's impossible!

M: I wouldn't be so sure. Actually, it's very possible. There was something on the news just the other day … a group of students learned the basics of Russian in just one week, in a sleep-learning lab.

F: For real? Maybe we should get some more information. Might be a fun way to learn French!

Conversation 3 [M = Punjabi]

F: Here's something I'd really like to try!

M: What is that?

F: A speed-reading course. They can train you to read a 200-page book in an hour!

M: I don't know. I find that kind of hard to believe. I mean, I've heard of improving your reading speed, but 200 pages in one hour—it just doesn't seem likely that anyone could do that.

F: Yeah … it does sound a bit much.

UNIT 6

Page 66. Exercise C.

Conversation 1 [M1 = Slovak]

M1: I wonder if you could please do me a favor.

M2: I'll try.

M1: Well, I've been waiting in line here for a really long time now, and … well … I'd like to use the bathroom. Do you mind?

M2: No problem, no problem. Go ahead.

M1: Thanks a lot. You won't forget me when I get back, will you?

M2: Of course not. Don't worry about it.

Conversation 2 [F2 = Arabic]

F1: Unnh. What was I thinking?

F2: Do you need help?

F1: That would be really nice. Do you mind?

F2: Of course not … On a count of three, OK?

F1: OK.

Both: One. Two. Three. Uhnn.

F2: Oh! This is heavy. What's in this thing?

F1: Sorry. I packed a lot of books in there. Listen, I really appreciate it.

F2: My pleasure. Really.

Conversation 3 [F = Spanish]

M: Excuse me. Do you speak English?

F: Yes.

M: I'm afraid I'm a little lost. I'm trying to get to the Prado Museum.

F: The Prado? You are lost. OK. Let me see … Are you walking?

M: Yes.

F: OK, then you need to take the bus. There's a stop about three blocks from here.

M: Oh. Which way is that?

F: That way. Just walk straight up this street for about three blocks till you see a small café. Sorry I can't remember the name. The stop is right in front of the café.

M: Oh, OK.

F: The bus will take you right to the Prado. OK?

M: Thanks so much for your help.

Conversation 4

F: Hank, I'm sorry to bother you, but could you do me a favor?

M: Of course. What's up?

F: I just want to go grab a cup of coffee. Would you mind watching these?

M: These?

F: Yeah. I'll only be a minute.

M: Susan, don't worry about it. Take your time.

Conversation 5

M: Excuse me … excuse me … thanks … excuse me … Uh, excuse me. Do you mind?

F: Yes?

M: Your suitcase?

F: Oh, I'm sorry! Let me get that out of the aisle.

M: Thanks so much! Excuse me … excuse me … excuse me …

Conversation 6

F: What did he say?

M1: I don't know. I didn't hear.

F: Something about a storm.

M1: A storm? When?

F: Excuse me.

M2: Yes. What can I do for you?

F: We can't hear the TV. It's too low. Can you reach it?

Page 70. Exercises A and B.

[F = British English]

M: I saw this show last night about incredible stories of things that happen to people on vacation. It was called "When You Least Expect It." It was very interesting. It's amazing how you can be enjoying a vacation one minute, and the next thing you know—everything's changed.

F: What do you mean?

M: Well, you know how you are when you're on vacation. You're so carefree; you never expect anything serious to happen to you. I still keep thinking about all the stories of those tourists who were on vacation in Asia when that monster tsunami hit. Well, actually, the first story on that show was about that. There was this girl from England. Umm … Tilly Smith …

F: What happened to her?

M: Well, here's this ten-year-old girl who, like, saved her parents and dozens of other people who were all on the beach in Phuket … in Thailand, because she'd learned about tsunamis in school.

F: What did she do?

M: She was playing in the sand on the beach, and everyone saw the water acting strangely and they were fascinated. So they started walking toward the water to look at it, but Tilly was screaming to get off the beach. At first everybody ignored her, probably because she was just a kid, but she didn't give up. She just kept screaming "It's a tsunami. Run!" So finally, they took notice and ran. Within seconds, the beach was deserted. Umm … yeah, everybody had left for the safety of the hotel. And it was a good thing. It turns out that this was one of the only places along the beaches in Phuket where no one was killed or seriously injured.

F: Gosh! It's … it's kind of shocking that out of all the people on the beach only a ten-year-old knew anything about tsunamis.

M: Yeah, isn't that surprising? But very encouraging that this ten-year-old kid was able to make such a difference.

F: I'm sure all those people will be changed forever by that experience. What a close call! … You know … I know some people who were there, too. Well, not in Thailand, but in India. In the south, in some beach town, I don't know what it's called. These friends of mine—Shira and Dan—have a daughter, Liore, who was doing some community service in India, and they were spending their winter vacation with her.

M: Umm, what happened to them?

F: Well, they were all having breakfast at their hotel when they heard a hotel employee telling everyone to run. They turned around and saw a wall of water coming straight at them. At first they were so shocked by the scene that it fascinated them and they didn't move. But then, all of a sudden, they realized they were in danger. They ran to their van and drove away as fast as they could, up to the hills where the water didn't reach them.

M: Whoa, that was a close call too!

F: But that's not the end of the story.

M: Really? What happened then?

F: They thought it was all over and they went back to the hotel. Unfortunately, they didn't really understand the seriousness of the situation.

M: Wasn't it all over by then?

F: That's probably what most people would think. But when they got back to the hotel, the water was rushing towards them again. Shira thought that they would all die. Her whole life passed in front of her eyes. They were really desperate at this point.

M: What a horror! How did they get out?

F: They ran for their lives back to the van. And they started driving again. On their way, they picked up old people who couldn't run. Finally, the van couldn't hold any more people. Somehow they managed to drive back up to the hills again.

M: Wow.

F: My friend says that those few hours changed her life forever. She says that never again will she take life for granted. She'll always think of how fast things can change. And she'll always remember how precious every minute is.

Page 73. Exercise A.

M: Welcome to "Trip Advisor." I'd like to read you two letters I received recently about travel nightmares. Here's the first one, from Kevin Root of Banbury, England.

Dear Trip Advisor,
I am writing to tell you about a travel nightmare that happened on our recent vacation. On the flight home, my brand-new, black vinyl suitcase was lost. A bag that looked similar to mine was unclaimed, so the airline believes that another passenger may have taken my bag by mistake. The airline has suggested that I wait to see if

this other passenger will return the luggage. However, it has been several weeks and the bag has not turned up. You can bet that the next suitcase I buy isn't going to be plain black!

Now here's the second letter, from Irene Karameros, from Ontario, Canada.

Dear Trip Advisor,
Here's a travel horror story for you. I recently took a flight for a business trip. When I arrived at the luggage claim area, my checked suitcase was completely smashed and torn open, and my clothing was lying all over the luggage carousel! It looked like a wild animal had attacked my bag. I guess I'm partly to blame, as I did pack the bag pretty full and had to sit on it to close the zipper. Still, don't you think that baggage handlers should treat our property with more care?

Page 73. Exercise B.

M: Well, Kevin and Irene—thanks for sharing your stories. Your travel nightmares are unfortunately common ones. Statistics show that about 0.5 percent of all checked bags are lost or damaged. With roughly 1.5 billion airline passengers each year, that translates into several million lost bags every year. The good news is that 98 percent of the time, lost luggage is located and returned in the first 24 to 48 hours.

Of course, there's nothing you can do to prevent your luggage from getting lost or damaged. However, there are some things you can do to reduce the likelihood of this happening and also to minimize the inconvenience when it does.

First off, most luggage looks alike. To avoid having another passenger grab your bag by mistake, try making your bag as distinctive as possible. For example, if you've got a black nylon bag like everybody else, tie a brightly colored ribbon to the handle or mark the exterior with colored tape. And, as Kevin recommended, the next time you buy a suitcase, consider a color other than black!

As you're packing, make a list of what goes into each bag. That way, if you have to file a lost luggage claim, you'll know what you lost. Be sure to pack anything especially valuable, such as prescriptions, electronics, or jewelry, in your carry-on bag. And pack enough clothing and essentials in your carry-on to last 24 hours. That way, if your bags do disappear, you aren't stuck with just the clothing on your back.

And never check baggage that won't completely close. As Irene can tell you, if your bag is too full to close, it's better to remove some items than to have the bag pop open when it's being loaded into the airplane. Also, to avoid damage to checked luggage, remove any shoulder straps or other loose elements that could get caught on a luggage conveyor belt.

Be sure that your correct name, address, and telephone number appear on the luggage tag on the outside of your bag. You'd be surprised how many bags have outdated or incorrect tags. As an added safeguard, pack this contact information and also your flight and hotel itinerary inside your bag, too, in case the label on the outside of the bag gets torn off.

UNIT 7

Page 82. Exercise C.

Part 1

M: As you know, the theory of multiple intelligences provides one way of looking at human intelligence. Well, the concept of genius provides yet another way of approaching this topic. As you can probably imagine, this, too, is a controversial topic, and there are different theories supporting opposing views.

So, what is genius? There's a lot of disagreement on this. To a lot of people, a genius is simply a person with a high IQ. Average people have an IQ that can range from 85 to 115. But a genius is a person with a score over 145. For example, Albert Einstein—who I'm sure you're all familiar with—is estimated to have had an IQ of 160. But many people disagree with this definition of genius. For them, genius is not related to IQ. At the beginning of the twentieth century, American psychologist Lewis Terman selected 1,500 gifted children—children with IQ scores of 140 or more—who were then followed through middle age by a group of psychologists. None of these people actually stood out; none went on to become great inventors or brilliant thinkers. To the psychologists who studied them, this is proof that a person may have a high IQ and still not be a genius.

Page 82. Exercise D.

Part 2

M: Now let's move on to another area of controversy concerning this topic. Is genius determined by the environment? Or is it passed to us by our parents through genes? To some scientists, intelligence is determined by the environment—that is, the education we get, the books we read, or the food we eat. Identical twins have the same genes, but do they also have the same abilities? Well, they often don't. And why is this? Well, some scientists believe that twins have different talents because they are exposed to different environments. What supports this view even further is the fact that if genius were inherited, every genius in history should have had gifted ancestors—his or her parents, grandparents, great-grandparents—they would all have been geniuses too. And this—we all know—is far from true.

Now, what do supporters of the opposite theory say? Of course, that genius is not determined by the environment but inherited from our parents. There are families of geniuses—for example, the Bachs, who were all excellent musicians. Supporters of this theory would argue that such families exist precisely because talent is passed through genes. Another example in support of this theory is the mathematical genius, Srinivasa Ramanujan. He was raised in a poor hut and had almost no mathematical education. Scientists who support this view claim that if genius were determined by the environment, this man's genius would be impossible to explain.

Now scientists have proposed other explanations of genius, but these are the two main theories—greatly simplified, of course.

Page 85. Exercise A.

1: Liza

F: Well, unfortunately, Liza is really struggling in French and Italian. She clearly does not have a knack for languages. But she is wonderfully imaginative! And she shows a real flair for creating stories and writing poetry.

2: Ben

F: Ben needs to pay more attention to his academic subjects, especially math and science. He's not doing well in those areas, I'm sorry to say. However, he does show real artistic talent, especially with crafts and design. He's been making beautiful sculptures and jewelry, and his woodwork is very skilled.

3: Stella

F: I'm happy to tell you Stella is a very strong student, and she's doing well in all her subjects, especially German. After only two years of German, she speaks it quite fluently! Her only weakness is in music. Her lack of interest in this area really surprises me, because she has such a good ear for languages.

4: Steven

F: Steven is really smart in math. He understands the concepts immediately, and he's comfortable with numbers in a very practical sense: His ability to solve problems in his head is extraordinary. He's a bit shy, though, and is having trouble making friends and working with his classmates.

5: Sophie

F: Sophie really shines in her music and art classes. She shows a natural ability in both these areas. As I'm sure you've noticed, even though she just started piano classes, she's able to play pieces easily and with great skill. It's amazing how sometimes she can play a piece after hearing it only once or twice.

6: Dan

F: Well, no surprise here. What Dan seems to enjoy most is working with cars and engines … figuring out how they work. The only problem I see is that he often works too quickly and doesn't pay enough attention to the little things. That can really create problems when you're trying to repair a machine!

7: Karen

F: Karen's power of observation is really well developed for a child of her age. She notices every single detail. Karen really stands out in that area. Where she has difficulty is in communicating her ideas. Her written work could be a bit stronger.

8: Sam

F: I find it fascinating how Sam seems to be able to know what other students are thinking before they even speak. But I'd like to see him develop his social skills more. Sometimes he gets a little impatient when one of his classmates needs him to explain something. He's great when he's on his own, but he's having trouble working well with the other students.

UNIT 8

Page 90. Exercise C.

Joke 1

M: Listen to this. A guy asks a woman, "Do you know where Fifth Avenue is?" So she says, "Yes" and walks away.

F: [laughs] Cute.

M: [laughs] I don't know why, but that just tickles me.

F: I can see why. That's really a hoot!

Joke 2

F: Here's a good joke. Knock knock.

M: Who's there?

F: Banana.

M: Banana who?

F: Knock knock.

M: Who's there?

F: Banana.

M: Banana who?

F: Knock knock.

M: Who's there?

F: Orange.

M: Orange who?

F: Orange you glad I didn't say banana?

M: You've got to be kidding me. That is so lame.

Joke 3

F: Wanna hear a great joke?

M: Sure. Shoot.

F: A guy drives up to the curb and asks the policeman, "Can I park here?" The policeman says, "No." So the guy asks, "Well, what about all these other cars?" The cop says, "They didn't ask!"

M: They didn't ask? That just cracks me up.

Joke 4

M: Did you hear the one about the couple with the perfect marriage?

F: No.

M: Well, he's deaf and she's blind.

F: What's that supposed to mean?

M: Get it? He's deaf and she's blind.

F: Uh, that's really offensive.

M: Oh. Sorry.

Joke 5 [F2 = U.S. regional]

F1: Know any good jokes?

F2: Umm … Yeah. Here's a good one. An old man goes into a restaurant and orders some soup, and the waiter brings it to him.

F1: And?

F2: Well, after a minute the old man calls the waiter over and says, "I want you to taste my soup." The waiter says, "Is it cold?" The old man says, "I just want you to taste my soup."

F1: How weird.

F2: So the waiter says, "Oh, I can't do that, sir. But I'd be happy to get you another bowl if there's something wrong." So again the old man says, "I want you to taste my soup."

F1: So?

F2: So finally the waiter says, "OK, OK. I'll taste your soup. Where's the spoon?" The old man says, "Aha!"

F1: That's it?

F2: Yeah.

F1: I don't get it.

F2: What do you mean you don't get it? "Aha!" … He didn't have a spoon!

F1: Oh … That's pretty silly, if you ask me. Sorry!

Joke 6 [M1 = Australian English]

M1: You know the one about the woman who calls her lawyer?

M2: No. How does it go?

M1: She calls her lawyer and the man who answers says, "Smith, Smith, Smith, and Smith." The woman says, "Let me talk to Mr. Smith." He says, "I'm sorry, he's on vacation." "Then let me talk to Mr. Smith." He says, "He's on a big case, not available for a week." "Then let me talk to Mr. Smith." He says, "He's away. He's playing golf today." "OK, then, let me talk to Mr. Smith." "Speaking."

M2: Now that's funny!

Page 94. Exercise B.

F: I've got a good one. My dad was famous for playing jokes on people. Usually they were in pretty good taste, but this one may have crossed the line.

M: Really? What did he do?

F: Well, I'll tell you the whole story. My dad was the chief of staff at Claremont Hospital—you know, they have a huge psychiatric ward with patients who have to be kept under lock and key. Well, one day, this young doctor, Dr. Adams—the butt of the joke—asks my dad to arrange for him to visit the ward.

M: Uh-huh.

F: Well, my dad invites him to come to the ward at three. But before Adams gets there, my dad goes to the guard at the ward and tells him that he's going to admit a patient who thinks he's a doctor. My dad says to just go ahead and let this guy examine the other patients.

M: Oh, no. I can see what's coming!

F: Yeah. So, at three, my dad brings Dr. Adams to the ward and then leaves. Adams starts examining the patients, and at four o'clock he asks the guard to let him out.

M: Uh-oh!

F: Uh-oh is right. Adams tells the guard, "OK. I'm ready to go now." And the guard says, "Sit down. You're not going anywhere." So Adams says, "But I'm Dr. Adams." And the guard says, "Yeah, right. And I'm Napoleon."

M: That's terrible!

F: Well, maybe so. Anyway, eventually my dad came back to the ward and straightened everything out. It's a good thing Adams could take a joke.

M: I would have killed him! Adams was a really good sport.

Page 94. Exercise D.

Speaker 1 [F = Spanish]

F: You won't believe what my friends did to me last night. You know, I just got a new car, and I was so excited. I invited a couple of friends out to dinner to celebrate. So when we get to the restaurant, they tell me to park in the lot instead of on the street. The car will be safer there, they said. Well, you know how it is with a new car. You really don't want anything to happen to it. So we finish dinner and when we get to the car, there's this note from some woman apologizing for scratching my car. I couldn't believe it. So I start walking around the car looking for the damage, but I can't see anything wrong. Then my friends all start cracking up. It turns out they had left the note on the car as a joke. It was all made up. Boy, did I feel dumb. But no harm done. Once I got over the shock, I was fine. Those guys! Don't worry. I'll get even with them some day.

Speaker 2 [F = U.S. regional]

F: A couple of years ago, my friend Alex helped me get a job as a salesperson where she worked—over at Lakeside Department Store. Well, on my first day on the job, Alex was showing me the ropes, and she asked me if I'd been told yet about the "first year reward" program. I said no. And she seemed kind of surprised. So she tells me that on your first day, new employees get to pick out something from the store worth up to $500, and at the end of the year, if you make your sales quota, you get to keep it—for free—as a sort of reward. So Alex tells me I'm supposed to walk around and choose something and then let the manager know what it is. It was still early and the store was pretty empty, so I figured it'd be a good time to browse. All of a sudden, the manager shows up and asks me what I'm doing walking around looking at everything. Why aren't I at my counter waiting for customers? I wasn't sure what to say. I mean, it dawned on me that this was some big joke—on me—so I figured I'd better say something. I just told him I wanted to get familiar with what the store was selling so I could do a good job. But inside, I was pretty ticked off at Alex. I could have gotten fired! Oh … did I mention that Alex is my ex-friend?

Speaker 3

M: Someone actually played a practical joke on me at the office about a month ago. I got in early because I'd gotten some e-mail attachments I needed to download and wanted to print out the files for the general manager. She was gonna make some big PowerPoint presentation that afternoon. So I turn on the computer and I can't get any of the files to open. I'm about to panic when all of a sudden this message comes on the screen saying, "I'm taking a break. Be back in a half an hour." I thought, "What?" And then I totally freaked. How am I going to get this done in time? So I get up to ask this guy who sits right across from me if he could give me a hand, when all of a sudden he starts laughing his head off. It seems the jerk had unplugged my mouse and keyboard and plugged his mouse and keyboard into my computer as some kind of practical joke. I should have known—he's always doing this sort of thing. I have to admit, it was pretty clever. And in retrospect, it was pretty funny. But what a jerk!

Page 97. Exercise A.

Example 1

M: One day these two guys wanted to play a joke, so they went out and bought one of those benches—you know, the kind they have in the park, where people sit and have their lunch, read the paper, whatever. So the two guys carry the bench to the park and put it down, just as if it were a regular park bench. And they sit down and have lunch. After a while, they see a policeman walking toward them. So they pick up the bench and start running away with it, one guy at each end of the bench. The cop sees them and yells, "Hey! Where do you guys think you're going with that bench?" One guy says, "It's our bench." The

cop says, "You guys are under arrest." At that point, the second guy takes the sales receipt for the bench out of his pocket. And of course, what could the cop do? Pretty funny, right?

Example 2

M: Did you hear the one about the intelligence test?
F: No. How does it go?
M: One day this guy comes home and his wife says, "Wasn't today the day everyone at the company was supposed to take an intelligence test?" He says, "Yes, that's right." "Well," she says, "did you take the test, too?" "Absolutely," he says. So she asks him, "How'd you do?" So he says, "Well, let me put it to you this way. It's a good thing I own the company!"

Example 3 [F = French]

F: How many letters are in "the alphabet"?
M: Twenty-six.
F: Wrong! There are eleven letters in "the alphabet."
M: I don't get it.
F: Eleven letters! T – H – E – A – L – P – H – A – B – E – T.

UNIT 9

Page 102. Exercise C.

Conversation 1

M: If they can make a copy of a sheep and a cow, why can't they do the same thing with a human?
F: Good question. But it's still pretty controversial.
M: I actually don't see what's so wrong about it. People would be able to live twice. Sounds pretty good to me!
F: Don't you think that's playing with fire?
M: Not really. I think it's a personal choice.

Conversation 2 [F = Arabic]

F: Can you believe all these stories in the news about people's personal information getting stolen?
M: I know. It's kind of scary. I've heard once someone's got your personal information, they can spend all your money and pretty much ruin your life. Too bad they can't prevent it from happening in the first place.
F: Actually, they say they can. But you have to put this little tracking device under your skin. That way, no one can get away with trying to be you.
M: What? Would you have one of those things implanted?
F: Me? Over my dead body! That's going too far. I can't even believe it's legal.

Conversation 3 [F = Italian]

M: I think it's morally unacceptable to combine plant and animal genes.
F: Why's that?
M: Well, putting the genes of a fish into a tomato can lead to nothing but trouble. The Creator made fish and tomatoes —not fishamatoes.
F: That's true, but that kind of technology can do a lot of good, too.
M: Like what?
F: Well, they've used it to create bacteria that can clean up oil spills by consuming the oil. And apparently it's economically feasible.
M: Hmm.

Conversation 4 [F = U.S. regional]

M: I read that a French doctor working in a New York hospital operated on a patient in a hospital in France.

F: How did he do that?

M: With some newfangled technology and videoconferencing. The surgeon in New York guided the surgical instruments—electronically—in France.

F: That's pretty weird. Sort of like an e-mail operation! I wouldn't want that done to me!

M: And pretty impractical … unless you're in outer space, I suppose!

Conversation 5 [F = Korean]

M: I want to get one of those chess games that you play without a partner.

F: How does that work?

M: It makes chess moves based on your moves. They say it's great—better than most humans.

F: And does this thing actually think?

M: No. But it instantaneously computes the best move based on hundreds of thousands of potential moves.

F: That's awesome.

Page 104. Exercise B.

Conversation 1 [M = Indian]

M: You know, in this country, there is a falling fertility rate.

F: What exactly is a fertility rate?

M: It's the number of children per family. Fifty years ago, the average family had 3.2 children. Today, the rate is only 1.9.

F: What do they think is the reason for that change?

M: Apparently there are a number of factors. But the most important is that the country has changed from a mostly rural farm economy to a mostly urban technological one. Farm families need a lot of kids to help out. But children are just an added expense for urban families.

Conversation 2

F: Can you believe that Rongovia has only a 20 percent literacy rate?

M: That's horrendous. No wonder they've got so many problems. There's no way to improve the situation if so many people can't read or write.

F: True. But this article says the rate's been increasing. Five years ago it was just 10 percent. And it's going up at a rate of 2 percent a year.

M: At least the trend's in the right direction.

Conversation 3 [M = British English]

M: Just look at this statistic! There were over a thousand assaults in the city this year. That's an increase of 50 percent over last year.

F: That is pretty steep. Does the article say why they think the crime rate is rising?

M: They think it has something to do with the changing demographics in the area.

F: What's that supposed to mean?

M: Well, lots and lots of young men have moved here to work at the chemical factory that opened this year. The percentage of young men in the population has risen over 100 percent in just one year. And since the crime rate is generally higher among young men, that seems to account for it.

Conversation 4

F: This country's going to the dogs!

M: Why? I don't think it's so bad.

F: Well, have you read this morning's paper?

M: What are you talking about?

F: They say the divorce rate's rising and the birthrate's declining. If this keeps up, there won't be enough people around to keep things going.

M: Oh, lose the gloom and doom, would you? Tomorrow there'll be another study that says we're overpopulated.

Page 104. Exercise C.

F: Population Trends Through 2015

The world in 2015 will be populated by some 7.2 billion people, up from 6.1 billion in the year 2000. The rate of world population growth, however, will have decreased from 1.7 percent annually in 1985, to 1.3 percent today, to approximately 1 percent in 2015.

Increased life expectancy and falling birthrates will contribute to a shift toward an aging population in high-income developed countries. Beyond that, demographic trends will sharply diverge. More than 95 percent of the increase in world population will be found in developing countries, nearly all in rapidly expanding urban areas.

India's population will grow from 900 million to more than 1.2 billion by 2015; Pakistan's probably will increase from 140 million now to about 195 million.

Some countries in Africa with high rates of AIDS mortality will experience reduced population growth or even declining populations despite relatively high birthrates. Regarding mortality rates in South Africa, for example, the population is projected to fall from 43.4 million in 2000 to 38.7 million in 2015.

Russia and many post-communist countries of Eastern Europe will have declining populations. As a result of high mortality and low birthrates, Russia's population may drop from its current 146 million to as low as 130 to 135 million in 2015, while the neighboring states of Central Asia will experience continued population growth. Populations in Japan and West European countries such as Italy and Spain will also decline because of falling birthrates and low immigration.

North America, Australia, and New Zealand—the traditional destinations for immigrants—will continue to have the highest rates of population growth among the developed countries, with annual population growth rates between 0.7 and 1.0 percent.

Page 109. Exercises A and B.

Conversation 1

M: What's incredible to me is that computers can be programmed to recognize your voice. It's amazing how smart they're getting. They say the technology is as accurate as a fingerprint.

F: When would they use something like that?

M: On the phone. Like if you call the bank, you don't even have to tell them who you are. The machine can identify you from your voice.

F: I find that a little sketchy. I mean, couldn't someone imitate your voice?

M: Oh, come on! It doesn't scare me at all. Stop being such a worrywart!

Conversation 2

F: I'd hate to live out in the boonies. I mean, I like wide open spaces, no crowds and all that, but what happens if you get sick and need surgery? I just feel more secure living in town.

M: Well, one day they'll be able to operate on you from anywhere.

F: I've read about that, but I think it's just pie in the sky. It's too impractical. It'll never happen.

Conversation 3 [F = Spanish]

F: Did you hear they found that little boy who'd been lost?

M: That's great. How did they find him?

F: Through a signal from one of those implants. They received it at the police department, and they were able to locate him in the mall.

M: Is he OK?

F: Yes. He'd just wandered off.

M: You know, I have mixed feelings about those things. They say it's the wave of the future, but I'm still on the fence about it. It sounds great, but I just can't make up my mind whether it's OK.

F: Really? This has totally convinced me it's a great thing.

Conversation 4 [F = Australian English]

F: No way am I gonna drink this milk. Look at what it says: "This milk produced under modern dairy technology including the administration of bovine growth hormone."

M: What's wrong with that? That's progress. It's great that they can improve animals so they produce better.

F: You know—you buy everything hook, line, and sinker!

M: That's not fair. I'm actually very skeptical about a lot of things, but not about this.

UNIT 10

Page 117. Exercise F.

Conversation 1

M: Did you hear that my brother got laid off last week?

F: Are you serious? That's terrible!

M: I know. They're closing his factory and moving all the jobs overseas. So now practically the whole town is out of work.

Conversation 2 [M = Portuguese]

F: How was your trip?

M: Frankly, it was a little shocking. I wasn't expecting the people there to be so poor.

F: Things were pretty bad, huh?

M: Well, I mean, many of the people we met didn't have the most basic necessities like clean water, food, medicine, shelter.

Conversation 3 [M, F = British English]

M: How come you're buying that beef? This one is so much cheaper.

F: I never buy foreign beef.

M: Why not? It's almost half the price.

F: I don't care about the cost. In other countries, they treat beef with growth hormones, which can cause cancer. I just don't feel it's safe. I'll stick with the local stuff, even if it's more expensive.

Conversation 4 [M2 = Mandarin Chinese]

M1: Do you think it would be worth putting money into a horse farm in Ireland?

M2: Definitely. I know someone who did that a few years ago, and he made a huge profit.

M1: How would you like to go in on an investment with me?

M2: Maybe. Do you happen to have a copy of the annual report?

Page 118. Exercises A and B.

Speaker 1 [M = Arabic]

M: I really love watching Hollywood movies, American and British TV shows, the news on BBC and CNN—it really maximizes the amount of time I get to hear spoken English. Sure, there's always something I don't understand. Look, I don't think I could ever know every word or expression there is to know in English, but it really feels good to be able to understand as much as I do. As a matter of fact, when I watch TV shows in English, I try to learn all the latest expressions so I can use them and sound up-to-date, and I try to improve my pronunciation as well. To me, being able to speak English makes me feel really good.

Speaker 2 [F = Russian]

F: I use English as a tool. I have to communicate with people from all over the world, so it's just a necessity in my life. But I really couldn't care less about U.S. or British culture. I mean, it's interesting, but I don't really have time to spend learning about it. What good does knowing about U.S. culture do me if I'm using English to communicate with someone from China, right? And I certainly don't need to sound like a native speaker. Just give me the vocabulary and grammar I need. Like I said, it's a tool for me to utilize as I see fit.

Speaker 3 [M = Korean]

M: I know a lot of people think English has kind of taken over the world—that it's basically an extension of the dominance of the United States economically and culturally. I mean, after all, you see evidence of this dominance everywhere—in movies, clothing, fast foods—you name it. But actually I don't see English that way. It seems to me that using English is a way of neutralizing communication. I mean, it makes people more equal. For example, I'm Korean. And if you're, say, from the United Arab Emirates, we don't have to negotiate which language we're going to use—whose language is going to be the "important" one. If we use English, neither of us is on top, so to speak. It really is the language of international business, not U.S. business—in the best sense.

Speaker 4 [F = Italian]

F: I'm glad I learned English because it's really helped me a lot. I'm able to keep up with international journals and attend international conferences in my field. But from what I hear, English may not always be the number one international language. You know, a century ago, everyone needed to speak French to get along in the world. So who's to say English will always be the language to learn? For instance, they say Chinese may one day surpass English as the primary language of the Internet. And with China becoming the dominant Asian economy, who knows? Maybe we'll all be speaking and reading Chinese someday.

Page 121. Exercise A.

Report 1

F: According to an annual report prepared by the Worldwatch Institute, we need to pay attention to the impact of increased consumption on the environment. Worldwide, nonessential goods are still purchased primarily by the United States and Western Europe, but developing countries such as China and India are quickly catching up. Globalization is making goods and services previously out of reach in developing countries much more available. Items that were once considered luxuries in these countries, such as televisions, cell phones, and computers, are now viewed as necessities, and the increased production of these goods is putting more pressure on the Earth's supplies of water and natural resources. Gary Gardner, director of research for Worldwatch, believes we need to figure out how we can provide all people with an adequate standard of living, using the lowest amount of resources. If we fail to do this, supplies of natural resources may be threatened.

Report 2

M: Given the fact that globalization has been such a controversial topic over the last decade, it's somewhat surprising to find out that, generally speaking, people around the world seem to be welcoming it. This is according to the Pew Global Attitudes Project, which conducted its research in over 44 countries around the world. However, research also showed that people continue to be concerned about worsening problems in their lives—lower incomes, deteriorating working conditions, higher health-care costs, and the growing gap between the rich and the poor. Yet, despite that, people are not inclined to blame such troubles on globalization.

Report 3 [F = British English]

F: Starbucks Coffee Company, the U.S.–based company that has opened its highly recognized coffee shops worldwide, is celebrating its thirtieth birthday today. The first Starbucks opened in the city of Seattle, and since then, the company has grown to over 4,600 stores in 21 countries on four continents. From Switzerland to Saudi Arabia to Korea, Starbucks has changed the way the world sees coffee. Starbucks Chairman Howard Schultz describes their success this way: "Starbucks has a universal language because of the quality of the coffee, the social atmosphere, the romance—all of these things are as relevant in Singapore and China as they are in Zurich or Seattle." Starbucks also presents itself as a socially conscious company, giving to local charities and working to preserve the environment. The company is hopeful that its image will also catch on in Latin America, where coffee is already a way of life.

For some general guidelines on using the *Summit TV* interviews and documentaries, see the Teaching Ideas document in the *Summit TV* Activity Worksheets folder on ActiveTeach. **Note:** The Answer Keys provide answers to the Activity Worksheets exercises from ActiveTeach. Printable unit video scripts are also available on ActiveTeach.

UNIT 1
Dreams and Goals

On-the-Street Interviews:
I have a couple of dreams ...

PREVIEW

• Ask students the following questions:
> *What are some of your short-term goals?*
> *What are some of your long-term goals?*
> *What life goals have you already achieved?*

Write students' answers on the board.

VIEW

Ask students to focus on a different topic each time they view. Some ideas:

• Write on the board, in three columns: *Career*, *Family*, *Other*. Ask students to listen for the types of goals each interviewee talks about.

• Ask students to listen for specific details about career goals.

• Ask students to listen for specific details about family or other goals.

If you decide to use the optional Activity Worksheet, ask students to read each activity before viewing.

REVIEW

• Ask comprehension questions. Play the video segment again if necessary. (Answers may vary—some possible answers are included here.)
> *Why does Vanessa want to run the New York City marathon?* (to be able to say she completed it)
> *Is running the marathon a short-term or long-term goal?* (a short-term goal)
> *What is Vanessa's long-term goal?* (to open an agency for special-education children)
> *What kind of a career is Rob considering changing to?* (landscape architecture)
> *What is he doing to make that dream happen?* (taking a class)
> *What other dream does he have?* (to be an opera singer)
> *How does he plan to follow that dream?* (He plans to take a voice lesson.)
> *Is Joe satisfied with the goals he has achieved in his life?* (Yes. He has moved to the city, has a good job, and he's comfortable with his life.)

> *What other goal does he have?* (to find someone to share his life with him)
> *What is Jessica's career goal?* (to open her own restaurant)
> *What are her personal goals?* (to be happy and have a family, to be tolerant and honest, to listen to people, and to be someone people can rely on)
> *What does Lorayn say about having a family and parenthood?* (that she would like to have a family and that she hopes to be as good a parent as her parents were)
> *What is Alvino's long-term goal?* (to own his own clothing line)
> *How does Alvino plan to attain this goal?* (by developing marketing skills, doing research, and saving money)
> *Does Alvino think he will be successful?* (Yes. In ten years he plans to be opening his fifteenth shop in the New York area.)

EXTENSION
Oral work

• Discussion. On the board, write: *Future Goals*. Then have students recall the goals mentioned in the interviews. Write them on the board. Have students compare their own goals with those in the interviews.

• Pair work: role play. Have pairs of students choose one of the following interviewees from the video segment: Rob, Alvino, Jessica, or Vanessa. Tell them to role-play the short conversation between the interviewer and the interviewee and to extend the conversation with more detailed questions about career goals. For example, *What type of restaurant would you like to own, Jessica?* or *How did you become interested in landscape architecture, Rob?*

Written work

• As a class, summarize Lorayn's comments regarding children and parenthood. Then tell students to write a paragraph describing the influence their own parents had on their lives. Invite volunteers to read their paragraphs to the class.

• Pair work. Replay Alvino's comments. Then ask *Do you think it's likely that Alvino will be opening his fifteenth store in ten years? Why?* Have students work with a partner to write up a detailed plan for Alvino's long-term goal. Write the following questions on the board to help them:
> *What can Alvino do to develop his skills?*
> *What kind of research does he have to do?*
> *How much money does he need to save? How can he do this?*

Invite students to share their plans for Alvino with the class.

- Have students write a paragraph describing their own short- and long-term goals. They should include what they can do or intend to do to achieve those goals and, if applicable, the time frame in which they hope to do so.

LANGUAGE NOTE: When Rob says *I don't know how far I can take that* when talking about his dream of becoming an opera singer, he means that he isn't sure how successful he'll be in achieving this goal.

VIDEO SCRIPT

Interviewer: Could you tell me something, a dream or a future goal that you have for yourself?

Vanessa: I want to run the New York City marathon. I want to be able to, maybe not come in first, but at least be able to say that I completed twenty-six point one miles in a certain time, so that's my goal for the future. That's my, I would say, my short-term goal. My future goal would be to open up an agency of my own, for children, special-education children. That's my long-term goal.

Rob: I have a couple of dreams that I'm pursuing. One of them is to look into a different career, possibly landscape architecture. So I'm taking a class at the New School to explore that. Another dream of mine is to be an opera singer. I don't know how far I can take that, but I plan to take a voice lesson very soon.

Joe: I have to say that I think I have succeeded in a lot of goals that I've set for myself to this point in my life. I . . . since I was very young, I always wanted to move closer and closer to a city. And now I've done that and I live in a city. I have a great job and I'm very comfortable in my life. As for goals, I'd like to continue with that. I wouldn't mind finding someone to share that life with me. But as for attaining any goal, I think that's possible as long as you set your mind to it and that's what you really want.

Jessica: My goal in life is to be happy and to have a family, to have two kids. And my other goal, like career-wise, is to have my own restaurant. That might be a little difficult to combine, but I think I can make it, and it's . . . yeah, that's . . . these are my, like my first-priority goals. And also one of my first-priority goals is to make like, to try to make everybody else happy, like to be tolerant, to listen to people, to be honest and, yeah, to be somebody who people can rely on. So I think that's the most important thing.

Interviewer: How about family or other goals besides work?

Lorayn: Family, like I said, I would love to have a family one day. When that's going to happen, I don't know. I don't think a person is ever fully ready to commit to having a baby. I think it's something that you have to work through as you go through it. But I would love to have a family one day. And I would . . . I hope that I could be a parent as good as my parents have been to me. If I'm half as good, I think I succeeded.

Alvino: I would like to own my own clothing line and to attain it I think I would develop my marketing skills and research . . . and save money.

Interviewer: So what do you think you'll be doing in ten years?

Alvino: Ten years? Opening my fifteenth shop in the New York area.

ANSWER KEY
A. 1. c 2. a 3. b 4. d
B. 1. False 2. False 3. True 4. False 5. False
   6. True 7. True 8. False
C. *Individual responses should include variations on the following:*
   Jessica: Jessica wants to have a family and two kids. She thinks this might be difficult to balance with her other long-term goal of having her own restaurant, but she thinks she could make it work.
   Lorayn: Lorayn wants to have a family one day, though she doesn't know when. She's not yet ready to commit to having a baby. She hopes to be as good a parent as her parents were to her.
D. *Answers will vary.*

UNIT 2
Helping Others

TV Documentary:
Dr. Torstveit's Vacation

PART 1

PREVIEW
- Ask students *Would you ever consider using your vacation time for volunteer work? What would you think of a person who did just that for the last ten years?*

VIEW

Ask students to focus on a different topic each time they view. Some ideas:

- Write on the board: *the problem*. Ask students to listen for the problem Dr. Torstveit is trying to address by spending his vacation time in Sri Lanka.

- Write on the board: *the solution*. Ask students to listen for what Dr. Torstveit would like to achieve by using his vacations to work there.

- Ask students to listen for what influenced Dr. Torstveit in his life to want to help people.

If you decide to use the optional Activity Worksheet, ask students to read each activity before viewing.

REVIEW

- Ask the following comprehension questions. Play Part 1, or segments of Part 1, again if necessary. (Answers may vary—some possible answers are included here.)

  What is the problem Dr. Torstveit is trying to address by taking his vacations in Sri Lanka? (Thousands of children who could be helped with heart surgery are dying from heart defects each year.)

  What would Dr. Torstveit like to achieve by using his vacations to work there? (He hopes to save the lives of children who need heart surgery, but more importantly he wants to train other doctors to be able to perform the surgery when he isn't there.)

  What first convinced Dr. Torstveit to go to Sri Lanka to learn about the situation there? (He was persuaded by a colleague who came from Sri Lanka and who encouraged him to visit and see if heart surgeries, which are routine in the United States, were possible there.)

  What made him decide to return to perform heart surgeries? (He couldn't accept seeing thousands of children dying from heart defects that could easily be corrected through surgery.)

  How many children are waiting to have heart surgery in Sri Lanka? (over 2,500)

  How many trips does Dr. Torstveit make to Sri Lanka each year? (usually two)

  How many Sri Lankan surgeons has Dr. Torstveit trained in this technique so far? (three)

  How many heart surgery operations are performed on Sri Lankan children each year? (400)

  How much do the children's families have to pay for each surgery? (Nothing; the surgeries are free of charge.)

  On this trip, how much time does Dr. Torstveit have for traveling to and working in Sri Lanka? (a week)

  What's the first thing he does when he arrives at the hospital in Sri Lanka? (He meets with the staff to give them a morale boost.)

  How did Dr. Torstveit's family influence his thinking about giving? (His family thought helping others was extremely important.)

LANGUAGE NOTES: The expression *Never mind that . . .* is used in the report to emphasize Dr. Torstveit's willingness to do his work despite the difficulties.

When Dr. Torstveit says *We normally gave until it hurt,* he means they donated time and money until it truly became a sacrifice to do so.

CULTURE NOTE: When Dr. Torstveit says *We weren't people that gave on Sunday,* he is referring to the Christian tradition of giving money for the poor every Sunday at church. He is saying that his family didn't limit themselves only to Sundays, but believed in giving every day.

VIDEO SCRIPT

Chris Bury: For the last ten years, Dr. Jeremy Torstveit has spent his vacations in Sri Lanka, the island nation near India once known as Ceylon. Like many surgeons, he has a reputation for being a cool, difficult, and talented perfectionist. He is obsessive about his life's work: repairing heart defects in children. In this country, such operations have become almost routine. But ten years ago, on his first vacation to Sri Lanka, Dr. Torstveit discovered that his specialty was virtually unknown there. Children born with heart defects simply died—thousands of them every year. For this driven doctor, that was just unacceptable. Since then, he developed a new obsession: performing heart operations on children who have no chance to live without them.

Stephenie Hollyman: Torstveit is a cardiac surgeon who gives children born with severe heart defects every reason to expect a normal life.

Jeremy Torstveit: Everything's in place in the United States for heart surgery. So what else can I do, you know? I don't build roads. I don't teach school. This was a natural thing for me to do.

Stephenie Hollyman: At the National Hospital, the waiting list for children with heart defects numbers over 2,500. Torstveit learned about all of this from Dr. Dudley Halpe, a colleague in Phoenix, who is a native of Sri Lanka.

Jeremy Torstveit: He encouraged me to come and see if . . . if it was possible to operate on the literally thousands of children that were dying of heart disease untreated in this country.

Stephenie Hollyman: Torstveit usually comes twice a year at his own expense, participating in twenty to thirty operations a week as surgeon or instructor. Most of his time is now devoted to training Sri Lankan doctors in the lifesaving procedures. Three surgeons perform 400 operations a year, free of charge.

Tuesday, 6:00 A.M. This time, one week is all Dr. Torstveit can spare from his busy Arizona practice. A week to travel there, work, and fly back, halfway around the world.

The sun is rising over the Indian Ocean. Never mind that Torstveit has been flying for twenty-seven hours now.

Jeremy Torstveit: Time to get going. Don't have a lot of time to waste. And I feel fine, so I'm ready to go.

Stephenie Hollyman: Never mind that for Torstveit, it's 3:00 A.M., body time. The beleaguered staff wants a few minutes with him, always a morale boost.

Jeremy Torstveit: Everybody you meet here is . . . that I've run into, that I've worked with . . . everyone is so genuine that you really miss them when you don't see them. And they are your family, and you want to get back and see them. I came from a family that believed in giving and really giving a lot. We weren't people that gave on Sunday. We normally gave until it hurt. We believed in . . . in helping people out. And there's always a way. There's always a way to find a way to help people out. And I think I grew up with that tradition, and I think that I felt that I should do this.

ANSWER KEY

A. b

B. 1. Dr. Torstveit usually makes two trips a year to Sri Lanka. 2. There are now three Sri Lankan doctors who are qualified to perform the surgeries. 3. Doctors in Sri Lanka perform over 400 heart surgeries a year. 4. The surgeries are free of charge. 5. Dr. Torstveit's body feels like it's 3 A.M., because that's the time it is in the U.S.

C. *Individual responses should include variations on the following:*
1. In the United States, the surgeries are routine. In Sri Lanka, thousands of children die from heart disease every year. These deaths could be avoided with surgery. 2. A colleague from Sri Lanka told him about the problem and encouraged him to go and see what he could do to help. 3. His family had a strong tradition of giving, even when it wasn't easy to do.

PART 2

PREVIEW

• Ask students *How much of an impact do you think Dr. Torstveit's work has on the lives of people who live in Sri Lanka? Do you think his work is worth the effort?*

VIEW

Ask students to focus on a different topic each time they view. Some ideas:

• Ask students to listen for what Dr. Torstveit considers an ideal patient for the first heart surgery on this trip to Sri Lanka.

• Ask students to listen for how Dr. Torstveit describes how he feels about helping others.

• Write on the board: *ripple effect*. Ask students to listen for information that will help them define this term.

If you decide to use the optional Activity Worksheet, ask students to read each activity before viewing.

REVIEW

• Ask the following comprehension questions. Play Part 2, or segments of Part 2, again if necessary. (Answers may vary—some possible answers are included here.)

   What type of patient does Dr. Torstveit consider to be the ideal candidate for the first heart surgery on this trip to Sri Lanka? (a child whose surgery will not be complicated and who can recover quickly)

   Which do you think Dr. Torstveit considers more important: finding a child who needs the most help or finding a child he can help the most? (a child he can help the most)

   How long has Nadisha been waiting for heart surgery? (two years)

How will Nadisha benefit from the surgery? (She will grow up, be able to have children, and have a normal life.)

Why does Dr. Torstveit consider heart surgery so economical? (Because the child can recover in three or four days—a very short time—yet be fixed forever.)

How does Dr. Torstveit describe how he feels about helping others? (He finds it very rewarding—that the rewards far outweigh the sacrifice. He thinks you just have to get to work, no matter how overwhelming it might seem.)

EXTENSION

Oral work

- Have students tell the class about a person who volunteers his or her time to help others. They should use personal experience, or do research on the Internet or at the library.

- Pair work. Write Dr. Torstveit's quote on the board: *So what else can I do, you know? I don't build roads. I don't teach school. This was a natural thing for me to do.* Have students discuss with a partner what the natural thing would be for themselves to do if they were going to donate their time to help people.

- Discussion. Ask *Do you believe Dr. Torstveit's criteria for choosing a child for heart surgery is appropriate? Why or why not?*

Written work

- Have students write a report describing Dr. Torstveit's work and why he has chosen to do it.

- Have students write a conversation between Dr. Torstveit and Dr. Halpe, his colleague from Sri Lanka, at the U.S. hospital where they both work. Dr. Halpe describes the situation in Sri Lanka to Dr. Torstveit.

- Ask students to write a paragraph or two describing either how their family influenced the choices they have made in their lives or what have been the greatest influences on their lives.

- Write on the board: *Give a man a fish; you have fed him for today. Teach a man to fish; and you have fed him for a lifetime.* Ask *How does this saying apply to Dr. Torstveit's work in Sri Lanka?* Have students write a paragraph answering the question.

LANGUAGE NOTE: To *dig in* can be used to mean to begin working hard.

VIDEO SCRIPT

Stephenie Hollyman: For the last three days, Torstveit has been trying to find the best candidate for the first surgery on Monday.

Jeremy Torstveit: Put her name down there and what you're going to do next to that.

Stephenie Hollyman: Heart defects often pass detection in Sri Lanka until too late. He looks for a child whose correction won't be complicated, a case that, after surgery, will enjoy a quick transition through intensive care. Torstveit finally finds his candidate, the one child he can help the most. He selects a farmer's daughter who has a hole in her heart. She's called Nadisha.

Chandama Aramasena: She's a straightforward case. That's why we selected that girl. And she has waited . . . waited on the waiting list for two years.

Stephenie Hollyman: Monday, 8:00 A.M. Dr. Aramasena will perform the operation with Dr. Torstveit assisting. This senior surgeon for the National Hospital trained three years at Oxford University. Nadisha's father carries his precious cargo to the operating theater from ward twenty-five.

Dr. Perrera: . . . now we have the intravenous line in . . .

Jeremy Torstveit: This very simple operation will allow this child to have children, grow up, have a normal life, statistically. And without that, this child would be having significant problems fairly soon. This is a very large defect. This is why heart surgery is so economical in the long run. This little girl spends three or four days recovering, and that's . . . and she's fixed forever.

Chandama Aramasena: If it is all right, go on one. Go to thirty-two, please. Drop the off-flow, please. Clamp it off.

Jeremy Torstveit: We're just making sure there's no air inside the heart. OK, we're going to come off the heart-lung machine now. OK, go ahead.

Stephenie Hollyman: The hole in Nadisha's heart is fixed. It's almost time to head home.

Jeremy Torstveit: Everything went fine. Everything went fine. I truly believe that you can get a ripple effect in reality, a really, truly, tangible ripple effect. And I think you can show other people that this can be done. You know, what I've found here is that this has been rewarding to me beyond measure. This . . . the rewards have been far greater than the sacrifices. Rabbit. Can . . . can she smile? The attitude of "Well, you know, it's too much. There's too much to do" never will work. You have to just dig in and go.

Chris Bury: Since those vacations to Sri Lanka began ten years ago, his priority has changed from performing surgery himself to training the doctors and nurses there in his specialty. In so doing, the ripple effect of his gift, his obsession, is that much greater.

ANSWER KEY

A. a

B. 1. She's been waiting for two years. 2. It will take three or four days. 3. She will be able to grow up, have children, and lead a normal life.

C. *Individual responses should include variations on the following:* A ripple effect is when one person's actions cause others to act, and those peoples' actions cause even more people to act.

D. *Individual responses should include variations on the following:* The rewards are greater than the sacrifice. He says that one's actions can have an effect on other people, causing them to help others too. That way more and more people are affected by one person's actions.

UNIT 3
Frightening Experiences

On-the-Street Interviews:
I could have died . . .

PREVIEW

• Ask students to brainstorm dangerous things people do—for example, rock climbing or racing cars. Write student responses on the board. Then ask *Has anyone done any of these things? Why did you do it? Would you do it again?*

VIEW

Ask students to focus on a different topic each time they view. Some ideas:

• Ask students to listen for what activity the interviewee was doing in each story.

• Ask students to listen for what made each experience dangerous.

• Ask students to listen for specific details that describe each story.

If you decide to use the optional Activity Worksheet, ask students to read each activity before viewing.

REVIEW

• Ask comprehension questions. Play the video segment again if necessary.

> *What dangerous thing did Catherine and her husband do?* (They explored an area in Hawaii where a volcano had just erupted.)
>
> *What happened to Catherine and her husband?* (They watched the volcano while standing on a cliff made of lava. Nothing hit them, but they were very nervous.)
>
> *How does Catherine describe the experience?* (as dangerous but incredible)
>
> *What dangerous thing did Christine do?* (She went skydiving.)
>
> *What did she think the experience would be like?* (She thought it would be fun and exciting; she did not think it was dangerous.)
>
> *What does* go tandem *mean when referring to skydiving?* (to strap yourself to your instructor and jump out of the plane together)
>
> *What happened to Christine and her instructor?* (They started to spin uncontrollably; they needed to use the reserve parachute; they crashed; the instructor disappeared.)
>
> *How did Christine feel?* (She was in shock.)
>
> *What dangerous thing did Angelique do?* (She jumped onto train tracks to pick up money that had fallen out of her bag.)
>
> *What happened next?* (Two men pulled her up from the tracks before the train came.)
>
> *What did Angelique learn from this experience?* (to stuff her money deep in her bag)

EXTENSION

Oral work

• Pair work: role play. Have students take turns role-playing the conversation between the interviewer and one of the interviewees. Tell students to include as many details of the story as they can remember.

- Discussion. Ask:

  Which of the three experiences do you think was the most dangerous? Why?

  Who has had a similar experience?

  Were these dangerous experiences avoidable?

  Why do you think some people put themselves in dangerous situations?

  Do you ever put yourself in dangerous situations? Why?

Written work

- On the board, write: *Which of the people do you think might repeat the dangerous activity? Explain.* Have students write a paragraph responding to the question. Then call on students to share their paragraphs with the class.

- Tell students to write about a dangerous experience that they or someone they know has had. Ask them to include as many details as possible.

OOPS! Angelique says that the wind *threw* her envelope *into* the train tracks. She means to say that the wind *blew* her envelope *onto* the train tracks.

VIDEO SCRIPT

Interviewer: Have you ever done anything that was genuinely dangerous? What happened? What were the consequences?

Catherine: OK.

Interviewer: And how did you feel about it? Was it a positive or a negative experience?

Catherine: I . . . I did do something that was genuinely dangerous once. I look back at it and I think, yeah I could have died, but the experience was incredible. My husband and I, just before we got married, went to Hawaii and we rented a car and we went out into this area where the volcano had taken out a whole neighborhood. So we hiked out there at night. There's no lights. It's just black. To the edge of this cliff and watched . . . it was incredible, watched the lava just coming out. But we're standing on a cliff that's made of lava, and lava's very unstable and there's no warning. It breaks off. It falls into the ocean. We were, it felt like we were close. You could see the smoke. The sulfur was coming towards us but the ocean kind of, the waves kind of pushed everything up. So it didn't really hit us. I heard, I kept hearing popping noises. I was getting nervous. My husband was definitely nervous. That's probably the most dangerous thing I've ever done. But it was incredible. Incredible experience.

Christine: Well, I went . . . I went skydiving a few years ago. I actually did not think it was insane. I did not think that it was dangerous or anything. I went because I thought that it would be fun and exciting and I almost died. I went tandem, so that means that you have to actually strap yourself into your instructor and you jump out of the plane and dive with them. And we were supposed to have a thirty-five second free fall, and which basically means that you, you know, kind of enjoy the fall for thirty-five seconds before you have to release the chute. So when we jumped out of the plane, we started spinning uncontrollably for twenty-eight seconds. After twenty-eight seconds, he released the parachute and we jerked up into the air, and we thought everything was fine, and all of a sudden we started crashing to the ground again at a rapid speed. So he had to use his reserve parachute. So he opened up the reserve parachute just in time for us to go crashing into a cornfield, miles from where we were supposed to be. When I finally came to—I didn't pass out or anything, but I think I was just over-stricken with shock—I realized that my instructor was gone, and he was nowhere to be found. So I had to find my way out of the cornfield. It felt like it took hours. I don't actually know how long I was in there for, but when I finally found my way out, a Jeep came and found me, and it ended up being people from the sky-diving school.

Angelique: I was on the subway . . . I was in the subway, and I had picked up my money from work. And so I had my money in a little envelope, and I was walking down on the tracks, and da, da, da, da, da, and a gush of wind came, and it threw my envelope into the train tracks. So against my complete better judgment, and it was a horrible idea, but I jumped down on the tracks, got the envelope, and then had two men pull me up before the train got here. It's a bad mistake. Never, never do it again but I got my sixty dollars so, I don't know. And what I learned was to stuff my money deep in my bag, as opposed to right outside of my bag so it could fall out. But I'm safe 'cause it worked out.

UNIT 4
Handling Anger

TV Documentary:
Soothing the Savage Beast

PART 1

PREVIEW

• Ask students *Do you think that freely expressing your anger is healthy or unhealthy? What do you think is the best way to handle anger—to let it out, or to hold it back?*

VIEW

Ask students to focus on a different topic each time they view. Some ideas:

• Write on the board: *Jim Girgenti.* Ask students to listen for the ways he "lets off steam."

• Write on the board: *David Morgan.* Ask students to listen for what his business offers its customers and why.

• Write on the board: *Brad Bushman.* Ask students to listen for his point of view on the benefits of helping people vent their anger.

If you decide to use the optional Activity Worksheet, ask students to read each activity before viewing.

REVIEW

• Ask the following comprehension questions. Play Part 1, or segments of Part 1, again if necessary.

How does Jim Girgenti let off steam when he's angry? (He yells at other drivers when he's driving and he yells at his family when they make him mad.)

Does he think it's a good way to deal with his anger? (Yes. He doesn't think there's anything wrong with it and that it works for him.)

Where did David Morgan open his new business? (in Los Angeles)

What does David Morgan's business offer its customers? (For US$8.00, they can beat a dummy to vent their anger.) *Why?* (to reduce their anger and make them feel better)

What does John Stossel think about when he's hitting the dummy? (his boss and his older brother)

What makes Carolyn Amos angry? (driving in traffic, people cutting her off, delays)

What other methods has Carolyn Amos tried to deal with her anger? (She's tried walking and meditation.) *Have they helped?* (Yes, but not as much as hitting the dummy.)

What is Brad Bushman's point of view on the benefits of helping people vent their anger? (He says there's no scientific evidence to support it. He thinks it's bad advice and it's bad for society.)

Why does he think venting might be bad for society? (Because it makes the person behave more aggressively.)

LANGUAGE NOTES: To *hold one's temper, not blow a fuse,* and *keep one's anger bottled up inside* mean to keep oneself from expressing anger.

To *vent* or *let off steam* is to express one's anger.

To *lose one's temper* means to become so angry that one cannot control oneself.

A *pressure cooker* is a cooking pot with a very tight lid that is designed to use high pressured steam to cook food.

To *make believe* is to pretend.

To *fume at* or *about something* is to be very angry, but to say nothing about it.

When something *eats you up,* it means that it causes you a lot of distress.

VIDEO SCRIPT

Charles Gibson: We have all been told to hold our temper when we get angry. Don't blow a fuse. Of course, we're also told we shouldn't keep our anger bottled up inside. So which is it? John Stossel found some people actually taking lessons on how to lose their temper . . . or not. We'll let him explain.

John Stossel: Many people believe humans are a lot like pressure cookers, that we need to let off steam sometimes.

Woman at table: You didn't even say one nice word to them.

John Stossel: Jim Girgenti believes that.

Jim Girgenti: Make believe you have someplace to go. Come on!

John Stossel: Jim and his family live in Philadelphia, where Jim works for an Internet company. A lot of the time, Jim's a good husband and father.

Jim Girgenti: Get up, wise guy.

John Stossel: But he also spends a lot of time snapping at his wife, Jan, and their two kids.

Jim Girgenti: Whatever possessed you to do that? Sienna, I think you need to spend some time in your room.

John Stossel: Jim doesn't think there's anything wrong with his anger. He feels it works for him.

Jim Girgenti: And how come you're not out of your uniform yet?

John Stossel: And many people believe that this . . .

Jim Girgenti: Hello! You want to stay in your lane?

John Stossel: . . . is healthy. Ex-Marine David Morgan recently opened a new business in Los Angeles dedicated to helping people vent, though not at people. For just eight dollars, customers get to spend a few minutes beating on this dummy.

David Morgan: This is what this is for, the *bataka*. This can be a situation, an incident, a person.

John Stossel: I gave it a try. I thought about my boss and my older brother. (I like this.) It was a good workout, but would this reduce anger? Carolyn Amos says it does. She's tried all kinds of other techniques.

Carolyn Amos: I walk and I meditate, and they help. They help get the stress out. But it's nothing like . . . like hitting the dummy. I mean, you just really have to whack something.

John Stossel: She says she's always gotten angry in traffic, fuming at the delays, screaming at people who cut her off, until she did this.

Carolyn Amos: The anger just wasn't there.

Brad Bushman: It's a seductive theory. It does make sense. But it's a myth. There's virtually no scientific evidence to support it.

John Stossel: Brad Bushman's a professor of psychology at Iowa State. He's among a number of social scientists who now believe venting's a bad idea. Any kind of venting is bad, they say—venting at people or even inanimate objects. Sure, they say, it'll make you feel better. But the feeling won't last. It'll just make you more angry the next time. All the advice I hear is that if you're angry, you've got to vent it, or it eats you up.

Brad Bushman: It's bad advice. It produces harmful effects. It's bad for society.

John Stossel: Most researchers we talked to agreed with Bushman. And other studies have gotten similar results. But how does that explain the benefits people say they get from venting? I showed our tapes to Dr. Bushman.

John Lee: Hmm. How's that feel now?

Florence Brown: A lot better.

John Stossel: She feels a lot better.

Brad Bushman: She might feel a lot better, but what's happening here is she's learning how to behave aggressively.

PART 2

PREVIEW

• Ask students *What effect do you think anger has on family relationships? What do you think would be an effective way to handle too much anger?*

VIEW

Ask students to focus on a different topic each time they view. Some ideas:

• Write on the board: *overventers* and *underventers*. Ask students what they think these words might mean (An *overventer* always lets out his or her anger; an *underventer* rarely lets out his or her anger.) Ask students to listen for how experts think each type of person should be treated.

• Write on the board: *Ray DiGiuseppe*. Ask students to listen for what he thinks the negative effects of overventing anger are.

• Ask students to listen for the advice Ray DiGiuseppe gives Jim Girgenti in anger therapy.

If you decide to use the optional Activity Worksheet, ask students to read each activity before viewing.

REVIEW

• Ask the following comprehension questions. Play Part 2, or segments of Part 2, again if necessary.

How do experts think overventers and underventers should be treated differently? (They suggest that overventers need to learn to control their anger, while underventers need to learn to express it more easily.)

How does Jim Girgenti feel when he watches a video of himself with his family? (He feels bad. He wouldn't want someone to talk to him the way he talks to his son.)

What's the first thing Ray DiGiuseppe tries to show overventers when they begin anger therapy? (He tries to show them the negative effect their anger has on their interpersonal relationships.)

According to DiGiuseppe, what are the negative effects on a person's children from overventing anger? (Overventing doesn't help to get them to behave better.)

What advice does DiGiuseppe give Jim Girgenti for dealing with his anger when he's driving? (He should change the way he thinks by thinking first about what people might do that would make him angry. That way he can think about how he will respond without anger.)

What advice does DiGiuseppe give Jim Girgenti for dealing with his anger when he's arguing with his daughter? (When Girgenti's daughter refuses to do something he wants her to do,

DiGiuseppe suggests giving her a choice that shows what will happen if she doesn't cooperate.)

How many anger therapy sessions did Jim Girgenti attend? (four sessions over four weeks)

What does Girgenti think he learned from attending the anger therapy sessions? (that he should think first before venting his anger)

At the end of the report, how do the three news reporters say they deal with anger: as overventers or underventers? (All three say they hold it in, so they are underventers.)

EXTENSION

Oral work

• Discussion. Ask *Do you think venting anger can be useful, or is it better to hold it in? Do you agree or disagree with Brad Bushman's point of view?* Ask students to give specific examples to support their point.

• Pair work: role play. Have students role-play that they are customers at David Morgan's business in Los Angeles. They should tell Morgan why they are there and how they feel after hitting the dummy.

• Group work: role play. Have students work in groups to role-play an anger therapy session. One person is the therapist. Students should discuss how they handle anger. The "therapist" should give advice to the overventers and underventers in the group.

Written work

• Ask students to create an advertisement for David Morgan's business. They should tell potential customers what they can do and how it will benefit them.

• Have students write a letter to Jim Girgenti. They should tell him what they think of how he handles his anger and give him advice for controlling it better.

• Have students write two paragraphs describing how they handle their own anger in different social situations: at home, while driving, at work or school, while shopping, etc. Ask them to explain if there is anything they would like to change about how they handle their anger.

LANGUAGE NOTES: To *back off* means to choose not to be confrontational.

Connie Chung makes a joke by playing on words at the end of the segment when she says, "I could bash Charlie, but he's no dummy." A *dummy* is a model of a person, but it also means a stupid person.

A *stiff* can be a person who doesn't pay back money he or she has borrowed or someone who has no personality. It isn't clear which meaning was intended in the video segment.

VIDEO SCRIPT

John Stossel: Well, now some experts on anger say there are different kinds of anger disorders, that there are people who overvent and others who undervent, that these are different problems and therefore they should be treated differently. An underventer like Florence, who's mostly repressed her anger, may benefit from being encouraged to get it out in a safe way. On the other hand, an overventer like Jim, who already vents at the slightest annoyance . . .

Jim Girgenti: It's green!

John Stossel: . . . needs to learn techniques to control his anger. All the experts say venting at people, especially your family, is a bad idea.

Jim Girgenti: Son, I think you need to . . .

John Stossel: After awhile, as Jim watched himself on our tapes, he started to think that maybe he did have a problem.

Jim Girgenti: (And how come you're not out of your uniform yet?) I wouldn't want somebody talking to me that way. I've got to learn to back off.

John Stossel: Jim agreed to attend this anger management workshop at the Albert Ellis Institute in New York City. It's run by Ray DiGiuseppe, who tries to get people to exchange their angry reactions for something more useful.

Ray DiGiuseppe: So have you done much problem solving?

Jim Girgenti: Not to this point.

John Stossel: Comparative studies have shown that this kind of anger treatment clearly does work for overventers. First, Ray tries to show them how their anger affects their relationships.

Ray DiGiuseppe: The most negative consequence of anger is that it impairs interpersonal relationships, in the long run. In the short run, you get people to do what you want.

John Stossel: Jim, for example, uses his anger to keep his kids under control.

Ray DiGiuseppe: Yelling and screaming at them and embarrassing them isn't really going to solidify the relationship or get them to behave better.

John Stossel: In fact, Ray tells Jim, "Your anger actually keeps you from solving your problems." He asks Jim to try a different approach. "Next time," says Ray, "when driving home, change the way you think about things."

Ray DiGiuseppe: Let me expect that they're not going to do what I want, and let me figure out how I'm going to handle the situation.

John Stossel: In the next session he tells Jim, give your daughter a choice.

Jim Girgenti: Either clean it up, or you don't watch TV for a night, two nights. No computer . . . or something along . . .

Ray DiGiuseppe: Give her a real consequence.

Jim Girgenti: Right.

Ray DiGiuseppe: OK, now is there any way that she talks that I could do to be more like her?

Jim Girgenti: You can call me an idiot a couple of times as you're going up the stairs.

Ray DiGiuseppe: OK, ready? Oh, dad, you're such an idiot. Why don't you let me watch the TV? I'll do it when I'm done. I'll do it later. You know, don't bother me with that, Dad. I'll do it later.

Jim Girgenti: All right. That's it. No TV. Go to your room.

Ray DiGiuseppe: Oh, Dad, you're such an idiot.

Jim Girgenti: That's OK. You still have no TV.

Ray DiGiuseppe: How angry did you feel then?

Jim Girgenti: I felt no anger.

Ray DiGiuseppe: Why?

Jim Girgenti: Because I came to the realization that I was not going to accomplish anything by having a verbal battle. I know how to handle the situation.

John Stossel: Jim attended four of these sessions in four weeks. Have they helped?

Jim Girgenti: Absolutely.

John Stossel: What have you learned?

Jim Girgenti: That I should stop and think prior to acting.

John Stossel: You had to go to a workshop to tell you to stop and think?

Jim Girgenti: Well, sometimes you need the outside influence to make you see the light, as it were.

Connie Chung: John Stossel is with us now. Now, if you don't have a dummy to bash . . . I mean, I could bash Charlie, but he's no dummy. What do you do? How do you vent your anger?

John Stossel: Me?

Connie Chung: Yeah.

John Stossel: Like when you called me a stiff this morning on live TV?

Connie Chung: I was teasing. I didn't mean it.

John Stossel: I just . . . actually I hold it in. I give myself back pain, I think.

Connie Chung: I hold it in.

Charles Gibson: As do I. We're three for three on that score.

ANSWER KEY

A. *Individual responses should include variations on the following:* Some experts believe that overventers need to learn how to hold their anger in, and that underventers may need to learn to express their anger.

B. *Individual responses should include variations on the following:* He thinks it gets in the way of developing healthy relationships with children.

C. *Individual responses should include variations on the following:* 1. expect people to do things that make you angry, but be prepared about how you will respond. Change the way you do things. 2. give her a choice. Don't get angry. Show her that there are consequences for her behavior.

D. b

E. *Answers will vary.*

UNIT 5
Phobias and Superstitions

On-the-Street Interviews:
I'm afraid of falling . . .

PREVIEW

• Write on the board: *Phobias and Superstitions.* Have students brainstorm examples and write them on the board. Then invite students to share phobias and superstitions they have. (See Language Notes for definitions of *phobia* and *superstition*.)

VIEW

Ask students to focus on a different topic each time they view. Some ideas:

• Ask students to listen for the kind of fear or phobia each interviewee describes.

• Ask students to listen for the interviewees who describe how the fears or phobias affect their actions.

• Ask students to listen for the interviewees who describe how they deal with their fears or phobias.

If you decide to use the optional Activity Worksheet, ask students to read each activity before viewing.

REVIEW

• Ask comprehension questions. Play the video segment again if necessary.

  What is Deepti's superstition? (She has to wear her socks on the correct feet. If she doesn't, she believes something bad will happen.)

  What does she realize about her belief? (that it is irrational, but she still can't help it)

  What is Dan afraid of? (closed spaces)

  What is the scientific term for this phobia? (claustrophobia)

  What does he avoid? (tight spaces; even going so far as to keep from covering his face and mouth when in bed)

  What does he love? (open spaces)

  What is San's phobia? (She is afraid of water and of drowning.)

  Why does she get nervous when she is flying? (Because if a plane were to crash when flying over water, she could drown.)

  What is Christiane afraid of? (heights, falling from high places)

  What does she do to deal with her fear? (She makes sure to have things to hold onto and tries not to go to high places.)

  Why does Ian avoid touching doorknobs? (for health reasons)

  Why does he avoid walking under ladders? (Because he is superstitious.)

EXTENSION

Oral work

• Discussion. On the board, write the interview question: *Do you have any unreasonable fears, phobias, or superstitions?* (See Language Notes.) Have students discuss the interviewees' answers. Then ask:

  Which people talk about fears and phobias? (Dan, San, and Christiane)

Which people talk about superstitions? (Deepti and Ian)
Who has similar fears, phobias, or superstitions to those mentioned in the interviews?
How do you deal with them?

- Replay Dan's comments on his claustrophobia. Ask *What does Dan do to avoid feeling claustrophobic?* (He tries to be in large open spaces.) Have students brainstorm different phobias and discuss what people with these phobias might do to avoid them. For example, a person who has a fear of water prefers to be on land and might prefer to travel by car rather than by boat. Or a person who is afraid of the dark might avoid the dark and sleep with the lights on. Write student ideas on the board. Then invite students to respond to the following question: *Do you think it is OK to simply avoid one's fear, or should a person face a fear and try to overcome it?*

Written work

- Have students choose one of the following interviewees: Dan, San, or Christiane. Tell them to pretend they are that person and write a letter to a friend asking for advice on how to deal with their phobia. Encourage students to use the information from the interview as well as their own details in the letter. Then have students swap letters and write letters in response.

- Have students write a paragraph describing a fear, phobia, or superstition that they have. They should include its origins, if possible, and what they do to deal with it.

LANGUAGE NOTES: A *phobia* is a strong, usually unreasonable, fear of something.

A *superstition* is a belief that some objects or actions are lucky and some are unlucky.

When Dan says not being able to move really *freaks him out,* he means that it makes him very uncomfortable.

It's not my thing means It's not something I like to do or that I do well.

OOPS! Deepti says *I don't know to call it phobia or superstition . . .* She means to say *I don't know <u>whether</u> to call it <u>a</u> phobia or <u>a</u> superstition.*

VIDEO SCRIPT

Interviewer: Do you have any unreasonable fears, phobias, or superstitions?

Deepti: Yes, I do have this, I don't know to call it phobia or superstition, but it's with socks. My left sock has to go on my left foot and my right sock has to go on my right foot. I fear that if it gets switched, that my day would go wrong and I would step into a huge mess or something horrible will happen. I learned these things when I was a kid, and there is no reason . . . I mean, really rationally, there is no reason to believe in this, but I do because . . . I don't know why.

Dan: I have a fear of closed spaces, claustrophobia. I can't, I don't really know how to surpass it. I have . . . I can't even have the blanket or the sheet covering my mouth or nose when I'm in bed. The idea, the sheer idea of being in a very, very tight space and not being able to move, really freaks me out, even when I'm not in that kind of situation. And conversely, I really have a love of large open spaces. I like to be in very large open spaces to sort of counteract all of that.

San: I can't think of any off . . . oh, I do have a fear. I have a fear of water. Even though I can swim, my biggest fear is drowning. I don't know why, I just, you know, I'm always . . . that's why I think why I kind of get nervous when I fly, 'cause we're gonna go into the water if we crash, so my biggest fear is drowning. I don't go too far into the ocean, basically.

Christiane: I am afraid of falling—falling from higher places, from windows, or even from diving boards in the swimming pool. I am not very good with heights. Jumping off or falling down somewhere is a big fear of mine. So I try to always have something to hold onto or places where I don't have to go very much downhill, things like that. I don't like that, going down. It's not my thing.

Ian: I really don't have . . . you know, I'm not really too superstitious. I may be conscious not really to touch a lot of doorknobs, but that's, that's more of a health thing than anything else. I'm not really superstitious. I don't walk under ladders. That's something I'm conscious of. I don't walk under a ladder.

Interviewer: So is that for safety or just 'cause it's . . .

Ian: No. I'd say that's a superstition. I don't want to walk under a ladder. They always say don't walk under a ladder; it's bad luck. So I don't want bad luck.

UNIT 6

Air Travel

TV Documentary: *Travelers Beware*

PART 1

PREVIEW

• Ask students *Why do you think criminals would find it fairly easy to steal people's valuables at airports? In which parts of an airport terminal do you think travelers are most likely to have their things stolen?*

VIEW

Ask students to focus on a different topic each time they view. Some ideas:

• Ask students to listen for specific situations the report warns travelers to be careful about.

• Ask students to listen for precautions the report recommends or implies for each situation.

• Ask students to listen for what criminals look for when choosing someone to rob at the airport.

If you decide to use the optional Activity Worksheet, ask students to read each activity before viewing.

REVIEW

• Ask the following comprehension questions. Play Part 1, or segments of Part 1, again if necessary.
   According to the report, why are airport travelers such easy victims of airport crime? (Airports are noisy and crowded. Passengers are in unfamiliar surroundings and often carrying lots of valuables.)

Who is Kevin Coffey? (He's a police officer who lectures to corporations on travel security.)

What specific situations does the report warn travelers to be careful about? (getting out of taxis, standing in line, sitting in airport restaurants, standing at the ticket counter)

What is a mark? (It's a person whom a criminal has chosen to steal from.)

Which people in the report are marks? (the woman getting out of the taxi; the reporter, Arnold Diaz; the man waiting in line; the woman in the restaurant)

What does the woman who is getting out of the taxi do that makes her a mark? (She is dressed nicely, she shows the money in her wallet, and she shows where she puts her wallet.)

What is Arnold Diaz carrying with him? (a laptop, a wallet, a phone, and airline tickets)

How much are they all worth to a criminal? (about $US2,000 to $US5,000)

How does the man waiting in line get distracted? (Sergeant Coffey pretends to be a foreign tourist and asks the man in line for directions.)

And why does his bag get "stolen"? (Because he's distracted, another man takes the bag.)

How does the woman in the restaurant have her bag "stolen"? (One man distracts her by pretending to have an accident; the other takes the bag.)

What did Arnold Diaz do wrong at the ticket counter, according to Sergeant Coffey? (He put his bags down and didn't pay attention to them.)

What precautions does the report suggest for each situation? (Don't show your money or valuables, keep an eye on your bags at all times, be careful about unusual distractions, and keep your bags in front of you and close to you.)

LANGUAGE NOTES: *The pick of the litter* means having the first choice of a new set of kittens or puppies. In this context, it means there are lots of good opportunities for criminals at the airport.

To *rip someone off* means to steal from someone.

When Arnold Diaz says that the woman getting out of the taxi would be *easy pickings* for a pickpocket, he means that it would be very easy for a pickpocket to steal from her.

When the police officer says *You've just committed what we call a luggage felony*, he doesn't mean Diaz committed a crime. He is teasing Diaz by calling it a crime, but he means a big mistake.

The interjection *Bingo* is used to mean *Exactly!*

VIDEO SCRIPT

Arnold Diaz: In a survey, one in ten frequent travelers said they'd been the victim of airport crime. Airports are ideal places for criminals to operate. It's noisy and crowded. Passengers are in unfamiliar surroundings and often carrying lots of valuables. You're not thinking that perhaps you're being watched by professionals waiting for you to let your guard down.

Kevin Coffey: When the criminal element's out here, they basically have the pick of the litter.

Arnold Diaz: Los Angeles police sergeant Kevin Coffey lectures to major corporations on travel security. He showed us how passengers can become marks for the criminals from the moment they arrive at the airport. Let's look right behind us. This woman . . . is she a mark?

Kevin Coffey: Yes.

Arnold Diaz: Why?

Kevin Coffey: You take a look, she's . . . she's coming out of a taxi cab.

Arnold Diaz: Right.

Kevin Coffey: She's smartly dressed. She has her wallet out there. She's going to tip the guy. You can tell now how much money she might have inside her wallet. You know where she puts her wallet. Watch. Her wallet is going to go right into that bag right there. So now if I wanted to rip her off, I know exactly which bag has her wallet.

Arnold Diaz: Right. She'd be easy pickings for the skilled pickpockets working the airport.

Kevin Coffey: What are you carrying with you?

Arnold Diaz: I've got a laptop.

Kevin Coffey: Inside your attaché?

Arnold Diaz: I've got a . . . my wallet, my phone, my . . .

Kevin Coffey: Airline tickets . . .

Arnold Diaz: Airline tickets.

Kevin Coffey: You're probably carrying on you right now anywhere between $2,000 and $5,000, and you don't even realize it.

Arnold Diaz: So I'm a mark?

Kevin Coffey: Of course you are.

Arnold Diaz: But I feel secure because I'm carrying this, so I think there's no way they're going to make off with any of this stuff.

Kevin Coffey: Well, you're secure for the time being. Wait till we get inside, and I'll show you sometimes how you can become victimized right in front of your eyes.

Arnold Diaz: Inside, Coffey changes into street clothes and with his partner, Sergeant Andrew Smith, demonstrates what are known as distraction thefts. First, they choose a mark . . . in this case, a man with an expensive-looking briefcase. Smith moves into position directly behind the unsuspecting victim. Sergeant Coffey, posing as a foreign tourist in need of help, distracts the mark.

Kevin Coffey: Do . . . do you know . . . where this . . .

1st passenger: No.

Kevin Coffey: Sorry.

Arnold Diaz: The passenger panics as he turns to find his bag is gone. Look at it again. As Sergeant Coffey diverts the mark's attention, his partner reaches down, grabs the bag, and begins to move away. Coffey continues the distraction until the thief is out of sight. We step in to tell the victim what's happened. He never suspected that lost tourist was setting him up.

1st passenger: I was trying to be helpful. I didn't understand what he was asking.

Arnold Diaz: The criminals are counting on your good nature. Here, a woman is passing time in the airport restaurant waiting for her flight. Sergeant Smith takes a seat at the next table, his eye on the briefcase at her side. Now Coffey moves in to provide the distraction.

Kevin Coffey: Ow! Ah!

Arnold Diaz: His partner steals her bag right from under her—her attention diverted to this poor guy who tripped.

Kevin Coffey: I'm sorry.

2nd passenger: Are you OK?

Kevin Coffey: I'm sorry. I'm fine. Thank you, ma'am. I'm sorry.

Arnold Diaz: It was some time before she even realized the bag was gone, and we told her what happened.

2nd passenger: It worked very well. Very well. Thank you.

Andrew Smith: Yes. And I'm sorry. No hard feelings.

Arnold Diaz: On to the ticket counter, where many passengers are too preoccupied to worry about their bags. I have my ticket here. Going to New York.

Kevin Coffey: OK. You've just committed what we call a luggage felony, and you didn't even realize it. Think about it. You walked up to the ticket counter, and as you reached here, what was the first thing you did?

Arnold Diaz: I grabbed my ticket, put my bags down.

Kevin Coffey: Bingo. And as you're conducting this conversation here, somebody picks up this bag and walks away.

Arnold Diaz: A savvy traveler, he says, will put their laptop or briefcase on the counter and stack their bags where they can keep an eye on them. Everything in front of me where I can see it.

Kevin Coffey: Right.

ANSWER KEY

A. *The following choices should be crossed out:* b, d, f
B. 1. b 2. b 3. b. 4. c
C. a. *Explanations will vary.*
D. *Answers will vary.*

PART 2

PREVIEW

• Ask students *What other places at the airport do you think the report might talk about?*

VIEW

Ask students to focus on a different topic each time they view. Some ideas:

• Write on the board: *the metal detector, the phone banks,* and *the bathroom.* Ask students to listen for the crimes the report warns about in each location.

• Ask students to listen for the advice for travelers that is stated—or implied—by the report for each situation.

If you decide to use the optional Activity Worksheet, ask students to read each activity before viewing.

REVIEW

• Ask the following comprehension questions. Play Part 2, or segments of Part 2, again if necessary.
  According to the report, how can criminals steal your bags at the metal detector? (Two people walk ahead of you. One creates a distraction and keeps you from going through the metal detector; the other steals your bag on the other side and exits security.)

What advice does the report give to travelers in this situation? (Make sure no one is in front of you; keep your eye on your bags the whole time they are on the conveyor belt; and if someone gets in front of you, make sure you can see your bags.)

According to the report, why might security personnel not notice if someone is stealing your bags? (Because their job is to watch for bombs or weapons, not thieves.)

What was the bait the police used at the phone banks? (They put two cameras inside a bag. They put a name tag and phone number on it so an honest person could report finding it.)

What did they do with the bait? (They put it by a phone and left it there unattended.)

What did the woman who took the bag do with it? (She put it in a shopping bag and tried to take it on a flight to Los Angeles.)

What does the report warn travelers about in airport bathrooms? (When a person is sitting on the toilet, a criminal might try to steal his or her bag or purse.)

What does Sergeant Coffey say many people think when they see people trying to chase criminals who have stolen bags from the bathroom? (that they're crazy, because they're usually not completely dressed)

What are some airports doing to try and protect travelers in the bathroom? (They have installed a special place for putting a purse or bag that would be difficult for a criminal to reach.)

What advice does Sergeant Coffey have for travelers when they are using the airport bathroom? (keep purses and luggage beside you)

At the end, what general advice does the report have for travelers? (Don't put cameras or jewelry in your luggage, pick up your luggage quickly when arrive at your destination, and consider wrapping tape around your bags.)

EXTENSION

Oral work

• Group work. Have students work in small groups to prepare and present "news reports" warning travelers about how they may be vulnerable to crime at the airport.

• Pair work: role play. Have students role-play a conversation between an airport traveler and a police officer in which the traveler has just had a bag stolen.

• Discussion. Ask students to think of other travel situations in which they think travelers may be vulnerable to crime (at the bus or train station, at hotels, at tourist attractions, etc.).

Written work

- Ask students to write a report warning travelers about how they may be vulnerable to crime at the airport. They should give advice for how to avoid being a victim.
- Have students write an imaginary letter to a local newspaper, describing a bad travel experience in which they lost their bags. They should warn other travelers how to avoid the experience they had.

LANGUAGE NOTES: *A bunch of* is a colloquial way to say *a lot of*.

To *stick something on* is a colloquial way to say to put something on.

The report uses the words *bait* and *nibble* to describe the trap set by the police at the phone banks. These words are normally used to talk about fishing, but here they are used to enhance the description of the trap.

A *rash* of thefts means a series of thefts that occurred within a short time.

To *case an area* is to check it carefully for a certain purpose. In this case, the thief is checking the phone bank to see if it is OK to steal the bag.

CULTURE NOTES: Miami, Florida, is in Dade County. The *Metro Dade* police are the Dade County police.

20/20 is a popular ABC news program in the United States.

VIDEO SCRIPT

Arnold Diaz: The latest caper of these organized airport thieves is their most brazen distraction theft yet. It's happening right here at the screening stations, where they're stealing laptop computers and other valuable carry-on items right in front of the airport security guards. Here's how it's done. After you've put your bag onto the conveyor belt but before you go through the metal detector, two guys cut in front of you.

Kevin Coffey: Suspect one, he walks through with no problem. Suspect two, he gets delayed. He has a bunch of change, keys.

Man: Sorry about that.

Kevin Coffey: Now he delays you from going through. They're very apologetic. Sometimes it's a very attractive woman.

Arnold Diaz: And now I'm waiting. I'm watching him.

Kevin Coffey: You've got it. And now, the first suspect—he's gone through, and he's picked up your briefcase, laptop, carry-on bag and turned right around and exited the airport.

Arnold Diaz: By the time a passenger makes it through the screening station to retrieve his bags, it's too late. The luggage is long gone. Well, so what do you do? I mean, everybody's sticking their luggage on. I'm going to stick mine on. What can I do? First of all, the police say, make sure no one's in front of you. Then put your bag on the conveyor belt and don't take your eyes off it.

Kevin Coffey: As you walked through here, you didn't bother to look back. And as you can see, he was right behind you, and he pulled your machine right out. Or your purse . . .

Arnold Diaz: And if you're delayed trying to get through the metal detector, stay focused on your bag as it exits the machine. You may be surrounded by security guards, but you're still vulnerable to theft.

Kevin Coffey: The security station personnel here—they're here to make sure bombs and weapons don't get into the airport.

Arnold Diaz: Not to watch my luggage.

Kevin Coffey: Correct.

Arnold Diaz: At Miami International Airport, baggage thieves have been working the phone banks.

Vince Garcia: All right. Basically what we want to do is to duplicate the same scenario that occurs at every airport.

Arnold Diaz: Undercover detectives from the Metro Dade police have decided to set a trap. They prepare the bait—a bag with two cameras inside, valuable enough to make stealing it a felony. They attach to it a clearly marked name tag with a phone number that rings at the police station in case an honest citizen wants to return it. Today's location, Concourse D. A female officer moves into position.

Vince Garcia: She's going to make believe she's making a phone call. She's going to hang up the phone, and is going to leave the bag.

Arnold Diaz: The bait now in place, the police watch and wait. It takes about forty-five minutes before they get their first nibble. The woman standing to the left on the phone begins eyeing the bag. Lieutenant Pete Casanova believes she's casing the area.

Pete Casanova: And it's common for the distraction thieves and these type of people to go to these phone booths and pretend they're making a phone call and look around. And what they're doing is they're scouting the area also.

Arnold Diaz: What she doesn't realize is she's looking right at five undercover detectives and *20/20's* hidden cameras. She moves her bags a little closer to the bait bag, then signals her partner. They talk briefly. A few seconds later, she makes her move, snatching the bait and walking away with the police bag on her arm. The two suspects waste no time getting on line for a flight to Los Angeles, the stolen bait now hidden inside a shopping bag. As they attempt to board the plane, they're arrested. Police believe the team may also have been responsible for a recent rash of thefts in the men's and women's bathrooms. Yes, the bathrooms are another place where airport criminals could be lurking.

Kevin Coffey: You're sitting on the stool, and you've got your pants around your ankles, and all of a sudden somebody comes in the stall in front of you.

Arnold Diaz: Hey, now what do I do? Do you jump up and run after them?

Kevin Coffey: We've had a few incidents like that, and someone's kind of thought they were crazy people chasing out the hallway, and their underwear is up and their pants are around their ankles. Because it's basically their whole lives are going out this door.

Arnold Diaz: In women's bathrooms, it's easy for thieves to reach over the door and pull a purse off the hook, which is why some airports are now installing devices like these to keep valuables secure. In general, Coffey says, purses and luggage should be kept beside you in the bathroom and everywhere else at the airport.

Hugh Downs: There are a few other things you can do to protect yourself. First, don't put cameras or jewelry or other irreplaceable valuables in your luggage. When you arrive at your destination, go directly to the carousel to pick up your luggage. It's not a bad idea to have wrapped some tape around the whole bag to deter unscrupulous baggage handlers.

ANSWER KEY

A. *Individual responses should include variations on the following:* 1. One person goes through the metal detector, and another drops something so you can't go through. The first person takes your bag and exits from airport security. 2. Someone acts like he or she is talking on the phone in order to watch what is happening and to decide when it is safe to steal a bag. 3. When you're sitting on the toilet, someone comes and takes your bag from under the door. You're not able to chase the person.

B. *Individual responses should include variations on the following:* 1. Always keep an eye on your bags. Make sure no one is in front of you. Don't go through the metal detector unless your bags are already going through. 2. Always keep an eye on your bags while you're talking on the phone. 3. Put your bag beside you where it can't be grabbed from under the door. 4. Don't put cameras or jewelry in your luggage. When you arrive at your destination, go immediately to pick up your luggage. Think about wrapping some tape around the whole bag to keep anyone from taking things from inside.

C. *Individual responses should include variations on the following:* 1. Because their job is to keep the planes safe, not to keep people from stealing luggage. 2. a bag with two cameras inside 3. They have a special place for purses where a criminal can't grab them. 4. They think that the person is crazy because he or she is shouting and often isn't completely dressed.

D. *Answers will vary.*

UNIT 7
Strengths and Weaknesses

On-the-Street Interviews:
I'm really good at multi-tasking ...

PREVIEW

- Call on individual students to name strengths that they have. Write these on the board. Note if any students have similar strengths. Then ask individual students to name their weaknesses and write these on the board. Ask *What can you do to overcome your weakness?*

VIEW

Ask students to focus on a different topic each time they view. Some ideas:

- Write on the board: *Strengths.* Ask students to listen for the strengths the interviewees mention.
- Write on the board: *Weaknesses.* Ask students to listen for the weaknesses the interviewees mention.

If you decide to use the optional Activity Worksheet, ask students to read each activity before viewing.

REVIEW

- Ask comprehension questions. Play the video segment again if necessary.

  What are some of Emma's strengths? (She is very helpful; she works well under pressure; she's good at multi-tasking and getting things done; she deals well with people; she doesn't let her emotions get in the way of her work; and she is good with children.)

  What is Emma's weakness? (She is sometimes bad at listening.)

  What are James's strengths and weaknesses? (His strengths include patience and attention to detail; his weaknesses are that he is sometimes a bit too slow and painstaking.)

  What skills and abilities does Martin have? (He is an amateur photographer.)

  Does he consider himself a good photographer? (He says he is working on it.)

  What does it take to be an excellent photographer? (You have to really work at it; in addition to developing technique, you have to have a vision.)

  How can a person learn to be a good photographer? (by taking a lot of pictures, going to a lot of exhibits, looking at other photographers' work to get inspired)

  What are Angelique's strengths? (singing, dancing, and acting)

  How did she become interested in the arts? (She grew up singing in a church, at school, and in competition; she grew up with art around her.)

  What weaknesses does Angelique have? (She's bad at math, cleaning, taking care of her roommate's dog, and keeping in contact with people.)

EXTENSION

Oral work

- Discussion. Replay Emma's description of her strengths and weakness. Ask students:

  Do you think that Emma has a way with people?

  Do you think her difficulty listening to others could negatively affect her relationships with people? How?

  Based on Emma's response, what type of job do you think she has?

  What other kinds of jobs do you think she would be good at? Explain your answer.

- Pair work: role play. Have pairs role-play the conversation between the interviewer and Martin. Tell students to try to include all the information they discussed. Then have students take turns interviewing each other about a strength or ability they have. Tell them they can use the interviewer's questions below and/or make up their own.

  I want to ask you about some skills or abilities you might have. I hear you _____. Is that true?

  Are you good at it?

  Is it hard?

  So, how do you learn to _____?

Written work

- Have students write a paragraph describing the strengths and weaknesses of themselves or someone they know. They should provide examples.

- Have students imagine they are Emma's supervisor at work. The supervisor is concerned that Emma has difficulty listening to other people during meetings. Tell students to write an e-mail to Emma pointing out this weakness and offering her suggestions on how to overcome it. Tell students to use information from the interview to help them. Encourage them to keep the tone of the e-mail friendly and helpful.

LANGUAGE NOTES: *Multi-tasking* means doing many different things at one time.

To *get fired up* means to get passionate about something.

Painstaking means very careful and meticulous.

OOPS! Angelique says . . . *so I'm a singer and dance and theater* . . . She means to say that she is a singer, a dancer, and an actress.

James says *Weaknesses might be sometimes a little bit too slow and painstaking.* He means to say *My weaknesses might be <u>that I am</u> sometimes a little bit too slow and painstaking.*

Martin says . . . *if you want to be very good and excellent photographer* . . . He means to say . . . *if you want to be <u>a</u> very good and excellent photographer* . . .

VIDEO SCRIPT

Interviewer: Tell us a little bit about some of your strengths, your talents, your abilities.

Emma: I'm very helpful. I believe I work really well under pressure. Sometimes when I'm working, the phones are ringing and somebody wants a copy of this, so I'm really good at multi-tasking and getting things done, and just handling people and the way they speak to me. And sometimes it's not nice, but you know, you take it, and I think I'm good at holding back how I feel so that I can get the job done. What else am I good at? I'm good at taking care of people's kids. Like children, I love being around children and they love being around me. And I enjoy doing that.

Emma: What am I bad at? I'm bad at listening sometimes. That's not really good, but I tend to go on and the person that's talking with me sometimes, and I'm just not paying attention. And it's because sometimes I get so fired up, and I have a point, and I just, I just look right past what they're saying, and that's not a good thing. I like to . . . like, let's say, we're having a conversation, sometimes I'll just cut them off. That's not good.

James: Probably patience and attention to detail are my strengths. Weaknesses might be sometimes a little bit too slow and painstaking.

Interviewer: You know, I want to ask you about some skills or abilities you might have. I hear you're a photographer. Is that true?

Martin: Yes, I'm an amateur photographer.

Interviewer: And are you good at it?

Martin: I'm working on it.

Interviewer: Is it hard?

Martin: Depends. You can get to a certain level, but if you want to be very good and excellent photographer, then you really need to work on it. It's not just, you know, techniques. You also need to have a vision, also.

Interviewer: So how do you learn to be a good photographer?

Martin: I think you have to take a lot of pictures, and you have to go to a lot of exhibits, look at other photographers' work. That might inspire you, and I think that's actually very important.

Angelique: Well, I grew up singing in the church and at school and in competition so I'm a singer and dance and theater and all those things and art as well. But . . . yeah, probably just those. Probably just the whole artistic thing. I mean, my mother's an artist so it's kind of always been around me.

I am bad at math. I'm bad at cleaning. I'm bad at tons of things. I'm bad at taking care of my roommate's dog, very bad at that. I'm bad at keeping in contact with people I should keep in contact with, but it's just, I mean, just silly things like that.

ANSWER KEY

A. 1. Angelique 2. Emma 3. James 4. Emma
5. Martin 6. Angelique 7. James 8. Angelique

B. *Individual responses should include variations on the following:*
Strengths: Emma is very helpful. She works well under pressure and is good at multi-tasking and getting things done. She deals well with people and doesn't let her emotions get in the way of her work. She is very good with children.
Weaknesses: Emma is sometimes bad at listening. She often doesn't pay attention to what another person is saying to her, and she cuts people off in conversation.

C. *Individual responses should include variations on the following:*
Martin explains that to be a good photographer you have to really work at it. Not only do you have to learn techniques, but you also have to have a vision. He says that you learn to be a good photographer by taking a lot of pictures, attending exhibits, and looking at other photographers' work for inspiration.

D. *Answers will vary.*

UNIT 8
Humor

TV Documentary: *Clowns*

PART 1

PREVIEW

• Ask students *Who are some people you think are very funny? Why do they make you laugh? Do you think clowns are funny? Why or why not?*

VIEW

Ask students to focus on a different topic each time they view. Some ideas:

• Ask students to pay attention to the clown rehearsal. What are the clowns trying to accomplish? What's working and what's not working?

• Ask students to listen for how the audience plays an important role for clowns.

If you decide to use the optional Activity Worksheet, ask students to read each activity before viewing.

REVIEW

- Ask the following comprehension questions. Play Part 1, or segments of Part 1, again if necessary.

  What helps Glen Heroy develop his clown character? (He bases his character on his real personality in order to connect with his audience.)

  How does an audience help a clown in his performance? (The audience lets the clown know whether or not the act is funny. The communication between the clown and the audience helps the clown to be funny.)

  How much time do these clowns put in to develop and rehearse their act? (They rehearse for a month before the show.)

  What do they think the audience will find funny about the act they are rehearsing? (They are whistling a tune, but it is very difficult to whistle and eat a cracker at the same time.)

  What does the clown coach suggest to make the act work better? (He suggests not chewing the cracker right away and using his teeth instead of his tongue. Later he also suggests using a larger cracker.)

  What are some of the difficulties in developing the act? (The cracker is small and will be difficult for the audience to see clearly. The clowns don't know if the audience will think it's funny. During the rehearsal, none of the other people are laughing.)

  How many times will the clowns possibly perform this act in front of an audience? (Perhaps more than four hundred times.)

LANGUAGE NOTES: *A newbie* is an informal word that describes someone who is new at doing something.

To *go after something* is to try to achieve something.

Petrified means extremely frightened.

To get in touch with something is to try and experience and understand something.

Brutal is sometimes used to mean very difficult.

To *fly by the seat of one's pants* means to try doing something without a clear idea of how to do it.

A gig is an informal expression for a paid performance.

The expression that something *isn't going to read* means that it won't be understood.

CULTURE NOTE: A circus is a traveling group of entertainers that usually includes acrobats, animal acts, and clowns. Traditionally a circus has one or more circular "rings," or performance spaces, in which the entertainers perform their acts. In North America, the "three-ring" circus was common, in which three different acts were performed at once.

VIDEO SCRIPT

Glen Heroy: My name is Glen Heroy, and I am from New York City, New York. I am a newbie to the circus. I've been performing my whole life since I was four. But this is something I secretly have always wanted, but never went after. And I'm scared to death. I'm petrified. I try to find my clown from the inside out. It's just totally getting in touch with the inner core of who you are and speeding it up to a huge degree. Hopefully it'll ring true to the audience if it's coming from a place of honesty. . . .Where's my audience?

Young Clown: Let's do it.

Coach: The process of putting material together can be really fun, without a doubt, but uh there's nothing more pathetic than uh clowns rehearsing without uh costume, makeup, and an audience.

Young Clown: You don't know if you're funny or not unless the audience tells you. As a clown, as . . . as a writer, you don't know if anything's working until you put it in front of people.

Clown Coach: Um let's just work that moment . . . And you're overplaying a little bit. Just put it . . . put it in his mouth and leave it there, because as soon as you put it in your mouth, the saliva starts working on it. So you want it as dry as possible, if you know what I mean.

Glen Heroy: Clowns spend a lot of time in secrecy. We like to plot and plan. We like to create and then show.

Clown Coach: OK. Uh um it's getting there. I think you can chew way later. You could . . .

Young Clown: Really?

Clown Coach: Yeah! Absolutely, and when you chew, just use . . . try to use your teeth and not your tongue . . . I'm no longer surprised when things that I think are unbelievably funny get no response.

Director: This is amplified?

Clown Coach: We'll rehearse this show for one month with no audience, and it's . . . it becomes brutal for a clown because you . . . you cannot entertain the table of those people who know you extremely well, and they're not smiling or laughing. Their job is, "OK, we're timing you now . . ."

Young Clown: Clowning acts are very carefully structured but because you have this relationship with the audience, this communication with the audience, anything can happen, and anything will happen.

Clown Coach: So we're good.

Woman: Again.

Clown Coach: The clowns, we're out there flying by the seat of our pants essentially, making best guesses for an entire month.

Director: Thank you for getting this stuff here.

Clown Coach: Sometimes it gels very quickly, and we're right. And we put it out in front of the first audience and the four hundredth audience because you have to be successful for all of those audiences. And uh my job is to use the pressure that comes with that, um, to get better and to . . . and to work fast because it's embarrassing to go out there and it not work, but it's part of the gig. . . . So I think the cracker's too small. That's my feeling. It's really cute, but it's like . . . something this big.

Director: Unless we're gonna . . . Do I want to have a cracker? It's not going to read. I just don't think it's gonna read.

Clown Coach: OK. Let's move on.

ANSWER KEY

A. *The following should be crossed out:* a, c, e,
B. 1. if you're funny or not unless the audience tells you 2. As a clown 3. you don't know if anything's working until you put it in front of people 4. surprised when things that I think are unbelievably funny get no response 5. because you have this relationship with the 6. communication with the audience, anything can happen 7. anything will happen
C. 2. The audience won't be able to see the cracker and understand what's happening.

PART 2

PREVIEW

• Ask students, *What kind of person do you think chooses to become a clown? Do you think clowns are generally happy or unhappy people? Explain your answer.*

VIEW

Ask students to focus on a different topic each time they view. Some ideas:

• Ask students to listen for how the speakers describe what most people think about clowns.

• Ask students to listen for what the speakers say about the emotions and personalities of clowns.

If you decide to use the optional Activity Worksheet, ask students to read each activity before viewing.

REVIEW

• Ask the following comprehension questions. Play Part 2, or segments of Part 2, again if necessary.

Why does the woman give the example about bankers in order to comment on clowns? (She is trying to say that clowns are just like anyone else from any other profession.)

According to one of the speakers, how are clowns different from actors and comedians? (He says that actors and comedians play other people, while clowns play themselves.)

When one speaker says that clowns work against the rules of culture, what do you think he means? (He probably means that clowns do unexpected things that we normally would not do or be allowed to do. That's why we find them funny.)

When one speaker describes his clown act as "It's me times ten," what do you think he means? (He means that he uses his own personality and emotion in his clown character, but in very exaggerated form.)

Why might a clown want to leave the "negative parts" of who he or she is at home? (A clown might not want to include parts of his or her personality that are not so nice or not so funny.)

When one speaker describes a clown going "waka waka waka," what do you think he means? (He probably means that some clowns just focus on being silly and don't have developed personalities.)

When one speaker says that clowns are "not supposed to be regular people," what do you think he means? (He probably means that most people expect clowns to just be silly and make people laugh. If a clown has a fully developed personality, it surprises most people.)

What's the difference between being a clown from the inside out and being one from the outside in? (From the inside out means using one's personality and real nature to develop the clown's personality and humor. From the outside in means only using costumes and makeup to make a clown funny.)

EXTENSION

Oral Work

• Discussion. Ask students if the video segments changed their views about clowns in any way. Have them say which clown they found the most interesting or funny and why.

• Group work. Have small groups of students create a clown act. Then they can describe it or act it out for the class.

• Pair work. Have pairs of students make a list of funny actors and comedians they are familiar with. They should analyze why each is funny.

Written work

- Have students write a letter to Glen Heroy about the act with the cracker from Part 1. They should make suggestions for how to improve the act.
- Ask students to develop a clown character based on their own personalities and describe it in writing.
- Have students identify a funny character from TV or the movies and describe what makes that character funny.

LANGUAGE NOTES: Saying you *don't buy* an idea means you don't agree with it or believe it.

Sometimes people use *thing* to mean an idea, as in *the sad clown thing*.

The expression *writ large* means bigger than normal.

To be *just oneself* means to act naturally.

Neurotic means anxious or fearful.

A *nerd* is someone who doesn't fit in with most people socially.

To *touch someone* can mean to connect emotionally with that person.

To *identify with someone* means to share or understand that person's feelings.

To *be bitter* means to have resentments or angry feelings about the past.

To *be mean* means to be cruel or not kind to others.

To *have an outlet for something* means to have a way or place to express certain feelings.

Suspenders are a type of clothing accessory, worn over the shoulders, that hold up pants (worn instead of a belt).

CULTURE NOTES: The character of the sad clown was most famously portrayed in the Italian opera Il Pagliacci, in which a clown discovers that his wife is seeing another man.

In North America, parents often hire clowns to blow up and twist balloons into animal shapes at their children's parties.

VIDEO SCRIPT

Female Clown: The notion that clowns are happy on the outside and sad on the inside is kind of silly because that's like saying all bankers are happy on the outside and sad on the inside. It really varies from person to person.

Male Clown 1: I can see you have never dealt with clowns.

Male Clown 2: I don't buy the "sad clown" thing. Clowns are complete human beings. They have all the emotions of the human being, but they're writ large. They work against the rules of the culture. They are people that we laugh at and they are people that are necessary for our survival because the rules don't always work.

Male Clown 3: The difference between a clown and an actor: an actor plays a character or even a comedian can play a character, but a clown is just himself.

Male Clown 4: My clown, when you see me in the ring, it's me times ten, do you know? So I'm this neurotic little nerd who's shy around women. That's my clown because that's who I am.

Male Clown 5: It's taking some of the aspects that are me and leaving some of the more negative parts of who I am at home, because they're not so entertaining.

Male Clown 2: Clowns have to have all the human emotions in order to be effective, in order to touch us, in order that we identify with them. They're human beings.

Director: Do I want the guy in front of me going "waka waka waka!" or do I want the guy in front of me to be real?

Male Clown 6: Clowns are not supposed to be regular people . . . Clowns are not supposed to be angry. Clowns are not to be bitter. And everybody is bitter sometimes.

Glen Heroy: I have a really mean clown character who I didn't pack for this event (laughs), but he's really mean . . . and scary. It's nice to have an outlet for him, you know? . . . Often clowning gets perceived as becoming a clown from the outside in. You can put on a big ridiculous wig and, "Oh my God—look at these suspenders!" and "Hey, these pants are really baggy! Hey, I'm a clown! Let me twist some balloons!" And I try to find my clown from the inside out, where the truer and more vulnerable and more honest I can be, to experience something as a total innocent, where if I'm angry, I'm really angry, and if I'm hurt, I'm really hurt. It's just totally getting in touch with the inner core of who you really are and speeding it up to a huge degree.

ANSWER KEY

A. b.

B. 1. clowns are happy on the outside 2. sad on the inside is kind of silly 3. that's like saying all bankers are happy on the outside and sad on the inside 4. from person to person 5. The difference between 6. an actor plays a character 7. can play a character 8. a clown is just himself 9. that are me 10. leaving some of the more negative parts of who I am 11. they're not so entertaining 12. are not supposed to be regular people 13. are not supposed to be angry 14. are not to be 15. everybody is bitter sometimes

C. *Individual responses should include a variation on the following:* Developing a clown character from the inside out is about taking one's own personality and emotions and bringing that out in the clown character. Developing a clown character from the outside in is focusing on how the clown looks, such as wearing funny clothes and make-up.

D. *Answers will vary.*

UNIT 9
New Technologies

On-the-Street Interviews:
The problem's not technology ...

PREVIEW

• Ask students *What are some examples of popular everyday technologies?* (for example, the Internet, cell phones) *What are some ways in which these technologies have had a negative impact on modern life?*

VIEW

Ask students to focus on a different topic each time they view. Some ideas:

• Ask students to listen for which interviewees have a positive view about technology and which ones have a negative view.

• Write on the board: *Advantages.* Ask students to listen for the specific advantages of technology that interviewees mention.

• Write on the board: *Disadvantages.* Ask students to listen for the specific disadvantages of technology that interviewees mention.

If you decide to use the optional Activity Worksheet, ask students to read each activity before viewing.

REVIEW

• Ask comprehension questions. Play the video segment again if necessary.
  What annoys Rita about cell phones? (that there are people who are constantly talking on cell phones; that they allow cell phones to interrupt whatever they're doing)
  Does she think cell phones have any advantages? (Yes. She says that they're good for some professions and are handy.)
  What does Mauro say about the impact technology has had on modern life? (He thinks the problem is not with the technology, but with the people who use it.)
  What does Stephan think are advantages to the Internet? (It's a great source for gathering news and information; it's a way to communicate with other people.)
  What does Stephan think is the disadvantage? (The Internet can start to replace human contact.)
  According to Lisa, what is the advantage of the Internet? (easy access to things)
  What does Lisa say about children using the Internet? (that they still should learn how to find information the traditional way, in encyclopedias and in dictionaries)
  How has the Internet helped Matt the most? (with directions)
  Does he find the directions provided online reliable? (primarily, yes)

EXTENSION
Oral work

• Discussion. Replay Rita's complaint about cell phones. Ask:
  What do you think Rita uses a cell phone for?
  Do you agree that a cell phone should not interrupt life as much as it does?
  Which professions do you think Rita is referring to when she says cell phones are good for people in some professions?

• Discussion. Have students respond to Stephan's comments about the loss of human contact that happens because of the Internet. Invite them to give examples from their own lives or those of people they know to comment on Stephan's point of view. Then ask *Does anyone think that there are situations when less human contact is a good thing? Explain your answers.*

Written work

• Focus on Mauro's answer to the question *In what ways have everyday technologies had a negative impact on modern life?* Replay his answer or write it on the board: The problem's not technology. The problem is the people that use technology. Have students write a paragraph interpreting Mauro's statement. Tell them to give examples of problematic ways in which people use technologies, referring to the other interviewees' comments (e.g., Rita's and Stephan's) and/or their own ideas.

- Have students write two paragraphs giving their own opinions of new technology. The first paragraph should describe what they think are advantages. The second paragraph should describe disadvantages. Students should provide examples from their own experience or that of others.
- Write the interview question on the board:

  Everyone agrees that newer everyday technologies, such as cell phone and computers and others, have had great impact on modern life. In what ways have they had a negative impact on modern life?

  Have students work in pairs to write a paragraph summarizing all five interviewees' views on this topic. Tell students to focus only on the negative impact technology has had.

LANGUAGE NOTES: When Rita says *The one thing that really gets me going* she means the one thing that really annoys her.

To *get back* to someone is to call them back later.

To *go overboard* with something is to do it too much or more than is acceptable.

A *landline* is a line of communication on land, for example—a telephone plugged into the wall, as opposed to a cell phone.

To *suck you in* means to make you so interested or entranced that it is difficult to get away.

OOPS! Lisa says *So I think there's advantages and disadvantages.* She means to say *So I think there <u>are</u> advantages and disadvantages.*

VIDEO SCRIPT

Interviewer: Everyone agrees that newer everyday technologies, such as cell phone and computers and others, have had great impact on modern life. In what ways have they had a negative impact on modern life?

Rita: The one thing that really gets me going, and I have a cell phone, are the people who walk with cell phones attached to their ears. People who will interrupt a conversation to talk on their cell phone. I can't think of anything so, so important that you need to interrupt a conversation with a friend, that you need to interrupt a walk through a beautiful park, that you need to interrupt any part of life at all, with a cell phone. I mean there's always a time when you can get back to someone, when they don't need to talk to you right then and there. We survived for many years with just landlines, and I think a cell phone is an

advantage, of course, for people in some professions, and they're handy things to use, but I really feel that people have gone overboard with the whole technology thing.

Mauro: The problem's not technology. The problem is the people that use technology.

Stephan: I have quite a few friends who spend a lot of time on the Internet, and I've done that myself and I still do. I find it to be a great source of news gathering and information and a way to communicate with others. But I think if you're not careful, it can really suck you in. You can spend a lot of time just chatting with people you know or people you don't know, you'd like to meet. But then this sort of meeting takes place on the Internet. And this is sort of a loss of human contact that happens. You meet a lot of new people, but it's not in sort of a real-life situation. And a lot of people stop going out as much, stop enjoying a nice day, stop enjoying a nice dinner with friends, just because it's easier to sit on your couch and not have to shower and not have to wear nice clothes and interact with people in life. So I feel that it has taken away, the Internet has taken away from human interactions.

Lisa: Pretty much I think that new technology is a good thing. I think that it's up to the individual as to how they deal with it. For instance, like the Internet is great because you have easy access to things, but I also think that kids should still find information in encyclopedias and look things up in dictionaries and things like that. So I think there's advantages and disadvantages, but you just need to know how to kind of use a little bit of both.

Matt: Technology has definitely been beneficial for at least my generation. It's at least helped me not get lost as much. If you are able to surf the web and get information, you can find directions on how to get almost anywhere. And primarily it's reliable, however sometimes they will mention a street that no longer exists, but it's been a great tool to help make your time easier and not get lost.

ANSWER KEY

A. 1. c 2. a 3. d 4. b
B. 1. False 2. False 3. True 4. False 5. False
   6. True 7. False
C. *Individual responses should include variations on the following:*

Rita complains about people who constantly talk on cell phones. It annoys her when people interrupt something to talk on the cell phone. She feels you can always call someone back.

D. *Individual responses should include variations on the following:*
Advantages: The Internet is a great source for gathering news and information. It's a way to communicate with other people.
Disadvantages: The Internet can start to replace human contact. People stop going out as much, choosing instead to chat with people online. People meet people online more than in real-life situations.

E. *Answers will vary.*

UNIT 10
Global Issues

TV Documentary:
The Ndoki Rain Forest

PART 1

PREVIEW

• Ask students *Who knows what a "rain forest" is? What do you know about rain forests? What countries do you know of that have rain forests? Do you know of any problems that rain forests face? Do you think rain forests are worth protecting?*

VIEW

Ask students to focus on a different topic each time they view. Some ideas:

• Ask students to listen for the ways the Ndoki Rain Forest is unique compared to other places.

• Ask students to listen for what Michael Fay is doing in the Ndoki Rain Forest.

• Ask students to listen for why poachers hunt wildlife in the Ndoki Rain Forest and what conservationists want to do about it.

If you decide to use the optional Activity Worksheet, ask students to read each activity before viewing.

REVIEW

• Ask the following comprehension questions. Play Part 1, or segments of Part 1, again if necessary.
  What is unique about the Ndoki Rain Forest? (It's been untouched by human hands, there are animals and plants that have disappeared from the rest of the planet, the trees grow very tall, and the butterflies are as big as birds.)
  How long has Michael Fay been exploring the Ndoki Rain Forest? (eleven years)
  Where is he from? (He's from the United States, New Jersey.)
  What is Michael Fay doing in the Ndoki Rain Forest? (He's trying to protect it and the animals that live in it. He's helping to turn it into a national preserve.)
  Who is he working with to protect the forest? (He's working with Congo's government and the Wildlife Conservation Society.)
  Why do poachers hunt wildlife there? (It provides income and food.)
  What do conservationists hope to do about poaching there? (They want to cut it back, but they don't think it can be completely stopped.)
  What percentage of Congo's wildlife is being killed each year by hunters? (about ten percent)
  What other danger is there to Congo's wildlife? (Loss of their environment. The rain forests are disappearing.)

I **LANGUAGE NOTE:** *Poaching* is illegal hunting.

VIDEO SCRIPT

Sam Donaldson: Now, we here at *PrimeTime* have watched John Quinones go to many exotic locations over the years. But we, and you, have never seen anything quite like this. It's the story of one man devoting his life to preserving the way his fragile fellow creatures live theirs in a land half a world away—a unique and beautiful place on the African continent which humans have yet to plunder.

John Quinones: It is a jungle so remote that parts of it have never been seen by human eyes. Deep in the northern Congo, an enchanted world where butterflies grow as large as birds and trees rise as tall as buildings—a land where time has stood still. It's called Ndoki— the world's last virgin rain forest, a million acres untouched by humanity. A Noah's ark, where animals and plants that have disappeared from the rest of the planet remain undisturbed.

No one knows this hidden world better than Michael Fay, a forty-year-old American from New Jersey. He's been exploring this malaria-infested jungle step-by-step for eleven years, often wearing nothing more than a pair of shorts and sandals. So what's a nice guy from New Jersey doing here?

Michael Fay: Hiding . . . Four leopard skins . . .

John Quinones: Perhaps, but he's also trying to stop the widespread slaughter of endangered species, defending the jungle against well-armed poachers.

Michael Fay: This elephant gun has probably killed hundreds of elephants over the years.

John Quinones: It's all part of his mission for the New York-based Wildlife Conservation Society. Working with Congo's government, Fay and a team of his colleagues are turning Ndoki into a national preserve.

Sam Donaldson: In a remote jungle deep in the northern Congo, correspondent John Quinones already has been given a personal guide to its breathtaking beauty. But he's about to encounter the dark side of a peaceable kingdom.

John Quinones: You're on a deadly safari in the heart of Africa. These hunters are tracking chimpanzee just outside the limits of the Ndoki forest. Be warned that the following scenes are very graphic. The target is hit. It's an adult male. The body parts are taken to market and sold to local butchers as wild game or bushmeat. It provides income to hunters and the families who depend on them. This demand for bushmeat is strong, and though it's illegal, conservationists know that the trade can't be shut down completely. By some estimates, up to 10 percent of Congo's wildlife is being slaughtered every year, including some of Africa's most endangered species, like this baby lowland gorilla found dead in a suitcase. This one is still alive, rescued while on its way to the bushmeat market. But even if the fight to cut back on the bushmeat trade is won, conservationists know that the animals cannot survive without the rain forest. And every day, there is less and less of it. For Michael Fay, saving this forest is not just a battle, it's a war.

ANSWER KEY

A. *Individual responses may include variations on the following:* It has been left undisturbed by humans. Some parts have never even been seen by humans. It contains animals and plants not seen in other places.

B. 1. True. 2. False. He's been exploring it for eleven years. 3. False. Poaching or hunting has been killing them. 4. False. He's been working with Congo's government and the Wildlife Conservation Society. 5. False. They don't think it's possible. 6. False. Up to 10 percent is being killed.

C. *Individual responses may include variations on the following:* 1. They are hunting them for food and to make a living. 2. Ndoki's wildlife need the rain forest to survive, and the rain forest is disappearing.

D. 1. have never been seen by human eyes 2. grow as large as birds and trees rise as tall as buildings 3. time has stood still 4. untouched by humanity 5. animals and plants that have disappeared from the rest of the planet remain undisturbed

E. *Answers will vary.*

PART 2

PREVIEW

• Ask students *Do you think the work Michael Fay is doing is important? Do you think it's more important for the Ndoki Rain Forest to be saved as a preserve or to be used as a source of income and food for people?*

VIEW

Ask students to focus on a different topic each time they view. Some ideas:

• Ask students to listen for what dangers to wildlife the report mentions.

• Ask students to listen for what argument Michael Fay makes for why logging should not be allowed in the Ndoki Rain Forest.

• Ask students to listen for why elephants are being hunted in the Ndoki Rain Forest and why it is illegal to do so.

If you decide to use the optional Activity Worksheet, ask students to read each activity before viewing.

REVIEW

• Ask the following comprehension questions. Play Part 2, or segments of Part 2, again if necessary.
   What specific dangers to wildlife does this part of the report talk about? (logging and poaching)
   Who is cutting down huge numbers of trees in Congo's forests? (logging companies) *What for?* (to export wood to other countries)
   How much money does Michael Fay think the tree is worth? (about US$10,000)
   How old does Michael Fay think many trees in the forest are? (over a thousand years old)
   How much time would it take to cut this tree down? (about twenty minutes)
   What do they see from the airplane? (elephants that have been killed by poachers)

V27

How many dead elephants do they count in all?
(about 300)
*Where are the biggest markets for ivory from these
elephants?* (Europe and Japan)
*Why is hunting elephants considered illegal in
Congo?* (Because Congo signed an agreement
in 1989 with ninety-nine other countries
banning the ivory trade.)
*Who is buying the ivory sold in markets in
Brazzaville, the capital of Congo?* (mainly
European tourists)
*How much money does Michael Fay say it would
cost to protect the Ndoki Rain Forest?* (six
hundred thousand dollars a year)
*What percentage of the world's rain forests have
already disappeared?* (about 85 percent)

EXTENSION

Oral work

- Group work. Divide the class into two groups.
  Assign one group to argue for conserving the
  Ndoki Rain Forest; assign the other to argue for
  further development. Then have the class debate
  the issue.

- Discussion. Discuss how local economic needs
  might be balanced with the need to conserve
  natural resources. Ask students to consider, for
  example, what Congo might do to reduce
  poaching in the Ndoki Rain Forest while still
  meeting the needs of the local people for food and
  income.

Written work

- Have students choose a natural place in your
  country that some people want to develop and
  others want to conserve. Ask them to write a
  couple of paragraphs developing arguments for
  one of those positions.

- Have students write a letter to Michael Fay
  praising or criticizing his work in the Ndoki Rain
  Forest.

- Ask students to write a paragraph or two on their
  own ideas for what can or should be done (or not
  done) about poaching or logging in the Ndoki
  Rain Forest.

LANGUAGE NOTES: *Divvied up* is a colloquial way
to say divided between two or more people or
organizations.

The expression *You're talking . . .* is used
colloquially to mean *I'm going to estimate . . .*

Whacking is a colloquial way to say killing or
cutting down.

VIDEO SCRIPT

John Quinones: For Michael Fay, saving this
forest is not just a battle, it's a war.

Michael Fay: Most of the large blocks of forest in
Africa have been divvied up in the last twenty
years to logging companies. They have just
been invading the forest at an unbelievable
rate.

John Quinones: Last year, French logging
companies cut down 200,000 trees in this part
of Congo. The product—mahogany and
plywood, most of it for export.

Michael Fay: Let's just have one place on earth
where, you know, we're not thinking about
how much money we're going to make off of
it. Let's just say, you know, this is an amazing
place, and it's the last one left, so let's save it at
any cost.

John Quinones: This is what . . . a couple of
hundred feet tall?

Michael Fay: Yeah. It's probably . . . yeah . . .
about 200 feet.

John Quinones: How much money is there in
this?

Michael Fay: You're talking about $10,000 on the
open market for this tree. Not bad.

John Quinones: How old is this tree, do you
think?

Michael Fay: Well, nobody really knows the ages
of these trees. And we've had some dates that
have been over 1,000 years old. So, you know,
a tree that takes 1,000 years to grow takes
twenty minutes to cut down.

John Quinones: With the vigilance of a hawk, he
watches over hundreds of miles of forest and
its wildlife.

Michael Fay: I can see some buffalo down in the
river there. And I don't see any elephants.

John Quinones: We pass over a clearing where
elephants normally gather, but today, there is
something terribly wrong here.

Michael Fay: There's two of them here.

John Quinones: There's an elephant every ten
feet.

Michael Fay: The farther you walk, the more you
see. They're everywhere. This place is just
littered with carcasses.

John Quinones: The killers are a local network of
ivory poachers who ambush the elephants
with powerful ammunition, remove their
tusks, and then sell the ivory in bulk to Europe
and Japan. This was a small elephant.

Michael Fay: Yeah, very small. Which means that they're not being selective out here. It means they're just whacking any elephant they see.

John Quinones: This random slaughter of elephants, Africa's largest endangered mammal, was supposed to have ended in 1989. That was the year Congo joined ninety-nine other countries in banning the ivory trade. Within minutes, we count nearly 300 sets of remains—the biggest elephant killing field ever found. In the capital, Brazzaville, a few days later, we find markets teeming with ivory sold right out in the open. It's real ivory?

Merchant: Yeah.

John Quinones: Real? Not plastic?

Merchant: No.

John Quinones: Most of the customers here, we are told, are foreign tourists, mainly from Europe. Without the protection of conservationists, Ndoki would surely die. But the work of Fay and his team depends on funding, which is always uncertain.

Michael Fay: Six hundred thousand dollars a year to save, in my opinion, the last great wilderness in tropical Africa. And you know, we can't come up with the money? And that's . . . that's crazy. It's insane. It's just . . . it's unbelievable.

John Quinones: Eighty-five percent of the rain forests that once covered the planet have now disappeared. The world cannot afford to lose the treasures of Ndoki, says Michael Fay. For once lost, they can never be regained. It's hard work—one man trying to save the rain forest. How long will you keep going?

Michael Fay: Well, as . . . as long as it takes. If we lost this place, if all of those animals get poached out and logging occurs, no one will ever have seen it. No one will know what it was.

ANSWER KEY

A. *The following should be crossed out:* a, b, e, f, g
B. 1. about 200 feet 2. about $10,000 3. no one knows for sure, could be 1,000 years 4. about twenty minutes
C. 1. mainly logging companies. They do it to export wood overseas. 2. about 300 3. about 85 percent 4. *Answers should include variations on the following:* In 1989, Congo joined ninety-nine other countries to ban the ivory trade. 5. It's being bought by foreign tourists, mainly from Europe.
D. 1. one place on earth 2. how much money we're going to make 3. an amazing place 4. save it at any cost 5. Six hundred thousand dollars a year 6. crazy 7. insane 8. unbelievable
E. *Individual responses should include a variation on the following:* Most of the customers in the ivory markets in Brazzaville are foreign tourists. By purchasing ivory, they are supporting the poaching of Ndoki's elephants.

Summit ActiveTeach DVD-ROM

For Windows:
- Insert the **Summit ActiveTeach** disc into the DVD-ROM drive of your computer. On most computers, the ActiveTeach menu will open automatically. On most computers, the DVD video program will also open automatically (using your default DVD software player). Close the application you do not want to use.

If *ActiveTeach* does not begin automatically:
- Open "**My Computer.**"
- Right-click on the Summit_2_ActiveTeach icon. Click on **Open**.
- Double-click on the Summit_2_ActiveTeach.exe file to start the application. Do not remove the DVD-ROM from the DVD-ROM drive while using ActiveTeach.
- On the opening screen, click on the book image to start ActiveTeach.
- To watch the DVD video program, open the default DVD Player software installed on your computer.

For MAC:
- Insert the **Summit ActiveTeach** disc into the DVD-ROM drive of your computer.
- Double-click on the Summit_2_ActiveTeach icon on your desktop.
- Double click on the Summit_2_ActiveTeach launch file. Do not remove the DVD-ROM from the DVD-ROM drive while using ActiveTeach.
- On the opening screen, click on the book image to start ActiveTeach.
- To watch the DVD video program, open the default DVD Player software installed on your computer.

Note: The original *Summit ActiveTeach* disc must be in the DVD-ROM drive when you use this application. This application cannot be copied or used without the original DVD-ROM.

ON A DVD PLAYER
You can also watch the video program using a DVD player connected to a TV.

ActiveTeach System Requirements		
	For PC-Compatible Computers	**For Macintosh Computers**
Operating System	Microsoft Windows® XP, Vista, Windows 7	Mac OSX v. 10.4.x
Processor	Intel Pentium® IV 1000MHz or faster processor (or equivalent)	PowerPC & Intel processor 500MHz or faster processor (or equivalent)
RAM	512 MB RAM minimum or higher	512 MB RAM minimum or higher
Internet Browser	Microsoft Internet Explorer® 7.x or Mozilla Firefox™ 4.x, or higher	Safari® 3.x, Mozilla Firefox™ 4.x, or higher
Plug-ins	Adobe PDF 8	Adobe PDF 8
Hardware	Computer DVD-ROM drive, Sound card and speakers or headphones. External DVD Player can also be used to watch available video.	Computer DVD-ROM drive, Sound card and speakers or headphones. External DVD Player can also be used to watch available video.
Monitor Resolution	1024x768	1024x768

TECHNICAL SUPPORT
For Technical Product Support, please visit our support website at www.PearsonELTSupport.com. You can search our **Knowledgebase** for frequently asked questions, instantly **Chat** with an available support representative, or **Submit a Ticket/Request** for assistance.